ANTHROPOLOGY, ART AND CULTURAL PRODUCTION

GW00676304

Anthropology, Culture and Society

Series Editor:
Dr Jon P. Mitchell, University of Sussex

RECENT TITLES:

ANTHROPOLOGY, ART AND CULTURAL PRODUCTION

Maruška Svašek

Pluto Press
LONDON

First published 2007 by Pluto Press
345 Archway Road, London N6 5AA
and 839 Greene Street, Ann Arbor, MI 48106

www.plutobooks.com

British Library Cataloguing in Publication Data
A catalogue record for this book is available from the British Library

Hardback
ISBN-13   978 0 7453 1795 3
ISBN-10   0 7453 1795 2

Paperback
ISBN-13   978 0 7453 1794 6
ISBN-10   0 7453 1794 4

Library of Congress Cataloging in Publication Data applied for

10   9   8   7   6   5   4   3   2   1

Designed and produced for Pluto Press by
Chase Publishing Services Ltd, Fortescue, Sidmouth, EX10 9QG, England
Typeset from disk by Stanford DTP Services, Northampton, England
Printed on Demand in the European Union by
CPI Group (UK) Ltd, Croydon, CR0 4YY

CONTENTS

LIST OF ILLUSTRATIONS

ACKNOWLEDGEMENTS

This book has benefited from my many dealings with artists, art dealers and critics in Europe, the USA and Africa who are unfortunately too many to name here, but without whose assistance this book could never have been written. From the ranks of the many scholars who commented constructively on drafts of some early chapters I would like to thank Justin I'Anson-Sparks, Ferdinand de Jong, Frances King, Fiona Magowan, Laura Peers, Elizabeth Tonkin and Vera Zolberg.

I would also like to thank Johannes Fabian and Helena Spanjaard for the many helpful insights they gave during our conversations about the book's central themes, and Jeremy MacClancy and Michael O'Hanlon for their words of encouragement. Last but not least, Roger van Zwanenberg from Pluto Press deserves equal thanks for his enthusiasm and support.

For Justin and Tristan

Part 1

Theorising Art

1   INTRODUCTION

WHAT IS ART?

When considering the different ways anthropologists might help to explain what many of us regard as artistic behaviour, we would very likely ask them the question: what is art? The question can be interpreted in two distinct ways. On the one hand, it demands to know the criteria by which objects that are often seemingly incomparable, such as Michelangelo's *Last Judgement*, Damien Hirst's dissected cow in formaldehyde and Australian Aboriginal Dream Paintings can be similarly classified as 'works of art'. The pursuit of common qualities that can bridge the divide between such distinctly different objects is sometimes referred to as a *generalising* system. Adopted by many anthropologists in the past, this approach claimed that all societies produce artefacts that are considered valuable, and that, while the objects themselves might differ wildly, the common motivation to create such objects is derived from distinct human behaviour that exists in all societies. By analysing art in its correct cultural and social context, supporters of this approach argued that art can be compared across different societies, civilisations and nations, in a similar way to politics or religion. Melville Herskovits, for example, suggests that '[i]n the widest sense ... art is to be thought of as any embellishment of ordinary living that is achieved with competence and has describable form' (1948: 380).

Broad definitions such as this argue that, because art exists in all societies, it constitutes a universal category that can be used not only to explain what art is, but can also be used as an analytical tool to explore similar types of behaviour involved in the production, use, and consumption of objects and artefacts in different parts of the world. As Chapters 2 and 3 demonstrate, this perspective is problematic because it disregards the fact that art is *itself* a 'set of historically specific ideas and practices that have shifted meanings across the course of the centuries' (Errington 1998: 103).[1] In other words, taking art out of its social and historical setting to analyse and explain other social or cultural habits presupposes that definitions of art are somehow timeless and free from preconceived ideas, which clearly is not the case.

In their pursuit of a broad definition that would allow them to identify and compare different artefacts in different cultures and societies, supporters

3

of the generalising approach found that the broader their definitions, the more meaningless they became. The anthropologist Roy Sieber (1973b: 431), for example, proposed a definition of art that distinguished eight principal qualities, namely that art is man-made, exhibits skill, exhibits order, conveys meaning, is the product of conscious intent, is effective, conveys a sense of unity and wholeness, and evokes a response that is immediate. He believed that, if used sensibly, this list could be used to identify art in different cultural settings, but he was quickly forced to acknowledge that the list was inadequate and needed constant revision and adaptation.

More recently, Richard Anderson (2000) proposed a theoretical definition of art that outlined certain combinations of highly probable artistic features.[2] In the hope of avoiding the ethnocentric projection of one society's ideas of what constitutes art upon another, and aiming to challenge what he considered an artificial separation of high-brow and popular art, he argued that '[l]ike a chameleon, the word "art" takes on different colors, depending on the verbal foliage in which it is found' (2000: 5). He distinguished a number of what he defined as objective qualities in order to help scholars establish whether a particular artefact could be considered art or not.[3] Again, however, using a list of artistic qualities to determine what was or was not art soon proved highly unreliable. Anderson's own study of art in America revealed that, while his approach did indeed erase the divisions between high and low art forms, it failed to differentiate between art and a range of other activities that could not reasonably be considered to have any claim to be art at all. His attempts to evaluate art by appraising the artist's commitment to his medium for instance, forced him to concede that, on those criteria even a committed comic-book reader could be considered a great artist (2000: 107). By over-extending his classifications, his category of 'art' became meaningless.

In contrast to this generalising approach, this book offers an alternative answer to the question 'What is art?' Instead of considering art as a universal category, it instead stresses the *processual* nature of art production, and identifies the many different factors that influence the ways in which people experience and understand it. Instead of generalising definitions of art that often prove deceptive simplifications, which hide or distort complex historical processes, the book aims to analyse the conflicting definitions of art and aesthetics in specific socio-historical contexts.

OBJECT TRANSIT AND TRANSITION

When exploring why objects are considered art in a particular period and in a particular social setting, it is crucial to analyse two processes referred to in this book as *transit* and *transition*. Transit records the location or movement of objects over time and across social or geographic boundaries, while transition analyses how the meaning, value and status of those objects, as well as how people experience them, is changed by that process. The works of Vincent van Gogh provide a good example of precisely that type of change. During the artist's lifetime, his paintings were only appreciated by a small number of people and were not the highly valuable artworks they are today. Even though Theo van Gogh, Vincent's older brother, managed to sell some of the works through a gallery in The Hague, the paintings were not in high demand and therefore did not pass extensively through the hands of dealers in networks that invariably stretched across Europe and North America. Most art lovers were not enchanted by the paintings, and there was no shortage of art experts ready to dismiss the artist's technique as falling far short of the high standard required of 'fine art'. Yet, over time, as artistic fashions changed, the paintings gained in status and financial value, and were marketed and sold as leading examples of avant-garde painting. Eventually, they were sought out by influential collectors and prestigious museums in different parts of the world, and presented as aesthetically powerful masterpieces. In terms of the process of *transit*, from the moment van Gogh finished painting his canvasses, they were over time transported over ever greater distances to private collections and public galleries where, as part of the process of *transition*, their status and meaning shifted from relatively worthless objects attracting few collectors and viewers to priceless artworks recognised internationally as ranking among the most sought-after ever created.

The processes of transit and transition are always shaped by the different relations between institutions or individuals who produce, consume, give, take, buy, sell, use, or display artefacts (Marcus and Myers 1995; Price 1989; Steiner 1994). These relations might sometimes be of a purely business character, between art dealers for example, or characterised by dependency in the case of an artist and his dealer who sells his paintings or a private collector who supports him financially as a form of patronage. In the case of van Gogh's works, in terms of how they are bought and sold today, only a small circle of the super-rich or well-funded galleries can afford to purchase them, which, in terms of transit, determines the type of locations where they can be found. That limitation adds to their value by making them an important symbol of economic power and prestige that increases the owner's social status. This same mechanism of supply, demand and prestige attached to particular objects not only functions within art markets, but also in other markets with collectable items that can range from stamps, autographs and baseball cards, to almost anything that is available in limited numbers and deemed of value by the group of people who seek to own it.

POLITICAL DIMENSIONS AND OTHER CONTEXTUAL DYNAMICS

When artefacts are shifted from one location to another as part of the process of *transit*, or when the values of the society where they are located undergo *transition*, they can become entangled with national and international political or religious issues. Governments of countries that were once the colonies of former imperial powers such as Britain, continue to demand the return of artefacts considered of national importance. The Elgin Marbles, for instance, sculptures that once adorned the Athens Parthenon, were taken to Britain by Lord Elgin in the nineteenth century, and continue to be a source of contention between Greece and the United Kingdom. Similarly, one of Ethiopia's most sacred monuments, the Axum obelisk, which was taken to Rome by Italian soldiers in the 1930s, has recently been returned, ending decades of dispute. Why some of these objects are given back while others remain in the hands of their present owners, and to what extent these artefacts are symbols of domination or resistance are issues addressed in depth in Chapter 6.

As an example of how, by transition, the status of an *immobile* object can change due to a shift in the values of the society where it is located, one only has to consider the recent destruction of the giant Bamiyan statues of Buddha in Afghanistan. Located on territory controlled by the Taliban regime, which enforced a fundamentalist doctrine of Islam, giant statues carved out of mountainsides some 1,500 years ago when the local society was largely Buddhist, were destroyed on the grounds that they were now unacceptable to Islamic teaching. In contrast to the attitude of Western governments and the governments of Buddhist nations, which argued that the statues should be preserved as one of the artistic wonders of the world, their destruction was celebrated by Taliban supporters. The different ways in which artefacts can simultaneously be valued in religious, political, artistic, cultural and financial terms are addressed throughout the book, and highlight the importance of contextualising our understanding of artefacts.

In terms of identifying the location or milieu of an object, this book adopts a multi-layered, processual concept of what constitutes a context. Context should not be thought of as a static, secure box in which supposedly unproblematic categories of art are kept, but as a setting that is liable to change and that requires extensive social and historical knowledge to provide more complete theories about the interaction between artistic and non-artistic processes. Rather than the metaphor of a box, context might better be thought of as a river, which has the power to divert its own course or erode its banks and reshape the landscape.[4] Discourses about art, as well as the different ways it is practised and experienced, both influence and are influenced by wider societal processes. A more fluid perspective of contextual dynamics can provide insights into the production of art and its aesthetic values. The hierarchical observance of one aesthetic principle of art over another can also be used to promote values or justify conditions that are enforced elsewhere in society. As discussed later in the book, such examples can arise in many different forms, in particular where they are used to reflect unequal power structures as was often the case in former colonies where foreign governments sought to justify their rule over indigenous populations.

To illustrate the point, when Amon Kotei, an aspiring young artist studying at Achimota Art College in the British Gold Coast in the 1930s, sculpted a realistic and technically skilled bust of an African head, his angry

British teacher dismissed his efforts with the remark: 'This is *European* art!' (Svašek 1997c). The colonial staff insisted that African students refrain from imitating 'superior' Western art forms, and remain true to their own 'less sophisticated' tradition. Instead of indulging in realism, they were instructed to make traditional artefacts such as fertility statues and wooden stools, which, according to the colonial teachers, reflected norms and values that were timeless, unchanging and specific to Africa. In this particular case, Western artistic and cultural superiority was promoted by colonial art teachers through their promotion of certain aesthetic values and was part of a wider political discourse that sought to justify the British presence in what is now Ghana. Art education was just one of the many areas of social life on which the colonial power similarly sought to stamp its authority. At the same time, however, the decision by some students to oppose their teachers' instructions by continuing to produce 'European' art turned their work into an act of resistance indicative of wider political discontent with British rule. The pressure put on artists to remain true to their supposedly unchanging forms of traditional African art, and their resistance to these aesthetic norms, must be analysed against the context of political domination and resistance that characterised the period and society (Svašek 1997c).

The process by which art is conceptualised in a particular socio-historical setting, and how that conceptualisation relates to other activities and processes in a society, is another issue central to this book. The clash between African students and colonial teachers in the former British Gold Coast demonstrates how the concept of 'art' is often contested in thought as well as action. The two groups used the English term 'art' to refer to the same process of creating artefacts, but both had very different interpretations of the aesthetic definition of the word. Understanding the social setting of conflicts that might be predominantly intellectual highlights why context is vital to understanding how and why struggles over definitions of art come about. In other words, in seeking answers to the question 'What is art?' we need to examine the ways in which particular artistic discourses are shaped by political, economic, social and cultural factors that are historically specific.

It is not just in relations between different societies and cultures that we find conflicting ideas about what constitutes art. Definitions of 'art' are often just as fiercely contested by different groups within the same society, and often highlight the different forms of interrelation between art production, professionalisation and social distinction. Consider, for example, the case of Wim Delvoye, a Belgian artist who exhibited his controversial artwork entitled *Cloaca* in Antwerp's Mukha Museum in October 2000.

The exhibit was a costly working reproduction of the human digestive tract, complete with mouth, stomach, bowels, human enzymes, bacteria and a glass anus, which became popularly known as the 'shit machine'. Constructed at a cost of well over a £100,000, with the help of biologists, Delvoye's artwork was fed three times a day by a local gourmet restaurant on luxury foods that included champagne and oysters. At the end of each day, the glass anus ejected excrement that was then sealed in Perspex jars and sold to eager collectors at a price that quickly spiralled above £1,000. Not surprisingly, the artwork evoked a wide range of reactions among art critics and the public alike.

Some members of the public lavished praise on the work, while those hostile to the idea that excrement could be considered a valuable artwork suggested it was further proof of the debauched mindset of contemporary artists, who, lacking genuine skill to produce artworks worthy of past masters, had resorted to trading in toilet jokes. Critics opposed to the work claimed that the artist was engaging in an exclusive artistic discourse unintelligible to the non-cognoscenti. People who rejected the work did so for the most part because the artwork did not fit with their own aesthetic preferences and expectations about what constituted art. The amount of money spent on building it and the gourmet catering bills also caused many to draw comparison between the decadent waste of food and the plight of people starving in the Third World. The idea of *waste*, according to the artist, was central to the artwork: 'I wanted to emphasise that art in itself is a decadent business because no artwork has ever done anything to improve the world.'[5]

For some modern art supporters up to date with twentieth-century art, however, the work was considered more a cliché than shocking. The conceptual artist, in their view, was simply incorporating elements of early twentieth-century modernist movements, such as Dada and Surrealism. From an historical perspective, *Cloaca* was relatively conventional in its aim of shocking audiences by displaying a form of human excretion. Over 70 years before, the French artist Marcel Duchamp claimed he had transformed a urinal into art by exhibiting it in a gallery and, in the 1960s, the Italian artist Piero Manzoni had sold his own excrement as artwork in tins labelled 'Merde d'Artista'. For this reason, some artists and critics dismissed the work as *too* conventional. Despite vociferous public hostility, however, *Cloaca* attracted a record number of visitors to the museum and, even though many did not attach any aesthetic value to the installation, they considered it a spectacle worth viewing, if only to witness its artistic pretension.

The different evaluations of the work by different art specialists and members of the public reveals the degree of aesthetic disagreement between groups that represent the public and those representing the cultural elite and modern art networks. To some degree, by analysing the context of such works, perceptions of art can be seen to reflect and even reproduce social, educational, professional and generational distinctions, a theme that is explored later, particularly in Chapters 3, 5 and 8, and that has been central to the work of Pierre Bourdieu.

THE CASE FOR PROCESSUAL RELATIVISM

The examples above highlight the point that art is not a straightforward descriptive category of objects with inherent qualities that can be objectively isolated and compared. Instead, as artefacts are created by hand or design, they have what Igor Kopytoff (1986) calls their own 'cultural biographies', or what sociologist Vera Zolberg (1990) describes as their own 'careers' – descriptions intended to stress the movement of artefacts and their reception over time. During their career, they may lose or gain what the anthropologist Arjun Appadurai (1986) calls their 'commodity potential'. In order to examine the process by which the artistic status of an artefact can increase or diminish, it is vital to adopt an analytical approach that takes into account not only the concepts transit and transition outlined earlier, but also the processual nature of object production in terms of what this book calls *processual relativism*.

Processual relativism signals a paradigm shift in anthropology away from cultural relativism towards a more radical processual view. As will be explained in detail in Chapter 2, cultural relativist scholars introduced theories of 'bounded cultures' and used fixed definitions of culture as analytical tools to explore how art manifested itself in different societies. Defining art as a form of universal behaviour, they sought to describe and understand how art was shaped in different cultural contexts by making cross-cultural comparisons.

Rather than referring to one strictly defined theory, the term 'processual relativism' used in this book incorporates a number of intellectual trends concerning the process of art production, its functions and the different ways it is experienced. The shift towards processual relativism began in the late 1970s, when anthropologists such as Johannes Fabian, James Clifford and others, in addition to exploring issues of power in relation to object production, also began to criticise fixed notions of bounded culture and entrenched ideas about 'high' and 'low' culture.[6] In their critical writings they similarly questioned the intellectual foundations that allowed ethnographers to map, collect and display material objects, a process which unavoidably gave objects particular significance or provided interpretations for how they should be understood. Analysing the socio-political context of objects when they are produced, the networks and power relations that characterise the behaviour of the different agents inhabiting that context, and scrutinising the anthropologist's own ethnographic role, is central to their approach.

AESTHETICISATION: ART AND BEYOND

Several other processes have played a key role in the configuration and continuous reconfiguration of exclusive domains of 'art'. In this book I use the term '*aestheticisation*' to conceptualise the process by which people interpret particular sensorial experiences as valuable and worthwhile. Disconnecting the notions of 'art' and 'aesthetics', I shall argue that processes of aestheticisation take place within *and* outside artistic fields of practice.

The application of the term 'aestheticisation' in this book is very different to the way it is used in more traditional approaches on aesthetics that might be described as Kantian, in reference to the German Idealist philosopher Immanuel Kant who, in his principal work, *The Critique of Pure Reason*, further developed a system of aesthetics that had been invented by his predecessor Alexander Baumgarten to understand the elements that constitute beauty (see also Chapter 7, p. 157). By contrast, in this book, the perspective of aestheticisation focuses on the relation between certain types of sensory experience, and accounts and textual interpretations of them provided by artistic and other discourses. As argued earlier, it criticises approaches that use etic notions of art as tools of comparison and rejects the Kantian view of art as a category of objects with *inherent* beauty and transcendental powers. The latter view is problematic because it fails to provide artefacts with a context, ignores the impact of outside forces on people's experiences of material realities, and hence their understanding or appreciation of artworks (Preziosi 1989; see also Svašek 1997c: 29).

The term 'aestheticisation' in this book describes the process by which objects are perceived and the ensuing sensory experience used to provide a basis for descriptions of 'aesthetic experience', which in turn are used to reinforce abstract ideas or beliefs. That experience is often already influenced by additional knowledge about the object and its reported status, and by the spatial setting in which it is used or displayed. For example, if the strong imagery and colours in a painting by Vincent van Gogh evoke powerful feelings in a viewer who sees the work in a prestigious museum, they are likely to be attributed to its artistic power and to reinforce ideas about the power of art in general. That aesthetic experience is likely be conveyed to others in a verbal discourse that draws on vocabulary from artistic discourses to articulate and give meaning to it. The type of discourse used might depend on the viewer's own knowledge and background, or how publicly well known and well regarded the work is. If the same van Gogh painting, for example, were viewed in a flea market by someone unacquainted with the artist's work and fame, the experience and subsequent discourse on it would likely be very different from when the same person viewed the artwork in a hallowed museum where the artist was celebrated as an artistic genius.

It should be noted that aesthetic experience and discourses that employ descriptions of it, are not limited to our appreciation of artworks. The concept refers to a type of experience that can be similarly stimulated by religious feeling, music or even during some political rituals. A devout Catholic, for instance, could attribute an aesthetic experience stimulated by the atmosphere of a church service or religious effigy to the divine power of Christ, and use it to reinforce Christian ideals. The aestheticisation of an object is thus partly derived from sensation, but is also stimulated and reinforced by other factors such as, in this case, religious belief.

Similarly, as discussed in detail in Chapter 8, military units among the Fante ethnic group in Ghana known as Asafo companies, parade with specially made flags through territory that belongs to rival groups. For every new member of the Asafo, a personal flag is made that links him spiritually with his patrilineal ancestors, forms part of his initiation ritual into the group and is kept locked away in a special shrine when not being used. The sorts of feelings that are engendered when art devotees or Catholic worshippers interact with objects central to their value system are similarly at work in the Fante rituals. The physical sensation of dancing with flags, combined with the awe-inspiring sense of communion with their ancestors, is used to reinforce abstract ideas about what it is to be a good or loyal member of the Asafo. In other words, the Fante aestheticise the flags, perceiving them as the embodiment of their patrilineal ties.

The examples show that people's engagement with objects is both physical and mental, and often grounded in social practices. Through aestheticisation, artefacts and other phenomena are granted special status on the basis of people's contextually specific experiences, perceptions, expectations and interpretations. Only in certain settings, they are aestheticised as 'art'.

AESTHETICISATION AS ART

The concepts of art *by intention* and art *by appropriation* help explain why certain artefacts, and not others, are aestheticised as 'art'. As this book will show, these concepts are useful analytical tools when examining how changing intellectual trends and market forces are able to influence the different ways people perceive art. The terms, coined in 1998 by Shelley Errington, are based on the concepts of art *by destination* and art *by metamorphosis* used in 1965 by André Malraux in his book *Museum without Walls*.[7] Art by intention/ destination is used to refer to artefacts that were created with the specific purpose in mind that they should represent and be regarded as art by galleries and museums, and bought and sold on the art market. By contrast, art by appropriation/metamorphosis refers to objects that may have been created for a different purpose or to champion values primarily not artistic, but which subsequently are given the status of art and 'appropriated' by museums or dealers as tradable artefacts. The processual relativist perspective taken in this book is particularly interested in processes of appropriation, because they illustrate very clearly how contextual factors influence the changing meaning and efficacy of artefacts.

In terms of art by appropriation, Malraux argued that, from the nineteenth century onwards, objects such as royal portraits or religious paintings that were originally considered to belong to two very separate domains were similarly presented in museums as works of art. As discussed in depth in Chapter 6, by recontextualising objects that once had a very different purpose and location in new museum settings, the objects can effectively metamorphose into art, and the way viewers experience them can differ wildly from the way originally intended. As Malraux noted:

So vital is the part played by the art museum in our approach to works of art today that we find it difficult to realize that no museums exist, none has ever existed, in lands where the civilization of modern Europe is, or was, unknown; and that, even in the Western world, they have existed for barely two hundred years. They were so important to the artistic life of the nineteenth century and are so much part of our lives today that we forget they have imposed on the spectator a wholly new attitude toward the work of art. (1967 [1965]: 9)

The urinal which, as mentioned earlier, was exhibited by the French artist Marcel Duchamp in an art gallery in the 1930s, is a frequently cited example of how an object not created to be art can become art by appropriation. Supported by fellow avant-garde artists and critics, Duchamp succeeded in adding aesthetic and economic value to the object. Nevertheless, despite the fact the urinal was accepted as an artwork by some circles, there was far from universal agreement, which again illustrates the essential point that what constitutes art changes in tandem with changes in ideas of aesthetic value.

The anthropologist Arjun Appadurai (1986) applied Malraux's concepts in his theory of *commoditisation* to describe the process by which objects gain or lose the qualities needed to become a commodity, a process which he terms *commodity-potential*. Commoditisation is a central focus of this book, not least because it is a key element in the processes of transit and transition outlined earlier. Chapter 5, in particular, considers the role played by commoditisation and explores the ways in which aestheticisation and commoditisation are linked.

ATTRACTING CUSTOMERS AND OTHER FORMS OF EFFICACY

To understand why people are willing to buy or use art or other artefacts, and how they are affected by them, this book uses the perspective of *object agency*. It is an important perspective because, as will be demonstrated, the influence an object has is directly related to how it is aestheticised. First introduced by Alfred Gell in 1998, the concept describes the ways an artefact is able to impact upon a viewer both in terms of evoking certain emotional states and ideas, as well as sometimes motivating them to take different types of social action. Instead of considering art in terms of how well it conveys a particular message or achieves a particular aesthetic standard, Gell chose to concentrate on how successful it was in affecting the viewer in the way intended, similar in some way, perhaps, to trying to gauge the success of advertising in, for instance, a government anti-smoking campaign, by calculating the number of people who actually gave up the habit as a result.

[i]n place of symbolic communication, I place all the emphasis on agency, intention, causation, result, and transformation. I view art as a system of action, intended to change the world rather than encode symbolic propositions about it. (Gell 1998: 6)

The point is that, when interacting with artefacts, we attribute values to them but are often similarly influenced by the ideas or values they express. The ability of an image to achieve wide acclaim and transform the mood of an audience in the way intended, can empower its creator, or the authority that commissioned it, to directly influence the individuals of a group or nation. Consider, for example, the use of imagery by twentieth-century autocratic leaders such as Joseph Stalin, Adolf Hitler or Mao Zedong, who used cinematic images and artworks to create powerful personality cults. In addition to the use of such techniques, which can still be found in North Korea, Burma and elsewhere, the agency of objects also occurs in far less extreme situations. A painting of the white cliffs of Dover as a symbol of home will have particular influence on a Briton, and likely more influence on a Briton old enough to have witnessed the use of the image in songs and propaganda campaigns during the Second World War. Its aestheticisation as 'valuable art' is, in this case, related to its power to trigger experiences of beauty and evoke nationalist sentiments.

Countless emblems are able to evoke particular reactions due to personal experiences linked to them, such as to a special brand of cocoa or a school motto. The reaction can also be evoked by a general knowledge linked to them, such as to a nationalist flag or a Nazi symbol. But artefacts can sometimes wield powerful symbolism without any direct personal link to them or knowledge of particular events. A painting such as *The Scream* (1895) by the Norwegian painter Edvard Munch is instantaneously recognisable for almost all viewers as an expression of deep-seated human angst. How and why some people are moved by certain objects while others are not, however, is in part determined by aestheticisation, commoditisation and the context in which they are set. Why, for example, might one person wax with enthusiasm on seeing Duchamp's urinal presented as an artwork while another storms out in anger, disgust or disdain? It is certainly true that many emotional reactions are common to all, but this book will argue that the way we experience artefacts, and why one emotion rather than another might dominate the experience of a particular artefact, is also always influenced by social factors and a context that can, to a large degree, be analysed.[8]

Analysing the use of language that describes such emotional responses, however, is fraught with problems.[9] Whereas a negative reaction to Duchamp's urinal might be influenced by an individual's social or psychological make-up, a preference for realistic sculpture or a general dislike of avant-garde art, analysing an individual's choice of language to describe his reaction might reveal other factors or blur the comprehension of his response. Linguistic descriptions themselves need to be placed in their context to understand what Gell calls *enchantment*, the ability of an object to affect our emotional state of mind. Consider how the adjective 'beautiful' might be used to describe an array of different objects and experiences. A night in the company of a beautiful person is, for most people, a wholly different experience from a night in the company of a beautiful painting, a beautiful animal or beautiful piece of furniture. Hence describing something as beautiful, such as 'a beautiful example of Baroque architecture', 'a beautiful Minimalist painting' or 'a beautiful Dogon mask', raises very particular expectations as to what kind of emotions the object in question should evoke in the viewers.

Gell's broad perspective is highly relevant as it examines the interaction between processes of aestheticisation, commoditisation *and* enchantment. Unlike Gell's theory, however, this book rejects his sometimes overextended use of what he terms 'art' in order to analyse objects that do not exist in any identifiable form of art market, or which only occasionally have a marketable value, such as tattoos. By overextending the category to give it an etic dimension, it begins to overlap with the generalist approach discussed earlier, which presupposes a bound definition that is essentially timeless and neutral. As the book highlights, it is important to continuously analyse conflicting and changing uses of the term 'art' in the context of global art economies, and that is most effectively achieved by using analytical concepts which encompass the dynamic nature of transit and transition.

STRUCTURE OF THIS BOOK

Anthropology, Art and Cultural Production is divided into two parts, entitled 'Theorising Art' and 'Objects, Transit and Transition'. Part 1 includes this first introductory chapter and consists of two more chapters which critically discuss and compare anthropological theories of art that have been developed throughout the history of the discipline, pointing out their analytical strengths and weaknesses.

Chapter 2, 'From Evolutionism to Ethnoaesthetics', discusses the main theoretical developments from the early beginnings of the discipline in the nineteenth century to the late 1960s, and explains why cultural relativism became the dominant paradigm.

Chapter 3, 'From Visual Communication to Object Agency', points out how cultural relativism slowly gave way to processual relativist approaches as an increasing number of scholars began to attack cultural relativist notions of bounded culture and, more recently, started criticising their use of 'art' as a tool of cross-cultural analysis. Instead, it will propose an alternative relativist approach, which allows for the analysis of aestheticisation, commoditisation and object agency in contexts of power.

Part 2 begins with Chapter 4, entitled 'Performances: The Power of Art/ efacts', which focuses on object agency. Various case studies clarify how objects and works of art trigger quite specific emotional reactions in users and viewers, which often lead to social action that can also be politically relevant. The analysis points out that the efficacy of artefacts is influenced by context-specific processes of aestheticisation and commoditisation, and that the ways in which people experience and react to objects may change as a result of transit and transition.

Chapter 5, 'Markets: Art/efacts on the Move', looks in more detail at commoditisation processes, examining the development of changing markets of art and ethnographic objects. Building on some of the findings in Chapter 4, it explores the influence of exchange mechanisms on the ways in which objects are valued, understood and handled, also showing that marketing strategies often affect the ways in which artefacts are interpreted and experienced. The chapter gives numerous examples of art by appropriation, demonstrating that specific consumer expectations often influence, but do not fully determine object production.

Objects are also appropriated by a variety of museums, including ethnographic museums, folklore museums and museums of art. Chapter 6, 'Museums: Space, Materiality and the Politics of Display', examines the involvement of such museums in object transit and transition in nationalist, colonial and postcolonial settings. Numerous case studies explore the relation between representation, aestheticisation and issues of power, and contribute to an analysis of the impact of spatial and discursive recontextualisation on object perception and experience.

Chapter 7, '"Fine Art": Creating and Contesting Boundaries', develops one of the main arguments of this book, namely that 'fine art', though defined differently in different times and spaces, is always a category of exclusion. The analysis mainly focuses on the creation of boundaries between 'art' and supposedly non-artistic categories such as 'craft', 'kitsch', 'pornography' and 'propaganda'. Various case studies show how artists have tried to undermine these oppositions by appropriating elements of the latter categories into their art.

In Chapter 8, 'Processual Relativism: Fante Flags in Northern Ireland', a detailed case study of Fante flag-making and flag exhibition ties up the main arguments of the book. The chapter makes a strong case for the study of object transit and transition in local, national and transnational fields of power, focusing on the movement of material objects within and across historical, social and geographic boundaries, and examining transitions in terms of the objects' value, meaning and efficacy.

2   FROM EVOLUTIONISM TO ETHNOAESTHETICS

Changing definitions of 'art' and 'culture' have strongly shaped anthropological theories of art. But how have notions of 'art' and 'culture' been defined and related to each other in concrete cases, and how have particular theoretical positions been influenced by historically specific interests and processes? In this chapter, we shall focus in more detail on theories which dominated the anthropology of art from its early beginnings in the late nineteenth century until the 1970s. As we shall see, these theories promoted ideas about the objectivity of science, which strongly influenced their analytical perspectives and findings. The resulting studies ranged from accounts which claimed that the diversity of material expression proved the essential difference between peoples, to accounts which emphasised similarity, arguing that most if not all humans have the ability to create art. The majority examined objects as products of particular groups of people, conceptualised as 'racial groups' or 'cultures', and tried to grasp their meaning or function within the boundedness of such groups. As I shall argue, this meant that processes of object transit and transition were largely ignored or were regarded as irrelevant.

The discussion continues in Chapter 3 which will examine the theoretical developments from the 1970s until the early twenty-first century. Both chapters explore debates about form, function, materiality, meaning and power, and point out the weaknesses and strengths of particular concepts and perspectives. As we shall see in Chapter 3, scholars became increasingly interested in processes of transit and transition from the 1970s onwards.

EVOLUTIONISM: ART AS INDICATOR OF RELATIVE PROGRESSION

Anthropology emerged in the context of empire-building and colonial expansion, which was, of course, itself a project of modernity (see also Chapters 5–7). It was strongly influenced by a political meta-narrative of progress, which propagated the idea of linear progression from tradition to modern life. The ideology of human evolution stipulated that mankind could be divided into distinct groups, which had reached particular developmental stages. Non-European peoples, in particular, were regarded as savages who simply lived by natural instincts, were slaves to their wild passions and unable to produce culture (Svašek 2005a: 3–4). The *Encyclopaedia Britannica*, for example, claimed in 1884 that:

No full-blooded Negro has ever been distinguished as a man of science, a poet, or as an artist, and the fundamental equality claimed for him by ignorant philanthropists is belied by the whole history of the race through the historic period. (vol. XVII: 318, quoted by Jordan and Weedon 1995: 286)

Evolutionism was based on the idea that 'culture' could be possessed in different quantities. Distinct collectivities – imagined as 'races', 'peoples' or 'nations' – were thought to have inherent qualities which made them more sophisticated than others and, for various reasons, this quality could increase, decrease or even disappear (see Fabian 1998: xi). The fully evolved white upper-class man was thought to have reached the highest level of evolution. It is important to realise that evolutionist arguments were not only deployed to create distinctions between the 'civilised' European colonisers and the 'uncivilised' non-European colonised, but were also played out in gender politics and in the context of intra-European political processes. The following quote, taken from the political pamphlet *The Uncivilised Irish: Samples of Catholic 'Culture'*, provides a typical example of highly politicised, in this case anti-Irish, anti-Catholic evolutionist rhetoric.

The Celtic Catholic Irish are the lowest in the scale of all the races of Western Europe. They are a survival of the Dark Ages, with a minimum tincture of civilisation ... . A great mistake of our own English people has been the habit of judging the Irish as if they were approximately on the same development as ourselves, whereas *they are generations behind us*. (Freeman 1923: 1, 2, italics mine)

As the quote clearly demonstrates, central to the evolutionist argument was an image of historical process according to which all races would eventually progress through the same developmental states. Consequently, the study of the less developed races could be employed to gain knowledge about the past of the civilised nations.

Biological 'evidence' was commonly used to prove that certain groups or nations were inferior to others. C.I. Freeman claimed that:

[The Celtic Irish] arrested development is evidenced by its well known simian features of the small flattened nose, the large upper lip and clumsy jaw – features which have been seized on by the caricaturist as typically Irish; though even the caricaturists do not exaggerate it much. The type persists because the Anglo-Saxon population does not intermarry with it. (1923: 3)

Highly relevant to the arguments made in this book, the quantitative notion of culture was not only based on biological arguments. According to the evolutionist theoreticians, the civilised nations demonstrated racial superiority through their political, economic and religious systems, *and* through the production of 'fine art'. To stay with the Irish example, Celtic imagery – being apparently largely abstract and decorative – was dismissed as aesthetically inferior to the refined realism of European art (see also Chapter 7).

To gain a better insight into evolutionist discourses of art and culture, it is helpful to look at the life and work of the British anthropologist Alfred Cort

Haddon. Haddon had been trained as a biologist but had extended his research focus to the study of non-European artefacts. Besides studying zoological species and conducting craniological research, he analysed material objects, mapping the various stages of human evolution. During his research on the coral reefs of the islands of the Torres Straits, he developed a keen interest in British New Guinean native artefacts, and his research resulted in two major studies, *The Decorative Art of British New Guinea* (1894) and *Evolution in Art* (1895).[1] Heavily influenced by Darwin's theory of social evolution, and in the intellectual spirit of the time, 'Haddon's evolutionary theory paid less attention to particular forms of art than to their relative positions in a biological scheme of development' (Fraser 1971: 22).

In the introduction to *The Decorative Art of British New Guinea*, Haddon set out his universalist argument, claiming that an approach which classified objects according to 'the generally recognised rules of the country or race to which the critic belongs', should be rejected without reservation because it offered 'a purely subjective point of view' (1894: 1). Instead, he propagated an objective, scientific method which used 'a more precise system of analysis' by analysing art 'as if it were a branch of biology' (1894: 2).[2] Central to his method was the assumption that all humans evolved along the same evolutionary scheme, and that particular races and racial groups could be classified by examining the relative complexity of their material products.[3]

The following quote clearly demonstrates the extent to which Haddon was influenced by evolutionary biology:

When difficult problems have to be investigated the most satisfactory method of procedure is to reduce them to their simplest elements, and to deal with the latter before studying their more complex aspects. The physiology of the highest animals is being elucidated largely by investigations upon the physiology of lower forms, and that of the latter in their turn by a knowledge of the activities of the lowest organisms. It is among these that the phenomena of life are displayed in their least complex manifestations and they, so to speak, give the key to a right apprehension of the others. So, too, in studying the art of design. (1894: 2)

Haddon argued that it would be best to analyse the artefacts of those savages who were still relatively primitive but who had progressed far enough to have developed 'a true feeling for art'. He did not regard people's developmental stage as the only determining factor of artistic style, and argued that the function of objects and the tools with which they were made were also highly important. This was of course completely in line with the circular rhetoric of evolutionary theory, which defined technological advancement as a sign of progress.

Haddon's publications were based on a comparative analysis of objects from private collections and museums in Ireland, Britain, Germany, the Netherlands, France and Italy. He admitted that crucial information about the exact origin of the artefacts was often missing or possibly unreliable (1894: 8), but nevertheless claimed that his books provided objective knowledge, which could be used to determine the civilising potential of particular savages. Certain objects, he noted, showed 'loving, tender work' and 'infinite labour expended with observation', and, in various cases, 'intellects finding the crafty hands' produced results that he regarded 'with amazement and hope – amazement at the workers themselves, and hope for the future before them, *if the white man is content to lead them onwards*' (1894: 271–2, italics mine).

As the quote illustrates, in Haddon's account of native artistic potential, the presence of the white man was the condition for further progression, and this view justified the colonial project. Early anthropologists such as Haddon were thus actively involved in imperialist politics. The colonial system partially enabled them to do their work and ethnographic knowledge production helped to provide a scientific rationale for missionary and military activities.

RELATIVE COMPLEXITY: KUBA AND KETE ARTEFACTS

The materiality of artefacts was central to the evolutionist conceptualisation of 'art'. According to the evolutionist perspective, objects with similar features and technical complexity had been produced by equally advanced peoples.[4] As will be discussed in more detail in Chapter 6, this view was strongly propagated in ethnographic museums during the late nineteenth and early twentieth century, and shaped the practices of those who collected 'ethnographic objects'. The anthropologist and collector Emil Torday, for example, who travelled in the Congo during the first decade of the twentieth century, was influenced by discourses of racial typology. As noted earlier, the levels of evolutionary progression were thought to be dependent on people's physical characteristics, such as skin colour and facial features; on societal characteristics, including social organisation, political organisation, hygiene standards and the presence or absence of cannibalism; and on the forms, functions and technological advancement of their material products (Binkley and Darish 1998). Not surprisingly, perceived resemblances with the superior Caucasian (white, European) race indicated a higher level of progression. Consequently, 'Congo Pygmies' were regarded as the most primitive peoples in the region, who were progressively followed by 'Bushmen', 'Forest Negroes' and the furthest progressed 'Nilotic Negroes'. Evidently, these categories were European constructions. 'Nilotic Negroes' were thought to be a racial mix of African and Caucasian populations, which made them a 'superior [aristocratic negroid] type of humanity' (Binkley and Darish 1998: 39, referring to Johnston 1908: 702–3).

The Congo case clearly demonstrates that European notions of 'fine art' were central to racial classifications. Kantian notions of aesthetics which assumed that 'good art' had inherent qualities ignored the social and political dynamics of aestheticisation and represented high art as a signifier of racial superiority. European scholars believed that truly superior art could only

be produced by male white artists. As such, they constituted an exclusive
domain of 'art' against which products by other people were measured (see
also Chapter 7). The Kuba, one of the Nilotic Negro populations, produced
objects that were evaluated according to Western standards of artistic skill
and genius. In 1908, the British explorer Sir Harry Johnston argued that the
Kuba were less primitive than other tribes in the region. They were 'a very
powerful and industrious people, chiefly occupied in the ivory trade. ... They
smelt and work iron, weave cloths to perfection, embroider and dye them.
They also make large mats on a frame and carve woof with much artistic
taste' (Johnston 1908: 515–16, quoted in Binkley and Darish 1998: 39).

The discourse of Kuba advancement was reinforced by comparisons with
'inferior' neighbouring tribes, such as the Kete. One of the missionaries who
visited the Kete village of Bena Kasenga noted that:

[e]very corner and cranny in the town has its *nkissi* or image, and generally the rudest
you could fancy in construction. The features are portrayed by three cuts in a stick.
Two strokes make the mouth, as many each eye and the finish is planting it before
a house or at the cross-road. (Lapsley 1893: 166–7, quoted by Binkley and Darish
1998: 49)

Torday, who collected Kuba artefacts for the British Museum, believed that
the Kuba were one of the few remaining African 'golden civilizations' that
had not totally lost its power and glory, and had produced superior art. His
Romantic search for an antique culture strongly influenced the selection he
made as a collector of artefacts. He was solely interested in objects which,
in his view, demonstrated the aristocratic status and antiquity of the Kuba,
and ignored artefacts which were recently produced or 'spoiled' by over
decoration (Binkley and Darish 1998: 51). The most important objects of
Torday's collecting activities were *ndop*, royal king figures made of hardwood
with relatively realistic features. He enthusiastically described a statue of the
seventeenth-century ruler Shyaam aMbul a Ngoong as 'the most remarkable
work of art black Africa ever produced' (Torday 1925: 147, quoted by Binkley
and Darish 1998: 52).

The above demonstrates that the evolutionist understanding of art decontextualised artefacts by presenting them as examples of prototypical styles
which signified levels of progression. Anthropologists like Haddon and Torday
failed to examine local processes of aestheticisation and interpretation, and
ended up projecting rigid ethnocentric assumptions on the artefacts they
collected. Their theories constructed 'form' and 'technique' as units of
factual knowledge which could be measured through scientific methods,
and objectively determine the developmental stage of a certain peoples. As
noted in Chapter 1, this book argues by contrast that classification *is* interpretation, that ethnographers should acknowledge and reflect on their own
interpretative power, and study their own and other agents' involvement in
the dynamics of object transit and transition.

DIFFUSIONISM: DISTRIBUTION AND CULTURE CONTACT

Around the turn of the century, some German scholars, such as Adolf Bastian (1826–1905) and Friedrich Ratzel (1844–1904), began to criticise the evolutionist conceptualisation of art and culture. They rejected the argument that art and culture were related indicators of relative progression, and claimed that the formal similarities of artefacts produced in different geographical settings were generated by migration, trade and other mechanisms of transmission. Attacking the quantative notion of culture, they defined art as a pan-human phenomenon of production, distribution and imitation. In this 'diffusionist' perspective, stylistic likeness was an indicator of social interaction, and 'cultures' were distinct units of people who produced particular styles, which were often borrowed from other cultures.

Bastian and Ratzel developed their ideas during a period when nationalism became an important political force (Germany unified in 1871; during the second half of the nineteenth century the Habsburg Empire was troubled by the nationalist aspirations of the Slavic minorities). The image of culture as a binding force, propagated by the German philosopher Herder, became central both to nationalist thinking and in the emerging academic field of ethnology (see also Chapter 6).

Bastian (a physician who had travelled widely), fiercely attacked the evolutionist thesis which stipulated that 'primitives' were mentally under-developed and uncultured. He argued that all humans had similar mental capacities and shared basic ideas (*Elementar-Gedanken*) which were shaped within particular geographical contexts (Bastian 1860, 1871–73). He pointed out that fully developed ideas or 'culture traits' (*Völker Gedanken*) found their expression in man-made artefacts, and that specific culture traits were often spread out over large areas due to processes of migration and cultural borrowing. Consequently, geographic regions which produced similar artefacts (*geographische Provinzen*) sometimes stretched out over many hundreds of miles, and many regions showed a variety of different, often 'impure' cultural traits. In a similar vain, the geographer Ratzel distinguished particular 'culture areas' (*Kulturkreise*) by grouping artefacts that shared similar designs and styles. His ideas strongly influenced anthropological thinking during the last decade of the nineteenth century, and had a particularly strong impact on American anthropology through the work of Franz Boas (Boas 1927: 5).

As with evolution theory, diffusion theory was strongly influenced by the discourse of scientific objectivity, and often based its analyses on the study of spatially and historically decontextualised artefacts. This implies that, although the diffusionists acknowledged that objects move across time and space, they did not write critical studies of cultural appropriation. Form and function were at the centre of their analytical focus, and, as with evolution theory, the analysts were not particularly interested in local meanings. Central to diffusionism 'was the idea that humans were basically uninventive, so that most inventions were made only once and spread by migration and diffusion; in extreme form, from a single source' (Hatcher 1985: 245). As the following case demonstrates, this universalist assumption about the inevitability of cultural imitation was one of the weakest and most debatable arguments in diffusionist theory.

FRASER: THE DIFFUSION OF 'HERALDIC WOMEN'

A relatively late but typical example of diffusionism is Douglas Fraser's work on the image of the 'heraldic woman' (1966 [1941]). His analysis discussed the historical and geographical spread of representations of this female figure who, holding her knees apart, exposes her genital area. In most cases, two other figures – animals, birds, monsters or humans – symmetrically flank on her sides. According to Fraser, the image was historically and geographically widespread because it was extremely compelling: 'like the frontal face, it has the power to ensure the viewer's glance and hence capture his subjectivity or selfhood'. Interestingly, Fraser talked here about object agency, a perspective that would be further developed by Alfred Gell in the late twentieth century (see Chapter 3). Fraser also claimed that the image was widely reproduced in different cultural and historical contexts because it could be interpreted in different ways. Some saw it as a magical charm, which had the power to increase fertility, others wore it to guarantee safety and success in battle, and again others used it to ward off death in childbirth.

Fraser found examples of the heraldic woman in many different regions and periods, including Luristan (1000–600 BC), Etruria (600–500 BC), and in twentieth-century Cameroon, New Guinea, Borneo and Ireland. His Luristan example was a bronze pin which depicted a Mother Goddess holding her breasts while giving birth, with two beings rearing up on either side of her. According to Fraser, it was a fertility symbol as well as an erotic symbol, and a fusion of culture traits had taken place because the creators of the object had combined the two roles performed by the goddess Ishtar or Ishtar-Kititum in nearby Semitic Mesopotamia (as goddess of fertility and goddess of war).

He argued that:

[t]he fusion of these two images ... may have been abetted by the marginal position of the Luristan people. As a nomadic horse-folk living on the periphery of the Ancient Near East, they produced little themselves but imported metal workers from Mesopotamia and other areas to produce the luxury goods they required. Luristan art was therefore invariably less canonical than that of the settled populations of the Ancient Orient and often lagged behind the styles of the sedentary groups. Symmetrical flanking, for example, was obsolete in Mesopotamia when the Luristan bronze casters were still employing this device constantly. (Fraser 1966 [1941]: 39–40)

The above clearly shows that formal similarities and differences were taken as a direct proof of contact (or the lack of contact) between or amongst populations. Supporters of the diffusionist perspective were so convinced of this hypothesis that they often based their analyses on unproven facts, which sometimes led to fierce debates in which scholars accused each other of deliberately suppressing or distorting evidence.

Large gaps also appeared in Fraser's analysis of the heraldic women. One of the objects he included in his analysis was a twentieth-century West African image from Cameroon, which had been carved in the wooden door lintel of the palace of the Bamileke paramount chief. In Fraser's words, it showed 'two displayed female figures who subdue single leopards on either side of a central displayed figure, seemingly male, who controls two leopards', and he tentatively suggested that '[t]his scene *probably* represents the chief who with his first wife is supposed to become a leopard on occasion. As in Benin art, these leopard-controlling figures are *probably* intended to symbolize the power of the chief and his protection of the group' (Fraser 1966 [1941]: 46, italics mine). His strong belief in the premises of diffusionist theory was also reflected in the following statement:

Until more is known about the transmission of Mediterranean and Near Eastern ideas to West Africa, it is impossible to single out the precise source of these influences. But the multiplication of similarities makes the chances of independent invention and convergence relatively slight. (1966 [1941]: 47)

This again shows the stubbornness with which the diffusionists held on to the idea of cultural borrowing.

FRANZ BOAS: A CULTURAL RELATIVIST ANALYSIS OF 'PRIMITIVE ART'

As argued earlier, both evolutionist and diffusionist perspectives were based on universalist arguments. In the evolutionist case, ethnocentric aesthetic standards (reflecting the Kantian notion of inherent aesthetic value) divided the human races into a hierarchy of increasingly civilised species, and all humans (once progressed), were thought to eventually share the same aesthetic standards. The diffusionists, by contrast, distinguished a universal human tendency to copy and imitate, and used this perspective to make all sorts of hypotheses about culture contact. A radically different perspective, which combined universalist and cultural relativist arguments, was developed by Franz Boas (1854–1942), who attacked the evolutionist view on art and culture in a series of public lectures during the first two decades of the twentieth century. Having worked in the Royal Ethnographic Museum in Berlin from mid 1885 to mid 1886 as an assistant under Bastian (see also Chapter 6), he was influenced by diffusionism and strongly disagreed with the view that 'primitives' were backward irrational beings. In 1927 he stated that:

[a]nyone who has lived with primitive tribes, who has shared their joys and sorrows, their privations and luxuries, who sees in them not solely subjects of study to be examined like a cell under the microscope, but feeling and thinking human beings, will agree that there is no such thing as a 'primitive mind', a 'magical' or 'prelogical' way of thinking, but that each individual in 'primitive' society is a man, a woman,

a child of the same kind, of the same way of thinking, feeling, and acting as man, woman or child in our own society. (Boas 1955 [1927]: 2)

Boas's aim, however, differed from the diffusionist one. Even though he was interested in 'the regional distribution of folklore elements' (Stocking 1995: 12), his research amongst the Kwakuitl did not focus on imitation and contact, but rather examined the ways in which artefacts were used and given meaning in particular socio-cultural settings. Boas (1955 [1927]: 4–6) strongly criticised the diffusionist tendency to generalise,[5] and stressed that people who formed cultural units were not only influenced by outsiders but were also able to invent new forms independently. This implied that the existence of similar forms in different regions did not automatically assume cross-cultural distribution.

Boas's approach to art was strongly shaped by his belief in the importance of skill, and he regarded technical mastery as a universal feature of true art.[6] In this perspective, aesthetic value was only created when 'the technical treatment has attained a certain standard of excellence, when the control of the processes involved is such that certain typical forms are produced' (1955 [1927]: 10). Boas stressed that only skilled producers could set standards of beauty, and that non-specialists who lacked the necessary skills could not attain artistic perfection, but only strive for it. In his view, in all societies, at least some individuals developed artistic skills, and active bodily engagement with the material was vital to the learning process: 'The very fact that the manufactures of man in each and every part of the world have pronounced style proves that a feeling for form develops with technical activities' (1955 [1927]: 11). Boas defined aesthetic experience as 'elevation of the mind' through 'sense impression', a view which reflected Kantian ideas as well as Modernist notions of formal beauty (see in particular Chapter 7). Artistic effect, he argued, had a 'twofold source'; it was either produced by form alone, or by ideas associated with form (1955 [1927]: 13).

Boas's focus on form and technique meant that his analyses were not so much concerned with the analysis of content or expressive intention, which can be exemplified by his analysis of a Haida drawing in his book *Primitive Art*, which represented an eagle carrying away a woman. Noting that certain works of primitive art had a 'fair degree of realism' but were 'composed in ways that distort the natural form and which are perspectively impossible', he wrote:

The face of the woman is evidently intended as a three-quarter view. Facial painting will be noticed on the left cheek; the left ear only is shown as seen in profile; the mouth with teeth is placed under the nose in mixed full profile and front view, and has been moved to the right side of the face. In the lower lip is a large labret shown *en face*, for only in this view was the artist able to show the labret with its characteristic oval surface. The nose seems to be drawn in profile although the nostrils appear *en face*. (Boas 1955 [1927]: 71)

Arguing that the artist had chosen to show only the most essential charac-teristic features of the two figures, he argued that the method should not be considered as unrealistic (and therefore less civilised, as the evolutionists would argue). He argued that the essence of realism could be defined as 'the reproduction of a single momentary visual image', a representation of an experience during which only certain 'salient features ... attract our attention' (1955 [1927]: 72). Interestingly, this definition of realism was close to the approach taken by the Cubists around the turn of the twentieth century, when artists such as Pablo Picasso, inspired by 'primitive art', turned away from the classical Western art canon (see Chapter 5). Like them, Boas rejected the ethnocentric view of abstraction as failed naturalism and propagated a more inclusive approach to aesthetic quality.

STRUCTURAL FUNCTIONALISM: ART AS STABILISING INSTITUTION

As with evolutionism and diffusionism, Boas's approach to art was largely focused on style, form and technique.[7] In general, until the late 1940s, art anthropology was mainly led by an interest in the material aspects of art. Scholars failed to study the social conditions in which specific forms, designs and styles emerged. The development of structural functionalism in Britain in the 1950s, however, sparked off a new trend of research, which focused on the embeddedness of art in society. As Raymond Firth (1973a: v) argued, scholars began to realise that 'primitive art could not be understood without systematic examination of the structure of social relationships and concepts of the specific societies in which it was produced'.

The structural functionalists (most of them examining kinship systems) defined society as a structured system in which people's beliefs, actions and institutions maintained the social and political status quo. Besides 'religion', 'politics', 'economics' and 'kinship', 'art' was one of these institutions. Art anthropologists who were inspired by this new perspective, such as Roy Sieber, did not show much interest in the formal aspects of artefacts, but rather saw art as a social mechanism which helped to produce stability in society. In their view, the arts were 'for the most part oriented positively, that is, toward man's search for a secure and ordered existence' (Sieber 1971 [1962]: 205).

On the positive side, the functionalist approach to art refused to accept the ethnocentric Western definition of fine art as a category of artefacts with universal transcendental aesthetic qualities (see also Chapter 7). In Sieber's words, the arts were 'symptomatic of cultural values' and, since cultural values differed from group to group, it was of little value to project Western aesthetic systems onto non-Western societies (Sieber 1971 [1962]: 205). More problematic, however, was the functionalist linkage of art to culture. 'In emphasizing that an art form takes its meaning from its cultural context, that art is a mirror for culture and society, one may unwittingly imply that the essential reality, the "real thing" lies not in the art at all but in the context' (Flores 1985: 30). In this book, I aim to avoid contextual determinism through the perspective of aestheticisation, which explores how artefacts in transit (through time and space) are experienced and given meaning and value in changing social settings, and analyses the dialectics of materiality and interpretability (see Chapter 3).

In the functionalist perspective, 'culture' was not, as the evolutionists had suggested, an entity which existed in different amounts and levels of complexity. Nor was it, as the diffusionists had claimed, a process of spreading traits and styles. Instead, culture was a relatively unchanging, shared system of thoughts and practices which identified distinct groups of peoples. In the functionalist perspective, art not only helped to maintain social stability, it also reinforced cultural distinctiveness. The conceptualisation of culture as a closed unit of analysis was problematic, however, because it 'over-emphasize[d] the boundedness of particular cultures' (MacClancy 1997: 3). The mosaic perspective of a world made up of separate cultural wholes blinded the functionalists to dynamic processes of transit and transition, which meant that they ignored the impact of global economics on local artefact production (see Chapter 5). Another major weakness was the overemphasis on social stability and consensus. In the words of Toni Flores (1985: 30), 'there is a concomitant and very real danger of seeing art as mirroring, not tension and change, but the status quo, the official structure, the ideology of the dominant group'. Stylistic differences between individual artists were ignored (a view that persists),[8] and the fact that members of specific cultural or other groups do not automatically share the same thoughts and feelings, even if they outwardly conform, was not acknowledged.

ASHANTI ARTEFACTS AND POLITICAL CONTROL

To understand the impact of the ahistorical and overgeneralising functionalist view of art and culture on ethnographic interpretations of material production, it is useful to look more closely at a specific analysis. Not surprisingly, many functionalists were interested in cultural production in *hierarchical* societies, as they tried to understand how artefacts reinforced social stability and justified the authority of political powerholders. The West African Ashanti, ruled by a powerful class of royalty, were an attractive object of study (Anderson 1979).[9] In 1701, the Ashanti rulers had established a powerful empire when local leaders had formed a confederation of city states. Ashanti society was highly stratified and was headed by a hereditary king, the Asantihene. The political organisation was based on a matrilineal kinship system and a complex political hierarchy. Senior lineages provided village headmen who formed a council of heads with representatives of the other lineages; on a higher provincial level, each senior royal clan provided a chief who formed a higher-level council with other chiefs. The political system was protected by supernatural forces in the form of ancestor spirits (Cole and Ross 1977; Hatcher 1985: 213; Rattray 1927; Service 1963). The political powerholders employed specialised artisans to produce objects that symbolised their status and authority. The sacred Golden Stool was believed to enshrine and protect the soul of the nation, and other artefacts, such as ceremonial swords, staffs and carved stools, similarly objectified supernaturally sanctified political authority. As Evelyn Payne Hatcher (1985: 213) noted, '[m]any art forms were involved in the symbolic regalia that went with this system', and this 'was not just a matter of parading rank, but of visually proclaiming the social contract, the constitution of the nation'.

The functionalist perspective on Ashanti regalia provided a valuable insight into the political function of artefacts. Yet, as noted earlier, the reduction of 'art' to a purely functional realm of action underestimated the complexity of internal power struggles, and excluded the possibility of individual and collective resistance. In Hatcher's words:

> even though symbolic forms are important in maintaining society, especially when it is conceived as an organic whole, we cannot maintain that they always work, that each society is a smoothly functioning entity, existing in isolation. This being so, a full understanding of the social functions of art must include situations of competition, conflict, violence and war. (1985: 114)

In the Ashanti case, the functionalist perspective also ignored the impact of the global market on local artefact production (see also Chapter 5). During the colonial period, the market for Ashanti carving had widened as colonial officials and tourists became interested in African souvenirs. Responding to this new demand, individual carvers introduced new objects and styles (Silver 1983). Some of the new artefacts, such as small-size wooden replicas of royal stools, may have referred to the importance of the Asantihene to the Ashanti people; yet, as commodities which left Ashanti territory, they did not, of course, reinforce his local authority, but rather signified his declining power as a result of colonialism and global capitalism.

The above demonstrates that functionalist theory used a combination of universalist and cultural relativist arguments. On the one hand, it claimed that the world could be conceptualised as a variety of bounded entities, namely cultures, and that art, regarded as a social mechanism of aesthetic behaviour, was prevalent in all cultures. Art was thus a universal phenomenon, and its function was similar all over the world. On the other hand, the functionalists claimed that even though art everywhere helped to create socio-political stability, its form and local meaning depended on the cultural context. As argued in Chapter 1, the usefulness of a generalising perspective is highly debatable, as the definition of art is often contested and its function variable, even within single socio-historical settings.

Many scholars who had been influenced by functionalist theory became conscious of (some of) its shortcomings during the 1960s and 1970s, and called for a more subtle analysis of art in society. In 1973, for example, Sieber attacked functionalism's ahistorical view of culture as a stable system, and emphasised that art forms should not only be examined in terms of function and style, but also as historically emerging cultural forms (1973a: 71). As we shall see in the next section, an increasing number of scholars began to attack the functionalist lack of attention to individual difference, and began to explore the tensions between social norms and individual creativity.

ART PRODUCERS AS INDIVIDUALS

A number of anthropologists who tried to determine the criteria of aesthetic judgement in particular cultures began to focus on individual artists and their public. In 1973, the editor of the volume *Primitive Art and Society*, Anthony Forge, stressed that individual artists had personal styles (1973a: xiv), and pointed at earlier studies by Himmelheber (1935, 1960), Fagg (1963), Fischer (1962) and Gerbrands (1967), which had already shown that tribal styles were not uniform or unchanging. He argued that:

[i]t seems obvious from the evidence available that all art systems, no matter how tied up with ancestral sanction and ritual functions, provide both stylistic limits, culturally determined but capable of change through innovation, and at the same time considerable freedom in selection of elements and in stylistic variation available to the artist working within these limits. (1973a: xv–xvi)

The anthology *The Traditional Artist in African Societies* was also published in 1973 and, in the introduction, Warren d'Azevedo (1973: 1) similarly called for a focus on individual artists, and complained that the actual creators of the objects collected by Western art lovers had remained 'largely anonymous'. One of the contributors, Frederick Dockstader approved of the focus on individual artists, but warned of the 'risk of building whole cultural concepts upon the work of a single artist in that culture' (1973: 125). In other words, the focus on specific artists should not lead to generalisation but, rather, to a more complex analysis of art in society, which would explore internal difference.[10] Various contributors to the volume analysed the evaluative criteria used by individual critics and consumers. Their perspective on art was quite close to the art world theory of art sociologist Howard Becker, who published his ideas in his book *Art Worlds* in 1982. As will be discussed in more detail in Chapter 5, Becker would argue that one should study the interaction of *all* actors in art worlds, including producers, critics, distributors and consumers.

Paul Bohannan had similarly claimed in 1961 that a sole focus on artists and their products was limited, and served to reproduce the Western myth of individual artistic genius (1971 [1961]: 173). When doing research amongst the Tiv, he had discovered that wooden artefacts were often carved by more than one individual, and that artists were influenced by other people's comments.[11] Rather tellingly, he recalled:

My most vivid encounter with such art criticism amongst the Tiv came when I was watching an artist – not a very good one – carve a wooden figure of a woman. The carving, which I had commissioned from him, was about eighteen inches high and, like all African sculpture, was worked from a chunk of log while it was still green. As he worked, and I sat by silently watching, a youngster from his compound appeared. The youngster said, by way of greeting, the equivalent of 'Grandfather, you are carving [creating – *gba*] a woman.' The old man replied that such was indeed the case. 'What are those three bumps on her belly?' the youngster asked. The old man laid down his adze and eyed the youngster who had interrupted him. 'The middle one,' he said impatiently, 'is her navel.' The boy was silent for a moment but spoke again just as the old man reached for his adze. 'Then what about the other two bumps?' The old man barely concealed his contempt for questions about so obvious a point. 'Those are her breasts.' 'Way down there?' the youngster asked. 'They've fallen!' the artist fairly shouted. 'But, grandfather, even if they had fallen, they would not ... ' The old man grabbed up his adze. 'All right, all right,' he muttered, and with three perfectly aimed blows the three bumps came off. (1971 [1961]: 175–6])

The above shows that during the 1960s and 1970s, certain anthropologists began to explore the social complexity of art production in specific cultures, while acknowledging the importance of individual difference and change. As we shall see in the following section, rather paradoxically, other scholars who developed the strongly influential theory of structuralism completely ignored the level of individual creativity.

STRUCTURALISM: OPPOSITION AND MEDIATION

We have seen that functionalism was a system theory that regarded culture and art as social mechanisms that served to reproduce society. Structuralism was a very different type of system theory, which based its arguments on the idea that human life was structured by mechanism of the brain. As with functionalism, structuralism combined universalist and cultural relativist arguments. The universalist argument was based on the view that *all* humans imposed a logical order on their experience. The relativist argument concerned the particularity of specific cultural forms of expression.

The central ideas of structuralism were introduced in the 1960s by the French anthropologist Claude Lévi-Strauss, who strongly disagreed with the evolutionist claim that non-Europeans were irrational beings who were unable to think logically. The main structuralist premise was that the human brain was organised by the rule of opposition and mediation, and that all social and cultural phenomena, including art, were expressions of underlying, unconscious mental processes (see Lévi-Strauss 1953, 1960, 1963). As Hatcher explained:

When we look at visual forms that already exist, and try to figure out what is being said, when we seek to analyze the visual using words, we often do so by making distinctions in terms of binary oppositions or polar oppositions. The structuralist form of analysis is based on an opposition theory that comes out of the effort to make distinctions, and so emphasizes the either/or sorting process as the basic organizing principle of human thought. (1985: 138)

Lévi-Strauss saw this structuring principle as an inherent part of human nature and the result of human evolution. He defined art as a typically human form of cultural expression, which reproduced the structuring mechanisms of the human mind (Lévi-Strauss 1963).

The structuralists were inspired by structural linguistics, in particular by Ferdinand de Saussure (1959), who had rejected the view that languages represented reality directly and that linguistic behaviour should be regarded as a purely conscious enterprise. Instead, de Saussure had claimed that the relationship between sound and meaning was arbitrary, and that all languages had logical structures which were based on contrasts and con-tradictions (*langue*) that were unconsciously reproduced by language speakers during speech (*parole*). De Saussure had introduced the terms 'signifier', 'signified' and 'sign' to analyse processes of linguistic signification. In his analytical framework, signs consisted of agreed-upon associations between sounds (signifiers) and mental images (signifieds). To give an example, in the English language the sound 'monkey' (defined as a signifier) is connected to a particular signified, namely the mental image of a monkey. The sign 'monkey' then consists of the relationship between the signifier and the signified, and is based on the cultural agreement that 'monkey' stands for a particular kind of animal that has two arms, two legs, a tail, that eats bananas, and so on.

The linguist convincingly argued that signs did not passively reflect reality but instead actively constructed reality through the systematic use of similarities and differences. In the case of monkey, the spoken word 'monkey' differs from 'mincky', and only some animals are classified as 'monkeys'. In the case of art, the spoken word 'art' differs from 'irt', and speakers of English generally connect the signifier 'art' to mental images of paintings and statues. Art is often opposed to other signs, such as 'craft', 'kitsch' or 'propaganda' and, in concrete socio-historical contexts, the choice to call something art (and not craft, kitsch or propaganda) reveals more about the perception of the speaker than about the object itself (see in particular Chapter 7).

Lévi-Strauss considered the structuralist approach to language a helpful conceptual model, which could also be used for the study of culture and art, as he argued that human products were only meaningful because they were shaped by underlying contrasts. In his view, common cultural binary oppositions were, for example, 'raw' versus 'cooked', 'culture' versus 'nature', 'man' versus 'woman' and 'human' versus 'supernatural'. In his analyses of artefacts, he looked for formal contrasts (light/dark, horizontal lines/vertical lines, angular forms/rounded forms, etc.) as well as for conceptual oppositional pairs which made art and other cultural forms, such as myths, meaningful.

Structuralism influenced numerous anthropologists, including Douglas Fraser (1974), who analysed African art in terms of meaningful oppositions, and James Fernandez (1971 [1966], 1973), who argued that the Fang used oppositional categories to shape social and symbolic forms, regarding them as mediating solutions. Referring to Fernandez' work, Hatcher (1985: 138–9) noted that '[s]tructuralist analysis fits the Fang case very well. Fernandez has so well documented many situations in which the Fang use symmetrically balanced social and symbolic forms and perceive them as solutions, that one is convinced of the meanings he gives us.' She added, however, that '[t]his is not always the case. The problem is the enormous number of polar dimensions that the analytic mind can discover in any visual form' (1985: 139). In other words, in the analysis, the line between Fang perception and the structuralist obsession with oppositional pairs was hard to draw.

Another important point of criticism was that structuralist theory completely disregarded historical change and individual idiosyncrasy. Clifford Geertz (1983 [1977]: 96), for example, strongly disagreed with the structuralist view that 'the whole secret of aesthetic power is located in the formal relations amongst sounds, images, volumes, themes, or gestures'. He argued that 'one can no more understand aesthetic objects as con-catenations of pure form than one can understand speech as a parade of syntactic variations, or myth as a set of structural transformations' (1983 [1977]: 98). As we will see in Chapter 3, this failure was sharply addressed by post-structuralist theorists. Stucturalist theory was also heavily criticised by scholars studying linguistic behaviour instead of formal classification. As early as 1969, J.R. Searle argued that speech (*parole*), and not the rules underlying languages (*langue*) had an empirical existence, and that individual speakers of single languages internalised these rules in different ways (Layton 1991 [1981]: 102).[12] The conceptualisation of culture as a process rather than a system, as a performative act which unfolded in real time and space, became central to the study of oral literature and in folklore studies (see, for example, Ben-Amos 1977). Chapter 3 demonstrates that the practice-oriented approach began to influence the study of material culture during the second half of the 1970s (see, for example, Fabian). The new paradigm led to a strong interest in the enactment of power through cultural discourse and practice.

OPPOSITIONS IN INUIT MYTHS AND MATERIAL CULTURE

Structuralism, although heavily criticised for its a-historical approach to culture, has been extremely influential. The following account will focus on a study by Susan Pearce (1987) of myths, rituals and artefacts produced by the Thule Inuit, and will point out some of the weaknesses of the structuralist premise.

Pearce's analysis was largely based on information gathered by Boas in 1883 and 1884. She argued that a particular series of oppositions underlay key concepts in Thule culture, and that these oppositions were also reflected in their material products. In the first part of her analysis, Pearce discussed the structure of Thule myths, distinguished opposed segments as binary pairs, and amalgamated the latter into single set of binary pairs, namely 'birdland/land', 'woman/man', 'geese maidens/salmon father', 'vulva/penis', 'feathered/naked', 'wife/husband', 'mother/father' and 'feathers/wood'. Daily life, she argued, was organised around the following opposed pairs: 'winter/summer', 'sea/land', 'sea mammals/caribou' and 'women/men'.

To assess the underlying structuring principle of Inuit artefacts, Pearce looked at number of collections of Inuit artefacts which, in her view, demonstrated 'a clear tendency for caribou hunting-arrowheads to be made of caribou antler and the artefacts of winter (snow and dog equipment), seal hunting, bird hunting, and of women (sewing equipment) to be made of sea mammal ivory or bone, a distinction which does not reflect practical considerations' (1987: 318). This, she claimed, suggested that the oppositions 'ivory/antler' and 'feather/wood' could be added to the set of binary pairs on which the myths were based. She concluded that her analysis demonstrated 'that material culture, which until recently has been given a rather low intellectual rating among social anthropologists, carries just as many social messages as myths or kinship systems, and should be an integral part of any overall cultural analysis' (1987: 319–20). Even though Pearce's plea for serious attention to be paid to the messages of material culture must be applauded, her analysis showed the weaknesses of orthodox structuralist theory, which tends to produce overgeneralised, a-historical representations of (in her case Inuit) culture and which fail to examine the ideas and practices of socially and historically situated individuals.

CULTURE, COGNITION AND ART: ETHNOAESTHETICS

Criticising the ethnocentric tendencies of the structuralists, numerous anthropologists who were partly influenced by cognitive psychology developed the field of 'ethnoaesthetics', a branch of the much broader field of 'ethnoscience' which examined indigenous systems of classification and knowledge.[13] Ethnoaestheticians defined culture as a system of knowledge (a cognitive map) which encoded culturally specific aesthetic codes and preferences within particular societies. Scholars taking this approach studied people's own criteria of beauty, arguing that only an emic perspective would enable them to avoid ethnocentrism (Flores 1985: 31; Kempton 1981: 3).[14] Evidently, the assumption that all members of a particular culture share the same cognitive map simplifies the dynamics of meaning production in contexts of power and historical change. Various scholars inspired by eth-noaesthetics, however, remained sensitive to historical process and individual difference, as demonstrated by the following examples.

In his study of culturally specific concepts of beauty amongst the Nilotic Pakot people, Harold Schneider (1971 [1956]) found that his informants used the term *pachigh* when talking about something pretty or beautiful, or about something unusual but pleasant to look at. Male Pakot, in particular, used this term to classify a number of different sensorial experiences which they valued positively, including the sight of women with firm round breasts, a light brown skin and even, white teeth. They also used it to express their admiration for the colours and shapes of cow hides. Yet not everybody agreed when evaluating something as *pachigh*, which pointed at individual perceptual difference. Schneider also found that matter could lose its perceived beauty over time.

'The glossy surface of "americani" cloth imported into the reserve is similarly considered pretty, but when it wears off the cloth becomes purely *karam*' (1971 [1956]: 57). His findings demonstrate the significance of historical process to the production of meaning, value and sensorial experience.[15]

Nancy Munn (1973a, 1973b), who examined the folk model of Walbiri Australian Aboriginal cosmology as expressed by visual and verbal signs, was also fascinated by the ways in which individuals manipulate visual symbols within the limits of culturally specific notions of art. According to Munn, 'a structural analysis of the representational system [was] essential not only to an interpretation of the dynamics through which the forms are generated, but also to an explanation of the relation between the graphic system and the wider sociocultural order' (1973: 3). She used componential analysis to explore the meaning of Walbiri women's body-painting, and found that the women made creative personal statements by combining a limited set of forms and playing with symbolic ambiguity (Munn 1962, 1973; see also Layton 1991 [1981]: 208).

Many cognitive anthropologists claimed to conduct 'scientific', value-free studies, and made cross-cultural comparisons to test their hypothesis. As will be argued in Chapter 3, their empiricist approach drew a strict boundary between themselves, as observers, and their object of study. They ignored the fact that ethnographic knowledge 'is grounded in ... practical, personal and participatory experience in the field as much as ... detached observations' (Jackson 1989: 3). John L. Fischer (1971: 141), for example, tested how the dominance of straight or curved lines in visual art could be related to the absence or presence of social hierarchy and male dominance.[16] His conclusions were strongly speculative and based on debatable statistical outcomes.[17]

Clifford Geertz (1973: 11) fiercely attacked the paradigms of ethnoscience and cognitive anthropology, and argued that the assumption that 'culture consists ... of mental phenomena which can ... be analysed by formal methods similar to those of mathematics and logic' was a 'fallacy'. He argued that human behaviour was not knowledge itself, even though certain types of knowledge were necessary for particular ways of acting. Instead, he stated, culture was formed actively through symbolic action in public. He also criticised empiricist claims to objectivity, arguing that 'cultural analysis is (or should be) guessing at meanings, assessing the guesses, and drawing explanatory conclusions from the better guesses, not discovering the Continent of Meaning and mapping out its bodiless landscape' (1973: 20). As we shall see in Chapter 3, his disbelief in the project of scientific objectivity was central to his view that anthropology was an interpretative science. This view represented a paradigm shift which strongly influenced the study of art and artefacts in during the last three decades of the twentieth century, moving the focus of inquiry to questions of power and representation.[18] As pointed out in Chapter 1, this interest in power has also informed my own approach, which highlights that experience and perception (including the fieldworker's experience and perception) is often influenced by previous knowledge, which is in turn shaped by individual life histories and socio-political processes.

'ART': A CATEGORY OF CROSS-CULTURAL COMPARISON?

The above showed that numerous anthropologists, who all criticised the evolutionist claim that only civilised Europeans had the ability to produce valuable art, searched for analytical tools to compare what they regarded as artistic behaviour. Several prominent theorists proposed definitions of art which could be used for cross-cultural comparison. Warren d'Azevedo (1973: 6) suggested that it was necessary to first identify 'a type of individual behavior and a type of social action' that could be 'designated as the loci of artistry'. Melford Spiro (1968: 91) also stressed that it was important to find a working definition of art that would allow scholars to make cross-cultural comparisons, but warned that:

[the] insistence on universality in the interests of a comparative social science is, in my opinion, an obstacle to the comparative method for it leads to continuous changes of definition, and ultimately, to definitions which, because of their vagueness or abstractness, are all but useless. (1968: 86–7).[19]

Spiro tried to solve this problem by constructing a checklist of certain art 'indicators' which were to be adjusted according to local conditions and understandings. In a similar vein, Roy Sieber (1973b: 431) distinguished eight 'congeries of qualities' (see Chapter 1, page 4). He believed that, if used sensibly, his list could identify art in different cultural settings, but he stressed that none of the indicators were indispensable as they could appear 'in no fixed number or fixed groupings' and be combined with 'as yet unidentified concepts' (1973: 431).

As already pointed out in Chapter 1, more recently, Richard L. Anderson (2000) proposed a theoretical definition of art that outlined certain combinations of highly probable artistic features.[20] Identifying himself as an anti-postmodern positivist,[21] he distinguished a number of objective traits that would help scholars to establish whether a particular artefact could be considered art or not.[22] As explained in Chapter 1, this book uses a perspective which emphasises that aesthetic values are the product of social process, and that objects can gain or lose the status 'art' (defined in different ways) as they follow individual trajectories.

Some scholars who have acknowledged that objects can be appropriated as 'art' in Western art markets, have nevertheless maintained that art is a cross-cultural category, arguing that only artefacts with certain aesthetic qualities can enter these markets. Jacques Maquet (1986) claimed that, although art has different forms in different societies, aesthetic standards and the criteria by which they are judged are universal. In his view, the main components of universal aesthetic quality are clarity, simplicity, integration of composition, expressive power and 'discontinuity with the everyday environment'.[23] His universalist argument was based on the idea of a shared human biological make-up. He argued that:

[b]ecause the human organism, particularly the nervous system, is practically identical among all living populations, we may assume that its main functions, such as acting, thinking, contemplating, being affected by feelings and emotions, are not limited to some human populations. As creation and appreciation of art are mental processes, it is not unwarranted to look at their manifestations in the whole gamut of cultures. (1986: 3)

Maquet's view is, however, problematic. First of all, his definition of aesthetic perception as a mental process wrongly creates an image of the mind as an isolated cognitive mechanism. Second, when analysing people's engagement with objects and images, it is hard if not impossible to separate the more general, physiological responses from particular ones that are shaped by group-specific dispositions and individual interests. As Jeremy Coote (1992: 247) has noted, '[w]hile our common human physiology no doubt results in our having universal, generalised responses to certain stimuli, perception is an active and cognitive process in which cultural factors play a dominant role'. Along similar lines, Howard Morphy argued that '[t]he physical properties have an effect on the senses, but it is the process of aesthetic transformation that gives a value to a property, a value which often becomes associated with an emotional response' (1993: 7).[24]

As noted in Chapter 1, in this book I refuse to identify art as a generalising etic category, based on material characteristics, social features or a shared biological make-up. Instead, I regard 'art' as a set of historically specific ideas and practices, and concentrate on conflicting and changing notions of art in concrete socio-historical contexts. Interested in processes of transit and transition that may or may not transform objects into 'art', this book is therefore primarily focused on the analysis of aestheticisation, commoditisation and object agency in changing historical contexts.

CONCLUSION

This chapter has demonstrated that specific notions of 'art' and 'culture' have strongly shaped the anthropological study of artefacts from 1850 to 1975. Even though the connection was not always straightforward, anthropologists' perspectives were influenced by particular historical processes, such as the development of colonial empires, the emergence of nationalism and the belief in scientific objectivity. Debates about 'art' were shaped by discourses of 'culture' which reflected conflicting ideas about the history and variety of human production.

Evolutionist scholars reinforced Western discourses of high culture which regarded fine art as an indicator of civilised refinement. This notion of art became dominant in the Europe when 'the fine arts' were professionalised as a form of high culture (see Chapter 7). The evolutionists transformed their elitist assumptions about artistic quality into scientific tools which created hierarchically ordered racial groups. Their analyses justified colonial practices and racial prejudices.

The diffusionists were also influenced by notions of 'more developed' and 'less developed' artistic styles, but their notion of culture *denied* that art was a sign of relative progress and, by contrast, linked objects and people to places. This is not surprising, because the formation of diffusionist theory coincided with the formation of nationalist ideology, which defined culture as an essential identity-place category. As with the evolutionists, the diffusionists claimed scientific objectivity through the careful study of formal similarity and difference.

Boas's theory of art borrowed ideas which were dominant in Western art education, namely that artists needed to develop technical skills to be able to realise their creative products. Yet while conventional art historians most valued the skills necessary to produce classical naturalist styles, Boas argued that non-representational imagery was similarly skilful and artistic. In this, he reflected some of the Modernist critique of classical aesthetic theory (see Chapter 7). Boas argued that unbiased studies of form and technique would produce objective analyses which showed how art existed within the context of culture. His emphasis on skill, however, was informed by the then conventional Western discourses of technical mastery.

Defining 'art' as an institution which created stability, the functionalists also projected Western categories on the empirical realities they studied. To them, culture was like a machine, producing order and repetitive movement. Their perspective illustrated the influence of industrialisation and mechanisation on their intellectual imagination. The functionalist use of the category of 'art' demonstrated a strong belief in the universal creative potential of all humans and criticised elitist discourses of 'fine art'. Myths of Western superiority and creative genius were further attacked by scholars such as d'Azevedo and Dockstader, who focused on the activities of individual artefact producers outside Europe.

The structuralist interest in the unconscious reflected the impact of psychoanalysis on anthropology. Lévi-Strauss and his followers represented themselves as objective scholars, who could unveil the structuring principles of unconscious binary oppositions because they had the intellectual power to unravel cultural complexity. Here, culture was also a mechanism, albeit not of society (as in the functionalist model) but of the human brain. Cognitive science and ethnoaesthetics explored the use of local languages to identify the structuring principles of language and art. Regarding cognition as a grammar-like cultural system, they ignored the pragmatic use of language.

The next chapter will demonstrate how system approaches to culture and art were attacked from the 1970s onwards. New theories have been developed, which have stressed the *processual* nature of artefact production, interpretation and experience. As we shall see, these theories have also criticised many earlier studies for their lack of interest in the ideological aspects of material production.

3 FROM VISUAL COMMUNICATION TO OBJECT AGENCY

During the past four decades, numerous influential scholars have questioned and attacked the cultural relativist paradigm, which, as we saw in Chapter 2, was introduced by Boas and reproduced in different forms by functionalism, structuralism and ethnoscience. Cultural relativism understood culture as a closed system in which art, defined as a cross-cultural form of action with particular features, took on culturally specific forms, meanings or functions that could be objectively studied and compared. By contrast, the scholars whose work will be discussed in this chapter have developed perspectives which analyse the historical and ideological aspects of cultural production, and often emphasise the processual nature of object transit and transition. In the words of Anderson and Field:

> No longer can the scholar speak of small-scale societies as if they were merely distant curiosities, exotic but nearly extinct cultural butterflies to be embalmed by the fieldworker's pen and ink, then brought back to the West for dispassionate dissection. To the contrary, new emphasis is being placed on what might be called 'the *ethnographic* beholder's share', that is, the ways in which Western culture influences, and is simultaneously influenced by, perceptions of the Other. (1993: 388–9)

Most theories which have been developed from the 1970s onwards have addressed issues of power and inequality, an aspect of object production that was largely ignored by previous theories.[1] Another feature which characterises more recent studies is the shift towards reflexivity, the acknowledgement that anthropologists themselves actively shape the production of ethnographic knowledge through their own representational power.

SYMBOLIC ANTHROPOLOGY: ART AS COMMUNICATION SYSTEM

During the late 1960s, studies of religion, myth and cosmology began to spark a growing interest in visual symbolism. As became clear in the previous chapter, structuralist anthropologists examined the ways in which mental processes structured social life, and some showed a particular interest in the underlying symbolic structures of visual imagery. Nancy Munn, who was strongly inspired by the work of Lévi-Strauss, argued that 'the framework of symbolic theory [can] integrate the study of social, religio-cosmological, and aesthetic systems' (1973: 2).[2] Munn was inspired by the structuralist method of componential analysis, but focused on meaning production in *concrete* social contexts. This meant that she avoided the danger of over-generalisation and abstraction.

Munn had conducted fieldwork from 1956 to 1958 amongst the Walbiri, an Australian Aborigine people who lived in the western desert region of Central Australia. The Walbiri produced sand drawings and totemic designs. The making of sand drawings was an inherent part of story telling, and the painting of totemic designs (on sacred boards or stones, and on their own bodies) were central to Walbiri ritual life. Munn distinguished types of visual elements and arrangements and analysed their meanings. Ancestral manifestations through dreaming were central to Walbiri thought and were key elements in Walbiri visual symbolism. Graphic designs which represented totemic ancestors were 'extensively elaborated and [formed] part of a wider graphic system with some of the structural characteristics of a "language"' (Munn 1973: 32).

Single semantic units in the Walbiri representational system were made up of a limited number of graphic signs. Different combinations of curved lines and circles could signify different scenes, such as 'a man or woman sitting at a water hole or a woman sitting digging for yams, a man and women sitting at fires or two women digging for yams, actors sitting with backs to the "item", or a number of actors doing different things – for example, women dancing around a fighting stick or people sitting at a fire' (1973: 79). Interestingly, the lines and circles did not form an independent semantic system, but functioned in the context of speech events. In sand story telling, for example, Walbiri women used the graphic images in combination with verbal narrative to teach their children about the ways of the ancestors. In Munn's view, this did not mean that the graphic signs were speech itself. Instead, the graphs had a pictorial and material quality which could not be reduced to language. As with the sand paintings, a limited vocabulary of basic visual elements was used to create a variety of meanings in ritual body painting. In *Yawalyu* (the designs and ceremonies over which Walbiri women exercised rights), for example, four parallel stripes could stand for rain falling, headbands, paths or teeth.

Walbiri women ritually communicated with each other about private dreams in which ancestors had manifested themselves. In the *Yawalyu* ceremony, they painted designs on their breasts, across the shoulders and on the upper arms, stomach and thighs. The women claimed that each design was unique, as it had appeared to a particular female in a particular dream (1973: 36–7). Women often dreamed about food-gathering events or about the performance of a *Yawalyu* ceremony, and associated themselves in their dreams with totemic ancestors through food consumption. In dreams about the honey ant, for example, they would dig up and eat honey ants, and their body painting would include honey ant symbols. In addition, the ritual would be accompanied by honey ant songs. The women believed that the ancestors themselves created the dreams, as well as the visual imagery and the songs (1973: 104).

Munn's interest in the dynamics of symbolic representation was shared by Clifford Geertz, one of the key thinkers who developed the field of symbolic anthropology. In 1973, he warned of the danger of treating culture as a closed symbolic system in which the internal relationships of isolated elements were the object of study. His own semiotic concept of culture was, instead, based on the idea that cultural forms found articulation 'through the flow of behaviour – or, more precisely, [through] social action' (Geertz 1973: 17; see also Otten 1971: xiv). The perspective of aestheticisation taken in this book similarly grounds meaning production in concrete action.

Referring to previous anthropological studies of art, Geertz attacked the scientist aims of ethnoscience and cognitive anthropology, and criticized the functionalist view of art as an instrumental phenomena, arguing that '[a]nything may, of course, play a role in helping society work, painting and sculpting included; just as anything may help it tear apart. But the central connection between art and collective life does not lie on such an instrumental plane, it lies on a semiotic one' (1973: 99). Geertz stated that art had primarily a symbolic value, as it communicated messages about the ways in which people experienced the world. He noted that to be able to understand how people communicated through art, the Saussurian definition of language as a semiotic system had clear limitations. Instead, it was necessary to examine the social reality of communicative practice.

Although revolutionary and insightful at the time, Geertz's approach has a number of analytical weaknesses. Communicative practice is not bounded by cultural boundaries, and Geertz has been attacked because, despite his interest in social practice and historical change, he failed to question the Boasian paradigm of cultural relativism. Geertz and his followers have often reified fixed identity-place notions of culture, a tendency which was strongly criticised by James Clifford (1988: 273), who argued that:

The concept of culture used by anthropologists was, of course, invented by European theorists to account for the collective articulations of human diversity. Rejecting both evolutionism and the overly broad entities of race and civilization, the idea of culture posited the existence of local, functionally integrated units. For all its supposed relativism, though, the concept's model of totality, basically organic in structure, was not different from the nineteenth-century concepts it replaced. Only its plurality was new. Despite many subsequent redefinitions the notion's organicist assumptions have persisted. Cultural systems hold together; and they change more or less continuously, anchored primarily by language and place. *Recent semiotic and symbolic models that conceive of culture as communication are also functionalist in this sense.* (italics mine)

As we shall see in the remainder of this chapter, by redefinining culture as a signifying process and examining objects in transit and transition, an increasing number of scholars have escaped the traps of cultural relativist theory.

MEANING PRODUCTION AS HISTORICAL PROCESS

Important developments in linguistic theory influenced the anthropology of art in ways which eventually led to processual relativism. During the 1960s, an increasing number of linguists and linguistic anthropologists had criticised the Saussurian approach to language and culture. J.R. Searle stressed in 1969 that speech had empirical existence, and that individual speakers of single languages internalised and used linguistic rules in different ways (Layton 1991 [1981]: 102). Dell Hymes (1983), one of the key figures of what became known as 'the anthropology of speaking', called for a focus on the historical dimension of verbal interaction.[3] Agreeing with Hymes, Johannes Fabian (1975: 10) stressed that a structuralist, taxonomic view of cultural production was fundamentally flawed because it historically decontextualised classificatory behaviour and ignored the issue of power: 'in ordering items man is ideological as well as taxonomic; he defines and creates entities apart from assigning relations'. In Fabian's view, knowledge production both articulates and produces reality, and therefore, culture should be defined as *formative* praxis (1984: 20; see also the discussion of Bourdieu's practice theory in Chapter 5).[4] This book strongly agrees with Fabian's view, and will show that knowledge about 'what is art and what not' often functions as a tool of division and selection, used to reinforce, justify or undermine existing power relations.

Using his perspective in an analysis of popular painting in Shaba, Fabian introduced the concept of 'genre' to explore the connection between the material form of art works (the signifier), the interpretation given to them (the signified), the socio-historical context in which interpretations were given, the wider process of signification in which the art works were given meaning and value, and – of crucial importance – the social position of the producers and consumers of the works (Fabian 1978: 319; see also Chapter 5). According to this model, the messages and functions of popular art in Shaba were encoded in concrete socio-historically situated products; not, as the structuralists would argue, in general taxonomic systems.

Fabian (1998: 51) found that the painters and their customers consistently 'defined the domain by a criterion of inclusion they called *ukumbusho*, a picture's capacity to activate memory and reflection', and within the domain, 'a limited, albeit never strictly defined, number of kinds of pictures were distinguished, almost always by commonly known labels'. All paintings somehow referred to experiences of oppression, violence or poverty. The genre 'Colonie Belge', for example, produced by mostly self-made artists and bought by the urban petit-bourgeois, triggered memories of political oppression in the context of Belgian colonial domination. The paintings, Fabian claimed, had a pragmatic as well as a semiotic function. They 'not only produce[d] images of power' but also 'created, within the overall practice of popular culture, a space of freedom from control by government or by the special interests pursued by large employers and the missions' (1998: 53).

POWER AND IDEOLOGY: BEYOND THE MARXIST APPROACH

Fabian had been inspired, but not fully convinced, by the Marxist view that cultural production reproduces power inequalities. Karl Marx had developed his ideas during the mid nineteenth century in a reaction to the effects of industrial capitalism, which had generated growing class differences between those who owned and controlled the means of production and members of the proletariat. The latter were economically reliant on their labour power, and were often underpaid or had to work under miserable conditions. Marx argued that class structures had been created by capitalism and that society was divided into an economic base and a cultural 'superstructure'. All cultural phenomena, including art, were ultimately determined by economic forces. In this perspective, producers who lacked power over the means of production could no longer realise themselves through culture and were therefore oppressed and alienated. In other words, art functioned as a medium of alienation by reproducing and mystifying the social reality of inequality (see also Chapter 5 and 7).

Two concepts were central in the communist critique of capitalism, namely 'cosmopolitanism' and 'formalism'. The first term had been introduced by Marx and Friedrich Engels to describe the formation of an international class of bourgeois entrepeneurs who fully controlled national and international economic processes. Communist aestheticians used the term to claim that artists who had necessarily 'entered the fully developed world of capitalist commodity production' (Fischer 1963 [1959]: 52), were increasingly subjected to the laws of competition, which meant that they were left to serve the interests of the international bourgeoisie. 'Cosmopolitanism', they argued, did not signify the freedom of artistic communication beyond national boundaries, but, instead, signified dependency and constraint. The second concept of 'formalism' was defined as 'a phenomenon typical of a social form no longer in keeping with the times, typical of the fact that a ruling class has outlived itself' (Fischer 1963 [1959]: 130). The idea was that while the content of social reality (class domination) was denied or mystified by capitalist culture, its form (its socio-political structures) was imagined as an eternal immutable state of being. Communist aestheticians saw this phenomenon reflected in art, and argued that 'formalist' artistic styles, such as cubism, overemphasised form at the expense of content, which resulted in an art that was inaccessible to the working classes (1963 [1959]: 127–30; see also Chapter 7). Marxist art historians, such as Ernst Fischer, argued that art should be defined as a means of building the socialist order. The economic restructuring of society would allow artists to free themselves from bourgeois oppression and the production of alienating cultural forms, and would stimulate them to create art with realistic content, which promoted the equality of a classless society.

The previous section demonstrated that although Fabian shared his interest in power and ideology with Marxist theoreticians, he offered a more dynamic theory which acknowledged that cultural production could function as a medium of domination and resistance, but which objected to the image of culture as a superstructure which simply reflected economic processes. During the 1970s and 1980s, numerous other scholars expressed the same view. Abner Cohen (1974: ix) argued that people actively construct meaning through the manipulation of symbols, and that, therefore, art was a productive instead of a reflective domain of action. Karin Barber (1986: 8) similarly stated that '[a]rtforms do not merely reflect an already constituted consciousness giving us window to something fully present. They are in themselves important means through which consciousness is articulated and communicated.'

SIGNIFICATION AS IDEOLOGICAL PRACTICE: DOMINATION AND RESISTANCE

From the 1970s onwards, the theory of semiology, developed by the French scholar Roland Barthes, strongly influenced anthropological thinking about visual representation (1980 [1956], 1977; see also Lidchi 1997: 164, 182). Criticising semiotics as a static model which ignored the pragmatics of knowledge production, Barthes defined culture as 'signifying practice' and emphasised its ideological nature. Many scholars, such as Howard Morphy (1991: 144; see also Chapter 4), agreed with Barthes' point that it was necessary to analyse continual processes of semiosis. Barthes' view also inspired anthropologists such as James Clifford and Ivan Karp to critically examine the politics of museum display (see below and, for more detail, Chapter 6); other scholars, such as Jeremy MacClancy (1997) explored the connections between art production and identity politics in national, colonial and postcolonial contexts.

Barthes had introduced the terms 'primary signification' ('denotation') and 'secondary signification' ('connotation') to point out that signification was a dynamic process, not a timeless system. He argued that existing signs (relationships between signifiers and signifieds, see Chapter 2) were often given new meanings, which meant that signs were transformed into signifiers as they were attached to new signifieds. Meaning, in other words, was not fixed, and objects could be interpreted in many different ways by different individuals in changing socio-historical contexts. Over 50 years earlier, the American philosopher C.S. Peirce[5] had already pointed out that signification was an ongoing process – Barthes emphasised the ideological nature of this process. Through secondary signification, he argued, people produced particular realities which were informed by myth and ideology.[6]

The ideological nature of signification can be illustrated by an analysis of the conflicting meanings of *Welcoming the Red Army*, a memorial statue which commemorated the liberation of the Czechoslovak town of Hranice by the Soviet Army in 1945 (Svašek 1995). The statue represented two persons facing each other: a soldier and a small girl of about eight years old who held out a bouquet of flowers. The soldier and the girl can be regarded as primary signs, which connect the visual images of 'military man' and 'female child' to the mental concepts of 'soldier' and 'girl'. As we shall see, secondary signification transformed the two figures into powerful signifiers of communist truth.

The context in which commemorative statues such as *Welcoming the Red Army* were commissioned was a time when Czechs and Slovaks vividly remembered how they had jubilantly welcomed the heroic Soviets who had liberated their country from Nazi rule. In 1948, not long after the ending of the Second World War, the Czechoslovak Communist Party took political power, portraying their Soviet ally as a nation which would continue to protect the communist Eastern bloc states. The iconography of *Welcoming the Red Army* shows how art was used to send ideological messages to the Czechoslovak people. The statue juxtaposes a tall, strong, male, adult military person to a small, female, civilian child. The soldier is intended to symbolise the political and military power of the Soviet Union, and the little girl embodies the powerlessness of the Czechoslovak state. Other visual clues reinforced the message of power inequality. The soldier carries a gun; the girl a bouquet of flowers. The soldier radiates strength and feelings of pride; the girl vulnerability and gratitude. The soldier receives a gift from the girl; the girl gives flowers to the soldier. These official interpretations clearly projected the communist image of the 'strong and caring' Soviet Union protecting a 'much weaker, dependent and grateful' nation. As an example of Socialist Realism, the statue also aestheticised reality in a rather particular way. It intended to evoke admiration in the viewers for the beauty of what was claimed to be a truthful depiction of communist experience.

Interestingly, the memorial in Hranice was only unveiled in 1984, at a time when the political climate in Czechoslovakia had considerably changed. By the end of the 1960s, Czechoslovak reformist communists had introduced what was called 'socialism with a human face', a form of state socialism that was less oppressive than the Soviet system. To suppress the liberalisation process, the Soviet Union invaded Czechoslovakia in 1968 and forced the country back into a Soviet-style political system. *Welcoming the Red Army* was commissioned by communist officials who supported this normalisation process. The statue intended to remind Hranice's citizens of the 1945 Soviet liberation, even though many citizens who had experienced the invasion had replaced the image of 'the liberating Soviets' with an image of the Soviets as 'unwelcome aggressors'.[7] In their interpretation, the strong soldier did not protect, but oppressed the little girl. Their understanding of the memorial as a sign of 'communist oppression' was an ideological act in which they resisted the one-sided communist truth.

When the memorial was unveiled in 1984 nobody protested in public as the inhabitants of Hranice were afraid of political persecution. Yet, soon after the 1989 Velvet Revolution, which brought an end to communism in Czechoslovakia, numerous people called for the removal of the statue from the city centre. After some public debate, the memorial was relocated to a more peripheral site in the city. Interestingly, this decision reflected a tension between the political and aesthetic evaluation of the memorial. Even though various commentators argued that the memorial had simply served as communist propaganda, and that, as an example of repetitive Socialist Realism, it was aesthetically uninteresting or worthless, Hranice's city representatives did not want to destroy it. They respected its status as a skilfully made work, and did not want to destroy art they did not like, as the Nazis and hardline Stalinists had done. Instead, they showed themselves to be cultured, and strategically moved it to the Military Academy, near another statue which celebrated the friendship of Czechoslovak and Soviet artillerymen. In this way, they expressed their critique of the communist past and protested against barbarism and oppression, while reinforcing their status as civilised Czechs. As such, *Welcoming the Red Army* was given new mythical power, signifying the restoration of democracy.

DISCOURSE THEORY: REPRESENTATION AND DISCURSIVE PRACTICE

The case above clearly demonstrates Barthes' view that signs have changing ideological meanings which may actively reinforce processes of political domination and resistance. Another influential theorist who was interested in the relationship between signification, power and ideology was the French philosopher Michel Foucault.[8] Foucault defined power as an element inherent in all social relationships, and emphasised that power was not just repressive, as the Marxists would argue, but was also productive and positive, being itself a necessary force behind the creation of social relations.

Fundamental to Foucault's notion of power was the concept of discursive practice. Interested in 'the way in which knowledge circulates and functions [and] its relation to power' (Foucault 1982: 212, see also Foucault 1972, 1980), he argued that discourses were not consciously produced by individuals but consisted of unwritten rules which regulate what can be written, thought and acted upon in particular fields of practice.[9] In his analyses, he looked for the epistemological order behind different, historically-specific discourses in an attempt to reveal the workings of power. He argued that particular discourses turned specific domains of social reality into objects of rational knowledge and presented them as objective representations of reality. In Foucault's view, discourses were propagated through technologies which were used to discipline, supervise, administer and shape human individuals. Through strategies of power, technologies became working practices and were used to exercise power. In the 1980s and 1990s, an increasing number of scholars began to apply Foucault's theory in critical analyses of discourses of art. James Clifford (1988), for example, explored how ethnocentric Western discourses of 'modern art' influenced Western perceptions of non-Western artefacts (see also Chapter 6). The following case study will elucidate the relationship between power, knowledge and visual representation in relation to the building of *Stalinův pomník*, the biggest Stalin monument ever built.

Stalinův pomník ('the Stalin monument') was unveiled in Prague in 1955. The monument was a product of historically specific discursive practice, informed by Stalinist politics and Marxist aesthetics; it formed part of Stalin's personality cult, which projected the image of the Soviet leader as an almost superhuman heroic political leader. The statue was a typical example of Socialist Realism, an artistic method which propagated socialist values in a figurative style (cf. Svašek 1966a, 1996b, 1997d). Highly placed members of the Communist Party had organised a competition open to all sculptors, and had decided which representation of Stalin was ideologically correct. Their choice had fallen on Otakar Švec's proposal, which placed Stalin at the head of a group of eight figures who allegorically personified the people of the Soviet Union and of Czechoslovakia (including male and female industrial workers, agricultural labourers, intellectuals and a soldier; see Figure 1).[10]

Figure 1   A proposal for the Stalin monument by Otakar Švec, published in 1950 in the journal *Výtvarné Umění* ('The Visual Arts')

Official discourse represented the monument as an excellent example of Socialist Realist art, and its meaning was supposedly unambiguous: the statue meant to reinforce the 'unquestionable' communist truth that the Czechoslovak people, perceived as a collective of workers who were loyal to the Communist Party, admired Stalin and approved of the Stalinisation of Czechoslovak society. People's sensory experience and perception of Socialist

Realism was of course informed by their knowledge of Soviet ideology. Since the communist coup of 1948, this truth had been communicated through various technologies which intended to discipline Czechoslovak citizens. The educational system, for example, was heavily politicised, and the art world had been restructured according to communist principles. Outwardly, it seemed as if all citizens had internalised the rules of communist ideology, accepting the communist take on reality as an objective representation which agreed with their personal experiences.

Yet outside official discourse, the monument was the target of heavy criticism, and was given new, subversive meanings. Some Czechoslovak citizens whispered that the statue could not be considered a 'work of art' because it was simply a tool of propaganda, as with all Socialist Realist products. People also secretly expressed their anger over the enormous sums of money that had been spent on the monument at a time when the national economic situation was disastrous. Referring to the half-empty shops and the amount of time they normally had to spend on buying the most common consumer goods, they jokingly said that the monument represented 'people queueing up at the butcher's shop'. Some added, alluding to the many economic advantages enjoyed by Party officials within the Communist system: 'And look who stands in front!' People also chuckled over the fact that one of the women behind Stalin seemed to have her hand on the genitals of the man behind her, as if their loyalty was only a pretence, and they were secretly involved in a sexual act.

Through such jokes, the seemingly fixed official meaning of the statue was challenged and replaced by new truths which corresponded more closely to people's experiences with Stalinism than the message 'Stalin is a hero'. In the first joke mentioned, the three-dimensional form of the monument was compared to the 'form' of a scene that they knew all too well in daily life: people waiting in a queue. The statue thus became a visual metaphor for the government's disastrous economic policy. In the second joke, a detail of the statue – the 'secret' position of the woman's hand – came to represent people's hidden resistance to the Party, which took place behind the backs of the powerholders. The jokes show that representation is a dynamic process of multiple signification, and that objects and images can never be protected from reinterpretation. The monument, as a signifier, was incorporated into conflicting discourses which constructed two alternative claims to truth. Connected to a new signified (the mental image of people waiting for a half-empty shop), it was incorporated into critical, anti-communist discourse. Evidently, in the context of the 1950s, this criticism was not expressed in public, or, using a theatrical metaphor, remained back-stage (Scott 1990). The Communists clearly controlled public discourse and practice.

GENDER: REPRESENTATION, POWER AND THE FEMINIST PERSPECTIVE

Not surprisingly, feminist scholars have been strongly interested in the embeddedness of artistic discourses and representational practices in contexts of power. They have not only criticised gender inequality in their own and other societies, but have also attacked their own professional fields for being male-biased. During the 1970s, feminist anthropologists convincingly showed that many ethnographic studies written by men had projected ethnocentric notions of male control and male creative power on the societies they examined. Women were often absent in these studies, or were portrayed as passive and obedient mothers, sisters, daughters or wives. Feminist anthropologists began writing alternative studies, highlighting female experiences and exploring the socio-cultural and political mechanisms of gender inequality. The key concept of 'gender' defined femininity and masculinity as culturally constructed categories instead of as essentially 'given' biological states. Most feminist studies have concentrated on issues such as sexuality, reproduction and violence, and only a few have paid critical attention to female artefact production or gender construction through visual imagery.[11]

Nancy Parezo (1993 [1982]) explored the impact of gender on the production of Navajo sand painting in the context of historical change. Navajo sand painters are traditionally male singers who invoke supernatural powers to cure the sick, sprinkling pulverised dry material on riverbed sand. Sand painting ceremonies must only be done in certain contexts and seen by certain people; many restrictions relate to the supposed weakness and polluting influence of menstruating and childbearing women. During the 1960s, some singers successfully created a new category of sand paintings in which sand and pigments were mixed with adhesive and stuck on board. Unlike the ceremonial sand paintings, which were destroyed after the ceremonies, the works on board were produced for an emerging tourist market. As the Navajo did not regard commercial sand painting as a sacred activity, both men and women became involved in the tourist trade. Consequently, commoditisation had a levelling influence on Navajo gender hierarchy.[12] Margaret Blackman found, by contrast, that when Northwest Coast Indian carving and painting was revitalised in the 1960s, even though several women trained and worked as professional artists, the art profession remained dominated by men. Most female producers of material objects made baskets, blankets and beadwork, products which were perceived and experienced as 'crafts' instead of as 'art' (Blackman 1993 [1980]: 243; see also Chapter 7 on gendered art–craft distinctions). These examples demonstrate, once again, that processes of aestheticisation take place in concrete contexts of power, and that object production and classification may reinforce or criticise gender relationships.

In an analysis of Western visual and textual representations of Pueblo women, Barbara A. Babcock (1997) noted that the women were commonly portrayed as symbols of unchanging tradition, wearing *mantas* (traditional clothes) and carrying pots on their heads. Numerous texts construed them as reminders of a European biblical past, and photographic images in tourist catalogues similarly referred to the supposedly pre-modern lifestyle and domestic virtues of Pueblo women. The exoticising discourse turned both women and pots into signifiers of stability and objects of Western desire. Referring to Said's *Orientalism* (1978), Babcock argued that these essentialising images reinforced a (neo)colonialist discourse, which placed the colonised outside history and industrial capitalism (see also Yegenoglu 1998). The discourse produced an image of Pueblo reality which was simply false:

For many decades now Pueblo women have rarely worn *mantas* on an everyday basis or walked around with pots on their heads unless they were paid to do so. Such 'picturesque' scenes exemplify 'aesthetic primitivism', which is a form of colonial domination. (Babcock 1997: 429)

In the nineteenth and early twentieth century, the tourist demand for Pueblo pottery was shaped by historically specific Western aesthetic preferences which were strongly propagated by the Arts and Crafts movement. The movement regarded 'premodern craftsmanship as an antidote for modern ills', and preferred simple abstract forms over figurative imagery (Babcock 1997: 430; see also Chapter 9). As a result, the female potters stopped making clay figures (such as mocking images of white men), and produced pots which, at least to their buyers, symbolised the timeless beauty of the 'authentic' Pueblo past. In 1964, however, Helen Cordero (one of the craftswomen) began making figurative objects which became a commercial success. This eventually stimulated the rediscovery of Pueblo figurative pottery (1997: 431).

From the 1970s onwards, feminist art historians have also mapped and analysed female creative production, criticising conventional art history which largely ignored women's artistic activities. *History of Art*, for example, written by the highly influential male art historian H.W. Janson (first printed in 1962 and a standard text in art history courses), did not include any reference to a single female artist. Janson defended himself in 1979, saying that he had 'not been able to find a women artist who clearly belong[ed] in a one-volume history of art' (Broude and Garrard 1994a: 16). Yet feminist art historians convincingly demonstrated that male-dominated art history was strongly biased because even those female artists who had been well known in their own day were deliberately ignored or forgotten (Chadwick 1990: 17).

Feminist scholars, such as Linda Nochlin and Gill Perry, began to rewrite art history from a female perspective by looking for marginalised female artists (such as Käthe Kolwitz and Frida Kahlo), and by showing that certain works produced by females (such as Judith Leyster) had been wrongly attributed to male artists. The result of the search for forgotten female geniuses was, however, disappointing. There simply did not seem to have been that many important female artists. This discovery led to the second, more radical phase of feminist art history which challenged the intellectual foundations of art history itself, and attacked its 'romantic, elitist, individual-glorifying, monograph-producing substructure' (Nochlin 1999 [1975]: 157; see also Chadwick 1990: 17; Pollock 1988, 1992). The discipline was uncovered as a field of knowledge production that served particular ideological causes, such as nationalism, elitism and, last but not least, male chauvinism. As also noted by feminist anthropologists, male scholarship had produced a gendered notion of creativity, which opposed images of superior male independent and productive creativity to images of inferior and largely passive female reproductive qualities.[13]

The focus of feminist art history shifted to gender representations in art and discursive and structural power in artistic fields (Nochlin 1989, 1999 [1975]; Perry 1999; Perry and Rossington 1994). Dominant Western images of females as weak, subservient, child-producing bodies, who were only very rarely capable of art production, were unveiled as particular cultural constructions which simply reinforced male domination. This more radical approach defined 'culture' as an ideological process of oppressive representation, attacked the image of masculinity as the only source of creativity and genius, and criticized artistic images which reproduced a particular male gender perspective. The latter was called the 'male gaze', a gaze which turned women into spectacles and projections of male sexual fantasy (Parker 1984; Parker and Pollock 1987, 1995; Perry 1999; Pollock 1988). Numerous female artists also participated in these critical debates, and their feminist works provided views on social reality which offered critical alternatives (see Chapter 7).

POSTMODERNISM: FRAGMENTATION, REPRESENTATION AND REFLEXIVITY

Feminist criticism highlighted the constructedness of social reality and the ideological nature of truth claims, especially concerning male and female identities and the inherent quality of fine art. These and other insights were central to the development of postmodern theories of art and culture.[14] 'Postmodernism' is a rather complex concept, with different, partly overlapping meanings (Wilterdink 2000). Amongst other things, it refers to a historical period after modernity; a particular style in art, literature and architecture; a political struggle of minority groups; a commercial trend; and – most relevant to this chapter – a philosophical statement about truth and science which has strongly influenced anthropological thinking.

The term 'postmodernity' suggest that modernity is a historical period with a beginning, a middle and an end. Modernity is generally characterised as a combination of historically specific processes, including industrialisation, urbanisation, the development of class-based societies, the growth of nationalism, the creation of national states and the construction of developmental ideologies which oppose notions of 'modern' and 'tradition'. In 1954, the historian Arnold Toynbee used the term 'post-Modern' to mark the end of modernity and the beginning of a new era, characterised by the growth of youth culture, the decreasing difference between urban and rural areas, the electronic revolution, increasing cultural plurality, transnational-ism, globalisation and the collapse of ideologies of progression.

Art history was an important field of intellectual production which promoted the ideology of cultural progression, shaping the history of art into a narrative of artistic movements, which almost naturally followed each other. Modernist art history, in particular, presented a chronological story of successive, avant-garde styles, which moved more and more towards abstraction (see Chapter 7).[15] In the second half of the 1970s, certain artists,[16] architects[17] and writers rejected the strict dictum of Modernism which propagated artistic authenticity, and required purity and simplicity. They proclaimed the 'death of the avant-garde', and began to use and combine elements of different past styles, claiming that the quest for endless innovation and purity of style was a Modernist myth. In their view, all acts of creation were necessarily citation and pastiche. Criticising Modernism's elitism, they also broke the Modernist divide between 'high art' (the fine arts) and 'low art' (mass-produced popular art, kitsch, souvenirs, craft and pornography) (see Chapter 7). In 1980, the Italian art critic A.B. Oliva introduced the term 'transavantgarde' for the new movement, but the term 'postmodern' became more common.

The term 'postmodernism' also referred to a philosophical approach toward truth and science which was highly influential. In 1979, the French philosopher Jean-François Lyotard defined 'the postmodern condition' as the end of a belief in meta-history and grand narratives. Single explanatory narratives, such as evolutionism, Marxism or Modernist aesthetics, he noted, were no longer convincing because of the fragmentation and specialisa-tion of knowledge production. He therefore proposed an approach which deconstructed the claims of science to a single truth. According to Lyotard, scientists could no longer claim to *objectively* represent reality; instead, they could only produce context-specific narratives and representations.

Influenced by and contributing to these views, a growing number of anthropologists have rejected essentialist views of knowledge production and have argued that anthropologists themselves play an important role in ethnographic research and writing. As already noted in the previous chapter, in 1973, Clifford Geertz attacked the notion of scientific objectivity, arguing that anthropology should be considered an interpretative science, 'whose progress is marked less by a perfection of consensus than by a refinement of debate' (1973: 29, 1985).[18] In 1975, Fabian advocated the elimination of the 'timeless ideal speaker' in ethnographic texts, and undermined images of a 'timeless ideal relationship between informant and analyst' (1975: 14). Both informants and researchers, he noted, give shape to the communicative events which make up fieldwork, and their historical co-presence should be made explicit in ethnographic texts. Today, it is widely accepted amongst anthropologists that reflexivity, the critical awareness of the researcher's impact on the production of ethnographic knowledge, must be an inherent part of doing ethnography (Clifford and Marcus 1986). As James Clifford (1988: 41) noted:

[i]t becomes necessary to conceive of ethnography not as the experience and inter-pretation of a circumscribed 'other' reality, but rather as a constructive negotiation involving at least two, and usually more, conscious, politically significant subjects.

The reflexive turn has also stimulated scholars to think about the ethical dimensions of fieldwork, and the fact that informants and people in their communities may or should be confronted with the ethnographic product. Fred Myers (2002), for example, showed his concern in his study of Aboriginal acrylic painting, stressing that '[t]his book contains images and names of deceased people that may be sensitive to some Aboriginal communities in Central Australia. Please consult with knowledgeable local people before sharing it with members of the community.'

REFLEXIVITY AND ETHNOGRAPHIC STYLE

While many anthropologists of art and artefacts have sided with the project of reflexivity, only few have acknowledged this in the presentation of their ethnographic material. Babcock (1997: 20), for example, claimed that her essay on Pueblo pottery was 'a pastiche of images, quotations, and reflections – the shreds of over a decade of studying ceramics and culture', but her analysis reads much like a conventional anthropological work. By contrast, in *Remembering the Present: Painting and Popular History in Zaire*, Fabian (1996) took the challenge of postmodern calls for 'heteroglossia' (Clifford 1988: 51), and made explicit that the knowledge he presented was the result of situated interaction and multiple authorship.[19] He employed a variety of representa-tional styles to create an insight into the intersubjectivity of fieldwork.[20]

Fabian's book is made up of different sections in which he presents interview transcriptions, images of paintings made by the painter Tshibumba Kanda Matulu and the painter's explanatory words about the meaning of individual paintings, and, in a separate last part, ethnographic essays about issues such as history, memory and the genre of popular painting. One of the interview fragments clarified Fabian's role in the production of the paintings, in which Tshibumba represented the history of his country:

F: We can begin with the story, or maybe let's start with a little conversation about how you got the idea to produce this history; how you first thought of it. This idea to do a series, right? A sequence like the one you've done now.
T: Yes.
F: Was this a thought you've had since long ago?
T: I have had the idea since long ago.
F: I see.

    T: But I did not have anyone come to me and ask me to work, the way you have asked me to now.

    F: I see.

    T: Yes. When you asked me, I got the strength to tell myself: I should work [to show] how things used to be. It is the story of the whole country. Every country has its story.

Fabian had in fact commissioned Tshibumba to make the paintings, so not only their conversations, but also the paintings themselves were the result of their cooperation.

    Although Fabian has noted that he fully agrees with postmodern revisions of boundary-maintaining notions of culture, he has also emphasised that 'the counterimages of pluralism, multivocality, playfulness, and anarchy should not lead us to ignore boundaries and exclusion in cultural practices where they exist, including those that occur in popular culture' (1998: 54). His understanding of meaning production as a historical grounded praxis, embedded in fields of power, has allowed him to analyse both the liberating and the oppressing effects of signifying practices, and has led him to examine processes of inclusion and exclusion.

MATERIALITY, INTERPRETABILITY AND EXPERIENCE: THE LIMITS OF LINGUISTIC METAPHORS

As we have seen, when examining meaning production through artefacts and art, a focus on semiosis and discursive practice is clearly extremely helpful. It is, however, important to realise that, when applied to material objects, these approaches also have their limitations. After all, artefacts consist of matter and take up space and speak to the senses, a reality that is largely ignored by studies which use linguistic metaphors to analyse the communicative aspects of material production (Svašek 1996b). The remainder of this section will show how various artists and scholars have problematised the 'thingness' of artefacts.

    In 1965 the American conceptual artist Joseph Kosuth put an installation together which was called *One and Three Chairs*. It consisted of three objects: a wooden chair, an almost life-size photographic representation of the chair, and a photograph of the dictionary definition of the word 'chair' (Lucie-Smith 1995 [1969]: 183). The artist's intention was to create an awareness of the underlying relations between material objects and their visual and textual representations. *One and Three Chairs* highlighted the tension between the concept 'chair' and its existence in three forms: as a three-dimensional object, as a photographic image, and as a word in spoken and written language. The installation challenges the spectator to think about the relationship between the three objects in the installation. Several questions come to mind. Do the chair, the photograph, and the text necessarily refer to one single concept? To what extent do the linguistic concept 'chair' and the photographic rep-resentation of the chair convey the existence of the real chair? Are the three-dimensional chair, the two-dimensional picture and the text perceived and experienced differently, and if so, what consequences does this have for their interpretation?

Questions of this kind have frequently been discussed by artists, aestheticians and philosophers. In 1973, Foucault (1983 [1973]) raised the issue by referring to the painting *The Treason of Images* by the Belgian painter René Magritte. This work, painted in 1928–29, contained the realistic image of a pipe, accompanied by the words 'This is not a pipe' (*Ceci n'est pas une pipe*). The written refusal to acknowledge the pipe as being real, was intended to highlight the illusory character of realistic painting and the materiality of canvas. In his discussion of *The Treason of Images*, Foucault analysed how the combination of the visual image and the text created meaning, and he distinguished four different possibilities: (1) 'this is not a pipe but a drawing of a pipe', (2) 'this is not a pipe but a sentence saying that this is not a pipe', (3) 'the sentence "This is not a pipe" is not a pipe', and (4) 'in the sentence "This is not a pipe," *this* is not a pipe: the painting, the written sentence, the drawing of a pipe – all this is not a pipe' (Foucault 1983 [1973]). By pointing out the arbitrariness of the relationship between the drawing and the sentence, Foucault showed that words and things cannot simply be reduced to each other's terms (Tilley 1990: 283).[21]

Taking the example of a pipe, one could say that pipe-as-a-material-object and pipe-as-a-word have distinct qualities. On the one hand, the materiality of a three-dimensional pipe means that it can be picked up, and is functional as a 'thing with which to smoke tobacco'. Smoking a pipe is an event which stimulates the senses of touch and smell. The experience of holding and smelling the object, and the physical effect of nicotine cannot (fully) be captured in words. On the other hand, the word 'pipe', perceived by the senses of hearing (speech) and sight (reading), can 'magically' evoke the image of a pipe without its material presence being necessary. It can also be used as a metaphor for other words in complex linguistic combinations, and may be given a great variety of meanings in different socio-historical contexts. The static matter which makes a 'real' pipe cannot capture the dynamic use of pipe-as-a-word.[22]

The tension between the materiality of objects and their interpretability is also present in the production and consumption of art. To gain a better understanding of how the dialectics find their expression in concrete empirical cases, two questions are fundamental. First, how are particular discourses translated by artists into two- or three-dimensional matter? And, second, in what sense does the materiality of art convey meaning and experience that cannot be reduced to linguistic metaphors, and, of course, vice versa? Further analysis of the Prague Stalin monument (see also pages 46 and 47) will help to answer these questions. To start with the first question: how did the Czech sculptor Otakar Švec manage to translate communist ideology into a separate material reality? Evidently, the sculptor was not the only producer of the statue and relied on others to realise it in its final version.

Personally, he used his ability to shape matter with his hands and tools in order to produce the small-size model. Control over matter (skill) was thus vital to the creation of the visual signifier. The stonemasons and sculptors who produced a giant version of the model in granite also knew how to handle their tools and tackle technical problems. The sound of their hammers and the feeling of stone dust between their teeth was an intrinsic part of their work, and they necessarily had a well-developed sense of dimension. Their multi-sense experiences cannot be fully represented through the analysis of signification processes.

Materiality in the Marxian sense of the term, control over the means of production, was a precondition of the building of the monument. The Czechoslovak Communist Party controlled the financial means, the manpower and the architectural space necessary for the eventual realisation of the large-scale project. The question of control over matter in space was another aspect of the monument's material existence. Because of its size and central place in the capital, the Party officials who had ordered the statue 'forced' people to see it. It was a permanent part of the city-scape until the government decided that it could no longer be interpreted in an ideologically correct way. Interestingly, despite the power of language to call up imaginary worlds, the monument could not be argued away, even though, as this chapter showed earlier, its meaning could be radically changed through humorous comparisons (see page 47). When the statue was finally redefined as a national disgrace during the period of de-Stalinisation, the only way of changing its meaning forever was through physical destruction (see Figures 2 and 3). Non-linguistic sensorial experiences, such as the sounds of the blasts and the smell of the explosives were intrinsic to its eradication.

The case of the Stalin monument not only shows that the materiality of art is central to the way people experience it, but also points out that materiality and interpretability are dialectically related aspects of artefacts. First of all, the freedom to shape matter was limited by norms generated through language as the statue was created in response to Stalin's personality cult and the design was selected on the basis of communist discourse. Second, new and subversive interpretations of the monument were formed partly in response to its material form. As such, the object's existence as a fixed three-dimensional form restricted the variety of possible interpretations. Third, the material existence of the monument ended as a direct result of the inability of the powerholders to find an acceptable interpretation of the monument in changed political circumstances. In other words, although on a theoretical level different aspects of art production can easily be separated into 'processes of signification' and 'experiences of materiality', they cannot, in any specific socio-historical context, be analysed in isolation from each other.

MATERIAL CULTURE STUDIES: CONSUMPTION AND APPROPRIATION

Daniel Miller (1987), one of the main representatives of a field of investigation that has become know as 'material culture studies', also fiercely attacked the analytical transformation of matter into a text-like reality by semiology and discourse analysis. He argued that the material reality of commodities is crucial to the ways in which they are used and manipulated by consumers.[23] Miller developed a theory of material culture which placed consumption and consumer goods in a positive light, rejecting negative Marxist images of the modern consumer as a passive, alienated victim oppressed by the destructive forces of capitalism. Miller stressed that buyers of consumer goods are engaged in processes of active appropriation when they create material environments in which they are able to express and experience specific images of self. In other words, consumption creates (instead of destroys or de-authenticises) culture. In his own words:

[t]he authenticity of artefacts as culture derives, not from their relationship to some historical style or manufacturing process – in other words, there is no truth or falsity

Figure 2   The destruction of the Stalin monument in 1961 [I] (photograph by Josef Klimeš), courtesy of Josef Klimeš

immanent in them – but rather from their active participation in a process of social self-creation in which they are directly constitutive of our understanding of ourselves and others. (1987: 215)

Miller's focus on appropriation is useful because it helps analyse the ways in which people are actively engaged in processes of identification through the material, spatial and interpretational manipulation of matter. His theory rejects dualistic 'subjects-versus-objects' perspectives, which conceptualise individuals as independent entities who are unaffected by supposedly objective material realities. Instead, Miller argued that relationships between subjects and objects are mutually constitutive. His theory defined culture, not as a signifying process, but as 'the externalization of society in history, through which it is enabled to embody and thus reproduce itself' (1987: 33). His culture concept focused on the constitutive practice of 'objectification',

Figure 3   The destruction of the Stalin monument in 1961 [II] (photograph by Josef Klimeš), courtesy of Josef Klimeš

defined as a fundamental relationship between human development and external form. He argued that this relationship was:

... never static, but always a process of becoming which cannot be reduced to either of its two component parts: subject and object. The action of externalization and sublation is always constitutive, never merely reflective, and is therefore not a process of signification. (1987: 33)

In this perspective, the materiality of artefacts – the fact that subjects relate to artefacts in three-dimensional space and experience them through sensorial engagement – becomes extremely relevant.

When thinking about the ways in which people use and experience artefacts on a daily basis, an obvious area of research is the manipulation of objects in domestic spaces. In an analysis of the material culture of everyday life in modern Britain, Judy Attfield (2000) objected to studies which merely examine stylistic and aesthetic features of designed objects, and argued that such approaches ignore the ways in which domestic artefacts are actively used by people in specific socio-spatial settings. Attfield suggested that a less biased view would 'not even call upon aesthetics as a major arm of analysis, but [use] a material culture framework in which things are referred to as the objectification of social relations' (2000: 29). Stressing the significance of object–subject dialectics, she noted that '[t]hings lend orientation and give a sense of direction to how people relate physically to the world around them, not least in providing the physical manifestation, the material evidence of a particular sense of group and individual identity' (2000: 14).

Attfield's study convincingly demonstrated that her informants used artefacts not only to adorn themselves and to beautify the domestic spaces they lived in, but also to mediate their own identities in changing historical contexts. Their perceptions of 'good design' were influenced by a preoccupation with authenticity, ephemerality and containment – historically specific themes which, she claimed, were central to their experiences of modernity (2000: 97). Even though different groups of furniture makers and their clients, for example, differed in opinion about the type of style and technique of authentic furniture, they all expressed 'a desire for an encounter with a raw sense of reality that has not been contaminated by artificial refinement' (2000: 97).[24] As noted earlier, a similar desire also helped to shape the production of Pueblo pottery. In the chapters that follow we shall see that the discourse of authenticity has indeed strongly affected the perception and production of artefacts and art.

BEYOND 'ART': THE AESTHETICS OF EVERYDAY LIFE

The above has shown that, especially from the late 1980s onwards, various scholars (anthropologists, cultural theorists and others) began to examine people's relationships with everyday artefacts in Western contexts, freeing themselves from the legacy of conventional art historical traditions to discursively construct artefacts as isolated objects of analysis. At around the same time, anthropologists interested in visual perception began to doubt the validity of etic notions of art, arguing that 'art' referred to a rather particular practice and thus unavoidably shaped analytical definitions. Jeremy Coote (1992), for example, argued that anthropologists had hampered the study of visual perception by projecting, perhaps unconsciously, Western aesthetic preferences on the societies they examined. In Coote's words:

In their accounts of the aesthetics of other cultures, anthropologists have concentrated on materials that fit Western notions of 'works of art', at times compounding the problem by making the focus of their studies those objects which are 'deeply prized' by the Western anthropologist, rather than those most valued by the people themselves. (1992: 245–6)

Coote and Shelton (1992) pointed out that anthropologists should focus instead on 'aesthetics', defining it broadly as valued human perceptual experience. As such, they revived pre-Kantian notions of aesthetics which referred not to art, but to more general processes of perception and valuation.[25] As noted earlier, although I welcome Coote and Shelton's understanding of aesthetics, I prefer the term 'aestheticisation' because it emphasises the processual nature of perception and interpretation, and can be used to explore the ways in which material realities may be aestheticised or de-aestheticised, for example when artefacts gain or lose the label 'art'.

In his study of Nilote everyday aesthetics in southern Sudan, Coote (1992: 247) defined 'aesthetics' as the 'valued formal qualities of perception', thus producing a theoretical tool which would be able to examine the relation between perception, evaluation and social life. His approach rejected biological approaches to perception as reductionist, and emphasised the impact of culture.[26] More problematic, Coote's perspective was also formed by the hypothetical assumption that '[p]eople act in the world to maximize their aesthetic satisfaction' (1992: 268). In my view, without any providing any evidence, this assumption essentialises humanity as an entity with a rather particular aim.

Not surprisingly, Coote's insightful study did not start off with a formal analysis of a particular set of objects, but instead focused on the everyday experiences and evaluative discourses produced by the cattle-herding Nilotes, whose lives centred on the breeding, milking, herding, and exchange of animals. The Nuer, Dinka, Atuot and Mandari cattle-herders highly appreciated certain visual characteristics of their cattle, such as the colour configurations and the sheen of the hides, the shape of the horns, and the size and fatness of the hump. The different populations used between several dozens to hundreds of different names for specific colour patterns, and particularly valued some of the less frequent configurations. Other 'qualities' that were strongly appreciated were glossy hides, large wobbly humps and horns cut in particular shapes.[27] The valuation of their sensorial experiences clearly resulted from their daily interaction with the cattle. This process was intensified through discursive practice about the beauty of the animals.

AESTHETICISATION AND COMMODITISATION

This book uses the concept of aestheticisation to examine the dialectics of people's sensorial perception of objects and the formation of abstract ideas about their meaning and impact. Examining aestheticising processes, it is also necessary to explore objects' spatial and temporal movement through networks of producers, dealers and consumers, as market influences have increasingly influenced object perception and experience (see Chapters 4 and 5). As already pointed out in the introduction, Arjun Appadurai has provided a useful theoretical framework for the study of object transit and transition through market forces. In the introduction to *The Social Life of Things* (1986), he rejected essentialist definitions of commodities as a particular type of things and proposed instead a more dynamic approach which looked for the 'commodity-potential' of all phenomena:

Let us approach commodities as things in a certain situation, a situation that can characterize many different kinds of thing, at different points in their social lives. This means looking at the commodity potential of all things rather than searching fruitlessly for the magic distinction between commodities and other sorts of things. It also breaks significantly with the production-dominated Marxian view of the commodity and focuses on its *total* trajectory from production, through exchange/distribution, to consumption. (1986: 13)

One of the perspectives that had inspired Appadurai was Maquet's distinction between 'art by destination' and 'art by metamorphosis' (see Chapter 1). Appadurai argued that some commodities could be considered 'commodities by destination', which he defined as 'objects intended by their producers principally for exchange'. Other commodities were 'commodities by metamorphosis' or 'things intended for other uses that are placed into the commodity state' (1986: 16). Appadurai's theory added two sub-categories. 'Commodities by diversion' were 'objects placed into a commodity state though originally specifically protected from it' and 'ex-commodities' were 'things retrieved, either temporarily or permanently, from the commodity state and placed in some other state'.[28] This book will show that the dynamics of commodification often coincide with aestheticisation, as artefacts gain commodity value when they come to be experienced as beautiful or otherwise significant objects.

A focus on commoditisation forces us to analyse histories of cultural production, marketing and consumption, which, instead of projecting generalising, humanist aesthetic perspectives on material realities, critically examines how markets create and reinforce particular aesthetic discourses. Fred Myers (2002), for example, showed, in a critical study of the marketing of Aboriginal art in fine art markets, that consumers' knowledge (or lack of knowledge) about Aboriginal life shapes their perception of 'genuine Aboriginal art'. My own work on the commoditisation of Ghanaian art and artefacts similarly demonstrated that many Western buyers wish to take home an object that allows them to continue their experience of 'the exotic' (Svašek 1990; 1997c). The link between commoditisation and aestheticisation will be further explored in Chapter 5. The following section discusses the idea that material objects can exercise power over human beings. As pointed out in Chapter 1, this perspective is highly relevant to the approach put forward in this book.

THE EFFICACY OF OBJECTS

Like most of the scholars discussed in this chapter, the British anthropologist Alfred Gell was critical of the effect that the linguistic turn had had on the anthropology of art. Like Clifford, he also criticised the cultural relativist aim of studying indigenous aesthetic systems because 'such a programme is exclusively cultural, rather than social' (1998: 2). In Gell's view, the definition of art as a semiotic or symbolic system had drawn attention away from what he called the 'agency' of material objects – their ability to emotionally engage the viewer and generate social action.[29] As indicated in Chapter 1, according to Gell both human beings *and* their material products are engaged in instrumental social action, and the latter embodies complex intentionalities and mediates social agency.[30]

To illustrate the potential social and emotional efficacy of artefacts, it is helpful to look at the Yoruba production of twin statues. In Nigeria, it has been common practice for Yoruba mothers of twins to commission sculptors to produce such statues, to which they make ritual offerings. Robert Farris Thompson (1973), who asked female owners of such statues to express an aesthetic preference for individual twin figures, noted that appreciation in terms of relative beauty was entirely irrelevant, and even regarded as dangerous:

Years of ritual had made these images seem alive. In point of fact, twin mothers handle their statuettes lovingly. Some explain that they are alive. One cannot expect a mother in such circumstances to play favorites. To do so is positively dangerous; the spirit of the slighted twin may strike the mother with sterility or cause her to 'swell up' and die. (Thompson 1973: 27)

Gell (1998) claimed to be the first to have formulated a truly *anthropological* theory of art, which refused to be lured by aesthetic arguments. Like Miller, he conceptualised subject–object relations as a dialectical process in which subjects produced objects but also used objects to construct social selves. Gell, however, emphasised that people could extend their selves through the workings of artefacts. He introduced a number of terms to clarify his theoretical argument.

'Primary agents' are intentional beings who, through their actions, cause causal reactions in others. Secondary agents are artefacts 'through which primary agents distribute their agency in the causal milieu, and thus render their agency effective' (1998: 20). Central to the idea of secondary agency is the concept of 'index', a visible, material entity which generates causal inferences and responses – 'abduction' – in the viewer. Smoke, for example, automatically evokes the image of fire, a process that cannot be fully understood through semiotic analysis. Similarly, a smiling face may trigger the inference that the smiling person is in a friendly mood.

In Gell's theory of art, art objects are material indexes of agencies that are able to trigger abduction in viewers. Gell used the example of a suggestively chipped stone, found on a beach by a passer-by to explain this process. The finder is somehow abducted by the stone, and wonders whether the object might be a prehistoric hand axe. These thoughts transform the stone into an index of the agency of a possible prehistoric stone carver. In addition, placing the stone as an ornament on his mantelpiece at home, the finder also transforms the stone into an index of his own agency as a person who has made an important discovery. Alternatively, if he decides that the stone is not a real prehistoric tool, but has an interesting shape, he transforms the item into an index of his own aesthetic judgement (1998: 15–16). In a similar vein, a painting hanging on the wall is an index of the agency of the artist who produced it, *and* of the person who hung it there. It may also be indexical of other social agencies, such as related kin if the painting was inherited, or of other art collectors if the history of ownership is known. A past of possession by prominent individuals will obviously increase the painting's power and status, and its ability to influence social action.

Gell was not the first to note that objects are often powerful because they influence people's thoughts, feelings and actions. Munn, for example, had noted in 1973 that Walbiri visual representations were highly efficacious and that their impact depended on certain contextual factors.[31] Yet while Munn focused primarily on communicative systems and practices, Gell placed object agency at the centre of his theory. Some scholars, such as Shirley Campbell (2001; see also Chapter 4), applauded Gell's interest in the social interplay between art and human actors, but argued that his approach could be combined with other lines of investigation. In her view, Gell had demonstrated this himself, by 'incorporating varying levels of function, interpretation, evaluation, and meaning' in his work (Campbell 2001: 134). Thomas (2001: 6) similarly noted that the book *Art and Agency* had not only introduced the theory of object efficacy, but also 'tackle[d] the question of familial relations among art works, and seem[ed] to shift back to conventional ground, in engaging with the concept of style'.

The example of the Prague Stalin monument referred to earlier in this chapter can again be used as a case study, this time to illustrate Gell's theoretical arguments. At the time of its unveiling, the monument, regarded as a secondary agent, was indexical of the primary agency of a number of individuals and social groups. First, the statue embodied the power of the Soviet leader Stalin. His 'physical' appearance in the centre of Prague caused emotional responses (of admiration, fear, contempt or indifference, depending on social position, political outlook and psychological make-up of the viewers). Being an iconic prototype, the statue was able to motivate particularly strong emotional abductions. The monument was also indexical of the agency of the artist who had created the work, and – when they made secret jokes about the monument – of the agency of critical citizens. The power of objects is, of course, always related to the historically specific relations of power in social and political contexts. In the Stalinist 1950s, the most effective social actors who distributed their agency through the statue were, therefore, the government and Communist Party officials, who had proved their authority through the realisation of the monument.

The above has shown that material objects distribute the primary agency of their producers and users who experience and construct them as mediators of their own desires, fears and convictions. Objects are often perceived as subject-like forces, which – like human subjects – exist in time and space, and are experienced through the senses. Expressing and evoking particular feelings, they make themselves 'known' as bodily-felt and imaged internalised presences (Svašek forthcoming). This theme will be further developed in the next chapter.

CONCLUSION

As with the previous chapter, this chapter has demonstrated that historically specific notions of 'art' and 'culture' have strongly shaped the anthropological study of artefacts and art. From the late 1960s onwards, scholars were increasingly unwilling to accept essentialising notions of culture and began to question the cultural relativist stance which defined culture as a bounded domain in which 'art' (however defined) manifests itself in culturally specific ways. Inspired by influential scholars such as Barthes, they produced more dynamic analyses which emphasised the processual and ideological nature of cultural production. The post-structuralist attack on cultural essentialism took place in the context of increasingly active feminist, gay rights and ethnic minority movements. Public debates about social inequality in the context of increasing ethnic pluralism created an intellectual climate in which the notion of bounded culture could no longer be maintained.

Semiologists, feminists, discourse analysts, neo-Marxists and practice theorists (as well as scholars who combined these approaches) placed the issue of power at the centre of their theoretical concern. Their interest in the oppressive impact and liberating potential of ideology was partially fed by dissatisfaction with governmental politics. Protests against foreign military involvement (US involvement in Vietnam) and neocolonialist economic strategies further stimulated scholarly fascination with the workings of power. In studies of artistic and other visual representations, anthropologists examined how historically situated signifying practices were embedded in contexts of local, national and global politics. Postmodernists deconstructed narratives of modernist progression, undermining myths of unilinear progression and male creative genius. Research into the ideological nature of representation led to the acknowledgement that anthropology itself was a discourse that needed to be deconstructed as a productive process, affected by the intersubjectivity of fieldwork.

Especially from the 1980s onwards, the use of linguistic metaphors (communication, signification, discourse, representation) in analyses of material culture was criticised. Some scholars pointed out that material realities had qualities which could not be understood in terms of language-like communication. Others argued that cognition and interpretation were shaped by multi-sensorial perceptual experience, and that bodily perception should therefore be included in the theoretical framework. This book uses the concept of aestheticisation to understand these dynamics, arguing that intense sensations that are generated by interaction with objects are often connected to abstract ideas, which discursively construct them as powerful and highly valuable experiences. As we shall see in the following chapters, defined as a process which links up the experiential and discursive aspects of object perception, aestheticisation is clearly central to the functioning of contemporary 'fine art' worlds, but also reaches beyond the limits of historically defined artistic fields. It can also be used to examine the impact and meaning of 'non-artistic' artefacts, and can help to explain why certain things (and not others) are appropriated as 'art' through commoditisation and techniques of display.

Part 2

Objects, Transit and Transition

4 PERFORMANCES: THE POWER OF ART/EFACTS

Social actors do not just produce and use artefacts, but are also impressed, captivated, motivated and manipulated by them. Material objects, whether inside or outside the domain of 'high art', can be powerful communicative instruments which may actively evoke emotional responses and generate social and political action. Using Gell's (1998) notion of primary and secondary agency, this chapter examines the impact of concrete artefacts on social realities, analysing the ways in which their efficacy has been shaped and affected by context-specific processes of aestheticisation and commoditisation. As emphasised in the previous chapters, 'aestheticisation' refers to sensorial experiences and the dynamics of perception and interpretation in more general terms – not to experiences of timeless beauty.

The dynamics of emotional life is an important theme in this chapter. I shall argue that artefacts can be active triggers and mediators of a wide variety of emotions, defined as interactive, partly mental, partly physical processes which undermine rigid theoretical distinctions between 'mind' and 'body', 'the individual' and 'the social', and 'intrapsychic realms' and 'extrapsychic, external worlds' (see Svašek 2002, 2005b). Emotions are regarded as experiential and interpretational processes in which individuals actively relate to their human and non-human environments through discursive practice and embodied experience. These dynamics are intersubjective because individual beings influence each others' emotional dispositions, generating new meanings and feelings as they live their social lives. This chapter will show that artefacts play an important role in this process (see also Svašek forthcoming).

'Performances', the title of this chapter, points to the performative nature of objects as social and emotional agents. The concept of performativity used here does not intend to create a clear-cut opposition between staged (fake, inauthentic) performances and 'real-life' behaviour. Instead, it argues that *all* human activities, including dealings with matter and materiality, produce and enact changing identities and social roles (Lemon 2000). This means that artefacts do not passively express ideas, but, instead, have the power to shape and transform social life. The political dimension of objects' social impact is crucial. After all, artefacts are used by individuals and groups as pragmatic tools and performative agents to stimulate, enchant and manipulate their own and other people's feelings and resulting behaviour. As the examples in this chapter will demonstrate, objects as varied as headpieces, monuments and children's dolls may reinforce or undermine existing power relations. It will also become clear that, as particular artefacts appear in different times and social spaces, their power to stir up politically relevant emotions may increase or decrease.

RITUAL PERFORMANCE: THE AGENCY OF DOGON MASKS

In May 1989, a ritual speaker in the Dogon village of Amani (Mali) proclaimed:

God, thank you, it all depends on you. This is not a thing of ourselves, but a thing of old, a thing found. You have danced well, this we could not do, it is the force of the village that could dance. May God bless you, give you many children. (van Beek 1991: 65)

He addressed a gathering of young men who took part in *dama*, a ritual organised by Dogon villagers about once every 13 years. As we shall see, specially made headpieces play a crucial role in the dance, and help to propagate a dominant male perspective on social life. This ideological aspect of the ritual is already apparent in the quote above, as the references to 'a thing of old, a thing found' and 'the force of the village' serve to deny individual agency to the dancers, identifying them as manifestations of an abstract ancestral force.

The men were gathered at the dancing-ground altar, and had just performed an important part of the ritual event, namely their first entry from the bush into the village. They wore impressive plaited or carved headpieces and other items of ritual clothing, such as wide trousers, skirts and arm adornments made of red and black fibres. Headpieces are an important part of *dama* outfits and are regarded as extremely powerful objects in the context of the ritual performance. Interestingly, as separate artefacts they have no efficacy at all, which sharply contrasts with their existence as commodities in the global network of 'African art'. I shall later look in more detail at this process of transit and transformation, and in particular at experiential contrasts between the headpieces as ritual agents and the objects as works of art.

It is important to note that the notion of *emna* includes the whole person dancing in a costume, and that the headpiece is just one part of it. In the context of Dogon ritual life, a 'good' mask is not a 'beautiful' mask but an object that conforms to ritual expectations and dances and performs well. In other words, an exceptionally well-carved piece of headwear will not be appreciated when its wearer is performing badly. 'Artistic' criteria do not exist as a separate domain of experience and judgement. Consequently, Dogon headpieces must be analysed in the framework of bodily movement and ritual activity; not as static objects with inherent qualities (for comparison, see also Chapter 8 on the Fante flags). This does not imply that the Dogon fail to perceive the difference between skilfully and less skilfully made headpieces. Their production involves a level of technical ability and the

Dogon acknowledge that some masks are harder to make than others. Men participating in the ritual are expected to produce their own masks and their choice is partly dependent on their technical skills.[1] Another factor that influences their choice is their ability to dance, because each mask is associated with a particular performance. Rabbit masks, for example, are popular among young boys because the dance is easy and can be performed in a group (van Beek 1991: 58).

But what is the ritual power of the dancing masks, how do they abduct the viewers and acquire affective agency? And how is the mask's performativity related to the enactment of power relationships amongst the Dogon? Interestingly, the headpieces are only thought to come to life when danced by Dogon men. Disguised in their dancing costumes, the men extend their male social selves through the performance. In other words, their own primary agency as males and the secondary agency of their costumes merge in the material manifestation of their appearance. The dancers also embody ancestral power and represent mythical figures. This turns the *emna* into agents of deceased kin and non-human beings, who exercise their authority by demanding the onlookers' acceptance of norms and rules. According to the myth of the masks' origin, the masks were first owned by bush spirits and found by a woman who, disguised in one of the masks, scared her husband. When the man was told about his wife's secret by an old woman, he put on the costume himself and used the mask's power to dominate his wife. Since that time, only men wear masks and use them to control women. The *dama* ritual thus enacts culturally specific ideas about gender and spiritual power (van Beek 1991: 66). Through the dancing *emna*, male agency is acted out as a force that does not depend on female procreative power.

the whole mask and *sigi* [ritual language] complex may be seen as a male appropriation of fertility, in which the role of women is ritually marginalized, and men, by transforming themselves, become self sufficient in procreation. In the masks, men claim to control the sources of fertility, of power, of life. (van Beek 1991: 67)

A perceived opposition between the village and the bush is also central to the performance. The bush is an ambiguous place where dangerous spirits may attack and harm people, but it is also a source of wisdom and power. During the *dama* ritual, masks embody the spiritual force of the bush, and women in particular are expected to show feelings of awe and admiration.[2] An important intended effect of the performing masks is thus to generate gender-specific emotional processes that help to reproduce a social structure in which male dominance is ensured. On the one hand, men use masks as instruments to reinforce their authority. On the other, masks are powerful, indexical agents, as their material presence actively produces particular emotions in women and men. Perceived as manifestations of ancestral power, the masks are aestheticised as objectifications of spiritual truth.

When commoditised as souvenirs or works of art, the headpieces enter new contexts and have a rather different 'social life'. Walter van Beek (1991: 57) noted that:

[t]ourists, art dealers, and museum curators routinely call Dogon head coverings 'masks'. For the Dogon themselves, however, the notion of *emna* includes the whole person dancing in a costume of which the headpiece is just one part. Masks are not worn; masks dance, perform, and shout.

Collectors of African artefacts, however, perceive the headpieces as separate artefacts that have inherent aesthetic values. Sold to outsiders, the masks are presented as aesthetic or ethnographic objects to be admired in the spatial context of public museums, or as souvenirs and part of collections in people's private homes. Aestheticised as 'art' or 'souvenirs', the complex and dynamic multi-sensorial ritual experience of the headpieces is replaced by an experience that is mainly visual, and informed by a discourse of beauty, style, and authenticity. The headpieces are turned into static objects, lose their ritual efficacy and their ability to reinforce gender differences. They do, however, gain the power to enchant new audiences (see also Chapter 5).

The following example looks at another case of material performativity and ritual efficacy in highland Papua New Guinea. As we shall see, here the main social aim is the management of inter- and intra-group rivalry, and the attraction of wealth and potential spouses. Unlike the Dogon headpieces, these decorations have not been transformed into 'Primitive Art'. Yet, from the 1960s onwards, performance artists have found inspiration in the self-decorative practices of people such as the Dogon, turning self-decoration into a form of 'art'.

HAGEN SELF-DECORATION: THE POWER OF ORNAMENTS

Hageners, who live in the Mount Hagen area of the New Guinea highlands, do not carve and paint wooden ancestor statues as is common in other regions in Papua New Guinea, but use complex forms of body decoration as an inherent part in social life (cf. O'Hanlon's [1989] study of adornment and display among the Wahgi). Andrew and Marilyn Strathern (1971: 1) argued that Hageners produce 'art objects of a kind, but the objects are human beings'. In my view, their use of the label 'art objects' is rather confusing because, even if it is not intended, it calls up an image of aesthetic appreciation that is typical in professional art worlds. As explained in the previous chapters, I rather use the notion of 'aestheticisation', which assumes a process of focused sensorial perception and experience, which may (or may not) include conscious appreciative discursive practice.

Amongst the Hageners, acts of self-decoration do not only *express* religious ideas and political convictions, but, more importantly, *shape* social relationships within and between clans. The management of emotional dynamics is a significant element in this process. Hagen society is characterised by a 'big-men' system, in which small political groups are headed by self-made leaders. Male Hageners are engaged in *moka*, a 'ceremonial exchange system in which groups try to outdo each other by the size of their gifts of shell valuables and pigs' (Strathern and Strathern 1971: 3). Inter- and intra-clan rivalry and pride are central dimensions of the exchange system, and the pragmatics of self-decoration stimulate these politically relevant feelings. Inter-clan exchange ceremonies are held to keep the peace between antagonistic groups, but also give expression to competition, as the groups try to outdo each other not only through the size of their gifts, but also through the brilliance of their self-decorations and the success of their visual performance. When a ceremony is organised, big men normally decide on the style of the decorative outfits, but individual clan members can distinguish themselves and compete through some element of personal effort and choice. Individuals are personally responsible for their own outfits and the necessary ornaments. To obtain the items, they are engaged in the exchange of valuables, and need to trade, hunt and borrow objects from relatives. Commoditisation through exchange, sometimes directly for money but more often indirectly for other goods and services, is one of the ways in which men get hold of the necessary objects and substances. Successful results indicate both individual prosperity and the prosperity of the clan (Strathern and Strathern 1971: 17). In other words, decoration as a form of material practice has wider political significance.

The main items used for self-decoration are shells, plumes, firs, wigs and aprons. Other accessories are drums, weapons, bones, oil and pig-grease, cane, vine, leaves, grasses and earth paints. More recent items are trade-store paints, cloth and beads (1971: 19). Transformed into parts of ritual 'costumes', the objects and materials gain value and symbolic power. Some of the items, such as shells, have become increasingly available since contacts with the Europeans, who have traded them in exchange for labour and food. Others, like industrial paints and cut-out shapes of cigarette packs, have been brought in from outside the region. This shows that Hagen decorative practices have been increasingly influenced by the workings of inter-local and global economies.

Notions of beauty are not irrelevant to Hagener perceptions of self-decoration. When being asked for their critical opinion about other people's outfits, one man noted that some people failed to create nice contrasts because they did not blacken their faces enough with charcoal. Others commented negatively on the distinct styles of other groups, finding them visually unattractive (Strathern and Strathern 1971: 127). These judgements were, however, closely related to the perceived agency of the ornaments. To produce an effective ritual outfit, technical expertise was not regarded essential. Instead, the ability to acquire the right objects was of major importance, and a successful style commanded other people's respect.

Certain objects and substances used in the outfits were thought to have particular visual qualities that were not just pleasing to the eye, but, more importantly, highly effective. Bright plumes, shells and body paint, for example, were thought to attract wealth and women, and therefore, men aimed for ultimate brightness. Other items indicated the support of the ancestors, which turned decorations into instances of spiritual agency. A good number of feathers, for example, showed that men had been successful in hunting, a success which, as Hageners believe, can only be reached when ancestors assist during the hunt (Strathern and Strathern 1971: 22). Using Gell's perspective, the performing ornamentations are thus not only the agents of individuals and clan groups, but are also the agents of ancestor spirits. As the ancestors are thought to be able to affect processes of rivalry, decoration must be analysed against the background of concrete political struggles.

Bodily decoration also re-enacted gender differences, but, by contrast with the previous example of Dogon ritual outfit, the main aim of the Hageners is to attract members of the other sex. Certain colours and substances are thought to overpower females. During pig-killing festivals, some of the Central Melpa groups, for example, drip the melted resin from the *kilt* tree on large wigs, which makes them bright and deep red. The belief in the efficacy of the bright colour is based on a metaphoric association between the powerful red *kilt* flowers, which attract birds, and the bright redness of the wigs, which is believed to captivate women (Strathern and Strathern 1971: 92). This process of aestheticisation – the association of the sensorial experience of this particular red with ideas about forms of attraction in nature – is central to Hagener decorative practice. As we will see, similar metaphoric associations are also important in Trobriand experiences of canoe design. The Hageners also think that the power of objects used in self-decoration can be weakened when men have sexual intercourse with women while making them. This alludes to their belief in the polluting force of women, an ideology frequently expressed through material expressions in numerous other societies.

KULA CARVINGS AND DESIGNS: MAGICAL POWER

The two previous cases showed how objects which appear within the territorial boundaries of small-scale groups can effectively influence social and political life. The next example will discuss how particular canoe designs have been used as a performative tool by people who live on distant islands, maintaining political and economic connections. Unlike the previous two cases, in this case the producers of the carvings are trained specialists who are thought to have magical power.

When, on a trading expedition or as a visiting party, a fleet of native canoes appears in the offing, with their triangular sails like butterfly wings scattered over the water with the harmonious calls of conch shells blown in unison, the effect is unforgettable. When the canoes then approach, and you see them rocking in the blue water in all the splendour of their fresh white, red, and black paint, with their finely designed prowboards, and clanking array of large, white cowry shells – you understand well the admiring love which results in all this care bestowed by the native on the decoration of his canoe (Malinowski 1984 [1922]: 108).

The above statement clearly demonstrates the anthropologist Malinowski's outright admiration for the colourful canoe designs produced by Trobriand master carvers. No doubt, the sight of the painted canoes would catch anyone's eye, simply because the human species is innately sensitive to tonal contrasts and bright colours. Yet as Alfred Gell (1992: 45–6) argued, to be able to understand why the Trobrianders grant strong magical power to the decorations it is necessary to go *beyond* biology and focus on the wider performative context in which the canoes obtain secondary agency. To understand why particular designs are effective, it is also necessary to find out who produces the canoe designs, how the Trobrianders perceive and evaluate particular combinations of forms and colours, and how specific meanings are encoded and experienced in the broader context of Trobriand life (Campbell 2000: 6).

The carving and painting of Trobriand canoe designs needs the hand of a trained master carver (*tokabitam*). To become master carvers, apprentices 'must undergo a series of initiation rites, accompanied by magical spells and substances to make them receptive to the acquisition of the knowledge they seek' (Campbell 2000: 54). The initiates are taught carving and painting skills, and knowledge about colours and designs, and learn the magical incantations which directly empower the canoes as ritual agents. They have an important political role as their products are expected to enchant *Kula* exchange-partners, thereby forcing them to hand over desired valuables.

Trobriand society is characterised by a matrilineal system, meaning that descent is traced through the female line. This implies that men belong to their mother's descent group or *dala*, and are – in contrast to women – unable to continue their lineage through reproductive behaviour. Men, however, use *Kula*, a complex system of inter-island exchange, to immortalise their names. The colourful canoes have a key function in this exchange system. The social dynamics of *Kula* allow men to create alliances outside the matrilineal clans and permits them to gain social status 'regardless of the constraints binding them into social groupings defined by women' (Campbell 2000: 175). Through the temporary possession of highly valued *Kula* shells, they accumulate social and symbolic capital, and construct the image of a competing male descent system which is able to reproduce itself. The successful operation of a *Kula* exchange is called a 'marriage' which produces 'offspring' in the form of new shells that are drawn into the exchange system (2000: 170–1).

The representations on the canoe gain agency in the context of everyday life experiences. The Trobrianders grant a special status to particular animals through sensorial experience of the animals and the attribution of particular meanings to them. The osprey (*buribwari*), for example, is aestheticised as a very powerful being. Known as an effective hunting bird that lives off fish, it is thought to be very competent and wise, and is a major figure in Trobriand iconography. Carved on the canoe's prowboard, curves represent the bird's head, beak and neck, and transmit its power to the boat. The carved osprey personifies *mwasila*, a form of magic that is used to evoke admiration in *Kula* exchange partners, and forces them to hand over valuable shells (Campbell 2000: 157–8). A small packet of magic herbs, placed near the carved osprey, makes the representation even more effective, 'unleashing [the *Kula* partners'] desire to give up their shell valuables easily' (2000: 99). The highly schematised representation of the osprey is clearly inspired by a particular perception of the animal which expresses and reinforces ideas about magical efficacy. Even though only master carvers are able to transfer powerful images to the boats and make them ritually effective, in principle, all men have access to the boats and can thus use the powerful designs during *Kula* expeditions.

CAST REALITIES: SADDAM HUSSEIN'S PERSONALITY CULT

The cases discussed so far have shown how male adults in three different societies have used material objects as performative agents to increase their power as individuals and members of particular groups. While some men were more successful than others, all males were in principle able to use the politics of aestheticisation and abduction – the struggle to cause particular desired responses in others through the handling and manipulation of matter in space. By contrast, in the following case a single powerful male exacted public obedience through the creation of a personality cult, which found its ultimate expression in the building of a gigantic monument. The construction of the monument was also a clear case of spatial politics, of exercising power through the transformation of the urban landscape. As Jon Mitchell (2006: 349) noted:

[i]f performance involves a transformation of the person and of objects, then the same is true of space. Through performance, space is transformed from the relatively neutral space of the lived environment to the symbolically and often politically charged space of performance.

In the previous chapter, I already gave an example of how Prague was transformed into a Stalinist landscape in the 1950s with the building of the Stalin monument.

The Victory Arch was conceived by the former Iraqi President Saddam Hussein in the 1980s, and celebrated Iraq's victory over its arch-enemy Iran. The monument was unveiled in Baghdad in 1989. Four years earlier, the President had described his design as follows:

The ground bursts open and from it springs the arm that represents power and determination, carrying the sword of Qadisiyya. It is the arm of the Leader-President, Saddam Hussein himself (God preserve and watch over him) enlarged forty times. It springs out to announce the good news of victory to all Iraqis, and it pulls in its wake a net that has been filled with the helmets of the enemy soldiers, some of them scattering into the wasteland. (Hussein, quoted by al-Khalil 1991: 2).

The monument was realised by two renowned Iraqi sculptors, Khalid al-Rahal and Mohammed Ghani, and represented the President as the embodiment of Iraqi heroism and national pride. Much of the symbolism was created through mimesis, the direct imitation of phenomenological reality. Saddam

Hussein's forearms (holding swords in his fists) were cast in plaster, and enlarged at a bronze foundry in England. The President thus reproduced himself in material form, using the bronze arms to demonstrate his political power. In this respect, the Baghdad Victory Arch differed considerably from the Prague Stalin monument, discussed in Chapter 3. Whereas Saddam Hussein's statue showed only a fragment of his body (his arms), the Stalin monument depicted the Soviet leader from top to toe. The muscular arms metonymically symbolised the essence of the Iraqi President, his strength, which reflected in the victorious nation. The casting technique created the impression of authentic presence. These were 'real' arms, showing the 'real' strength of a 'true' leader.

The 'perfect copy' indeed enthralled Saddam Hussein's admirers: 'The knowledge that in every little bump and squiggle which can be seen, felt and may even be stroked, these were, are and will always remain His arms is mesmerizing' (al-Khalil 1991: 7). The knowledge that the arms were 'Saddam Hussein's' directly empowered the monument, turning it into an effective secondary agent. The monument's efficacy was also attained by the use of emotionally highly evocative substances. The stainless steel of the sword blades and the Iraqi flag that was placed on the top of the monument consisted of melted-down broken machine guns and tanks that had been used in the war against Iran. Furthermore, a net was added with a bronze cast of 5,000 Iranian war helmets. Samir al-Khalil noted that this super-naturalism was highly effective.

To look at the helmets in the knowledge that their scratches, dents and bullet holes were made by real bullets, that actual skulls might have exploded inside, is just as awe-inspiring as the knowledge that these are not anybody's arms, but the President's own. Or, for that matter, that not any old steel was used in the sword blades, but only that taken from Iraqi 'martyrs'. (1991: 8)

The colossal monument formed a powerful ritual setting and had a definite performative quality. Although it consisted of unmoveable matter, it existed in time and space, and was surrounded by thinking and feeling subjects who interacted with its presence. The passage on the road under the Victory Arch symbolised a metaphorical move into freedom, and when the President inaugurated the monument, he rode under the monumental arches on a white horse, which alluded to the steed of Hussein, the Shi'ite Muslim martyr who had died at nearby Kerbala (www.globalsecurity.org/military/world/iraq/images/gaghdad-966422.jpg). The monument was thus a multiple secondary agent and enacted not only the power of the President himself, but also the power of those who supported him. The Victory Arch, however, did not only evoke admiration and support. Known for his ruthless oppression of political opponents and members of particular ethnic groups, such as the Kurds, to many, the monument was a symbol of terror, which triggered feelings of fear, anger and contempt.

Large sums of money had been used to realise the building of the Victory Arch, which had not been a problem in a state that was led by a powerful dictator. Considerably less expensive images of the President were also produced, for example, large-scale billboards paintings, smaller painted or photographic portraits, and miniature photographs inserted into golden wristwatches (al-Khalil 1991: 45). Both state commissions and the dynamics of state-controlled supply and demand thus strengthened the personality cult.

Interestingly, in 1991, the US army had planned to destroy Victory Arch during the last days of Desert Storm. Yet, even though the destruction of the monument would have been a symbolically powerful military act, it was decided that the Victory Arch should be protected under provisions of the Law of War. Obviously, through this act of non-iconoclasm, the Americans attempted to give new secondary agency to the monument and its site, empowering it (at least to themselves) as an advocator of their own respectful, democratic nature.

MORE WAR HEROISM: COMMODIFYING THE IMAGE OF GEORGE W. BUSH

Ironically, during the more recent war against Iraq, which resulted in the capture of Saddam Hussein by the Americans and their allies, the American toy industry began to produce an Action Man-type doll that depicted the American President George W. Bush in military costume. The outfit referred to his trip to visit his troops on 1 May 2003, when, after landing on the flight deck of the USS *Abraham Lincoln*, he appeared in a military flight suit, declaring the end of fighting in Iraq. His presentation was widely seen as a strategic move to boost his own standing with regard to the next elections and was therefore strongly criticised in the press.

Maybe partly as a result of the media commotion, the Bush doll was successfully commoditised and sold to large numbers of American children. The artefact proved to be able to evoke a wide range of emotions, which was cleverly stressed in the text that advertised the toy:

Perhaps never before in the history of American politics has one president set political parties against another as much as George W. Bush. The Conservatives love him and the Liberals hate him. Most of the Republican Party supports him while most of the Democratic Party criticizes his every move ... . Praised for his support of the troops in Iraq while at the same time being lambasted by his political critics for using the opportunity to boost his political career, President Bush remained as unflappable as ever. (see http://www.talkingpresidents.com)

The allusion to the radically different perceptions of George W. Bush suggested that the toy could be used in all sorts of fantasy plays, leaving it to the player to turn him into a brave hero or an opportunistic villain. The manufacturer was, however, clear about the image it intended to reinforce:

The figure captures the good ol' boy essence of the original George, from his rugged Texas back country good looks and characteristic placid political face. Its resemblance to the 43rd President is amazing, duplicating his crystal blue eyes, engaging smile and chiselled features.

It is interesting to compare the realisation of a gigantic political project, such as the Victory Arch, with the mass-production of the Bush doll, even though the comparison is in many ways problematic. Despite the obvious differences, however, there are some striking similarities in the use of imagery and agency. First, even though the toy's face was not a direct cast, its likeness was strikingly realistic (slightly improving his features) and the connection to the 'real' Bush was enhanced by a photograph on the toy's box, which showed the President during his visit to the USS *Abraham Lincoln*. Secondly, as with Saddam Hussein in the Victory Arch, Bush was depicted as an armed warrior who had triumphantly beaten the arch-enemy. In the context of the 'war against terror', the doll claimed the agency of a heroic fighter against pure evil.

Compared to the performative nature of Victory Arch, the Bush doll had rather different capacities. The free market system ensured that the image of 'Bush, the hero' could enter the private domains of family households and, in the hands of many American children, the doll performed the role of an adventurous superhero with superhuman qualities, similar to Action Man and Spider-Man. In this role, it was potentially capable of strengthening uncritical, patriotic feelings.

As with images of Saddam Hussein, 'Bush' also came disguised as art. The website that sold the Bush doll, for example, also offered 'original fine art prints' which portrayed the American President. The poster 'There's a New President in Town', for instance, showed two merging portraits of the President. One depicted him as romantic cowboy and in the other he looked like a friendly but determined leader. As with the Bush doll, the art prints reproduced both the agency of 'Bush, the hero', and the agency of the consumer who had bought and displayed the image in his or her home (for an interesting analysis of the use of objects and images in American homes, see Halle 1993).

The above again demonstrates that the power of objects to generate social action depends largely on their ability to generate and influence emotional dynamics. The Victory Arch was able to evoke emotional memories of the Iran-Iraq war, stirring up feelings of loss, hatred and triumph. At the same time, it produced contradictory emotions of affection and fear for Saddam Hussein. In a different context, the Bush doll managed to excite American children, because it could draw them into an world of danger, aggression and adventure. Their images of war and terror were, at least partly, informed by the media and by their parents', teachers' and peers' comments on the war in Iraq. Identifying with the doll, or imagining it as their ally or opponent, they could use it to perform a variety of social, emotional and political roles.

ARPILLERAS: GRIEF, ANGER AND RESISTANCE

As the previous examples clearly demonstrated, artefacts often evoke emotions that are politically highly relevant. This can also be illustrated by Chilean *arpilleras*, patchwork wall hangings that were first produced by working-class women in Chile during the military regime of Pinochet. The case will focus in particular on the ability of objects to express anger and criticism. The *arpilleras* depicted what was officially played down or denied by the repressive government: the detention, disappearance and death of large groups of mainly male civilians (Adams 2001; Rowe and Schelling 1991: 186–8). The women, who mostly worked together in small workshops, used scraps of textile and wool to create images of everyday oppression and suffering. The artefacts were bought and exported by the Catholic Church, which provided a highly necessary income to the *arpilleristas*. The demand from outside the country for handicraft products and anti-Pinochet visual statements thus stimulated their local production, and allowed the women to reproduce and export their critical agency.

The process of patchwork-making helped the women to express and share their personal sorrow, and evoked grief and anger in others. By turning their suffering into a public political statement, the *arpilleristas* actively resisted and openly criticised the dictatorial regime. Their critique was also expressed during protest actions, which extended the visual symbolism of the *arpilleras* to even more visible performative contexts in their own country. As members of the Association of Families of the Detained/Disappeared, established in 1974, the women participated in numerous forms of public protest. In 1978, for example, they 'formed a human chain connecting the capital, Santiago, with a mine in which a mass grave containing the partially burned bodies of "disappeared" farmers was found' (Rowe and Schelling 1991: 187). Rowe and Schelling argued that the gender-specific female language of highly personal feelings and experiences could express concerns in ways that were impossible to Chilean men. Interestingly, the common expectation that female handicraft products are friendly and innocent artefacts, made the *arpilleras* even more effective. When unexpected, the imagery of terror and misery was often experienced as a shock to the system. Inviting, colourful shapes depicted, for example, mass detention centres with desperate relatives waiting for news of their beloved and human corpses stacked up in army trucks.

Arpilleras have become internationally known statements of female resistance and emancipation, and women in other parts of the world have found inspiration in the technique and the politically conscious content of Chilean patchwork-making. Some have been confronted with *arpilleras* through people like Irma Prado, a politically engaged Chilean woman who left Chile in 1973 and settled in Belgium. Through clandestine contacts with Vicaria de la Solidaridad in Santiago, she managed to bring *arpilleras* out of the country to Belgium and, in 1984, she founded the studio Arpilleras de Chile. In 2004, she told me that she intended to create a podium for 'intercultural exchange, dialogue, and creativity with content', mainly addressing themes such as 'racism, the environment, Third and Fourth World, multiculturalism and peace'. She explained:

First I tell workshop participants about Chile, about its history and the period of dictatorship. Then I tell them about the women who produce *arpilleras*, and try to explain the significance of this form of expression to these women. After that I ask the group to come up with a theme that concerns them personally. Then they are asked to explore that theme in the same way as is done by the *arpilleristas* in Chile.

In November 2004, for example, Prado organised the workshop '"Arpilleras de Chile" – Small Tapestries of Hope, Threats of Love' in the Oxfam shop in Heist-op-den-Berg. The participating women empathised with Prado when she told them about the *arpilleristas*, which shows that empathy or sympathy, understood as a 'realignment of one's own affects to construct a model of what others feel' (Leavitt 1996: 530) can be an important motive for people to take certain actions. In the *arpilleras* case, the recognition of Chilean suffering and strength, as communicated by Prado and the handicraft products, inspired and empowered the Belgian women to express their own feelings of hope and resistance in a material form.

FEMINIST ARTISTIC OUTCRIES

Women have not only produced material culture to protest against oppressive state politics; they have also created works to express their anger about gender inequality and to move other women to acts of resistance. As noted in Chapter 3, from the late 1960s onwards, feminist artists in the West began to use art as a powerful medium to criticise the oppression of females in male-dominated societies. Unlike the case of the *arpilleristas*, these were often academically trained professionals who intended to change social reality on the level of local, translocal and transnational politics, improving the position of women across the world (Broude and Garrard 1994a).[3] As discussed in more detail in chapter seven, they pushed the boundaries of Western fine art, transforming it into a domain of active politics.

Some feminist artists turned to the more traditional artistic media, such as painting and sculpture, to bring about the feminist revolution, and produced evocative images in which females were sources of power and creativity instead of powerless beings. In the painting *God Giving Birth*, Monica Sjoo depicted God as a woman, who demonstrated her creative powers through childbirth. In this and other works, the Swedish artist offered a matriarchal perspective on human life and the supernatural, which counteracted the anti-female bias in common Western narratives. While growing up, she had been confronted with the inequality within the Swedish art world; her parents were both artists but only her father had become successful. Her feminist approach had partly been a result of that experience. In an interview with Moira Vincentelli, Sjoo noted that she felt that her mother had been 'killed by patriarchy. She was destroyed by the male-dominated art world' (Robinson 1987: 82).

Other artists used the medium of photography to criticise dominant gender expectations. Alexis Hunter, for example, made the photograph *Approach to Fear XIII: Pain-Destruction of a Cause* in 1977–78, which showed a female hand holding a high-heeled shoe that had been set alight. Like Sjoo, Hunter commented on the discrimination of women in the established art world:

From 1972, when I first came [from New Zealand] to England, women artists who tackled feminism as a subject were treated as lepers. This exposed the most abusive misogyny within the art scene – in colleges, among reviewers and in the Arts Council especially. (Robinson 1987: 64)

Several female artists who participated in feminist discussion groups found out that many non-artist participants regarded art as an elitist, male-oriented medium, unsuitable for the feminist struggle. Despite this scepticism, in different locations female artists grouped together and organised feminist artistic projects, often in the form of artistic performances which were documented on camera. Performance art in particular undermined the Modernist myth of creative aura and stylistic progression (see also Chapter 7), and often sought active interaction with members of the audience. It replaced the Modernist emphasis on formal purity with an interest in the content and politics of everyday reality. Feminist performance artists used the dramatic effect of rituals and the theatre to act out their feminist politics. The American artists Judy Chicago, Suzanne Lacy, Sandra Orgel and Aviva Rahmani, for example, performed the work *Ablutions* in 1972, in Los Angeles in the feminist centre Womanhouse. The work addressed the issue of rape. Arlene Raven described the performance as follows:

A woman was tied into a chair and then tied to everything else in the vast room. After being 'bathed' in raw eggs, earth, blood. The sound was a taperecording of women telling about their rapes. At the end of the piece, the last voice repeated over and over, 'I felt so helpless all I could do was lie there and cry'. (Withers 1994: 168)

Aestheticisation was here clearly based on multi-sensorial experiences (seeing, hearing and smelling) and the politics of emotional shock. To some extent similar to Hagen self-decoration, the efficacy of the spectacle was in part dependent on the combination of different symbolically powerful objects and substances.

Performance art was also used by African American feminists to criticise the bias in the art world against their work. In 1980 and 1981, Lorraine O'Grady performed the work *Mlle Bourgeoisie Noire Goes to the New Museum*. Dressed in a gown and cape made of 180 pairs of white gloves, she disturbed the opening of an exhibition, shouting angry poems which condemned the art world's racial politics (Withers 1994: 173). Her work reminded the audience that it would be naïve to assume that all women occupied the same position in society, as other factors, such as ethnicity and race were also influential.

Female African American artists have also incorporated negative images of 'blacks' in their art works, in an attempt to criticise dominant white ideology, and to make black viewers politically more aware, evoking their anger. The method of citation (depicting the offensive imagery) did, of course, carry the risk of reinforcing the offensive views. The insulting visual signs were, however, appropriated and changed, either through visual means or simply by appearing in the context of the art gallery – an environment which stimulates reflection. As such, they were transformed into tools of emancipation and resistance (Cooks 1997). The work *The Liberation of Aunt Jemima* (1972) by Betye Saar, for example, transformed the image of a 'happy mammy', a female house slave depicted as a submissive, docile, satisfied woman. Saar provided critical visual commentary, portraying her as an armed warrior, aiming to undermine offensive sexist, racist discourse. Obviously, her work also intended to evoke empathy for the difficulties faced by African Americans in a dominantly white society.

PIEDMONT: EMPATHY AND RELIGIOUS INVOLVEMENT

Empathy can also be consciously evoked by powerful institutions to attract and involve engaged followers. In the case of the *arpilleras*, the Catholic Church was only indirectly involved in the production of fellow-feelings, through its involvement in the export of the artefacts. By contrast, in the case of two- and three-dimensional representations at Christian pilgrimage sites, the Church has used the dynamics of empathy as a direct emotional tool to deepen religious feelings and convictions.

A good example is the *sacro monte* near the Italian town of Varallo in Piedmont, a mountainous site with a number of chapels, which confront the visitor with familiar biblical scenes (Freedberg 1989: 192–201). In 1486, the Friar Minor Bernandino Caimi obtained papal permission to build the first chapels, and more chapels were added in the eighteenth and nineteenth centuries. The aim was to present the scenes as vividly as possible in an attempt to teach the wider public about the Bible, and to induce pious responses and activate 'proper' emotional engagement. Painted settings and real objects and substances, such as furniture, clothes and human hair, were used to increase the effect. As a nineteenth-century commentator said:

The object is to bring the scene as vividly as possible before people who have not had the opportunity to realise it to themselves, through travel or general cultivation of the imaginative faculties. How can an Italian peasant realize to himself the Annunciation so well as by seeing such a chapel ... ? (Butler 1881, quoted by Freedberg 1989: 199)

Many of the chapels showed horrific scenes, such as the Massacre of the Innocents. According to the art historian David Freedberg, such displays reveal the power of objects, because they *automatically* generate emotional involvement:

we spontaneously draw back from the bloodied bodies of the infants, and ... the pain that registers on the faces of the distraught mothers becomes, perhaps only momentarily, the pain we feel ourselves. (1989: 200)

As was shown earlier, feminist representations of rape were similarly aimed at causing direct emotional engagement. In Freedberg's view, experiential effects cannot be understood by formal, stylistic or semiotic analyses of visual imagery, because they deny 'some of the most fundamentally spontaneous elements of the relations between feeling and perception' (1989: 200–1).

Freedberg has acknowledged that emotional responses to images are, at least to some extent, conditioned by socio-spatial contexts. He argued that a painting presented as 'a museum masterpiece' would be likely to produce feelings of admiration amongst the museum public, because they expect to see 'great art'. He insisted, however, that:

however much we intellectualize, even if that motion is spontaneous, there still remains a basic level of reaction that cuts across historical, social, and other contextual boundaries. It is at precisely this level – which pertains to our psychological, biological, and neurological status as members of the same species – that our cognition of images is allied with that of all men and women, and it is still this point which we seek. (1989: 22–3)

Freedberg's argument for the potential emotional power of objects is convincing and underlines Gell's theory of secondary agency, even though his suggestion that human emotions are universal may seem rather naïve (cf. Milton and Svašek 2005). His claim concerning species-specific responses, however, only refers to 'a basic level of reaction', and leaves room for cultural and historical relativism: 'No claim is to be made here that twentieth-century beholders respond to sixteenth-century images in the way sixteenth-century beholders might have (although we well may)' (Freedberg 1989: 23).

To understand Freedberg's highly innovative position within art history, it is important to realise that historians of 'fine art' have often argued that quiet contemplation and mild, controlled feelings are the proper responses to *and* indicators of fine art. As will be discussed in more detail in Chapter 7, many have ignored the study of strongly evocative images by placing them in 'non-artistic' categories, such as 'sentimental popular imagery', 'primitive idols', 'crude propaganda' or 'amoral pornography'. The following example, however, demonstrates that some contemporary artists have purposely used emotional shock-effects to draw the attention of the public. In the case study that follows, the Catholic Church actively opposed the showing of a work that they regarded as highly offensive.

'PISS CHRIST': OBJECTS AND MORAL OUTRAGE

In May 1989, the American artist Andres Serrano exhibited the work 'Piss Christ', a photograph in warm red, orange and yellow shades, of a crucifix submerged in the artist's urine. Serrano received $15,000 for the work through the National Endowment for the Arts. Soon after the opening of the exhibition in New York, the Republican Senator Alfonse M'Adamato began to receive letters, phone calls and postcards from constituents who were strongly offended by Serrano's work. Their reactions clearly showed that emotional discourses are often statements about morality (Rosaldo 1984). M'Adamato raised the issue in the US Senate, saying that the work was a 'deplorable, despicable display of vulgarity' (Congressional Record 1989). In a letter sent to the National Endowment for the Arts, he argued that '[t]his work is shocking, abhorrent and completely undeserving of any recognition whatsoever. Millions of taxpayers are rightfully incensed that their hard-earned dollars were used to honour and support Serrano's work' (Congressional Record 1989). In his speech to the Senate, M'Adamato emphasised that '[i]f people want to be perverse, in terms of what they recognize as art or culture, so be it, but not with my money, not with the taxpayers' dollars, and certainly not under the mantle of this great Nation'(Congressional Record 1989).

In an interview which originally appeared in *High Performance* magazine in 1991, Serrano argued that the opponents to his work had simply misunderstood his intentions:

One of the things that always bothered me was the fundamentalist labelling of my work as 'anti-Christian bigotry'. As a former Catholic, and as someone who even today is not opposed to being called a Christian, I felt I had every right to use the symbols of the Church and resented being told not to. (Fusco 2002)

In 1997, however, when Serrano's 'Piss Christ' was exhibited in the National Gallery of Victoria in the Australian city of Melbourne, numerous visitors seemed to agree that the work was highly offensive. The exhibition had opened despite legal attempts by the Catholic Church to prevent it. The Australian judge who dealt with the case had refused to grant the injunction, partly on the basis of the work's accepted artistic merit. His evidence was that the National Gallery of Victoria was generally considered an institution of very high standard, and that 'Piss Christ' had been included by the widely respected art historian Robert Hughes in his book *American Visions: The Epic Story of American Art* (see Arts Law n.d.). During the first weekend of the opening, however, a 51-year-old man took the work off the wall and tried to kick the glass frame to pieces. The next day, two teenagers managed to distract the guards, one of them attacking Serrano's photograph of a member of the Ku Klux Klan, while the other smashed 'Piss Christ' with a hammer. The three offenders were charged with criminal damage and burglary.

Timothy Potts, the director of the gallery decided to close the exhibition to protect the exhibition hall and the safety of his staff (see Art Crime n.d.). In the *Herald Sun*, Australia's biggest selling daily newspaper, various people gave their opinion about the 'Piss Christ' case. Archbishop George Pells proclaimed that the Catholic and Anglican churches would never accept art that was as blasphemous as 'Piss Christ', while the feminist Germaine Greer called the closing of the exhibition a 'pathetic' move. Other commentators also called for the protection of artistic freedom, and one noted that '[a]s a Catholic I feel the name "Piss Christ" was not in good taste. However, as a person who believes in freedom of expression I believe people should have had the right to view Serrano's work if they wanted' (Piteri n.d.).

Interestingly, in the interview with Fusco, Serrano suggested that 'Piss Christ' had the power to generate a positive visual experience *despite* negative moral evaluations of its content, and that this was why it was so unbearable to some. 'My work does more than just shock. It also pleases – and that really fucks with [right-wing politicians'] heads' (Fusco 2002 [1991]). This claim, which reflects the Freudian view that people actively suppress unwanted thoughts and feelings, suggests that material objects can be quite seductive and work against conscious aims and convictions. This theme will be further explored in Chapter 7 in a discussion of the shifting boundaries between art, pornography and kitsch.

THE VISUAL IMPACT AND INTERPRETATION OF YOLNGU BRILLIANCE

Australian museums do not just exhibit the work of internationally known artists. They also show works by local painters, sculptors and performance artists, which includes Aboriginal 'art by intention' (artefacts made as 'art' for the art market) and 'art by appropriation' (artefacts produced outside 'high art' contexts but appropriated as art, see Chapter 1).[4] The recontextualisation of Aboriginal artefacts as 'art' implies a radical shift in spatial appearance and social existence. As already alluded to in the discussion of the commoditisation of Dogon headpieces, when objects are appropriated as art, the locality in which they are presented and the type of viewers who experience and interpret them are often rather different. The obvious question is then, of course, to what extent 'art world' and 'non-art world' actors perceive and experience these objects in different or similar ways. How are objects in transit aestheticised differently within art worlds and non-art settings?

Howard Morphy, in a study of paintings produced by the Yolngu, Australian Aborigines from north-east Arnhem Land, also dealt with this question, arguing that:

[a]esthetic motivations are seldom acknowledged by the Yolngu as a purpose behind the production of works of art. However, the Yolngu clearly are concerned to produce effects on the senses by which the success of the work can be judged and which Europeans would interpret as aesthetic effect. Indeed, I do not wish to exclude the possibility that Yolngu art may have certain expressive characteristics that are universal in their effect, and which have been utilized by artists of many different cultures throughout time. Such properties are properties of form that may have an effect on the senses in an analogous way to the effect of heat on the nerves – in other worlds, they do not have to be interpreted in order to have an impact. (Morphy 1992: 182–3)

The properties of form that Morphy had in mind were what the Yolngu call *bir'yun*, a concept that can be translated as 'brilliance'. It refers to the visual impact of light refractions and other intense sources, and is used to describe the effect of fine cross-hatched lines that cover the surface of sacred paintings (1992: 189). The Yolngu experience the sensual effect of the design as the working of ancestral power.

To understand how Yolngu artefacts function as ancestral agents that influence emotional dynamics, it is necessary to know more about Yolngu religious views. Central is their belief in a sacred law (*mardayin*), which is reinforced through songs, dances, sacred objects, ritual incantations and paintings that are all associated with ancestral beings. Particular designs are regarded as manifestations of certain ancestors and provide a source of ancestral power that is used in rituals. In the eyes of the Yolngu, cross-hatching transforms paintings from dull, lifeless objects into brilliant manifestations of spiritual power and emotional force. The wild honey design of the Gupapuyngu clan, for example, represents light reflected by fresh water, eucalyptus flowers and the structure of beehives. One of the clan members described his reaction when looking at the design as a feeling of happiness (Morphy 1992: 192, referring to Thomson 1937). This is not surprising, because the wild honey myth refers to the finding of water and nectar by particular bees, which is essential to their survival. *Bir'yun* can, however, also evoke negative emotions, such as fear, and can have a destructive effect on the viewer. Shark images, for example, can be dangerous for spiritually weak people, and to those who are young, ill or suffering from bereavement. Afraid of the destructive power of certain ancestral images, 'people avoid looking directly at painting that are being produced' (Morphy 1992: 196).

Like the other cases analysed in this chapter, the above suggests that sensual experiences of material objects and designs cannot be analysed in isolation from other contextual factors, even though certain visual features may attract the attention of most, if not all, viewers. The power of art/efacts is thus almost always dependent on people's prior experiences, even though certain visual impulses may have effects that seem to be mainly biologically based. A debilitating condition, for example, can be caused by the stroboscopic reflection of sunlight on rotating helicopter blades, which induces nausea and a tendency to faint in helicopter pilots. Such physiological effects seem to be rare, however, and are beyond the scope of this study.

CONCLUSION

Artefacts exist in performative contexts, whether moved around and manipulated in rituals or children's games, statically displayed in museums or shrines, or quietly standing on public squares. Even though lifeless things lack their own feelings and consciousness, they can be socially highly effective. Artefacts 'do' things: they reproduce the agency of their commissioners, makers and users; they evoke emotional reactions within and amongst individuals, and urge people to take certain actions and positions. Obviously, not all objects have equal impact, and their relative efficacy is directly related to the ways in which they are experienced and perceived by particular individuals and groups in specific environments.

As this chapter has shown, some artefacts or images exist both within and outside professional art worlds, thus crossing social and spatial boundaries. Several case studies demonstrated that the particularities of 'high art' settings influence their social and emotional impact. Yolngu brilliance, for example, may enchant members of the art public, giving them an experience that is understood to be an 'aesthetic' confrontation with beauty and skill. Yet gaining efficacy as 'art', they may lose other types of agency. While to the Yolngu, the artworks continue to effectively embody the power of the ancestors, this power is irrelevant to most non-Aboriginal audiences. Evidently, 'ancestral power' can be transformed from an active power into an attractive story, and this may increase the paintings' agency as exciting (exotic, ethnographic or aesthetic) artefacts. In a similar vain, Dogon masks and Trobriand canoes have been appropriated as 'art', aestheticised as beautiful, well-crafted objects to be displayed in museum settings. As such, the objects have lost their efficacy as agents of intra- and inter-clan rivalry, but have gained the power to express and evoke the desires of art collectors, museum curators and the museum public.

The controversies around Serrano's works showed that 'art by intention', even when accepted by influential art professionals and institutions, does not always convince the public, and may evoke anger and outrage. As will be further discussed in Chapter 7, the aim to shock has become a central feature in certain well-established contemporary art scenes. As the case of 'Piss Christ' demonstrated, controversial artworks can be extremely powerful agents, both of the supporters of the work and of those who criticise it. In both cases, public reactions to the artwork defined standards, projecting images of 'proper' behaviour.

The fact that artefacts' moral agency is often related to political views was clearly illustrated by the Chilean *arpilleras*, which expressed moral outrage about political injustice. The works distributed the agency of their makers and convinced many buyers of the brutality of Pinochet's regime. By contrast, artefacts may also be instrumental in the enactment of state power. The case of the Victory Arch demonstrated that only an extremely powerful state leader could have found the means to realise such a large monument in the centre of the state capital. Objects can, however, become new political agents when interpreted in different times and spaces. Today, the Victory Arch (or rather, its remains) no longer signifies Saddam Hussein's power, but rather reminds people of his downfall.

This chapter has paid some attention to commoditisation. As most societies are nowadays part of local, national or global economies, the making of artefacts often entails financial interactions. The case of Hagener self-decoration has shown that, to obtain the items necessary to produce effective objects and outfits, Hageners have often had to exchange goods. The examples of Dogon masks and Trobriand canoes have illustrated how artefacts made for ritual purposes have gained monetary value, and are nowadays sold to outsiders. The production of these objects has been influenced by particular consumer demands and expectations.

The next chapter will focus in more detail on the commoditisation of art and artefacts, further developing the processual relativist approach to material production.

5 MARKETS: ART/EFACTS ON THE MOVE

Exchanged for other goods, services or money, artefacts move in and out of different socio-historical, cultural and geographical contexts. But why are some objects successfully marketed as 'art', while others keep their 'non-artistic' status? And to what extent does their economic value, meaning and emotional impact change when they are identified as 'works of art'?[1] Discussing various case studies and theoretical perspectives, this chapter provides answers to these questions, critically exploring artefacts' 'transformative journeys' through local, national and global networks of exchange (Hart 1995). The account focuses in detail on concrete processes of transit and transition, and explores the changing ways in which particular objects have been aestheticised, gaining commodity value and making their way into the 'wider world'.

In Chapter 1, I defined 'aestheticisation' as a process of perception and interpretation, in which focused sensorial experiences (for example, seeing, hearing, smelling and touching a dancing, decorated body, or looking at a political monument) affect people emotionally, carry important messages to them, and may urge them to take certain actions. In the previous chapter, we explored the various ways in which aestheticisation can be linked to object agency. As already shown by the example of the Dogon headpieces in Chapter 4, being incorporated in dynamic market settings certain artefacts may gain the power to attract potential customers, but often lose the symbolic meanings and impact they had in the societies in which they were produced. The buyers and owners of such artefacts will mostly use and perceive their new possessions in novel ways. In this chapter, we will further explore these dynamics.

This chapter follows Fabian's view that artefacts are given meaning in concrete socio-historical contexts, and that the socio-economic positions of artefact producers and consumers influence signification processes. As this chapter demonstrates, the successful commoditisation of artefacts as 'valuable art' or 'valuable culture' often reinforces existing power relations. Introducing Bourdieu's analytical framework, I argue that power is also enacted within fields of production, marketing and consumption because both artefact producers and consumers often compete for status and economic gain. This implies that the workings of power are relevant at the level of wider societal structures, as individual consumers' aesthetic preferences are often influenced by socio-economic factors.

Evidently, markets for art/efacts are diverse and changing, and many actors are involved in their functioning and development. The analysis presents numerous case studies which look at the involvement of different groups of people in concrete markets of 'fine', 'primitive' and 'popular' art. The first part of the chapter focuses on the commoditisation of 'art by intention', and critically analyses the tendency amongst many fine art producers to deny that they are engaged in an economic activity. As we shall see, the taboo on economics is rooted in the mythical image of the 'creative genius' and the notion that 'true art' has timeless aesthetic value and power.

The second part of the chapter looks at some of the exchange mechanisms central to 'art by appropriation' and investigates the extent to which the development and differentiation of concrete trade networks have, at least in part, responded to buyers' expectations. At the same time, it shows that particular production and marketing strategies have influenced processes of aestheticisation, affecting buyers' perceptions and evaluations.

In the final section, the focus moves back to 'art by intention', in particular to the development of global worlds of contemporary art, in which works of art, art producers, audiences, dealers, curators and buyers move around and meet. As we shall see, their mobility must not be regarded as a free and unrestricted 'flow' of subjects and objects, but rather as a process of transit and transition that is both limited and made possible by the workings of socio-economic and political power.

ART MARKETS: ARTISTS AS ECONOMIC ACTORS

To be able to understand why certain art works enter contemporary art markets and others do not, it is important to get an insight into how these markets function. Who decides what is 'art' and what not? How do art producers gain or lose professional prestige as they develop their careers? Why do their artworks increase or decrease in value? Which key players affect artworks' aestheticisation as valuable and emotionally powerful cultural objects? And which other forces shape the trade of art and artefacts?

These, and related questions, have been tackled by scholars who have emphatically deconstructed the image of artists as 'creative geniuses'. According to this mythical image, genuine artists are isolated individuals who despise commerce and simply live for their art; they embody an ideal world, by escaping the negative impact of alienating capitalist forces (see also Chapter 7). In this perspective, money is 'a form of fiscal defoliant; set it among the fragile flowers of the art world and in next to no time you will have a wasteland' (Watson 1992: xxiii).

The myth of the artist as a non-commercial or even anti-commercial agent is a typical product of nineteenth-century Europe. Its genesis was directly related to wider economic changes which strongly affected the production and marketing of fine art: the decline of art patronage by rich aristocrats and the rise of industrial capitalism. As a result, a new system of art production evolved, which was largely governed by critics and dealers (Zolberg 1990: 53). Having lost their personal ties and direct contact with private patrons in the nineteenth century, artists became increasingly dependent on relatively impersonal market forces. Their marginalised position (in particular of poor, unsuccessful artists, whose talent was only discovered after their death) was strongly idealised by the Romantic notion of 'the true artist' as a suffering but persisting creator (Wolff 1981: 11–12). This image of artistic authenticity clearly denies the fact that most artists employ conscious economic strategies to ensure their survival as art-producing professionals. It denies their active involvement in commoditisation processes and denies the role of market mechanisms in the production (as opposed to the discovery) of aesthetic value.

It must also be acknowledged, however, that the image of the not-yet-recognised, suffering artist has strengthened numerous individuals in their persistence to continue with their artistic careers. As the Ghanaian painter, George Hughes, noted, talking about the role of poverty in becoming an artist:

I have always countered my worse experiences as an artist with the age-old romantic view of the assertive artist who keeps working diligently hoping that in the future his or her works will be appreciated and rewarded. With this self-imposed fantasy, I never hesitated several years back to wash the dishes, clean toilets, and stock merchandise in order to feed the family and art. (personal communication 2005)

The above shows that artistic 'marginality' can be a tough reality and that artists may go to great lengths in their attempts to 'make it' as successful professionals.

ART WORLDS AND ECONOMICS

A number of art sociologists who have influenced anthropological approaches to art, have analysed the socio-economic mechanisms of fine art production. In their view, to be able to understand the production of artworks and related aesthetic values, one should examine the practices of all social actors who are crucial to the functioning of the art market, including artists, dealers, critics and buyers. As such, they criticised dominant trends in art history to solely focus on artists themselves. Kurt Lang and Gladys Engel Lang (1988), for example, analysed the rise and fall of artistic reputations among nineteenth-century etchers and found that the persistence of reputation was not defined by a supposedly 'inherent aesthetic quality' of the etchings (the Kantian perspective, see Chapter 1) but by a combination of the etchers' own professional strategies and the efforts made by relatives and art dealers after their death to exhibit and sell the works. This shows that the creation of the etchings' artistic value was strongly influenced by social and economic practices. In a similar vein, Raymonde Moulin (1987: 153) concluded in a study of the development of the French art market that specific economic developments in the nineteenth and twentieth century, namely the 'acceleration of capitalist transformation of the art market' had made it 'increasingly difficult to separate aesthetic from economic values', partly because of the uncertainty amongst buyers about the value of contemporary art works (Moulin 1987: 153).[2]

If artistic prestige and aesthetic values are, at least in part, actively created in art markets, it is of major importance to study carefully the interaction of key players who operate in these markets and to develop a theoretical framework that takes their interaction into account. In 1982, the sociologist, Howard Becker, introduced the concept of the 'art world', an analytical tool meant to examine forms of cooperation between artists and others involved in the art trade. Becker loosely defined 'art world' as:

a way of talking about people who routinely participate in the making of art works. The routine of interaction is what constitutes the art world's existence, so questions of definition can generally be resolved by looking at who actually does what with whom. (Becker 1982: 161–2)[3]

As pointed out in Chapter 2, the idea of expanding the study of art from a narrow focus on static artefacts to a much broader study of object production 'in society' was not new in anthropology.[4] It is not surprising, then, that numerous anthropologists have been influenced by Becker's study and have adopted the notion of the art world. Stuart Plattner (1996: 6), for example, has argued that Becker's approach has, 'the virtue of allowing us to get on with the job of studying the behaviour of people in the art world without getting bogged down in the seemingly impossible philosophical task of defining what fine art should be'. Interested in the status of contemporary art as a specific type of commodity, Plattner analysed the 'double existence' of art as aesthetic and economic product in a study of the local art market in the North American town of St Louis. In Plattner's view, the fact that art was 'sold like a commodity' but, at the same time, was 'produced like a religious calling, as an object of intense personal expression' formed an intriguing paradox (1996: 23). His research aimed to find out how artists, dealers and collectors in St Louis dealt with this paradox.

Plattner's study showed that the unpredictability of the status and price development of contemporary art works in St Louis was reflected in the sensitive and often tense relationships between artists, dealers and buyers. Those involved in the purchase of art took various risk-reducing strategies, including the establishment of long-term personalised economic relationships and the building of mutual trust with artists and collectors (1996: 199–202). A collector he spoke with said about the necessity of trust:

So you're really interested in not throwing your money away strictly on your visceral reaction. You go to dealers that you trust and that you know are the right dealers, and then anything you viscerally go crazy for, you can plunge in and afford to go. ... If you get a dealer you like and you trust and they have good access to the museums, you can have lots of fun, because you don't make mistakes. (1996: 136)

Plattner's study provides fascinating personal accounts by artists, dealers and collectors, and gives a good impression of the social dynamics of a local American art world. These dynamics are clearly influenced by the financial risks involved in the creation of artistic reputations amongst relatively unknown painters and sculptors. Anne Brydon (2001), however, has accused Plattner of economic reductionism and ethnocentrism. In her view, Plattner's proclaimed paradox is in fact an ideology that needs to be deconstructed as a culturally and historically specific discursive formation that defines art in a rather particular way. According to Brydon, the analysis of art worlds needs 'a more complex definition of human agency, wherein divergence from the idea of self-maximizing is not treated as a paradox in need of resolution' (2001: 327). She also accused Plattner of a bias towards painting and sculpture, art forms that are more likely to be commoditised than, for example, video or performance art.

Brydon's criticism is relevant to the perspective taken by this book, namely that art worlds are highly selective fields of production and interaction, not only in their everyday social dynamics but also in the ways they often reinforce particular discourses of art and aesthetic value (see Chapter 7). Evidently, scholars who study such fields should be reflective about their own perceptions of art, and deconstruct them as culturally and historically specific assumptions that influence their views.

ART SALES AND GLOBAL ECONOMIC FLOWS

Plattner looked at what is, in the context of the international art trade, a relatively insignificant market segment. In the St Louis case, to successfully commoditise the artworks, it was essential for artists to convince dealers and buyers of the aesthetic value and efficacy of their products. By contrast, in this section we will look at a different type of marketing mechanism, namely at the trade in well-established, internationally known artworks, where their 'aesthetic quality' is not or is no longer in question, and is regarded as a timeless power.

So what strategies are adopted when famous art works are sold and what forms of economic interaction occur? What kinds of individuals or institutes are involved in those types of interactions? Without pretending to give a full picture of the complexity of the more up-market *transnational* art worlds (see also Chapter 6), the following case study of the 1987 record sale of Vincent van Gogh's *Sunflowers* by the auction house Christie's will give some indication of the market mechanisms. We shall see that transit and transition are central to the process.

By the 1980s, the British auction house Christie's had begun to play a major role in the purchase of well-established art. At the time, competing top art collectors, especially from America, Europe and Japan, were prepared to pay high prices for well-known artworks and often turned to auction houses such as Christie's because they regarded them as trustworthy institutions.

Unlike the case of the St Louis art market, the major risk factor was not the unpredictability of the commodities' artistic status (after all, Christie's mostly dealt in products by artists who had already gained a place in the art history books) but rather whether the object on offer was the authentic masterpiece or a worthless copy. Public auction houses like Christie's employed highly respected art experts who could (so they claimed) easily spot forgeries and therefore they guaranteed authenticity. In other words, the transit of artefacts to Christie's, and their valuation by experts working for the institution, was of central importance to their subsequent sales.

It is of course necessary to contextualise the auctioning of *Sunflowers*. By the end of the 1980s, the high end of the market was dominated by American, Japanese and German buyers, so when the sale of van Gogh's painting was announced, it was expected that they would be amongst the potential bidders. In Japan, several economic developments had pushed forward the interest in visual art collection. When Japan experienced an economic boom after the 1973 oil crisis, large Japanese companies began to invest in already famous European art, especially in late nineteenth-century and early twentieth-century modern works. Company art galleries were established which, in line with Japanese company ethics, proclaimed that they display the works 'for the benefit of their employees and the wider public' (Watson 1992: 393). The collections were, of course, also important economic investments. A boom in the global fine art market in the 1980s ensured rising prices and, in addition, in 1985 the International Plaza Agreement revalued the Japanese yen, which strongly increased Japanese wealth, to the advantage of Japanese art buyers, who operated transnationally.

In 1986, the Japanese corporation Yasuda wanted to buy an impressive centrepiece for its company museum and became interested in the planned sale of van Gogh's painting. Christie's announced that the work would almost certainly go for '£10 million, maybe more – and maybe a lot more' (Watson 1992: 389). Evidently, Christie's speculations drove the price up in advance, as did the speculations of other art sales experts and the knowledge that other wealthy collectors wanted to purchase the painting. Having sought independent advice, the president of Yasuda, Hajime Goto, initially decided on a maximum bid of £21 million, but was informally told by Christie's that this might not be enough. Consequently, Goto settled on a much higher (but unknown) limit. Eventually, he managed to buy the painting for a record price of £24.75 million, outbidding a competitor.

Interestingly, the former owners of the painting, a British family, only received a fraction of the amount paid by Yasuda. The economist Peter Watson (1992) estimated that they had only received around £3,435,000, a mere 13.9 per cent of the sales price. Apart from needing to pay around 10 per cent of the sales price to Christie's for its services, the family had to pay a considerable amount of tax; in the end, it was the British state that profited most from the economic transaction. Interestingly, the record sale of *Sunflowers* also turned out to be advantageous to other owners of famous nineteenth- and early twentieth-century paintings, as it drove up their market value. Japanese museums were particularly fortunate, because many had imported European art works in the previous years.

The above shows that auction houses like Christie's have become key institutions which allow for the movement of famous art works from one owner to the next. As illustrated by the *Sunflowers* case, the works gain new symbolic, economic and often emotional values in the process. One of the added attractions of *Sunflowers* for the Japanese was its appeal to nationalist sentiments. Ownership of an important object of European cultural heritage not only signified that Japan was now a powerful actor on the global economic stage. Indirectly, it also evoked feelings of pride in Japanese culture, as it was widely known amongst Japanese art lovers that van Gogh had strongly admired Japanese woodcutting traditions and that, during a particular period in his life, he had been directly inspired by them.

THE LIMITS OF 'ART WORLD'

Becker's perspective of 'art worlds' has clear advantages, as well as some obvious limitations. The above-mentioned studies (Plattner 1996; Watson 1992) prove that a focus on networks and social interaction can produce valuable insights into commoditisation as a process of transit and transition, and into the involvement of institutions such as Christie's in the creation of aesthetic and monetary value. Yet the concept of art *world* may easily be misunderstood as a closed, geographically bound and internally united entity, and this can be misleading. The analysis of the *Sunflowers* auction demonstrates that art sales may temporarily connect people, places and objects that have rather different histories, aims and backgrounds, and in that sense, do not form a single 'world'. By contrast, they form historically specific fields of cooperation which may evolve from local to national and transnational levels of interaction.

In my own study of Czech art production from 1945 to 1992, I similarly noticed that artists, dealers and critics tended to form distinct groups with rather different aims, even though they all worked within the constraints of the same political economy. Individuals strongly disagreed about the definition and boundaries of valuable art, and were linked to different (and changing) international networks. This made the Czech art scene into a fluid, internally divided 'world' which had various connections abroad (Svašek 1996a, 2002).

Second, and perhaps more importantly, Becker's approach 'offers little guidance for understanding what impels the process of artistic creation and diffusion, stylistic choice in relation to extant styles, and innovation in general' (Zolberg 1990: 126). Too focused on everyday interaction and organisation, his analysis fails to give a wider perspective on the instrumentality of art as a tool of social and political distinction. In an attempt to tackle this problem in the analysis of the Czech state-socialist art world, I took a longer-term historical approach and constructed three levels of analysis. The first level examined the changing organisational dynamics of the Czech art world, the second the ongoing creation of social groups and hierarchies, and the third explored the formation of artistic discourses in the context of political change. What I found was a diversity of organisational, social and discursive processes, which revealed both politicising and de-politicising tendencies.

Political domination and resistance clearly shaped the production, marketing and consumption of art, and the analysis of the activities of artists, art historians, dealers and art policy makers during the communist period (1945–89) showed strategic manoeuvring in what was widely known as the Grey Zone (*Šedá zona*), a social space between the official state policy and unofficial counter-movements. From the late 1960s onwards, for example, critical art historians who worked in official state galleries managed to buy works by politically-suspect artists (who were not allowed to exhibit in public) for their collections (Svašek 1996a: 149–51, 2002). The art historian Jaroslav Rataj told me in 1992 that Jiří Kotalík, director of the National Gallery from 1967 to 1990, had been one of the people who had supported politically unacceptable art, even though he had been a party member. With a smile, he recounted one particular occasion when Kolalík, who had put him on a purchase committee which bought statues for the National Gallery, had succeeded in purchasing conceptual art works by the sculptor Jiří Seifert:

I remember that the sculptor and director of the School of Applied Arts Jan Šimota, the sculptor Josef Malejovsky, and other conservative [i.e. hardline communists] people like that also sat on the committee ... . I remember that among the art works which we had to decide about, were works by artists who weren't allowed to exhibit ... for example, works by Seifert called *Balíky* (Packages). They were packages of stones tied up with rope. Well, for Šimota and the other conservative artists this was totally unacceptable. But Procházka, Head of the Department, wanted to buy them. So I told him, Vašek, don't put it on the programme now, leave it till later when Šimota won't be here. Well at a certain moment Šimota and Malejovsky went out to the toilet and before they got back we'd bought all of Seifert's works. And they didn't know about it. It was quickly decided by vote, and when they returned, Seifert's work had already been taken away, it was no longer there. And afterwards they signed the protocol without reading what had been bought.

The above clearly shows both cooperation and tension within the Czech art world, as well as a partially 'hidden' struggle for influence and authority. This reinforces the view that it is crucial to take the issue of power into account when analysing the dynamics of the art trade. The case also demonstrates that object transit does not always occur 'in public', especially when the traffic is shaped by political censorship.

FIELD THEORY: A BROADER PERSPECTIVE

The highly influential scholar Pierre Bourdieu constructed a theory of art that not only acknowledges the importance of everyday social interaction to the art trade, but also incorporates the analysis of the historically grounded process whereby 'the hierarchical standing of social statuses, art forms, institutions, circles, and the changing nature and value of capital in all its forms, material or symbolic, come about' (Zolberg 1990: 126; see also Bevers 1993: 13). In an analysis of the aesthetic preferences of French art consumers, Bourdieu found a clear relationship between social class, lifestyle, and taste (Bourdieu 1984 [1979]; Bourdieu and Darbel 1969), which strengthened his view that people tend to internalise group or class-specific behaviour, thereby sharing the same 'habitus' (Bourdieu 1977: 72; see also Bourdieu 1979, 1993).

Rejecting the Marxist view that socio-economic circumstances alone determine people's thoughts and actions, and that culture just passively reflects political and economic processes, Bourdieu argued that people not only use economic capital to enhance their reputations and increase their power, but also utilise knowledge (cultural capital), symbols and rituals of acknowledgement (symbolic capital) and contacts with powerful others (social capital) for this purpose. In this perspective, knowledge about and ownership of 'quality' art is an important form of capital that boosts prestige in particular social circles. Knowing what to enjoy or aestheticising the 'right' kind of artefacts is then a crucial tool of power management.

Bourdieu introduced the concept of 'fields' – partially independent areas of social activity, which are 'structured according to a relational set of struggles that take place over currencies or resources particular to that field' (Prior 2002: 6). In the field of the art trade, the most important currency is of course the power to decide what is legitimate art and what not. In the case of St Louis, we saw that dealers played an important role in this decision process. The example of the *Sunflowers* auction illustrated the powerful position of respected auction houses.

In Bourdieu's theoretical framework, different agents occupy different, changing positions in the field, all striving for more authority. At the same time, works of art are in transit, gaining or losing aesthetic and monetary value. Successful agents must acquire insider knowledge about the functioning of the art trade and must create cooperative networks with other powerful agents, such as respected art critics. Successful agents mostly enter the field with 'historically given endowments (either in the dispositional form of the *habitus*, or in objectified form as material goods)' (Prior 2002: 6–7). As with artists, dealers and critics, art collectors – both individuals and institutions – also compete for power in artistic fields. When fine art became a commodity for financial investment and a way of affecting social distinction in the United States, for example, many of the new urban elite used their knowledge of art as a form of cultural capital to enhance their social prestige, collecting art and founding art museums and associations (Bennet 1995; DiMaggio 1986; White and White 1965). The newly established institutions further consecrated 'the fine arts', reinforcing and justifying the opposition of high and low culture (Gans 1974). The involvement of museums in cultural politics and class formation will be discussed in more detail in Chapter 6.

Gell objected to the institutional theories of art sociologists, such as Bourdieu (1984 [1979]) and also Berger (1972), arguing that they 'concern themselves with particular institutional characteristics of mass societies, rather than with the network of relationships surrounding particular artworks in specific interactive settings' (Gell 1998: 8). He noted that:

there are many societies in which the 'institutions' which provide the context for the production and circulation of art are not specialised 'art' institutions as such, but institutions of more general scope; for example, cults, exchange systems, etc. The anthropology of art would forever remain a very undeveloped field were it to restrict itself to institutionalized art production and circulation comparable to that which can readily be studied in the context of advanced bureaucratic/industrial states. (1998: 8)

Even though Gell convincingly claimed that we should not limit ourselves to the study of the institutionalised production and consumption of fine art, Bourdieu's theory offers a valuable framework for the analysis of specialised fields of art production.

ART BY APPROPRIATION: IDEOLOGICAL CONSTRAINTS

So far, this chapter has discussed the marketing of 'art by intention', of objects that are intentionally produced by professional artists for existing or developing art markets. Most anthropologists, however, have examined the marketing of 'art by appropriation' – artefacts that were not meant to be art at the time of their production, but that were at some point in their social life incorporated into art markets. Evidently, for artefacts to be commoditised as 'art', consumers need to perceive and experience them as having 'art-like' qualities. As we shall see, the ways in which particular objects have been perceived has not only been shaped by dominant discourses of 'art', but also by perceptions of human 'otherness'.

Non-European artefacts which began to be interpreted as 'primitive' art in the early twentieth century (see below), were for many centuries classified by Europeans as bizarre products made by strange, exotic beings. The following section and Chapter 6 outline how, initially, this led to their commoditisation as 'curiosities' instead of as 'works of art'. The analysis thus illustrates, once again, the selective working of artistic fields.

The European voyages of discovery, which started in the fifteenth century, coincided with the establishment in Europe of 'the fine arts' as a relatively separate domain of discourse and practice. In the eyes of the Europeans, the strange manufactures of the people they encountered had not much in common with the aesthetic creations of European painters and sculptors. Until the eighteenth century, the 'wild heathens' were more or less classified as a single category of beings, who differed essentially from the God-fearing European Christians. The artefacts the former produced were perceived as curiosities, which were soon in demand and displayed in special cabinets.

In the process of commoditisation, they were recontextualised, symbolising the strangeness of the pagans. This image was reinforced in travelogues and through visual depictions of the natives by European artists (see Chapter 6 for a more detailed discussion of this process). The viewers mainly experienced surprise and shock when seeing the items on display, and wondered about the strange nature of other, distant beings.

The perceptions of non-Europeans began to change when trade relations and other contacts in various part of the world intensified, which meant that the explorers, traders and missionaries gained more knowledge about local habits. The natives were no longer all placed in one undifferentiated category, and this changing view was also reflected in European artistic imagery. Some painters represented non-Europeans not as wild heathens, but as figures from an idealised European past. The painter William Hodge, for example, who travelled with James Cook to Tahiti in the 1870s, sketched natives from the Tonga Islands, and their facial expressions, postures and clothes looked strikingly similar to those in ancient Greek imagery (Rubin 1984: 6). European artists employed to document life in far-away places thus had a strong impact on the ways in which these people were imagined at home. Obviously, the artists themselves were influenced by European notions of humankind. Letters and travelogues also showed both negative and positive evaluations of native customs. Some accounts reflected a mixture of horror and fascination, whereas others expressed surprise and admiration. To give an example, various commentators praised the Sioux Indians for their courage, self-control and endurance (Kiernan 1990: 102), and some admired the liberal Tahitian attitude to sexuality (Porter 1990).[5]

The discourse of 'native life' became increasingly diverse and writers began to focus on the idiosyncrasies of distinct native peoples. This does not imply, however, that the natives were regarded as capable of art production, or that their products were perceived as art.[6] Instead, native products continued to be commoditised as curiosities in a growing market of exotic artefacts. Even when philosophers and writers such as Montaigne, Montesquieu, Diderot and Rousseau (who had never been outside Europe) found inspiration in the more positive accounts of 'native life', they did not think them capable of art production. The traveller J. Ives, who made a voyage to India in 1754, remarked, for example, that:

Upon the whole, though the Indian mechanics are by no means deficient in the handcraft arts, yet their talents seem to be only of a second rate kind. In many respects they certainly do not seem to come up to the dexterity of European artists, particularly in those works where great accuracy is required. They likewise labour under a poverty of genius which makes them dull at invention. (Ives 1773: 53, quoted by Marshall 1990: 57).

The 'noble savages', as natives were now often classified, were imagined as natural and free beings, an image which was used to attack European moral and political standards, and to criticise the stifling power of the Church and the aristocracy.[7] Evidently, the discourse of the 'noble savage', was as unrealistic and stereotypical as the discourse of the 'wild heathen'. Instead of demonising the natives, it propagated an idealised image which distracted from the historical reality of imperialism, capitalism and exploitation, and denied the natives their individuality and a place in real time and space. Influenced by the discourse of the 'noble savage', and the ideal of 'natural' truth and beauty, Romantic artists of the late eighteenth and early nineteenth century painted impressive landscapes, and some depicted peaceful natives, living in harmony with their, supposedly, untouched surroundings. Such images objectified them as passive elements of nature, not as active creators of culture.

The above quotes clearly show that ideological constraints propagated by imperialism, colonialism and racist ideology, hampered the aestheticisation and commoditisation of non-European artefacts as 'artistic objects'. As the following section discusses, this began to change when European artists re-identified certain types of objects as 'primitive art'. It is, however, rather telling that the classification 'art' was qualified by the word 'primitive'.

FROM PRIMITIVE ARTEFACTS TO PRIMITIVE ART: ESTABLISHING A MARKET

In the latter part of the nineteenth century, the French artist Paul Gauguin showed an interest in Polynesian artefacts, as part of his fascination with the lifestyle of the natives. His curiosity, however, was mainly generated by Rousseau-esque Romantic notions of natural freedom. Gauguin's book *Noa Noa* (1985 [1892]) made it crystal clear that he was not at all convinced whether the Polynesians could be considered as fellow artists. Commentating on locally produced stone statues, he seriously wondered whether the Polynesian producers had any sense of beauty (Fraser 1971: 23–4).

By contrast, during the early twentieth century, some Paris-based artists, including Henri Matisse, André Derain, Maurice de Vlaminck and Pablo Picasso, developed a strong interest in African and Oceanic artefacts, which they found in French curiosity shops and ethnographic collections. They admired the skills and artistic ingenuity of the non-European producers, and searched for ways of expression beyond the dominant, Western classical canon. In their view, the native carvings offered inventive formal and conceptual solutions (Rubin 1984: 5). In transition, the objects were appropriated and reclassified as 'primitive art', and helped trigger the artistic turn of events in Paris – called 'Primitivism' – which led to the development of Cubism, Surrealism and other innovative modernist styles.

It is important to note that the primitivists were most of all interested in the formal qualities of primitive art, not in original meanings or functions. Their aesthetic appreciation was clearly not a conscious, politically motivated attempt to reclassify the primitives as fully civilised human beings. In an interview with William Rubin, Pablo Picasso stated: 'Everything I need to know about Africa is in those objects' (1984: 74). As Anthony Forge pointed out: 'The modern artists were on the whole not concerned with meanings. They accepted the carvings that came their way as interesting and exciting in terms of form, basically as objets trouvés, on the same level as driftwood and other naturally occurring interesting shapes' (1973a: xiv). Intrigued by their abstract representation of reality, the European artists aestheticised the works as art, regarding them as agents of aesthetic power.

Even though Primitivism, a rather incoherent 'Rorschach of "the primitive"' (Clifford 1988: 195), also involved 'strong critiques of colonialist, evolutionist assumptions' (1988: 197), the movement was part and parcel of European imperialism. After all, it was European artists, actors in Western artistic fields, who decided to include a selection of non-Western artefacts in the domain of art. They did not actively involve non-Western object-makers, nor did they take non-Western forms of aestheticisation seriously. Instead, they projected ethnocentric notions of 'panhuman timeless beauty' onto the artefacts.

The revolutionary aesthetic views of the Primitivists generated a wider interest in non-European art and stimulated the establishment of a flourishing market (Rubin 1984: 11). It is interesting to look at the development of the 'Primitive art' market, and at the ways in which a growing number of European and American dealers were involved in transnational processes of object transit and transition. The Frenchman Paul Guillaume was the first professional African art dealer; he opened a gallery of African Primitive art in Paris in 1920. Evidently, he worked within the limitations of object availability, according to his own particular perception of 'Primitive art' and according to the expectations of his consumers. As a result, the gallery only accepted a selection of non-Western artefacts as 'authentic African art' and searched for artefacts that fitted in this category. The Primitivist, Modernist avant-garde artists were amongst the first buyers, who, as the legend goes, 'discovered' the timeless aesthetic quality of the objects. The Modernists preferred formal designs to more complicated ones, and their interest was also shaped by common Western distinctions between 'art' and 'craft', and 'ritual' and 'utilitarian' objects. As a result, when the market for African art began to develop in the 1920s, masks and fertility figures were in high demand.

From the 1920s onwards, Guillaume and a growing number of mainly European and American dealers established firmer links with colonial officials and African traders who helped them to acquire objects through extractive bargaining. At the same time, growing numbers of Africans began to produce artefacts in response to the growing demand (Steiner 1994: 6; see also Mount 1973). Today, 'the supply of objects that can be promoted as "authentic primitive art" is very much on the decline ... because the societies that formerly produced it have increasingly become part of the global economic system' (Errington 1998: 7). In the 1960s and 1970s, the market for old and new African artefacts experienced a boom. The European markets were now well established and the interest amongst African Americans grew as a result of the emancipation movement in the United States. At the same time, expatriates and a rapidly growing number of tourists became interested in African souvenirs. From the late 1970s onwards, however, there has been a downward turn, even though re-sales of old pieces from existing collections have made record prices (Steiner 1994: 6–7). While the latter pieces have entered the elitist world of the extreme rich, and function as material markers of wealth and artistic sophistication, the much lower-priced souvenirs have been used to evoke memories of exciting trips and exotic holidays. They are now sold in shops and galleries in different parts of the world, for example in the Heritage Gallery in Amsterdam (see Figure 4).

Figure 4 African masks on display at the African Heritage Gallery in Amsterdam, 2000 (photograph by Maruška Svašek)

ART AND SOUVENIRS: BARGAINING MECHANISMS

To make the transformative journey to 'art' or 'souvenir', artefacts must not only have commodity potential, their owners must also be willing to sell the items. When Christopher Steiner (1994: 65) interviewed the Hausa trader Malam Abukar about the supply of artefacts in the Bouna region in north-east Ivory Coast, he was told: 'I saw [Lobi] women there wearing ivory lip plugs and huge bracelets. But they wouldn't sell them for any price. It just makes you want to grab them right off their body. ... They didn't even understand what they were wearing.' The quote clarifies that, even though the objects had the potential to be commoditised, they did not enter the market because their owners refused to part with them. Appadurai noted that:

[t]he commodity *candidacy* of things is less a temporal than a conceptual feature, and it refers to the standards and criteria (symbolic, classificatory, and moral) that define

the exchangeability of things in any particular social and historical context. (1986: 13–14, original emphasis)

The Lobi owners clearly did not share standards and criteria with the trader, who regarded their jewellery as commodities because he knew about its appeal to foreign buyers. By contrast, the women saw their possessions as markers of personal identity and social status – as truly 'priceless' valuables which had power because they embodied the women's very own being.

Steiner was interested in the activities of dealers in African artefacts and examined the movement of their trade through local, national and transnational economies. His study shows the value of an approach that looks at object transit and transition, tracing both trade routes and changing ways in which objects are valued and experienced. Referring to the variability of object perception amongst the people he interviewed, he argued that, '[t]he perceived value of an item is ... wholly dependent on where one is situated in the chain of economic transactions, and each transaction is characterized by the logic of its own system of value and mode of bargaining' (Steiner 1994: 63). This finding reinforces the view, propagated by this book, that aestheticisation and commoditisation are dialectically related processes. After all, people's (changing) perceptions of particular artefacts may, or may not, push artefacts in and out of commodity status, and the possibility or impossibility of exchangeability may affect people's experiences and judgements of them.

But how are economic transactions shaped by object perception, and vice versa? Steiner's study provides some helpful insights. One of the activities Steiner examined was systems of 'bargaining' between different types of trading partners. As a market procedure, bargaining turned out not to be a straightforward reflection of abstract rules of supply and demand. Instead, bargaining procedures consisted of complex social interactions in which norms, values and expectations were actively created. Trading partners tried to influence each others' perceptions of the goods on offer, and thus attempted to maximise their own profit and satisfaction.

When Steiner conducted research in the late 1980s, several groups of buyers and sellers were involved in different bargaining mechanisms, which he called 'extractive', 'wholesale', 'retail' and 'performative' bargaining. In the case of extractive bargaining, African villagers owned objects that had not been produced as commodities but that had commodity potential. To the villagers, the objects had use value, for example, as items with ritual power or with the potential to increase their social prestige. African travelling traders recognized that these objects had exchange value outside the local context and tried to extract them from their local setting through exchange for money or other valuable goods, thus turning them into commodities. In the case of wholesale bargaining, commodities were sold and resold among African traders, and moved through a chain of rural and urban merchants. Exchange value was constructed on the basis of local criteria of supply and demand, which meant that most (especially the rural) salesmen were satisfied with a reasonable but not excessive margin of profit. Clearly, many merchants involved in wholesale bargaining were not aware of the high prices Western consumers were willing to pay for some of the artefacts. By contrast, in the case of retail bargaining African traders sold objects to Western collectors or dealers, and prices were negotiated in reaction to Western tastes and preferences. Steiner noted that in retail bargaining:

> there is always a tension between two systems of value. On the one hand, there is the African trade value (which is based on local supply and only a fragmentary or elliptical knowledge of Western demand). And, on the other hand, there is the Western trade value (which is based on gallery prices, auction records, and taste-setting trends/ perceived aesthetic value). (1994: 164)

The fourth bargaining mechanism was 'performative bargaining', the sale of artefacts to foreign tourists (as opposed to knowledgeable collectors). Here, the merchants actively reacted to Western desires to experience an 'authentic' African market place. They put up a performative act to convince potential buyers of the artefacts' value, telling interesting tales about exotic customs and hiding the fact that many of the objects were mass-produced by carvers and their apprentices who worked solely for the tourist market.

Steiner's analysis showed that markets for art and souvenirs have often been deliberately created, which is also illustrated by the following case study. In the early 1980s, the Italian entrepreneur Giovanni Franco Scanzi began to collect sculpted Baule slingshots in Ivory Coast, enlarging the category of collectable, and thus valuable, objects. Over a period of three years, he purchased over 1,000 items from about 20 traders. To strengthen the illusion of authenticity, he only bought unpainted slingshots, which looked older and more 'real' from a Western perspective. In 1987, he co-authored *Potomo Waka*, a catalogue which contained over 100 glossy colour photographs of slingshots from his private collection. The preface to the book 'carefully construct[ed] a case for the "authenticity" and "artistic" value of the objects' by presenting the slingshots as genuine works of art that were 'untainted by European influence' (Steiner 1994: 115). The writers claimed, for example, that rubber, which was produced after the establishment of contacts with Europeans, was not a necessary part of the slingshots because animal gut had been used in pre-colonial times (Delcourt and Scanzi 1987: 9).

The publication of *Potoma Waka* was essential to the successful commoditisation of the slingshots. It was for sale in stores and hotel gift shops in Abidjan, directing the attention of Western visitors to the artefacts. Interestingly, the book did not include the best pieces from Scanzi's collection. Steiner suggested that this was part of Scanzi's marketing strategy. At first, because they appeared in the catalogue, the objects of lesser quality were sold easily. Subsequently, after most of the slingshots from the catalogue had been bought, the better-quality pieces were valuable 'precisely because they [were] not in the book' (Steiner 1994: 117). Within a few years, the price of slingshots had increased dramatically. In response to the demand, more items began to appear on the market. To enhance their authentic look, traders sanded them down, and re-stained them with potassium permanganate, actively reacting to buyers' expectations.

COMMODITISATION AND QUESTIONS OF AUTHENTICITY

The example of the slingshots shows that the claim to 'authentic status' has been an important principle in the marketing of African and other indigenous artefacts. This principle has also been of major importance in the marketing of 'high' art, as was apparent in the *Sunflowers* case, in which the auction house Christie's guaranteed that the object on offer was a 'genuine' van Gogh. The belief that objects gain authenticity when they are produced and used by people who are thought somehow to be sincere, because of their artistic genius, wild exoticism or emotional purity, has given such objects a powerful aura (see also Chapters 6 and 7).

As was briefly discussed in Chapter 3, 'authenticity' has been an important aestheticising concept inherent in Modernism, which has strongly influenced the perspective and judgements of buyers of fine art and indigenous artefacts. The discourse of 'the authentic' created an opposition between the realms of 'honest, traditional engagement' and 'fake, commercial practice', projecting the former as a value-producing honest activity and the latter as a morally worthless enterprise. As Shelley Errington noted, in the case of pre-contact African 'primitive art':

[t]he message is that once upon a time Africans were great artists, now they are commercial hacks; once they lived in harmony, now they live in decadence; once their work was pure, now it is polluted. (1998: 72)

Evidently, the decision as to what is authentic African art and what not, implies a selection procedure. Following Bourdieu's perspective, it is important to examine who, in particular socio-historical contexts, has the symbolic, social and economic power to decide which objects can be classified as such and which cannot.

As noted earlier, the producers of African art objects have actively reacted to the expectations of a variety of customers in different markets. The example of the slingshots illustrated how the objects were made to look old and authentic through certain technical procedures, such as sanding and re-staining. An authentic feel is also created through choice of subject matter. Many Ghanaian artists trained at the art academy in Kumasi, for example, tended to portray images of 'traditional African culture', despite the obvious signs of modernity surrounding them (Svašek 1997c: 34–5).

THE IMPACT OF CHANGING MARKETS ON ARTEFACT PRODUCTION

Market mechanisms not only affect which kind of images are being produced, but may also influence the activities and status of image producers. This implies that object transit and transition not only recontextualises artefacts, it also affects the social and productive life of artefact producers. In a historical analysis of object production in the Trobriand Islands, Shirley Campbell (2002) provided valuable insights into the effect of European consumption on the position of Trobriand carvers (see also Chapter 4 on the efficacy of Trobriand canoe designs). Towards the end of the nineteenth century, the Trobrianders made a clear distinction between two types of carvers. While *tokabitam* carved 'with magic' and specialised in 'items of ritual and symbolic value', other carvers produced utilitarian objects, such as plates and walking sticks. The latter group included schooled carvers from the Kuboma district, and *tokataraki* – carvers who had not completed their training as *tokabitam* (2002: 41). The more prestigious *tokabitam* carved the prows and splashboards of the canoes that were used in *Kula*, a complex system of ritual exchange that was central to social, political, and ceremonial life (Malinowski 1984 [1922]; Weiner 1977; see also Chapter 4). They protected their status by each allowing only one apprentice to take on the status of *tokabitam*. As Campbell (2002: 43) noted:

Only a few *tokabitam* lived at any one time. Great lengths were taken to maintain the relatively low ratio of artists to non-artists; principal among them was the rule that a master carver could give his magic and training to only one apprentice. This was meant to ensure the elite nature of their profession.

The *tokabitam* were commissioned by members of the local community. By contrast, the carvers of the utilitarian artefacts also supplied people living on the other islands. The status of the *tokabitam* was considerably higher than that of the other carvers. The former were regarded as the owners of powerful designs and the possessors and mediators of magical power. Copyists were required to acknowledge their source and pay compensation. On some occasions, the locals commissioned the cheaper *tokataraki* to carve canoe prows and splashboards, but their work was considered 'less efficacious' because the *tokataraki* 'lacked the magic that would provide them with the "knowledge" held by the master carvers' (2002: 44).

From the late nineteenth century onwards, European traders, government officials, missionaries, and later tourists became interested in the Trobriand carvings, and a rapidly growing number of Trobriand men became involved in the lucrative trade, especially between the 1950s and the 1970s. European consumption not only influenced the type of objects that were produced, but also blurred the 'indigenous boundaries separating carver from non-carver and craftsman from artist' (2002: 46).

Looking at the interrelated processes of commoditisation, aestheticisation and object agency, a number of observations can be made. First, the Trobriand artefacts already had commodity status before entering the market economy. Functioning in a complex system of give and take, 'exchangeability' was an important aspect of their social and ritual life. Their entrance into the market economy, however, implied a fundamental change in the exchange system.

When sold to European customers, the carvings were exchanged for money instead of for local products and services, and disappeared from the Trobriand networks of circulation. Furthermore, the rules of demand and supply were increasingly decided by the global economy.

In the souvenir market, Trobriand perceptions of magic had no direct indexical relevance, in the sense that the objects did not affect the buyers in ways similar to the Trobriand *Kula* partners. Indirectly though, the Trobrianders' 'belief in magic' provided an interesting story, which could be told to potential customers and which increased the objects' attractiveness. The Europeans, however, did not know enough about Trobriand carving to be able to make a distinction between types of producers, and, consequently, the carvings produced by *tokabitam* were as much in demand as those produced by *tokataraki*. As a result, both groups of carvers began to produce similar objects that were similarly priced (2002: 46). Only on Vakuta, the island that was least visited by foreigners, the clear-cut distinction between *tokabitam* and *tokataraki* remained intact.

MONETISATION AND MARKET DIFFERENTIATION: YIRRKALA BARK PAINTINGS

In various cases, such as Trobriand carving, outsiders' demands for artefacts have drawn people (who, so far, had remained outside the monetary system) into the global economy. As this section illustrates, at times this has also stimulated the development of *diverse* networks of production and purchase, differentiating the market for indigenous artefacts into various, at times overlapping sectors, constituting multiple processes of transit and transition. Through their activities, anthropologists (as well as missionaries) have frequently stimulated this process. As argued in Chapter 3, it is important to have a critical awareness of their impact on social reality, as will be shown by the following example.

In 1967–70, Nancy Williams examined the production and marketing of Aboriginal art amongst Australian Aborigines in Yirrkala, Arnhem Land. Her analysis showed that the marketing of Yirrkala artefacts 'has been an important factor in the transition from a hunting-and-gathering economy to a cash based economy'(Williams 1976: 266). In Yirrkala, missionaries and anthropologists were active agents in the commoditisation of Yirrkala products. In the early 1930s, Yirrkala was still a relatively isolated area. In 1935, a Methodist mission was established, which introduced the locals to 'white' beliefs and practices, including Christianity, sedentary life and the market economy. Until the beginning of the 1950s, only a minority of Aborigines had small amounts of cash, which they earned through occasional wage labour at the mission station. Otherwise, food, clothing and tobacco remained the dominant items of exchange (Williams 1976).

Some white Australians showed an interest in indigenous beliefs and practices, such as ritual body painting. To be able to study and display signifiers of Aboriginal culture outside the Aboriginal context, these ephemeral practices needed to be transformed into durable, portable artefacts. During the second half of the 1930s, the anthropologist Donald Thompson asked a number of locals at Yirrkala whether they could make indigenous paintings on sheets of stringy bark. The recently arrived Reverend Wilbur Chaseling was also interested in the products, and both he and Thompson exchanged the items for trade goods and sold them to various Australian museums (Williams 1976: 272). It was essential that the products would satisfy the museum visitors' interests and expectations. Chaseling, for example, discouraged innovative designs to ensure 'authenticity'.

During the Second World War, military personnel who were stationed nearby occasionally bought souvenirs in Yirrkala. The trade began to expand after the mid 1950s when several missionaries at the mission station stimulated the production of bark painting because they regarded it as an important source of income for the locals. The lay missionary Douglas Tuffin was responsible for the sales, and he pushed the producers to introduce a number of changes that would enhance the objects' commercial success. As a result, some locals invented the 'split-stick binding technique', which kept the bark straight, thus preventing it from breaking easily. Infrastructural changes (e.g. more frequent visits by ships from urban areas and a more effective postal service) also helped to widen the market. In 1964, Keith Thiele took over Tuffin's position, and he approached businesses all over Australia to trigger interest in the artefacts. At the same time, he became more selective in his own purchases and created labels which ensured the 'authenticity' of the products. The commercial success of bark paintings can be measured by comparing gross sales figures. While in 1954 the sale of paintings produced in Yirrkala amounted to US \$291, in 1970 the figure was as high as US \$24,883 (Williams 1976: 275).

In the 1960s, the market began to differentiate into objects produced for the 'souvenir trade' and objects produced for galleries of higher-status 'primitive art'.[8] With regard to the souvenir trade, various businesses ordered mostly small and inexpensive works, which were sold to tourists in the main cities. The gallery trade was developed in 1962, when J.A. Davidson, a collector of 'primitive art' and the owner of a gallery in Melbourne, started commissioning large works. Interestingly, he had been approached by the Director of Social Welfare from the Northern Territory Administration to find out about the commodity potential of Aboriginal painting, which showed that the state was clearly concerned with its welfare budget and intended to stimulate the development of new job markets. Davidson exhibited and sold the works produced at Yirrkala to a growing group of interested urban buyers, whom, he claimed, 'he "educated" ... to appreciate the artistic qualities of the bark paintings and to have some understanding of the designs' (Williams 1976: 276). The latter again illustrates how middlemen (in this case anthropologists, missionaries and dealers) are often actively involved in aestheticisation processes as they try to influence not only artefact production, but also the expectations of potential buyers.

MONETISATION AND MARKET DIFFERENTIATION: INUIT SOAPSTONE CARVINGS

The previous case showed that, as markets for particular objects grow, they may differentiate into distinct segments, which constitute relatively separate trade networks. In his study of Inuit artefacts, Nelson Graburn (1976) also pointed out that market differentiation was an important phase in their commoditisation. In the Inuit case, it was an artist, and not an anthropologist, who played a crucial role in the process of transit and transition.

During the first decades of the twentieth century, the Inuit began to trade with white traders, exchanging skins for wooden boats, guns, store clothing and other foreign goods. The former decorated utilitarian implements, and carved soapstone and ivory *pinguak*,[9] as well as amulets and charms for their own use. They began to occasionally produce ivory and soapstone carvings in response to outsiders' demands (Graburn 1976: 39–40). A more regular market in Inuit artefacts began to develop in 1948, when James Houston, a visiting Canadian artist arrived in Port Harrison. He showed a number of drawings to the locals and asked them to copy these in soapstone. Houston's expectations of Inuit material culture – based on his own perception of 'traditional' Eskimo life – thus directly shaped the production of soapstone sculptures. After successful sales of the artefacts in Montreal, Houston returned to place a new order and, in 1949, the Canadian Handicrafts Guild granted US $3,000 to acquire carvings. As a result, an increasing number of Inuit became involved in the trade (1976: 45). During the 1950s, the local economy was increasingly drawn into the monetary system, and soapstone carving was essential to this process. As Graburn explained:

> Subsistence hunting required a monetary income and the by-product sale of skins became increasingly unprofitable, as did fox-trapping in many areas. The carving of small sculptures for sale had originally been a time-filling occupation between hunting and trapping expeditions, as in bad weather. Very soon it became a more important source of income for 'target marketing' when individuals or families wanted to accumulate enough money to buy particular items, such as a gun, a motor, or even a boat. (1976: 46)

Cash income per family grew from US $25 per month in 1949–50 to US $150 in 1976, with some individuals earning over US $1,000 per month (1976: 41). As in the Yirrkala case, aiming to keep welfare expenses low, the government urged unemployed Inuit to take up carving as a source of income (1976: 46).

The market began to differentiate when, in the late 1950s, a mission station in Povungnituk founded the Sculptors' Association. Only the better carvers could become members of this prestigious guild, which became an important site of contact with potential buyers. The other carvers continued to sell their works through the Hudson's Bay Company. In Graburn's view, this meant that a distinction was established between the souvenir trade, which was solely focused on outsider demand, and the production of 'bolder sculptures' which 'even when made entirely for sale, are important to the Eskimos and have become integrated into their modern culture' (1976: 55). For reasons of analytical clarity, Graburn (1976: 6) classified the work of the former as 'tourist art', a category of artefacts which is produced when 'the profit motive or the economic competition of poverty override aesthetic standards' and 'satisfying the consumer becomes more important than pleasing the artist'. By contrast, he classified the 'bolder sculptures' as works of 'commercial fine art', which 'although they are made with eventual sale in mind ... adhere to culturally embedded aesthetic and formal standards' (1976: 6). The repetitiveness of 'tourist art' and its strong response to outsider demand thus contrasted with the more inward-looking 'commercial fine art'. The analytical distinction between the two does, of course, reflect a rather particular notion of art, in which the extent to which object producers react to consumer wishes is an important tool of measurement, dividing different classes of objects.

PRODUCERS' AGENCY: INTELLECTUAL AND CREATIVE INDEPENDENCE

In view of dominant Western discourses of art, it is not surprising that the question of whether indigenous producers of artefacts necessarily become slaves of market demands, or whether they are able to maintain some intellectual and creative independence, has been central in numerous studies. In the case of Yirrkala bark paintings, Williams emphasised that, despite commercial constraints, the producers had their own political agenda. Their main concern was to avoid the loss of sacred stories, which reinforced their clan identity and expressed claims to territorial rights. So even though buyers' demands (for small, portable objects and 'traditional' designs) limited creative freedom, the producers' agency was essential to the production process. The reality of object transit and transition shaped, but did not fully determine the production of Yirrkala bark paintings.

In his study of Inuit artefacts, Graburn similarly argued that commercial carving reflected particular Eskimo concerns (1976: 49). The Inuit used the concept of *pinasuakpuk* to draw parallels between hunting, male socio-sexual behaviour and the carving of soapstone artefacts. In all three cases, the Inuit perceived the activity to be an exciting process with a prestigious product as end result. In the context of hunting, *pinasuakpuk* referred to the following and catching of animals, with the aim of producing food for family and friends. In relation to sex and gender, *pinasuakpuk* meant having intercourse and the subsequent birth of children. In the case of soapstone carving, the concept signified the 'attacking' of raw material with axes, chisels and knives, transforming it into a successful sculpture, which would bring admiration and prosperity. This knowledge was central to the ways in which the Inuit valued and experienced their own carving products. It is important to note, however, that even though the concept of *pinasuakpuk* clearly framed Inuit experience of carving, non-Inuit outsiders did not need this knowledge to be able to appreciate the statues. The latter's perceptions were mainly shaped by the image of unspoilt and authentic traditional culture. Ironically, but unknown to most buyers, this image was undermined by the very existence of carving practice; soapstone carving had emerged as a consequence of modernisation and the growing tourist industry.

BETWEEN REPETITION AND INNOVATION: THREE KAMBA CARVERS

Tourist demands have often directly stimulated the emergence of thematic and stylistic uniformity.[10] Yet, some souvenir producers have been more innovative than others, which makes it hard to draw a sharp line between Graburn's categories of 'tourist art' and 'commercial fine art'.[11] The following case of souvenir production in Kenya illustrates the variable degree of diversity and innovation amongst Kamba carvers. It illustrates that, when studying commodities in transit and transition, it is important to pay attention to the personal histories and changing intentions and abilities of individual producers.

Before the 1920s, the Kamba, patrilineal agriculturalists who inhabited the Ukamba Highlands, carved spoons, stools and small magical objects for local use. Over a period of five decades, an increasing number of men became involved in carving workshops, and many were eventually employed by cooperatives in Nairobi and Mombasa. The trade started when Mutisya wa Munge, a Kamba farmer and member of the Carrier Corps, was stationed in Dar es Salam during the First World War. During his stay, Mutisya found out that carving was an important source of subsistence for the Makonde and Zarano people in Tanzania. On his return, he began carving statues which depicted 'traditional African life', and sold them to European residents and travellers. He also taught the skill to relatives and friends, and, by the early 1950s, a small community of Kamba artisans near Mutisya's homestead carved figurines, decorated salad servers and miniature animals (Jules-Rosette 1984).

Initially, the artisans sold their products through informal trade connections in Nairobi, but by 1960 many had settled in Mombasa and the capital, setting up shops on street corners and offering their works directly to passers-by. The statues were strikingly uniform, as most carvers imitated existing designs, but some introduced changes in response to customers' requests (for example, by carving animals with their head turned backwards). During the 1960s and 1970s, some of the workshops were joined in cooperatives. The aim was to pool resources to buy wood, to improve working conditions and to introduce a more orderly marketing situation, with administrative offices to oversee the sales, showrooms to exhibit the products and work spaces for carvers, their apprentices, sanders, stainers and refinishers. The emergence of larger cooperatives thus meant a social transformation from an informal apprenticeship system to more complex division of labour. While apprentices and most carvers copied existing designs, some of the more experienced and imaginative artisans generated and responded to new trends.

In *The Messages of Tourist Art*, Bennetta Jules-Rosette (1984: 139) argued that Kamba carvers 'self-consciously set and modify technical standards and aesthetic conventions for their carvings'. She added that:

[O]nce the artist is technically proficient, he generates new aesthetic standards through interaction with his colleagues and the commercial milieu. Many of the Kamba carvers pursue self-improvement through increasing the range and diversity of their work. (1984: 139)

Amongst some of the more innovative carvers was Jonathan Kioko (*b.* 1948), who carved many similar-looking artefacts for the Chagamwe cooperative, but also sold more innovative works through middlemen in Nairobi. According to Jules-Rosette, Kioko's work illustrated 'the individual carver's transition from manufacture back to art' (1984: 127). Using conventional themes for commercial reasons, he introduced new designs that were sold in various venues. Dealers influenced the production of innovative works through commercial feedback, telling Kioko how their clients had reacted to particular works. Another innovative carver was Mili Kisweli (*b.* 1947), a female member of the Wamunyu Handicraft Cooperative. She joined in 1977 but also continued to work at the Nfanza Partners' shop, where she had trained as an apprentice. Kisweli spend much time on the details of her carvings and tried to give her figures emotional expression. Unlike most Kamba carvers, she only worked four hours a day, and stopped carving when she felt uninspired (1984: 131–2). A third example of an artisan-turned-artist is Safari Mbai, one of the managers of the Africa Arts Gallery in Nairobi who is also member of the Nairobi cooperative. In an interview with Jules-Rosette (1984: 132–3) he explained:

When I was seven years old, I used to sit under a tree at my father's feet. I watched him carve and began to copy him. His carving quality was poor. I learned that type of carving – lions, elephants, antelope, old Masai, Turkana. As my work became better, I began to change my carving of humans. About seven years ago, I developed a unique style. ... I used to carve six pieces a day, doing a donkey horse's work. Now I take a week or a month, depending on the style of the item.

Mbai referred to himself as 'artist-sculptor' and distinguished himself from carvers who were dependent on commissions from the cooperatives. His self-classification shows that 'art-versus-craft' discourses that have been so central to Western notions of art (see also Chapters 6 and 7), have been appropriated by artefact producers in Kenya. The 'art–craft' opposition has also, at least partly, shaped the development of a diverse market. Mbai's representations of animals and human beings showed motion and dynamism, unlike the mass-produced products of many other carvers. Because of his individual style, his works were perceived as 'authentic pieces', an important identifying feature of 'true art'. As with Kioko and Kisweli, Mbai successfully entered a more sophisticated segment of the souvenir market, which allowed him to spend more time on the carving of 'unique pieces' for a restricted audience of 'art lovers'.

CREATIVE AGENCY, MARKET MECHANISMS AND QUESTIONS OF POWER

The Kenyan case showed that sculptors who worked for the souvenir trade often moved to urban centres for strategic reasons, to be able to reach their tourist audiences. It made clear that commoditisation not only implies the transit of objects but, in some cases, also the more permanent movement of object producers to urban settings. And obviously, tourists on holiday travelled on a temporary basis to Kenya, buying souvenirs and taking them back home. African cities are, of course, also inhabited by other potential consumer groups, such as urban Africans wealthy enough to afford material objects. The following section will point out that some anthropologists invented new categories to classify this type of artefacts, such as 'urban' or 'popular' art.

When the anthropologist Johannes Fabian conducted fieldwork in Zaire and worked at the university in Shaba in the 1970s, he noticed that many members of the local middle class decorated the walls of their private homes with paintings. The works were produced by usually self-taught urban painters who worked 'with a minute profit margin and [had] to sell at least a painting a day to make a living' (Fabian 1997 [1978]: 20; see also Fabian 1978; Fabian and Szombati-Fabian 1980; Szombati-Fabian and Fabian 1976). Fabian classified the paintings as 'popular art made by popular artists' in an attempt to undermine ethnocentric oppositions of 'high elitist quality art' and 'low popular craft'. As such, he tried to avoid the image of artists as non-commercial creative geniuses, whose work was only truly appreciated by educated, sophisticated people with a superior knowledge of art and a sensitivity to timeless aesthetic values. He explained:

The attentive reader may be troubled when I speak here and elsewhere of the creators of popular culture as 'artists'. Am I lumping or confusing art and culture? There are several ways to meet this question. First of all, producers of popular culture, such as popular musicians, painters, and actors, speak of themselves as artists. When they reflect on what they do they often identify their practices and creations as art and, in that respect seem to set themselves apart from prophets, practitioners of magic, and historians. On the other hand, the historical juncture at which I encountered popular culture in Zaire does not permit the conclusion that art is perceived as a separate, let alone higher, domain of culture. If there are indications of an aesthetic distinction of art from mundane pursuits, there are many more indications of economic, practical inclusion. (1998: 16–17)

As already pointed out in Chapter 3, power has been the central focus in Fabian's exploration of popular culture. In his view, the post-independence phenomenon of popular painting in Zaire was a medium of resistance to colonial and postcolonial domination. The paintings in the *salons* of third- and fourth-generation urbanites actively evoked memories and more recent experiences of inequality, and the images transformed experiences of power and oppression into communicable expressions (1998: 18).

Depictions of *Mamba muntu*, an attractive mermaid accompanied by a snake, for example, referred to a story of danger, seduction, and magical good luck. In the popular myth, mermaids could drag boatman, fishermen and swimmers under water. Men who surprised a mermaid resting on shore, and were be able to obtain a lock of hair, her comb or a piece of her jewellery, would be visited by her in their dreams. 'In exchange for her belongings and a promise of silence and exclusive devotion to her (including abstention from all sexual intercourse)', a *Mamba muntu* would make her protagonist suddenly wealthy (Fabian 1997 [1978]: 20). In the paintings, Fabian argued, the mermaid became a metaphor for the 'situation of the urban masses ... a most eloquent "reminder" of the continued control exercised by anonymous foreign capital' (1997 [1978]: 24). From Gell's perspective, the paintings were popular because they had the power to evoke relevant memories and emotions.

Colonie belge, another genre of popular painting, had a more direct political message and was strongly emotive. Depictions of oppression in the context of the Belgian colonial system directly addressed the issue of power abuse. The painting *Colonie Belge, 1885–1959*, by Tshibumba Kanda Matulu, for example, showed a prison camp with a colonial official overseeing the beating of an inmate by a local policeman (Fabian 1996: 68). As the painter explained to Fabian:

The colonial period was a time of servitude. They put people in prison and beat them with canes. Yes, they were flogging people in prison. It wasn't the way it used to be in the village when you had transgressed and they would grab you and beat you. In prison, the flogging was like paying a fine when you had done something bad. The flogging took place during roll call. It could happen that you were in the line-up and did not quite understand what the supervisors said. Then they would beat you with a cane. (1996: 68)

It is clear that paintings such as the one described above are active visual reminders of past oppression. In Gell's terminology, they are powerful secondary agents that are able to evoke sadness and anger, and thus strongly differ from tourist images of traditional dancers and exotic beaches.

The concept of 'popular art' has also been used to categorise works by wayside artists who are informally taught as 'apprentices', learning the trade from 'master artists'. Attention to their socio-economic position and the conditions of their training explains why these artefact producers do not regard commercialism as a problem. Their professional outlook is, at least to some extent, similar to the disposition of European craftsmen before the separation of 'art' and 'craft' (see Chapter 7). The apprentices generally come from poorer families and get some pocket money during the time of their training. After about three years, the more talented boys become master artists themselves and set up their own studios.

Wayside artists often produce works on commission for local businesses or individuals with particular interests, expectations and historical experiences. In Ghana, wayside artists include, for example, sign writers, who produce all sorts of commercial bill boards, cement sculptors, who make decorative and funerary statues, and photographers, who make pictures of individuals and groups of people against elaborately painted backgrounds (Svašek 1990: 74). In this field of artefact production, successfully responding to market demands is not taboo, but instead a positive sign of achievement. As we shall see in Chapter 6, in the last decade numerous Western curators have expressed a strong interest in the work of some of these wayside artists, aestheticising their products as 'powerful works', giving them new meanings and pushing up their price.

'FINE ART' BY INTENTION: COLONIAL AND POSTCOLONIAL MARKETS

The final sections of this chapter focus on the establishment of 'fine art' markets in colonial and postcolonial contexts, and on the related development of formal art education, as opposed to the informal apprentice system. As we shall see, in markets for fine art, the 'fine art' status of commodities is a social attribution to artefacts rather than an inherent quality. Consequently, the boundaries between fine art and other artistic or non-artistic domains often change and overlap, as perceptions of art are unstable and conflicting. I shall emphasise that the production of 'art by intention' for fine art markets must be studied from the perspective of globalisation, as concrete, world-wide processes of transit (of people, objects, images, money) and transition (of ideas, values, practices and experiences) have been crucial to the formation of these transnational networks of exchange. It is crucial to find out to what extent globalising forces have generated similar ways of experiencing, interpreting and valuing similar types of artistic products in different localities.

It is necessary to historically trace the development of fields of contact, which led to the (anything between willing or forced) confrontation of people with other people's artefacts, artefact-related ideas and institutions. Here I shall concentrate on Western-style academic art education. In most of the former colonies, European artists and colonial officials were directly involved in the establishment of art schools and art academies, which were often modelled after European examples and ideas.[12] Even though, in some contexts, more formal systems of art teaching preceded colonial art education (for example, Mogul art), European presence in non-European localities stimulated the export of particular artistic ideas and art educational practices to all continents. Even though these ideas and practices were localised in different ways in distinct settings, some features, such as the notion of fine art as a relatively separate professional field, and the idea that fine artists from different parts of the world have something (however defined) in common, were spread on a global scale.

Despite significant differences, world-wide similarities in formal art education have influenced the development of transnational fields of art production that are based on interconnected local, national and global art critic–dealer networks. Fine art students all over the world receive at least some basic information about the field-specific forms of capital they need to enter fine art markets: knowledge about the marketability of particular artistic styles, organisational skills to advertise and exhibit their work, familiarity with the functioning of galleries and social skills to make contacts with dealers, critics and collectors. Evidently, in different fields of practice, the key to success may be rather specific. A Kenyan sculptor who lives near a popular tourist resort in Kenya and an urban-based Indonesian video artist will need to take rather different steps.

To give a more detailed example, in Ghana, recent art academy graduates often sell their products to different categories of foreign consumers, including tourists, expatriates and members of the Ghanaian middle class.[13] Painters and sculptors offer their works at various locations, ranging from tourist markets through government-funded National Art Centres and foreign cultural institutes (the Goethe Institute and the British Council), to a number of international hotels and fine art galleries in Accra. In Ghana, the gallery Artists Alliance, established in 1994 by the painter Ablade Glover, is the most prestigious and globally connected outlet. Unknown academy graduates often begin by selling their work in less prestigious tourist art shops. Some gradually move on to more prestigious markets as their work gains national and international status. A minority manage to make contacts with art dealers in Europe and the United States.

During my fieldwork in 1988–89, most visitors to the galleries and the National Art Centres were tourists in search of exotic icons, and the academically trained painters and sculptors were confronted with strong competition from the much cheaper souvenir market. To reach 'serious art lovers', the fine artists made personal contacts with local collectors and expatriates by inviting them to their studios. Some regular buyers became patrons, who tried to push particular artists in their own local and global middle-class networks. Not infrequently, the client artists would lower the price for their patrons, or even give them works for free, as a token of gratitude through which they hoped to maintain the supportive relationship.

In this situation, in which the actual boundaries between 'tourist art' and 'fine art' blurred, it is not surprising that the many formally trained fine artists emphatically denied that their work was influenced by commercial constraints. They reproduced the myth of the artist as 'free creator', arguing that, in contrast to the non-academic souvenir producers, who were 'just commercial artisans', they produced 'genuine art'. In reality, it was clear that academically trained artists had to adapt to the expectations of dealers and buyers if they wanted to survive economically. This was also suggested during their training. The art student Adam Agyeman, for example, who was doing his final exams at the Kumasi School of Fine Arts in 1989, surprised me when he made a figurative work while most of his earlier paintings had been abstract. He explained that his teacher Ato Delaquis had warned him that, if he continued to paint purely abstract works, he would risk not being able to live from the production of pictures. Delaquis commented that most Ghanaian and foreign art buyers do not perceive abstract painting as 'typically Ghanaian', and that Agyeman would therefore have 'no chance' in making any money if he stuck to abstract art. Even though Delaquis said that he stimulated his students to produce original, non-commercial works, he explained that he also had to prepare them for the reality of the market (Svašek 1997c: 42).

Globalisation has affected the development of the Ghanaian art market in several ways. As the above showed, during the colonial period, the British exported certain forms of institutionalisation (such as art education), which influenced the training and production of art producers. At the same time, drawn into the global market economy, art producers were and still are confronted with the expectations of foreign dealers and consumers, many of whom travel to or live temporarily in Ghana. In addition, through books and other media, local artists have the opportunity to find inspiration in images of art produced elsewhere in the world. And, finally, as the following section will demonstrate, Ghanaian artists themselves move across state borders in serious attempts to develop their careers.

ARTISTS ON THE MOVE: GEORGE O. HUGHES

Several successful Ghanaian artists who have managed to find professional recognition at home and abroad have lived and worked in Europe or the United States, widening their experience and enlarging their network of contacts with other artists, critics, dealers and buyers. The following section tracks the complex dynamics of their transformative journeys through the example of the career development of painter and performance artist George O. Hughes.

Hughes, who received a Bachelor of Arts in Painting and Drawing in 1989, and a Master's degree in Art Education in 1991 from the University of Science and Technology in Kumasi, did not come from a wealthy background. When I met him in 1988 in Ghana, he was a strongly devoted art student who had to sell paintings to be able to finish his studies. One of his teachers, the painter Ablade Glover, was impressed by his passionate efforts and occasionally bought works to support him. Hughes also sold works to European and American expatriates, and began exhibiting in The Loom (a privately owned gallery) and in the government-sponsored Art Centre in Accra. He explained to me in 2005 how he had approached them:

With the galleries, I made appointments, showed them samples of my work and they decided to sell my work on consignment. The individual collectors came to buy my work through word of mouth. A collector will buy a piece and that will lead to other sales.

Hughes' success made him hopeful about a possible career in Europe. He saved money and left Ghana for Paris in 1991. His departure was also stimulated because he 'tired of doing commissioned work for my clients who were mostly Europeans', clients who wanted a particular type of paintings (see Figure 5). The painter commented:

Only few of the European clients were interested in paintings beyond the norm. I wanted to do art that was personal and that had the element of surprise. I wanted to explore new subject matter in new ways that required enough time and isolation. I also think most of the clients wanted art that reminded them of their visit to Ghana, like souvenir-type art. On specific occasions I realised that some clients did not even feel comfortable meeting me or were not interested in discussing what the work they had purchased was about, but went on to form their own opinion (which later was related to me by another client). There were some special clients who were very interested in my work and commissioned works without any restrictions. Jean-Pierre Merchant, Gerald Marciniak and Jean-Pierre Boucheau were very open-minded and very helpful. They knew a lot about art. (personal communication 2005)

In an interview in 2001, Hughes argued that market demands hamper the aims of African artists, who aim to 'join the International Art Community'. Their problems, he noted, are also caused by a lack of serious engagement with African art, both in Africa and abroad:

Figure 5   Beach Scene (1989) by George Hughes. Oil and enamel on masonite (22 × 32 ins). Photograph by George Hughes

I think more African historians, critics and patrons should get involved in promoting both traditional and contemporary African art. It is a good thing that several books have been written about traditional African artists by Westerners. However, very little has been written about Contemporary African Art by both African and Western writers. There should be more institutions such as museums, galleries and organizations set up in Africa to compete with the few institutions abroad that specialize in African art. (personal communication 2005)

He admitted that the dire economic position of most African states was a major problem. 'It's easier said than done. Most African countries do not have the economic resources to fund and promote art.' In Europe, things were not as easy as Hughes had expected:

I told myself 'if I could sell that many paintings to Europeans in Ghana then I would even sell more in Europe'. I was wrong. Even though, especially in European capitals, there are plenty of art galleries, competition is high and none or only few specialise in African art. What is more, artists of African origin who aim to enter European art markets are often confronted with rather particular expectations concerning 'African art'. (http://outspoken.co.uk/forum/index.php?showtopic=67)

After a brief visit to Paris 'to see the works of the Modern Masters', Hughes moved to London, where he got in touch with Florence Benson, a Ghanaian art dealer whom he had met in Ghana. She was interested in his work and he sold several works at wholesale price. To survive in England, however, he could not depend on the limited income from these sales and he had to take up several menial jobs. When he met his future wife, an American sculptress, they moved to Ghana, but soon decided to settle in the United States in the city of Toledo.

At first we wanted to live in Chicago to be closer to the art scene, but we changed our mind because Jayne was with child, and it was cheaper to live in a smaller city like Toledo, which is where Jayne grew up, and her parents live.

A similar choice for living in a cheaper but more peripheral artistic environment was made by many of the artists in St Louis, in Plattner's study (see pp. 91–2).

As had been the case in Ghana, in Toledo, contacts and cooperation with other artists, dealers and collectors were essential to Hughes' career development. To gain entrance to the local Toledan art world, he decided to take part 'in every show that was advertised in the area'. He also went to most of the parties to meet people who were active in the local art scene. Befriended artists introduced him to gallery owners, and he slowly widened his professional network. In his own words, 'One show led to another.' Hughes also continued to exhibit in Ghana and became a member of the newly opened Artist Alliance gallery. 'I maintained my dealer in Ghana, Ablade Glover [the art teacher who had supported him earlier, see above], whose gallery, Artists Alliance, has represented me since 1994. Through Artists Alliance I developed a strong network of contacts.'

The Accra-based gallery had a global outreach. It was Hughes' connection with this Ghanaian gallery, rather than his move to the United States, which helped him to catch the interest of the American art critic Doran Ross, a respected and influential curator of the Fowler Museum (at the University of California) in Los Angeles. In 2001, Ross wrote a nine-page illustrated feature which was published in *African Arts*, a magazine that is widely popular amongst collectors of old and new African art. The article increased Hughes' reputation as a producer of quality paintings and portrayed him as a passionate artist who refused to be pushed by market forces. Ross (2001: 54) quoted the artist, for example, saying that '[a]uthenticity doesn't necessarily mean that we should paint what people expect you to paint'.[14]

The topic of buyers' expectations brings us back to the main topic of this chapter, the ways in which market mechanisms influence the production of artefacts and art. When I asked Hughes in 2005 whether he felt financial pressure to produce, at times, a particular type or size of work, he answered: 'Several years ago when I was a student at the College of Art in Kumasi I would do work that fits the market. Now I create art without recourse to a market.'

Hughes' earnings from teaching at the University of Toledo and Bowling Green University has made him financially independent, and this gives him space to experiment freely, without the need to give in to commercial pressures. This does not imply, of course, that his production is unaffected by more indirect economic dimensions of strategising in the artistic field. The article in *African Arts* was a result of Hughes' active maintenance of contacts in the Ghanaian art world. In the article, Ross wrote that Hughes' paintings of cars could 'easily be seen as powerful metaphors for contemporary society – its values, aspirations, and defeated dreams – as reflected in titles like Decadence, Apocalyptic Emblem II, Tow Away, Crow Bar and Red Car' (see Figure 6) (Ross 2001: 51).[15] It is likely that this serious evaluation of Hughes' work by a respected art critic has not only increased the commodity value of the car paintings, but has also inspired Hughes to continue painting more 'metaphors of contemporary society'. Evidently, on the one hand, the latter psychological effect of positive art reception cannot be understood as an economic strategy. Yet, on the other, it is not totally unrelated to market mechanisms.

Hughes' attempts to keep experimenting and circumvent commoditisation have also led to his involvement with performance art, which by definition only exists in saleable form as photographic (and thus replicable) documentation. On 16 July 2005, he did a performance in New York City on Park Avenue, entitled 'Dead Man' (see Figure 7), and explained that

[t]he idea was to test the boundaries of pedestrian reaction to a well dressed man dead on the pavement. Most of the passers-by avoided the dead body. Those who knew what was going on either posed with me or thought I was crazy, drunk or funny. This brings to mind that meaning is imputed by the individual based on one's knowledge of an experience. (personal communication 2005)

Figure 6   Red Car (1996) by George Hughes. Mixed media on canvas (69 × 96 ins). Photograph by Charles Rushton

Figure 7   Dead Man performance (2005) by George Hughes. Digital colour print on photo paper (8.5 × 11 ins). Photograph by Octasha

Hughes' case illustrates how the movement of artists and works of art across time and space can affect individual art production. His case also shows the need to undermine rigid theoretical distinctions between 'Western' and 'non-Western' (or 'African' and 'non-African') art, as they are based on unrealistic images of cultural boundedness and static identity.

CONCLUSION

This chapter has promoted a dynamic approach to artefact production, marketing and consumption, which undermines the notion of the non-commercial, purely creative artist and emphasises the dynamics of human and object mobility. It has argued that artefacts do not move through local, national and global networks because of inherent aesthetic qualities or innate enchanting powers. These qualities and powers are created in social settings of production, marketing and consumption, and are therefore context-specific and subject to change, as shown by the case of van Gogh's *Sunflowers* painting. Perspectives that acknowledge these processual dynamics, such as Becker's art world theory and Bourdieu's field theory, are useful tools that can be used to create a better understanding of object transit and transition through commoditisation.

The case studies demonstrated that 'aestheticisation' is an important element in the functioning of markets of art and artefacts. First of all, makers cannot produce objects without sensorial and semiotic engagement. They necessarily see, feel and smell the raw material they work with, and create meaning as they give shape to the final product. As 'individual artists' or representatives of particular 'tribes', 'ethnic groups' or 'cultures', they extend their agency to their products and aim to produce certain effects in their audiences. Evidently, in the context of the market, one of the intended effects is to attract potential buyers, to seduce them to spend money. Various examples made clear that buyers are mostly attracted by different types of objects when going to different parts of the world, which is partly dependent on their perception and knowledge of the areas they visit. It is, for example, likely that local buyers of 'art' in St Louis wish to buy an abstract painting, while, when they go on holiday to Kenya, they are more likely to be interested in wooden statues. Object producers often react to their clients' preferences through strategic choices of theme, style and exchange venue, and dealers aim to attract and convince their customers through particular bargaining mechanisms and forms of display. Anticipating customer experience and sensorial priorities, they may emphasise that a painting looks 'bright' or that a statue feels 'smooth', and that they are therefore 'good' or 'authentic'. Discourses of art thus become central to their marketing strategies. As Steiner showed, in West Africa the type of bargaining strategies used also depended on the position dealers had in a chain of buyers and sellers, and on the sort of market in which they operated. The purchase of van

Gogh's *Sunflowers* underlined that bargaining mechanisms may be highly institutionalised.

Market mechanisms not only affect what kind of objects are being produced and enjoyed, and what type of sensorial experience is prioritised, but may also influence the status of image producers, as shown by the Trobriand example. The Kenyan and Ghanaian cases pointed out that artists and artisans may decide to move to urban settings, or even emigrate to other countries, in an attempt to captivate the attention of new groups of potential buyers. Besides the transit and transition of commodities, the journeys and changing status of commodity producers thus provide an important focus of study.

Finally, this chapter has shown that people's interest in objects and images does not occur in a historical vacuum. The demand for 'primitive objects' occurred within the context of colonialism, and the souvenir market grew explosively when, especially from the 1950s onwards, people from richer countries had more leisure time and transportation systems improved and became cheaper. More recently, globalising forces have increasingly influenced the art trade. While artists such as Hughes have settled in America and gained direct contacts with local galleries and buyers, transnational auction houses like Christie's have opened offices in Asia and Australia and deal in 'ethnic' and 'aboriginal' artefacts. Such developments emphasise the need for a processual relativist perspective, which undermines simplistic classifications of art into 'Western' and 'non-Western' classes of objects.

The next chapter deals more specifically with the social, spatial and discursive recontextualisation of artefacts in museum settings. It further develops the perspective of object mobility, and examines the role of various types of collectors, curators, art historians and anthropologists in the politics of representation. As we shall see, museum policies are often directly intertwined with political processes.

6 MUSEUMS: SPACE, MATERIALITY AND THE POLITICS OF DISPLAY

One of the most basic characteristics of all artefacts is their relative material permanency; the fact that they can be moved from one place to another without changing their physical features. The question, however, is to what extent an object which moves through time and space, and appears in different locations, remains 'the same thing'. As was argued earlier, from the processual relativist point of view, which takes a wide variety of changing contextual factors into account, the object will almost certainly be presented, perceived and influential in distinct ways in different environments. While the previous chapter examined the connections between such transformations and economic processes, this chapter is particularly interested in representation, aestheticisation and issues of power, and in the spatial recontextualisation of objects in museum settings. Following James Clifford (1988) and Karp and Lavine (1991), I shall argue that exhibitions are never just 'neutral' spatial arrangements, because facilitators of object display are inevitably involved in representational politics.[1] Exhibiting selections of artefacts in particular combinations and spatial set-ups, they mostly intend to send rather particular messages to the viewing public and aim to move them in specific ways. As we shall see, through concrete practices of collecting and display, exhibition makers have often reinforced (or at times challenged) dominant discourses of 'art'.

When examining the changing meanings and impact of material objects as they are moved into and out of particular spaces, it is important to consider how concrete matter blends in or contrasts with the surrounding environment. Several questions are relevant. Does changing spatial and visual embeddedness affect the ways in which artefacts are perceived and interpreted?[2] Why and how does a single material presence – a wooden stick, a mask, a painted egg, an oil painting – move individual viewers in similar or different ways? And, last but not least, who are the main actors who influence, control or criticise processes of appropriation and the way in which recontextualised objects are experienced and understood?

The first part of the chapter investigates the movement of non-European objects to Europe from the sixteenth century onwards, and looks at the different ways in which particular artefacts have been classified and displayed. It explains why, initially, many objects were mainly perceived as strange rarities, and why, during a later historical period, they were incorporated into domains of 'culture' and 'art'. We already saw in Chapter 2 that anthropologists played a rather particular role in this process by creating theoretical paradigms which actively categorised artefacts. This chapter focuses in more depth on their involvement in the collection and exhibition of ethnographic artefacts, and looks at the wider political implications of museum practices in colonial and postcolonial contexts.

This chapter also demonstrates that the establishment of museums and galleries has been inherent in the politics of nation-building. As various examples will make clear, the aestheticisation of particular objects as symbols of nationhood and indices of national sentiments has often been an effective strategy to propagate loyalty to national states. Displayed as 'products of the nation' in symbolic spaces, such as national museums, exhibits have often reinforced nationalist sentiments amongst members of the visiting public. The analysis will show that, intended as performative secondary agents (see Chapter 4), collections of ethnographic objects, folkloristic items and 'art by intention' have all been used for that purpose.

The previous chapter showed that both 'art by intention' and 'art by appropriation', as well as the people involved in its production, marketing and consumption, frequently move across national boundaries through global networks of trade. Drawing on the perspectives of Howard Becker and Pierre Bourdieu, this chapter further develops the notion of transnational art worlds and artistic fields. We shall investigate the activities of a number of Western-based curators, who have brought together material products from different corners of the world within the spatial and discursive settings of single 'art' shows. Through processes of transit and transition, they have aestheticised them as collections of unique but comparable examples of 'contemporary art'.

As we shall see, object transit and transition has also been crucial to members of native populations who have claimed objects that once belonged to their ancestors from ethnographic museums. Returned items have a complex history of spatial existence, having first been moved from 'tribal areas' to museum contexts, and years later being re-appropriated and brought back to their places of 'origin'. As we shall see, returned artefacts often regain meanings and forms of efficacy that were lost in the museum setting, but they are also given new meanings and functions, as the geographical locations and socio-political spaces in which they were originally produced have drastically changed. Their past as 'lost-but-regained' artefacts can turn them into powerful agents of 'minority' or 'first nation' politics.

The chapter ends with a discussion of how, in recent years, various museums have used exhibition practices to create active dialogues with different communities, thus turning the museum space from a more conventional exhibition area into arenas of relatively open-ended interaction and critical reflection. Various case studies will show that such practices of cooperation and object performance have served particular political agendas within what have been conceptualised as 'multicultural' settings.

RECONTEXTUALISING MATTER: COLLECTING 'CURIOSITIES'

To be able to answer the question posed at the beginning of this chapter, namely to what extent objects which move through time and space remain 'the same things', it is necessary to take a historical perspective. Not claiming to provide a complete overview, this section will introduce the reader to some aspects of the history of collection and display that are relevant to the main theme of this chapter, the impact and significance of artefacts' spatial contextualisation and recontextualisation in changing socio-historical and political settings. The account will primarily focus on the politics of display in Europe and North America.

In the sixteenth, seventeenth and eighteenth centuries, when trade posts and other settlements were established along the coastal areas of the Americas, Africa and Asia, valuable materials, such as metals, minerals and spices were exported from these areas to Europe. European travellers, entrepreneurs and those who sponsored the voyages of discovery were also increasingly interested in indigenous man-made artefacts, or 'curiosities' (Feest 1984; Paudrat 1984; Peltier 1984). The expeditions were often financed by wealthy rulers and other members of the aristocracy who valued these artefacts most of all for their strangeness and rarity, regarding them as products manufactured by bizarre, Godless beings. In other words, in the hands of the Europeans, the objects were transformed into signifiers of exotic otherness.

The collectors, mostly rich and influential aristocrats, displayed the artefacts in special rooms and cabinets, together with natural history specimens, medallions and botanical rarities. The exhibition spaces were called 'cabinets of curiosities' (*Wunderkammer* or *Kunstkammer* in German, and *gabinetto* in Italian, see Prior 2002: 58). In their new spatial environments, exhibited amongst all sorts of other uncommon objects, the strangeness of the artefacts was emphasised. The cabinets not only reinforced the status of their owners; they also produced images of Europe as the civilised centre of a world in which those on the periphery led barbarous and mysterious lives (see also Chapter 2). In other words, they were powerful agents which evoked fascination and contempt in the viewers for people who inhabited far-away places; furthermore, they demanded respect for their wealthy owners.

Apart from their suitability as a sign of the bizarre, the objects' materiality constituted an important criterion of selection, which reinforces the view that materiality and interpretability are dialectically related aspects of artefacts (see Chapter 3). Many objects were simply too heavy, too large or too vulnerable to be transported to Europe. In some cases, the more interesting parts of larger structures were simply removed or chopped off and taken away. In other cases, artefacts were purposely changed to increase their exotic attractiveness. This shows that while the physicality of objects put certain limitations on collecting practices, material realities could be altered to accommodate the collectors' desires.

The search for curiosities was ambiguous in the sense that it was, on the one hand, driven by an infantile interest in anything new and strange and, on the other, informed by a serious attempt to map the world in all its diversity (Thomas 1991: 127–8). With the early development of European science, learned scholars became increasingly involved in the collection of non-European objects. Following the paradigm of Renaissance science, they differentiated matter into categories of the 'natural' and the 'artificial'. This distinction was in line with the dogma of Christianity, according to which God had created the natural, and had given mankind the ability to use and develop skills to produce the artificial. According to this paradigm, the displays of curiosities mapped the wonders of a God-created natural and artificial world. The 'natural' exhibits included biological samples, such as dried plants, stuffed animals, seeds and minerals, as well as drawings of mythical creatures such as griffins and phoenixes, which travellers claimed to have seen on their travels. The category of 'the artificial' consisted of man-made objects, such as clothes, utensils and religious objects (see Lidchi 1997).

One of the larger British collections of curiosities was started during the first decades of the seventeenth century by the botanist and gardener John Tradescant, who collected plants and natural specimens in Europe and along the Barbary coast. The items were exhibited together with a variety of artefacts collected by scholars and travellers who had been commissioned by the Duke of Buckingham. The result was a display which, as was common at the time, combined samples of the natural and the artificial.[3] As the curiosa collections grew, artefacts were also moved from one location to another. In 1628, the Tradescant collection, for example, was relocated to the new Musaeum Tradescantianum which was situated in South Lambeth near London. In 1683, the entire collection was donated to the Ashmoleam Museum in Oxford (Impey and MacGregor 1985). This shows that, being objects which moved through time and space, collections of curiosities had their own particular histories. In most cases, new artefacts were added over the years, but individual pieces or parts of collections were also given away as presents to other rulers, or disappeared when they were destroyed or stolen during war time. The collection of *künstliche Sachen* (artistic items) and *Seltenheiten und merkwürdige Dingen* (rarities and strange things), initiated by Kurfürst Joachim II von Brandenburg in the sixteenth century, underwent many transformations. During the chaotic Thirty Years War (1616–48) many pieces were lost and, between 1688 and 1713, the collection grew again from 320 to 1,500 artefacts. When Friedrich III von Brandenburg was crowned in 1701 and became the first King of Prussia, the collection's name was changed into Königliches Antiken-, Kunst, und Naturalien-Cabinet (Royal Cabinet of Antiques, Art and Natural Things). At the time, the 'ethnographic' part of the collection was still relatively small, but this changed when Jean Henry, a librarian and preacher from the French community in Potsdam, became involved, first as attendant and in 1816 as director. Henry acquired numerous objects from Tahiti, the Orient and India. During the Napoleonic Wars, however, the whole Cabinet was confiscated as war booty by the French. Eventually, only one-third of the collection was returned to Germany (Bolz 1999: 23–5).

SCIENCE, MATERIALITY AND OBJECTIVITY

As noted earlier, until the early eighteenth century, European scientists had regarded 'nature' as a divine realm of seemingly unlimited possibilities, and their main aim had been to discover more species. Towards the end of the eighteenth century, however, scholars who were interested in natural phenomena began to establish the disciplines of biology and geography and looked for *regularities* in nature (see Pomian 1990: 69). The natural specimens were no longer classified as strange but wonderful examples of God's creative power, but were instead presented as scientific objects of serious study. In the light of the newly developed theory of positivism, the material features of the specimens were of central importance. The scientists (mainly geologists, biologists and medical scientists) described, measured and compared their forms, sizes, weights and colours. In the case of animal and human species, they also examined physiological characteristics. The results were presented in newly set-up scientific displays, which represented neat scientific taxonomies and thus radically differed from the chaotic curiosa cabinets. Preserved plants, animals and other items were exhibited in orderly cases. Transformed into 'specimens' they were aestheticised as embodiments of 'objective truth'; presented motionless and behind glass, the sense of sight was prioritised as a primary source of object experience. Crucially, the displays served as powerful agents of professional and disciplinary authority, producing historically specific scientific norms and perceptions.

In the late nineteenth century, the collection, classification and interpretation of man-made artefacts became a central aim of a newly established scientific discipline, namely ethnography (see also Chapter 2). Influenced by the natural sciences, ethnographers transferred what they now regarded as the higgledy-piggledy collections of curiosa into rationally organised, ethnographic museums.[4] They were interested in natural specimens, but mostly focused on what used to be called 'artificial objects', redefined as 'ethnographic objects' (Bennett 1995: 40–1; Leyten and Damen 1992: 15–18; Stocking 1985). The first ethnographic museums were established during the first half of the nineteenth century in Berlin, Frankfurt, Paris and other important European cities, at a time when nationalism and colonialism shaped European politics, and intellectuals and academics gained political influence (see also Chapter 7).[5] Some of them presented science as a more rational alternative to religious belief, undermining the power of the church.

Modelling their practices after the natural sciences, ethnographers classified man-made objects through measurement (of size and weight) and by the definition of other material characteristics, such as shape and colour. Functionality was another important classificatory tool. Exhibitions suggested objectivity through the display of individual samples in particular material and spatial combinations. Ten wicker baskets arranged in a row of increasing complexity of form, for example, underlined factual relations of similarity and difference. The discourse of scientific objectivity was, however, reductionist, and denied the unavoidable subjectivity inherent in selection and categorisation.

As discussed at length in Chapter 2, early anthropologists recontextualised artefacts merely as signifiers of social evolution, which meant that much of the meaning, function and efficacy they had had in their original social settings was lost (see also Chapter 4). As pointed out by Barbara Kirschenblatt-Gimblett (1990), they presented only fragments of a much more complex material reality, partly because the format of museum display forced them to include certain material objects, and exclude others:

> The artfulness of the ethnographic object is an art of excision, of detachment, an art of the excerpt. Where does the object begin and where does it end? This I see as an essentially surgical issue. Shall we exhibit the cup with the saucer, the tea, the cream and sugar, the spoon, the napkin and placemat, the table and chair, the rug? Where do we stop? Where do we make the cut? (1990: 388).[6]

A processual relativist analysis of exhibition-making makes these 'surgical' practices explicit, and regards museums as professional fields in which socially-situated collectors, curators, directors and other relevant actors exercise their influence.

ANTHROPOLOGICAL THEORY AND MUSEUM PRACTICE

By the end of the nineteenth century, the ethnographic museums had become the main centres of anthropological professionalisation. As already pointed out in Chapter 2, the early development of anthropological theory was strongly influenced by museum practices, and vice versa. Between 1880 and 1920, during the four decades that have become know as 'the museum age' of anthropology (Sturtevant 1969: 622), strong links existed between university-based anthropologists and anthropologists who were employed by ethnographic museums.[7] Even though the relation of anthropology to these museums was not always unproblematic (cf. Chapman 1985: 16), museum anthropologists actively stimulated the development of anthropology as a university discipline, and anthropology lecturers and students who visited the museums for study and research purposes gave the museums an academic function.[8] Scholars employed by the museums sometimes managed to create new academic posts, and provided possibilities for anthropology students to conduct research and gain professional knowledge within the museum setting. The ethnographic museums, in their turn, visualised and materialised anthropological theories through particular exhibition practices. As such, they 'generate[d] representations and attribute[d] value and meaning in line with certain perspectives or classificatory schemas which [were] historically specific' (Lidchi 1997: 166; see also Vogel 1988).

In the late nineteenth and early twentieth centuries, ethnographic collections were mainly arranged according to 'typological' and 'geographical' models, or a combination of the two (Chapman 1985: 23). The ethnographer Pitt Rivers (Henry Lane Fox), for example, exhibited artefacts in the Pitt Rivers Museum at Oxford in a typological arrangement, grouping artefacts with similar forms and functions (see Figure 8). He collected systematically and intended to establish 'the sequence of ideas by which mankind has advanced from the condition of the lower animals' in the Pitt Rivers Museum in Oxford (Rivers 1874, quoted by Chapman 1985: 33). As was discussed in detail in Chapter 2, this type of arrangement reflected the then highly influential theory of social evolution.

German museums preferred to exhibit ethnographic artefacts in geographical or regional groupings, reflecting the perspective of diffusionism then dominant in Germany. As pointed out in Chapter 2, the American anthropologist Franz Boas, who worked from mid 1885 to mid 1886 as an assistant under Adolf Bastian at the Royal Ethnographic Museum in Berlin, was influenced by the German tradition. Back in the United States, he criticised the typological mode of exhibiting common there and propagated the geographical approach, calling it 'the tribal arrangement of collections'

Figure 8   The first curator of the Pitt Rivers Museum, Henry Balfour, in the Upper Gallery. Photograph by Alfred Robinson, circa 1890–95. Courtesy of the Pitt Rivers Museum, University of Oxford

(Boas 1887: 66–7, quoted by Jacknis 1985: 79). Employed by the National Museum in 1894, Boas set up 'life groups', three-dimensional naturalistic representations of natives who were engaged in daily activities.[9] He claimed that by culturally and situationally contextualising tribal artefacts, their meaning would be clearer to museum visitors. His aim was to stimulate their interest in other 'cultures', and he believed that objects should be shown in scenes that were as realistic as possible, demonstrating how people who formed single cultural groups lived their lives. In 1895, for example, he created the highly popular life-group exhibition of a winter dance ceremony (Jacknis 1985: 77). He had purposefully collected the individual artefacts during fieldwork on the Northwest Coast with his Kwakiutl assistant George Hunt. Both life-group displays and cases in which he showed artefacts produced by people who lived, as he argued, in single cultural settings, reinforced the discourse of culture as a separate, clearly delineated field of thought and action. As explained in Chapter 2, this image of culture was central to his highly influential cultural relativist approach.

Boas realised that he had to accept the limitations of realistic representation. Commenting on the naturalistic life-group displays, he noted that:

[i]t is an avowed object of a large group to transport the visitor into foreign surroundings. He is to see the whole village and the way the people live. But all attempts at such an undertaking that I have seen have failed, because the surroundings of a museum are not favorable to an impression of this sort. The cases, the walls, the contents of other cases, the columns, the stairways, all remind us that we are *not* viewing an actual village and the contrast between the attempted realism of the group and the inappropriate surroundings spoils the whole effect. (Boas, cited in Jacknis 1985: 101)

The above shows that both typological and geographical approaches to exhibition-making communicated particular ideas to the museum public about the development and the diversity of human civilisation. The modes of display reflected changing anthropological theories. While the typological model presented human evolution as a generator of radical difference, the geographical model emphasised cultural particularity. It is important to note that the design of the displays was also influenced by pragmatic considerations. Practical problems, such as the availability of artefacts and funding, the limits imposed by exhibition spaces and audience responses, and dependence on trustees and patrons, imposed clear limitations on museum practices. Both Pitt Rivers and Boas were, for example, forced to adopt their visions because of practical considerations (Chapman 1985: 34, 42–3; Jacknis 1985: 83; Stocking 1985: 8).[10]

COLLECTING AND THE COLONIAL PROJECT

As argued earlier, despite claims to objectivity, ethnographic museums were not neutral spaces. Ethnography was not, as it claimed, a 'science of discovery' but, instead, a 'science of invention' (Lidchi 1997: 161; Stocking 1985: 122,

263). As the following section emphasises, ethnographic imagination and representation were strongly influenced by the political dynamics of empire-building and colonial expansion.

In the nineteenth century, Britain had become a powerful colonial empire with possessions in many parts of the world. The establishment of museum collections was an important symbolic activity through which the empire displayed its power and authority. In 1851, for example, Lieutenant Henry Cole organised the Great Exhibition of the Industry of All Nations in the Crystal Palace in Hyde Park in London. The exhibition, which was held under the patronage of Prince Albert, displayed raw materials and artefacts from over 30 British colonies and dependencies, drawing the attention of the visiting public to the economic importance of the regions to the British Empire. The products on display represented the empire as a natural economic unity, as a political reality which had logically evolved as part of modernisation.

The success of the Great Exhibition led to the opening of the South Kensington Museum in 1857. This museum acquired many new objects from India, South-East Asia, China and Japan, cultures which, though not regarded as fully civilised, were admired for their old artistic traditions. The displays 'were deeply imbedded in the developing culture of Victorian imperialism' (Barringer 1998: 11). Initially, the artefacts were presented as examples of good design, and served as educational tools for contemporary British designers. Yet, as the British Empire became increasingly powerful, a process symbolised by the installation of Queen Victoria as the Empress of India in 1876, the exhibits were reinterpreted as signifiers of British superiority. As Tim Barringer argued, '[t]he procession of objects from peripheries to centre symbolically enacted the idea of London as the heart of empire' (1998: 11). The changing meaning of the artefacts showed that, as was argued in Chapter 3, objects are 'signifiers' that can always be tied to new 'signifieds'. I emphasised that a processual relativist approach to art and artefacts analyses signification through objects as an ongoing process, which takes place in concrete socio-historical and spatial settings.

In the 1870s the museum built impressive Architectural Courts, huge exhibition spaces which were filled with large casts of Indian ancient monuments and sculpture. The area was also adorned with a 33-feet-high copy of the Eastern Gateway of the Great Stupa at Sanchi. The copy not only generated interest in Indian architecture, it also meant to trigger feelings of pride and admiration for the efficiency and success of the British Empire. The original gateways had been discovered in 1818 by a British officer, and excavated with the help of the British army. The account in an 1870 issue of *Art Journal* of the discovery of the gateways and the making and trans-portation of the cast, produced a powerful narrative of British superiority. It 'underpinned a colonial hierarchy of expertise and authority, offering a microcosm of the colonial ideal, with an efficient military administration and native labour directing colonial production to the home market' (Barringer

1998: 19).[11] Obviously, the decision to display a copy of the gateway in the museum had been politically motivated.

COLONISATION, CONVERSION AND MISSIONARY COLLECTIONS

As discussed in Chapter 5, missionary activity was an important element of European imperialism. Since the early voyages of discovery in the sixteenth century, Christian missionaries had viewed native populations as inferior 'heathens' who could only be 'saved' through contact with and conversion to Christianity. Obviously, this belief was politically highly relevant, because it justified the political domination by the European powers of non-Christian regions. Highly relevant to this book, many missionaries were ardent object collectors, and in their European and North American home-bases, they often presented them as signifiers of their own missionary aims and outcomes. In this case, object transit and transition served to validate the missionary project.

The Scottish explorer David Livingstone, for example, sent objects back to Scotland that had belonged to his one and only African convert, the Kwena chief Sechele. The latter had been baptised in 1848 and, some years later, Livingstone sent his stool, rhinoceros horn stick, sandals, a ladle and a number of private 'charms' to the Royal Scottish Museum. Recontextualised as former possessions of a new convert, the objects marked the explorer's success as a would-be missionary. The confiscated charms signified Sechele's former status as a pagan, which indirectly proved the supposed victory of Christianity over local religious beliefs. In a catalogue, produced in 1913 for the Livingstone Centenary Exhibition, Sechele was described as 'an intimate friend of Livingstone', which suggested that the explorer had been very close to the African, and had truly convinced him of the superior truth of Christianity (Cannizzo 1998, 161–2).[12]

In a similar vein, the Canadian missionary Walter T. Currie collected artefacts from Ovimbundu converts during the late nineteenth and early twentieth century, which, according to the original museum catalogue, included a 'fetish outfit belonging to an Ovimbundu chief ... who embraced Christianity' (Cannizzo 1998: 160). Again, the fact that the chief had apparently abandoned his belief in the power of fetishes signified the success of Currie's missionary activities and transformed the exhibits into 'trophies of his victories on spiritual battlefields' (1998: 163). From the perspective of Gell, the items had been turned into agents of the Mission. Displayed in the spatial and social setting of Canadian Sunday schools, they urged members of congregations to give their moral and financial support in the form of generous donations.[13]

ETHNOGRAPHIC MUSEUMS AND THE DISCOURSE OF AUTHENTICITY

While the missionaries were mainly interested in objects that signified 'despicable pagan beliefs' and 'successful conversion of the natives', curators of ethnographic museums aimed to acquire older-looking artefacts which were examples of 'traditional culture'. They particularly favoured objects with physical signs of ritual and other use, such as traces of blood or smoothness resulting from frequent handling. These material characteristics were interpreted as indicators of 'authenticity'. The previous chapter already pointed out that the ideology of the authentic strongly shaped the commoditisation of non-European artefacts. Ethnographic museums emphatically rejected objects which had been intentionally produced for the curio market. Evidently, they did not always recognize these intentions, and numerous objects in their collections had actually been produced in a reaction to the increasing European demands.

As noted in earlier chapters, it is important to realise that the discourse of authenticity was formed in the context of modernisation and Western imperialism (see also Chapter 7). The oppositional ideology of 'the authentic versus the inauthentic' was reinforced by the belief in scientific objectivity, which created exclusive realms of truth (the authentic) and falsity (the inauthentic). The concept was also easily projected onto moralising political discourses which made sharp distinctions between 'right' and 'wrong', and which, rather paradoxically, reinforced an ideology of unilineal progression (from primitive to civilised) and primitive static tradition. The paradigm was used as a political tool to classify the natives into neat, tribal groups. Anthropological theories which identified markers of authentic style or culture stimulated and justified these politics.

Anthropological approaches based on notions of cultural or ethnic purity assumed that genres of artefacts which did not have clearly distinguishable stylistic features signified 'loss of tradition'. The underlying assumption was that experts on culture and style (i.e. anthropologists) could demonstrate whether tribes, artefacts or ethnic groups were authentic or inauthentic, using expert knowledge and objective standards. The collection and display of presumably authentic artefacts in ethnographic museums further institutionalised the notion of cultural authenticity, an image which also had important political connotations. In the colonies, for example, identified tribal-specific styles were used as objective indicators to establish administrative units and plan labour policies.[14]

The above makes clear that the image of exclusive realms of authenticity justified the professional authority of respected, established ethnographers who claimed superior knowledge about the relative purity of particular genres of artefacts. In Bourdieu's terminology, they had the cultural, symbolic and social capital to decide which artefacts were authentic and which were not. Crew and Sims (1991) have emphasised the dimension of power. Reflecting on claims to authenticity by museum curators, they pointed out that:

[a]uthenticity is not about factuality or reality. It is about authority. Objects have no authority; people do. It is people on the exhibition team who must make a judgement about how to tell about the past. Authenticity – authority – enforces the social contract

between the audience and the museum, a socially agreed-upon reality that exists only as long as confidence in the voice of the exhibition holds' (1991: 163).[15]

COLLECTING: ECONOMIC DIMENSIONS

The museum demand for authentic items and the development of trade and exchange relations in the context of European imperialism strongly shaped the practice of ethnographic collecting (Fabian 1998: 88). The previous chapter explored in detail the impact of consumer expectations on the supply of artefacts. The following example will make clear that, in the case of collecting expeditions, other economic dimensions also shaped the trade.

To make a collecting expedition practically possible and financially feasible, it was crucial to secure enough funding to buy the necessary food and equipment and hire local assistants. The ethnographers Emil Torday and Leo Frobenius, who collected artefacts during the first decade of the twentieth century in a rubber-producing region that was part of the Belgian colony, the Congo Free State, worked under different financial conditions. Torday's expedition was directly financed by the British Museum, so his situation was relatively straightforward. Frobenius, by contrast, used his own money as well as goods donated by German manufacturers and a number of grants from various foundations to fund his trip, and, after his return to Germany, he managed to sell the artefacts he had collected to the ethnological museum in Hamburg (Fabian 1998: 83).

Interestingly, financial and institutional support in Europe did not guarantee the success of an expedition. Equally important was the willingness of the locals to part with the objects the Europeans were interested in, and their familiarity with processes of commodification. In Appadurai's words, the commodity potential of things is partly dependent on the attitudes of their original owners. Hilton-Simpson commented in 1911 about his collecting experiences amongst the Batela: '[t]he people, as a rule, were perfectly willing to sell their belongings (at their own price!), and only upon one occasion did we meet with a Batela chief who declined to sell curios' (1911: 176–7, quoted by Fabian 1998: 89). In line with this comment, Fabian argued that in the Central African context the global spread of capitalism was far more important to the commoditisation of native artefacts than the establishment of effective colonial bureaucracies.

At the time when Frobenius and Torday organised their expeditions, while the Belgian state did not yet have much political power in the area, the natives were familiar with market mechanisms. Their willingness to part with their own products, and exchange them for European commodities, was essential to the development of a more permanent market for ethnographic objects. As Stocking noted, '[w]hile many ethnographic objects were acquired by expropriative processes involving no element of exchange, many others were acquired by batter or purchase' (1985: 5; see also O'Hanlon 1993).

Evidently, there are numerous cases when objects were simply stolen; brutally taken as war trophies and triumphally displayed in Europe as signifiers of successful colonial military action. In the 1870s, for example, the South Kensington Museum exhibited the royal regalia of King Theodore of Abyssinia, which had been seized during a military action in 1867, and possessions of the Ashanti leader Kofi Kari-Kari, which had been captured during a bloody campaign in 1873–74 (Barringer 1998: 21–2).[16] Yet in many other cases, collectors did not simply take what they wanted, but dealt with locals who actively negotiated about terms and prices.

NATIONALISM AND THE ROLE OF ETHNOGRAPHIC COLLECTIONS

Collecting had another political dimension, which was related to the intense economic and political competition amongst the European imperialist powers within and outside Europe. When states (such as France) and emancipating cultural groups (such as the Czechs and Slovaks) began to redefine themselves as 'nations' from the late eighteenth century onwards, ethnographic collections became important symbolic tools that helped to create and mark national identities. In many cases, ethnographic collections became part of national museums which were sponsored by the nation-state. These institutes' ability to acquire and exhibit objects from all over the world triggered nationalist pride and boosted the status of individual states at the international level.

Before looking at the significance of the politics of collecting in terms of national strife, it is necessary to identify some of the characteristics of nationalism itself.[17] Nationalism was an inherent part of modernisation, a historical process characterised by industrialisation, urbanisation and the declining power of the aristocracy and the Church. Improving transportation systems, printing techniques and more efficient state bureaucracies increased communication between state centres and their peripheries. Other important aspects were the socio-economic transformation of society through capitalist forces, increasing class divisions between the bourgeoisie, the petit-bourgeoisie and the proletariat, and efforts by intellectuals to (at least symbolically) overcome these divides through notions of communality and unity. In the Americas, an added factor was the increasing unwillingness, in many regions, to be ruled by European powers, while in Central Europe the cultural emancipation of the Slavs played a crucial role.

Key events during the first phase of nationalism were the French Revolution of 1789, American and Mexican independence in 1783 and 1821, the unification of Italy between 1859 and 1870, the unification of Germany in 1871, and the creation of Czechoslovakia, Hungary and Austria after the fall of the Habsburg Empire in 1918. The second phase was marked by most of the European colonies becoming independent during the second half of the twentieth century. The creation of new European nation-states after the collapse of the Soviet Union and the war in Yugoslavia represented the third phase.

During the nineteenth and early twentieth centuries in particular, competition between nation-states was played out in collecting practices and the establishment of prestigious ethnographic museums, a process that took place in the context of imperialist aims.[18] Displays of Chinese artefacts in London, for example, exhibited in the British Museum and in the Victoria & Albert Museum, framed the objects as material signifiers of British national superiority and imperial identity; they symbolised the British military victory of 1842 which brought an end to the Opium Wars (Clunas 1998: 43). After this, British fascination for China and Chinese commodities grew rapidly. The displays of objects from China in British museums gave the public 'a chance to display its national pride by patronising an exhibition of objects from a country defeated' (Paganini 1998: 37). Chinese people were represented as an inferior race,[19] and gifts from Chinese subjects – for instance a large bronze bell that had been presented to Queen Victoria in the 1840s – symbolised British superiority as it signified the powerful political presence of Britain in Asia (1998: 34). As we shall see in the next section, national sentiments were also triggered by collections in museums of fine art.

NATIONALISM AND THE ROLE OF FINE ART COLLECTIONS

Displays of European fine art also served to demonstrate the power and glory of national states. During the eighteenth and nineteenth centuries, the royal galleries, which had been used by European aristocrats as reception halls to impress visitors during the sixteenth and seventeenth centuries, were transformed into symbols of nationhood and equal citizenship. The French revolutionary government, for example, had nationalised the king's art collection after the French Revolution, and had turned his palace, the Louvre, into a public art museum. The objects in the museum no longer signified royal power, but were redefined as national property. The space itself was transformed, and symbolic and material strategies were used to turn a visit to the museum into an emotion-evoking experienced that celebrated shared nationhood (Duncan 1991).

To understand why fine art exhibitions played such an important role in nationalist movements, it is helpful to use Benedict Anderson's definition of the nation as 'an imagined political community – imagined as both inherently limited and sovereign' (1991 [1983]: 6). Anderson regarded nationalism as a sentimental belief in a shared past, present and future, and argued that imagined unity could only be reinforced through symbolic means, such as the invention of nationalist symbols like national flags and anthems.[20] The fine arts was one of the fields in which powerful nationalist symbols were produced. Numerous contemporary painters, sculptors and graphic artists, whose work was included in the exhibitions in the national galleries, used their art as a political medium to create national consciousness. In Europe, the participation of visual artists in nationalist discourse reached its apex in the late eighteenth and nineteenth centuries, when Neo-classical and Romantic artists respectively, sought to express 'the beliefs, hopes, fears of [their] own time and country' (Honour 1979: 16).

National museums of history and art (which were sometimes combined in a single institution) presented themselves as domains of objective secular scientific truth, reflecting the ideals of the Enlightenment. They were institutional frameworks for the display of historical and art historical knowledge, and for the preservation of what was regarded as cultural heritage, which embodied the spirit of the nation. The often impressive architectural features and the carefully orchestrated suggestion of sacredness forced museum visitors into a mood of quiet contemplation, and this increased the exhibits' power to trigger feelings of admiration and national pride.[21]

France was relatively early to establish a national museum (the Louvre). The rest of Europe followed the French example during the first half of the nineteenth century. By around 1850, almost every Western nation had a national museum or gallery, and there were strategically used as instruments of internal integration and international competition. Some museums were instrumental in the actual formation of the nation state. The Germanische Nationalmuseum, for example, opened in 1853 in Nuremberg, 18 years before German unification. It 'intended to create a history for a nation that did not yet exist' (Haskell 1993: 282).

In the Czech context, the opening of the Národní Museum (the National Museum) in 1891 to the wider public also pre-dated the establishment of the Czechoslovak state (which happened in 1918). In 1891, the Czech lands were still part of the Habsburg Empire, but since the early nineteenth century, Czech cultural life had been increasingly influenced by the Czech Revival Movement (*Obrození*). Under Habsburg rule, German had become the official language of the Czech lands, and Czech culture had been extensively Germanised. The Revivalists fervently criticised this, and demanded the use of Czech in secondary and higher education. Nationalist historians, most importantly František Palacký, began to write historiography from the perspective of Czech nationhood. The publication in 1948 of his first two volumes of *History of the Czech Nation in Bohemia and Moravia* boosted the nationalist movement.[22] During the nineteenth century, Czech fine artists were increasingly preoccupied with the struggle for Czech cultural emancipation.[23] Art associations that functioned as social spaces in which Czech nationalism was debated and visualised were established in various Bohemian and Moravian cities.[24]

The Národní Museum had been founded in 1818 by Count Kašpar Šternberk as a scientific institution, but Palacký and other nationalist intellectuals soon transformed it into a centre of Czech cultural and political activity.[25] Its new building, built and opened in 1891, was an important nationalist symbol. The impressive architectural structure overlooked Wenceslas Square, a site where Czechs had regularly protested against the domination of German culture. Stloukal (1994: 1) noted that '[t]he ideal location and imposing aspect of the building were intended to emphasize the symbolism that here was the greatest wealth of the nation, its national heritage'. The exhibitions had a clear nationalist message. The objects, texts and images on display represented Czech (as opposed to Habsburg) history, culture and art. The museum included various sections, namely the History Museum, the Natural History Museum and the National Museum Library. The History Museum was made up of various departments and archives, all devoted to particular themes and historical periods (Stloukal 1994).[26] Czech arts and crafts were important items in the exhibitions. In the context of the National Museum, all exhibits, whether fossils, stuffed animals or portrait paintings, were transformed into politically highly relevant signifiers of Czech national identity. The simple fact that they were on display in the building gave them the status of national heritage and turned them into powerful agents that triggered nationalist sentiments.

With the establishment of new nation-states, museums such as the Czech National Museum reinforced the progressive image of the new political order, as they claimed to preserve past, present and future national achievements.[27] Artworks were redefined as products of both individual *and* national genius, and self-celebratory exhibitions triggered feelings of pride and patriotism. Nationalist discourse combined the myth of artistic genius and inherent aesthetic qualities with a belief in authentic nationhood and notions of *communitas* and equality. According to this ideology, all citizens had access to art, and would enjoy and be moved by exhibitions in the national galleries and museums. Yet the ideology of equality stood in sharp contrast with the reality of class difference – the fact that the fine arts were a tool of social distinction. As Nick Prior argued:

Typical of the ambiguities of the modern museum project, though, nineteenth century conditions of formation pull in opposite directions. While the state constitutes the institution as a fully democratic free and open realm of national glory, as extolling the values of citizenship, civic improvement and moral refinement, the art museum, as an essentially bourgeois institution, remains an exclusionary and limited enclave. (2002: 38)

From Bourdieu's perspective, this implies that art museums have reinforced, rather than undermined, socio-economic distinctions.

NATIONALISM AND THE GLORIFICATION OF FOLK CULTURE

Nationalists believed that their community could only survive through cultural continuity. The search for the roots of the nation generated a strong interest in past and present rural traditions. As noted earlier, the Industrial Revolution had accelerated urbanisation, increasing the difference between urban and country lifestyles. Life in the country, by contrast to city life, became defined as a timeless zone that had preserved the authentic ways of the nation. References to traditional folk culture were common in nationalist discourse, and folklore provided a source of inspiration for artists and writers alike. Folk traditions were thought to provide a firm foundation for modern national identity. Paradoxically, the interest in folk culture, while generated by modernisation, was also a reaction against it. The products of country people were believed to have qualities which modern urban culture had lost.

Folkloristic scenes were depicted by visual artists, and folklore was studied by scholars and displayed in newly established folklore collections. To return to the Czech case, especially after the independence of Czechoslovakia in 1918, numerous folklore museums were established and the collections were presented as important cultural heritage.[28] One of the messages was that Czech folklore should serve as an important source of inspiration to contemporary artisans and fine artists, who should be conscious of their national identity and produce work in a nationalist spirit, maintaining the essence of Czech culture and further developing it for the sake of future generations. As noted earlier, during the nineteenth and early twentieth centuries, Czech fine artists had already participated in nationalist discourse, and depicted images which intended to express Czech identity. Fine artists, such as Josef Mánes, painted famous historical scenes and scenes from old legends, such as Čech, the forefather of all Czechs, who had climbed the mountain Říp and decided that this was where his people would settle.[29] Nationalist artists also depicted romanticised rural landscapes, inhabited by people in folk costumes, engaged in 'traditional' activities. Collections of folklore helped them to visualise such scenes. (For a comparison with Indonesia, see Spanjaard 1998, 2003, 2004.)

The folklore museums collected information about folk music, folk dance, folk speech, folk architecture, traditional customs and *Výtvarná kultura*. The latter term can be loosely translated as 'material culture' and is linguistically related to the concept of *Výtvarné Umění*, 'the fine arts'. While the shared adjective *Výtvarná* means that both material culture and the fine arts are made by productive, skilful human beings, the art/culture distinction suggests an essential difference between, on the one hand, refined aesthetic production by academically trained creative professionals and, on the other, possibly (but not necessarily) crude but authentic production by common people. As we shall see in the next section, art/culture discourses have reinforced underlying ideas about authenticity and artistic genius.[30]

Czech folklore museums collected artefacts, such as painted Easter eggs, embroidered clothes and handkerchiefs, ceramic pots, plates and jugs, decoratively painted wooden cupboards, and locally produced religious paintings and statues. The museums also acquired photographs of folk products and production processes, for example of decorative wall paintings on the door posts of rural houses, or of women doing an embroidery course around the turn of the nineteenth century (Kubíček 2000).[31] Folklorists presented their scholarly analyses in academic journals, such as *Český lid* ('The Czech People'). Their intellectual interpretations strengthened the belief that Czech culture was diverse but united through shared nationality. It is important to note, however, that there has also been disagreement about the inclusiveness of Czech culture. In particular the question whether 'Slovak culture' should be considered as part of Czech culture has been hotly debated. This shows that folklore exhibitions do not automatically instil ideas about shared identity in the minds of the audiences. Visitors could of course (openly or quietly) disagree with the curators' intentions, something that also happened when, soon after the communist coup of 1948, the official aims of Czech folklore studies were redefined in terms of Marxist ideology (Kunz 1954: 33, 36).[32]

COLLECTING: THE ART/CULTURE SYSTEM

Objects collected and displayed in museum settings have often been classified as either 'art' or 'culture'.[33] The distinction reflects a separation between the fields of art history on the one hand, and anthropology and folklore studies, on the other. While objects of art historical relevance have been exhibited as 'art' in museums of fine art, ethnographic objects and folklore have been displayed as 'culture' in ethnographic and folklore museums. 'Decorative art' is a more ambiguous category, which has been studied and exhibited in all three professional settings.[34] The discursive and spatial recontextualisation of artefacts has not only marked the boundaries of the three professional fields; it has also produced a hierarchical classification which has reproduced racial ideologies, the myth of the artistic genius and a gender bias. According to this hierarchy, objects of fine art are most valuable, followed by decorative art, folklore and, finally, non-Western artefacts.

James Clifford (1988: 223) convincingly argued that the practice of classifying objects as art or culture (the 'modern art/culture system') has reflected the historically specific preoccupation with the authentic. In other words, and as was explained earlier in this chapter, the discourse of the authentic has strongly shaped the evaluation and institutional appropriation of artefacts. Clifford's diagram of the art/culture system (1988: 244) shows that, according to the logic of the system, artefacts reside in and move through four zones, which label them as 'art' or 'culture' and as 'authentic' or 'inauthentic'. In the authentic zones, objects are either 'original, singular authentic art' (acknowledged by the art market and displayed in museums of fine art) or 'traditional, collective authentic culture' (ethnographic objects, folklore and craft, displayed in ethnographic museums and museums of history and folklore). In the inauthentic zones, artefacts are either 'inauthentic commercial "not-art"' (artefacts that were not, or not yet, accepted by art connoisseurs), or 'inauthentic "not-culture"' (artefacts that have not, or not yet, been accepted by anthropologists as culture).[35]

Not surprisingly, the collecting and exhibition policies of conventional ethnographic museums reflect the workings of the art/culture system. In 1991, Clifford compared the representational practices of two majority museums (established and controlled by white Canadians) and two minority museums (established and controlled by native minority groups). The two majority museums – the Museum of Anthropology at the University of British Columbia and the Royal British Columbia Museum – presented individual pieces as top examples of native Canadian production and as instances of human genius (Clifford 1991). In 2003, the website of the former claimed that '[t]he objects in the collections originate from many different cultures. They provide a view of the world's peoples and their lifestyles, and attest to the ingenuity and creativity of humanity and its cultures' (http://www.moa. ubc.ca/Collections/collectview.html, accessed 06/02/03). The optimistic discourse of human creativity stressed the notion of universality and played down the reality of economic and political inequality inherent in the history of the collections.[36]

It is important to note that Clifford's art-culture system mapped synchronic as well as diachronic processes. Over time, he emphasised, objects may move between categories, such as when recently produced commodities, which were initially perceived as commercial souvenirs, are re-evaluated and enter the zone of art. Giving the example of Haitian 'primitive' painting, Clifford noted, however, that non-Western 'art' objects are often still evaluated as cultural artefacts. 'Though specific [Haitian] artists have come to be known and prized, the aura of "cultural" production attaches to them much more than, say, to Picasso, who is not in any essential way valued as a "Spanish artist"' (1999: 255). This, he claimed, reflects underlying assumptions about Western superiority, as Western great artists are thought to stand out by their individual (as opposed to collective) creativity.

The art/culture distinction has also been institutionalised through exhibition design. Art museums often display works of art in relatively empty spaces, with plenty of wall or floor space around the individual works. In art exhibitions, it is common practice to provide only limited information about the objects – mainly the name of the artist, the year of production, the title of the work and the chosen technique. The underlying message is that these are aesthetic objects which have the transcendental power speak for themselves (at least to those who listen). By contrast, ethnographic artefacts are often presented as 'works of culture'. They frequently appear in textual and material settings, with elaborate labels, surrounded by other objects, or as part of a life group. These explanatory tools aim to elaborate on the exhibits' meaning and function. The underlying message here is that ethnographic artefacts are hard to understand and lack the instant aesthetic power of art.[37]

As noted above, the art/culture system is not a fixed, a-historical system, and this becomes clear when looking at more recent trends in the politics of display. Since the 1980s, anthropology museums and fine arts museums have begun to influence each other, showing 'signs of interpenetration' (Clifford 1999: 228).[38] Numerous ethnographic museums, such as the Tropenmuseum in Amsterdam, have exhibited artefacts as individual objects, increasing their potential aesthetic efficacy. They have also organised temporary displays of works by professional artists from Africa, Asia and South America, with the intention of showing that 'non-Western cultures' also produce fine art. At the same time, as will be discussed in more detail in the next section, some museums of contemporary art in the West have opened their doors to artefacts produced outside Europe and America. Interestingly, these artefacts include both 'art by intention' and 'art by appropriation'.[39]

LES MAGICIENS DE LA TERRE: QUESTIONS OF POWER

In 1989 the exhibition Les Magiciens de la terre, organised by the French curator Jean-Hubert Martin, was opened in the prestigious Musée d'Art Moderne at the Centre Pompidou in Paris. The show was 'the first attempt at a giant, worldwide ecumenical survey of contemporary art in a major art museum' (Hart 1995: 135). To select works for the show, Martin had travelled widely. Although he had consulted some local people, his choice was mainly based on his own personal judgement and taste. Crucial to him was the object's or image's ability to convey meaning without the necessity for additional information. Presenting the works as 'art' in the context of exhibition, he aimed to offer what he regarded as a purely aesthetic experiment. Labels only provided basic information, as is common in high art exhibitions, and a dot on a world map indicated the artist's country of origin. Information was also provided about the artist's date of birth, place of birth, region, state and nationality, and about the works' titles, size and the materials used.

Numerous commentators argued that Les Magiciens de la terre misrepresented most artefacts (many of which where 'art by appropriation') by ignoring the meanings they had in their original context. When interviewed by Benjamin Buchloch in 1989, the curator defended his approach, saying that 'whatever meaning a practice has for its practitioners is not relevant to us if it cannot be communicated to us [by the object itself]' (Martin, quoted in *Art in America* 1989). He added that he did 'not really see how one can avoid an ethnocentric vision', and that it was better to accept and acknowledge subjective authority than to strive for objectivity. In a critical reaction to the exhibition in the journal *Art in America*, James Clifford suggested an alternative approach, which acknowledged the subjectivity of exhibition-making, but refused to lose the sound of local voices. Exhibitions, in his view, should be 'translation experiments', which would aim to 'keep the discrepancy between different meanings or messages – different contexts around the object – rather than thinking of them simply as art with more or less powerful communicative power' (Clifford 1989: 152).[40]

Analysing the recontextualisation of several Hindu paintings at Les Magiciens de la terre, Lynn Hart (1995) compared the meaning of the designs with their significance in the context of traditional Hindu households.[41] The works in question had been made by Mithila women from the Indian state of Bihar, and their original meaning was informed by kinship practices and religious values. The designs were normally used in frescoes, which decorated the walls of family homes, and were also painted on paper, papier-mâché objects and baskets (Hart 1995; Vequaud 1977: 17). Their abstract and figurative imagery referred to Hindu mythology, and, as objects of exchange, the works were used in courtship and wedding rituals. In the words of Vequaud, '[e]ach painting is a prayer and an accompaniment to meditation. If the painting is well executed and in accordance with ritual, the deity invoked will inhabit it' (1977: 21).

In Martin's exhibition concept, the paintings were transformed into works of 'fine art', and much of their social, ritual and iconographic meaning had become irrelevant; As Hart (1995: 137) noted, 'a whole new set of cultural meanings has invaded the piece[s]'. The commoditisation of Mithila painting (which was partly stimulated by the examples in the exhibition), also meant that, having become an 'intensely fetishised object of occasional exchange and elegant connoisseurship, it has gained an altogether new market and new respect' (1995: 138).[42] Even though Les Magiciens de la terre proved to be a popular attraction, the project clearly revealed the unequal distribution of power in the global field of contemporary art (see also Chapter 5). Martin, an established and respected European art historian, had created his own exhibition concept, selecting objects on the basis of his own aesthetic preferences. His outlook was strongly influenced by a postmodern notion of aesthetics, which attacked the idea of originality and authentic value, and aimed to break down the boundaries between 'high' and 'low' culture. Equally important, he had the position and contacts to find funding for the project and persuade an important museum to house the exhibition. In Bourdieu's terminology, he was a powerful actor in the artistic field, with plenty of the required cultural, social and symbolic capital.

Martin ignored the opinions and expertise of respected African and other locally based art historians, despite the fact that the artefacts he selected came from their areas. Not surprisingly, numerous local art experts and artists felt that the Frenchman had sidelined them, especially when they found out that he had chosen artefacts that had not been produced as fine art. In Ghana, for example, Martin had picked the brightly painted wooden coffins by Kane Kwei – funerary artefacts in the shape of airplanes and other objects. The curator had not shown any interest in artworks considered important by Ghanaian art historians, such as Kojo Fosu. Instead, he had been attracted by a type of artefact which was spectacular and interesting from the perspective of postmodern aesthetics. This angered the professional fine artists, who saw Kwei's transformation into a representative of Ghanaian contemporary art as totally inappropriate. In their view, the lack of interest in Ghanaian art history was a clear sign of Western arrogance and global inequality.

The exhibition South Meets West, which showed contemporary art from Southern and West Africa, triggered a similar critical response. It was held in 2000 in the National Museum in Accra, and later moved to Switzerland to Kunsthalle Bern. The Ghanaian painter Rikki Wemega-Kwahu noted that, although the exhibition had aimed to promote contemporary African art:

the African representation among the curators was disproportionally small in comparison to their Western counterparts. In a situation like this, it is certainly difficult to discuss dispassionately and promote authentic African art when our critical input is so small in number; the exchange of opinions can never be fair. There will always be an imbalance and the Western opinion will hold sway. (2002: 14)

He pointed out that many of his colleagues had been shocked by the exhibition, regarding the postmodern works as 'too alien and uninspiring for their liking. Not something they would want to embrace as a new form of expression' (2002: 15).[43] Also referring to other recent exhibitions of contemporary African art, (the Dak'Art Biennale, the Carnegie International, and the Whitney Biennale), he wondered whether 'globalization in art [has] become a new form of colonialism', and stressed that the Dak'Art Biennale should 'find its own unique voice and not become like one of the many biennales on the international art circuit, displaying always the same things wherever' (2002: 15).

The above clearly shows the functioning of power in transnational artistic fields, with established experts in New York, Paris and other major Western cities making decisions about the programming of major exhibitions. It should not be forgotten, however, that power is also enacted by people in the more peripheral art worlds, which have their own centres and peripheries. In Ghana, for example, some artists, such as Ablade Glover, have a powerful position in the Ghanaian art market, and use their own selection criteria to push the work of particular colleagues. Their authority is limited, however, and so far has not affected international art events such as the Dak'Art Biennale and Les Magiciens de la terre. As we have seen, this is partially related to the relative lack of interest of Ghanaian artists in the latest global artistic trends.

QUESTIONS OF OWNERSHIP: SOURCE COMMUNITIES AND ENGAGEMENT WITH LOST POSSESSIONS

As shown throughout this chapter, curators and museum institutions exercise professional power as they collect, buy and display artefacts according to their own aims and visions. In recent decades, however, curators' claims to professional authority and the issue of cultural ownership have become topics of critical debate.[44] Western museums of contemporary art have been accused of strongly disadvantaging non-white and female artists in their exhibition policies. As we shall see in Chapter 7, this has in some cases led to more frequent inclusion of artworks by these groups.

Ethnographic museums have been criticised by members of 'source communities', groups of people from whom the ethnographic collections originate (Peers and Brown 2003).[45] Members of these communities have accused museum staff of dubious collecting practices and ethnocentrism in the handling of their collections. Critical reflection on ethnographic display has also come from academic anthropologists, who (after a period in which museum management and academic research were rather separate fields of action), began to regain an interest in museum studies during the 1980s.[46] As we shall see, in several cases the attacks on conventional ethnographic exhibition-making have resulted in the establishment of minority museums, the repatriation of artefacts, and the emergence of the museum as a place of consultation and collaboration.[47]

Claims of cultural ownership by Canadian 'First Nation People' were central to the establishment of two minority museums, the Kwagiulth Museum and Cultural Centre (established in Cape Mudge in 1979) and the U'Mista Cultural Centre (established in Albert Bay in 1981). A major motivation had been the confiscation in 1921 of artefacts which had been part of an illegal potlatch, an exchange ceremony which traditionally marks important ritual events.[48] The prohibition of the ceremony and the confiscation of the objects had been part of oppressive Canadian cultural politics, which forced native people to adopt the ways of the dominant whites. As explained by the U'mista Cultural Society:

[a]lthough there was no immediate opposition to the potlatch at the time of initial contact with the white man, such opposition began to grow with the coming of missionaries and government agents. Frustration over unsuccessful attempts to 'civilize' the people of the potlatch led officials, teachers, and missionaries to pressure the federal government into enacting legislation prohibiting the ceremonies. (http:// www.schoolnet.ca/aboriginal/umista2/potlatch-e.html, accessed 06/02/03)

The return of their lost treasures was a major concern to the community and their efforts to repatriate the objects were eventually successful. In the 1970s, the Board of Trustees of the National Museums Corporation agreed to return many of the confiscated items (namely the ones held by the National Museum of Man), but only under the condition that new museums would be built to preserve and display them. After the completion of two museum buildings, each received approximately half of the returned objects (http://www.schoolnet.ca/aboriginal/umista2/potlatch-e.html, accessed 06/02/03).

The experience of loss and recovery was highly significant to members of the two communities, so it is not surprising that the exhibitions in both museums commented on the oppressive political context in which the confiscation had taken place. The displays challenged the notion of a unified Canadian history and undermined the idea of universal humanity. In other words, the message radically differed from the message given by the exhibitions of native Canadian artefacts in the earlier mentioned majority museums, the Museum of Anthropology at the University of British Columbia and the Royal British Columbia Museum. As Clifford noted, the two minority museums did 'not aspire to be included in the patrimony (of the nation, of great art, etc.) but to be inscribed within different traditions and practices, free of national, cosmopolitan patrimonies' (1991: 226). The art/culture distinction was of little relevance to their identity politics. Instead, the main aim was to evoke memories, generate stories and trigger emotions which would help reinforce community dynamics and ensure the intergenerational transmission of local knowledge and values. In response to the display of the repatriated objects in the U'mista Cultural Centre, Clifford commented that:

[t]he display's effect, on me at least, was of powerful storytelling, a practice *implicating* its audience. Here the implication was political and historical. I was not permitted simply to admire or comprehend the regalia. They embarrassed, saddened, inspired, and angered me – responses that emerged in the evocative space between objects and texts. (1991: 240, original emphasis)[49]

It is important to note that the two minority museums differed in a number of ways, engaging differently with the wider world. The Kwagiulth Museum and Cultural Centre was a more inward looking village-centred space of belonging, which presented the repatriated artefacts as family property and community memorabilia. By contrast, the U'mista Cultural Centre served a larger group of people, including well-known Native American artists who used the Centre to gain artistic recognition, both locally and globally. The Centre had local and regional significance, and was linked to a wider network of Canadian museums.[50]

MUSEUMS AND COMMUNITY COLLABORATION

The last decades have not only seen the establishment of minority museums. In the same period, some majority museums have introduced particular policy changes. Faced with changing demographics and decreasing visitor numbers, the latter have been faced with the necessity of finding strategies to attract and involve new audiences. John Kuo Wei Tchen (1992) has spotted two innovative trends. The first, a less revolutionary transformation, has been a move from inward-looking, collection-driven approaches mainly concerned with the preservation and display of existing collections, to inquiry-driven policies which, informed by new historical insights and debates, use a 'coordinated planning process for exhibitions and collections development' (1992: 290).[51]

The second trend is a more radical change towards active dialogue with museum audiences, especially with people who live in the areas surrounding the museum and with members of source communities. Redefining their relationship with the outside world, museums have had to rethink their position and reshape their attitude towards the collections. As Peers and Brown (2003: 2) argued, ethnographic museums that have taken a dialogical approach 'are no longer the sole voices of authority in displaying and interpreting [their collections], but acknowledge a moral and ethical (and sometimes political) obligation to involve source communities in decisions affecting their material heritage'.

Various scholars have argued that dialogue with audiences is most effective when the relationship goes beyond one-sided consultation, and when it involves true power-sharing and longer-term commitment (Peers and Brown 2003; see also Ames 2003: 172). Some curators have acknowledged that more radical institutional change can be hampered by an unwillingness of museum personnel to share power. Curator Peirson Jones (1992: 240) argued that this can be caused by internalised professional standards and insecurity, as curators are trained 'both to be authorities and to exercise authority, and sometimes find it hard to move away from these positions when they find themselves on unfamiliar terrain'.[52]

A good example of successful museum consultation, yet without more radical institutional transformation, is the realisation of Gallery 33: A Meeting Ground of Cultures in 1990, an exhibition curated by Peirson Jones herself. Gallery 33 was set up as a new permanent anthropology exhibition of the Birmingham Museum and Art Gallery. Conscious that a quarter of the Birmingham population originated from former British colonial territories, the museum had intended to create an exhibition and performance space that would attract local visitors and encourage them 'to examine assumptions they make about their own and other people's cultures' (Peirson Jones 1992: 222).[53] The exhibition intended to explore anthropological themes at a popular level, integrating artefacts from contemporary minority and majority groups in Birmingham with the historic museum collection.[54] Eight advisers from various professional and ethnic backgrounds were commissioned to discuss the content of the exhibition. They were also asked to communicate with representatives of the various local communities, to think about educational programming and to review the exhibition script. Bearing the advisers' recommendations in mind, the curator and exhibition designers finalised the project.[55]

One of the aims of the project was to unveil the collection history of some of the museum's possessions. Peirson Jones explained that '[a] few examples taken from the Birmingham collection will demonstrate how the examination of an artifact's history reveals the values and motivations of the collectors, places British colonial history on the agenda, and exposes the anthropological museum as a colonial construction' (1992: 232). Like Peirson Jones, several other anthropologists have argued that the complexity of cross-cultural contact and power difference inherent in collecting practices is often lost in ethnographic displays, and deserves more attention.[56] Clifford (1991: 229) suggested that, to escape the myth of objective exhibition-making, 'it is important to resist the tendency of collections to be self-sufficient, to suppress their own historical, economic, and political processes of production'. Stocking (1985: 6) emphasised that museums' institutional history should be examined seriously, and argued that the meaning linked to individual collectors' experiences, investigations and activities is often lost.[57] Chris Gosden and Chantal Knowles (2001: xix–xx) similarly pointed out that:

[t]he study of collections necessitates consideration of all the parties contributing to them, their interests, ambitions and failures. The collectors themselves are documented through their own recording activity and we need to take their intellectual interests, institutional histories, economic resources and social skills into account in understanding what they collected and why.

The above makes clear that Peirson Jones' aims were strongly informed by current anthropological debates and concerns.

In Gallery 33, a diorama called 'The Collectors' featured three collectors, and an accompanying text raised questions about their motives and selection criteria. An interactive video exhibit invited visitors to find out more about the background of four other collectors and offered different interpretations.[58] In addition, a commentator informed the audience about the role of the museum in the context of mission activity, patrimony and economic development, and confronted the visitor with critical questions (Peirson Jones 1992: 229–30). A second interactive video exhibit, called 'Archives', featured 117 images of objects in the collection, and provided information about geographical location the collector's name and other relevant issues. The technology allowed visitors to go round at their own pace and follow their own interests.

Interestingly, despite the museum's good intentions and the many enthusiastic responses from members of the public, some visitors argued that Gallery 33 should have focused more on 'the heritages of local black and ethnic groups', instead of paying so much attention to the museum's history. In their view, the institution should have truly opened its doors to people from these communities, allowing them not just to advise, but to have an active role in the shaping of its policy.

Commenting on the project, Steven D. Lavine (1992) criticised another aim of the exhibition, namely the intention to stimulate cross-cultural communication by emphasising similarity instead of difference. This was done, for example, in the section called 'The Decorated Body', which included a wide variety of images of body decoration, including Italian plastic surgery, ancient Egyptian face paintings, British Sikh turbans, Japanese, Maori and British tattoos, African hairstyling and modern cosmetics (Peirson Jones 1992: 227). Lavine argued that:

[o]ne might view this as an appropriate civic policy for forging a larger community out of smaller communities, all of which have their own different (and perhaps unavoidably conflicting) interests. On the other hand, one might argue that this emphasis emerges out of the interests of the dominant fraction of the population and is more acceptable to them. The dominant fraction of the population need have no fear that their distinctive characteristics and perspectives will be ignored, whereas subordinated elements of the population are alternatively encouraged and pressured to adapt and assimilate. (1992: 140)

The above clearly reflects an issue that has been central to anthropology and ethnographic display from its very beginning: the right to represent the human species in all its diversity.

MUSEUMS AS CONTACT ZONES: FROM CONSULTATION TO DIALOGUE

In Lavine's view (1992: 142), if museums want to represent a pluralistic society, exhibitions should 'turn from monologue to conversation' and truly cooperate with their audiences. Discussing the implications of such a paradigmatic shift towards dialogue, Ruth B. Phillips (2003: 156) compared a conventional opening ceremony (with the museum director, the curator, the chairman of the board and some other stakeholders making polite speeches while the other guests sip wine and nibble canapés) with the opening in 2002 of Kaxlaya Gvilas: The Ones Who Uphold the Laws of Our Ancestors at the University of British Columbia Museum of Anthropology. The ceremony was dominated by Heiltsuk hereditary chiefs, dancers, artists and community members from urban reserve communities, who enacted their own traditional protocols and ceremonial rules.

The ritual performance translated the basic principles and components of the potlach of the Northwest Coast First Nations into the language of a museum opening – or vice versa – and the brief speeches by museum, university, and sponsors' representatives which normally provide the substance of a museum opening were decentred and became enfolded within an indigenous Heiltsuk ceremonial event. (2003: 156)

In another case, members of a native Canadian source community were invited to Germany to engage with objects that had been taken from their region a century before. In the 1880s, Adolf Bastian, director of the Royal Ethnological Museum in Berlin, had commissioned Johan Adrian Jacobsen to collect artefacts from America's Northwest Coast. Jacobsen came back with, amongst other things, over 2,000 artefacts from Yup'ik communities, who lived on the shores of the Bering Sea. In 1994, the anthropologist Ann Fienup-Riordan travelled to Berlin to select a number of Yup'ik masks from Jacobsen's collection for an exhibition she organised in Anchorage in 1996. She was astonished by the number and quality of the Yup'ik artefacts and, a year later, returned with four Yup'ik elders to explore the collection in Berlin. The Royal Ethnological Museum gave the delegation the time, space and privacy to freely engage with the objects; the curators handed their responsibility for the objects over to the Yup'ik elders, understanding that unrestricted access was essential. According to Fienup-Riordan, this was indeed extraordinary. She reflected:

I have accompanied Yup'ik elders on visits to museums thousands of miles from home and watched as their days in collections shrank to hours as they waited for museum handlers to access objects, present them one at the time, and remove them before going on to the next piece. (2003: 40)

By contrast, in Berlin the Yup'ik elders were allowed to touch, move and interact with the objects as they wished, an opportunity that triggered valuable memories, stories and songs. Through 'visual repatriation' (Fienup-Riordan 1996: 23–30), they were able to 're-own the knowledge and experiences that the objects embodied' (Fienup-Riordan 2003: 39).

The last example of museum–community dialogue in this section demonstrates how times have changed since the mid nineteenth century. In 1999, the Victoria & Albert Museum, which featured earlier in this chapter as an instrument of imperialist politics, opened The Arts of the Sikh Kingdoms, an exhibition which coincided with the 300th anniversary of the founding of *khalsa*, a central event in Shikh history.[59] The exhibition was the result of ongoing dialogue between the museum and South Asian individuals and communities, and triggered new community engagement. In the 1970s, the then keeper of the South Asian collections Robert Skelton had already 'recognized the need to make the V&A's "Indian" collections more accessible to the UK's growing South Asian community', and in the 1980s and 1990s, various community projects had been organised (Nightingale and Swallow 2003: 57). The Arts of the Sikh Kingdoms project, however, generated an ever more intense collaboration with the community. In preparation for the exhibition, museum staff attended numerous Sikh events throughout Britain. At the same time, members of the British Sikh community cooperated with the curators, providing valuable information and co-designing the exhibition and the educational programme. In addition, Sikh volunteers provided information to visitors each weekend during the exhibition.

Positive feedback showed that the exhibition had been effective in 'increasing Sikh audiences, bestowing cultural authority and contributing to enhanced self-respect within the Sikh community' (Nightingale and Swallow 2003: 64). After the event, community involvement was further stimulated through lecture series, a one-day conference and the development of a website with, amongst other things, an online story telling activity. Further projects, such as touring photographic exhibitions, followed. The museum also co-hosted a Sikh heritage desk, which, amongst other things, planned to 'identify and connect every location in the UK – from the Isle of Wight to Perthshire – which reflects the shared history of the Sikhs and Britain' (2003: 68). It may be clear that, in *this* history, the objects taken during the annexation of the Punjab in 1849, including the highly symbolic Golden Throne of the last independent Sikh ruler Maharaja Ranjit Singh, no longer signify British superiority, as they did 150 years before. Instead, they were presented as Sikh cultural legacy and signified the complexity of centuries of British–Sikh relations. The objects no longer intended to evoke colonialist sentiments, but rather aimed to produce respect for Sikh transnational culture, both amongst minority and majority groups. The changed policy clearly reflected the new trend in anthropology and museum studies towards reflexivity. In its own way, it also showed how those in authoritative positions in the museum world use museum policy to send out certain messages, even if that means giving up some of their power.

CONCLUSION

This chapter has shown that objects in museum collections should not be considered as static, lifeless matter, but rather that collections have complex pasts, presents and futures. Their histories reveal that, although artefacts may have relative material permanency, they have dynamic lives as material signifiers and as social or political agents. Within the context of changing professional fields that include anthropologists, art historians and curators, specific objects may be appropriated as works of 'art' or 'culture'. Museum practices thus reinforce historically specific and exclusive discourses of art.

The perspective of 'aestheticisation' has helped to unravel the dynamics of object collection and display. Those who order or acquire particular artefacts have particular desires and expectations that are, at least in part, based on previous knowledge and understanding of the material world. These expectations are shaped by a variety of dispositions related to, for example class, ethnicity or professional interests. They affect the collectors' or curators' sensorial engagement, and narrow their focus when looking for 'good', 'representative' or 'interesting' samples. Furthermore, their outlook influences the way in which found items will eventually be spatially contextualised when put on display.

The example of the cabinets of curiosities showed that, especially when objects were unfamiliar to collectors, they were regarded interesting. Most of all, curiosities needed to have strange forms and structures, as their *visual* characteristics were prioritised when statically displayed and shown to viewers. Brought together in singular spaces, their seeming uniqueness and exotic nature was emphasised to increase the artefacts' ability to surprise. By contrast, in the case of the early scientific museums, collections intended to unveil the underlying structure of nature. Influenced by a belief in evolution, the museums looked for specimens that could show the stages of evolutionary change, and the items were neatly displayed to map the laws of nature. Early ethnographic exhibitions emphasised similarities and differences in the exhibits' forms and functions, mapping histories of productivity as successions of cultural borrowing. Displays of similar-looking objects that originated from different parts of the world aimed to convince the viewers of the scientific significance of their hypothesis. Another strategy of ethnographic display, which became increasingly popular, was to bring together different types of artefacts used in single communities, mapping what became known as 'cultures'. Especially from the 1970s onwards, ethnographic museums began to offer multi-sensorial exhibitions, with things to see, hear, smell and touch, intending to give visitors a more 'realistic' experience of human life in its cultural diversity. The visual has, however, remained a dominant mode of perception in ethnographic museums, which has evidently shaped collecting practices.

The chapter has clearly shown that processes of transit and transition are central to museum practices. Individual objects are acquired, moved and spatially recontextualised, as they are put behind glass, mounted on pedestals, arranged in life-groups exhibitions and placed in alternative spatial set-ups. Individual exhibits as well as whole collections are often moved from one museum location to another. Presented in different times and spaces, and within different thematic exhibitions, they frequently lose and gain particular meanings, and are turned into different agents. To be able to understand this process, it is crucial to analyse the aims and interests of collectors and exhibition-makers, as well as their participation in professional and political discourses and practices.

Various examples in this chapter pointed out that exhibition-makers and those who own or sponsor museums aim to produce certain effects in members of the visiting public. This was clearest in the examples of the South Kensington Museum in London and the Národní Museum in Prague. In both cases, state politics encoded the intended message of the exhibitions, turning the exhibits into agents of government politics. In the former case, the museum was an outlet for colonial propaganda; in the latter, it was an instrument of nationalism.

The enactment of power is particularly obvious when exhibitions have conscious political goals. Yet, even when this is not the case, the display of objects presupposes selection and interpretation, as most curators want to tell particular stories. As pointed out in Chapter 3, however, discursive freedom is always limited by material reality: materiality and interpretability are dialectically related processes. A label with the text 'Clay pot 4000 BC, Middle East' placed under van Gogh's *Sunflowers* will never turn the painting into an object of clay. Similarly, if an eighteenth-century Dogon mask, after precise technical investigation, turns out to be a twentieth-century fake, it can no longer be presented as an original piece. In other words, material reality may resist certain interpretations.[60]

It is also important to realise that exhibitions do not automatically mould the perception and evaluation of the visiting public in ways intended by the exhibition-makers. After all, individuals are self-conscious beings who are at least potentially able to formulate their own thoughts and have their own emotional reactions. Earlier in this chapter, I pointed out that displays of war trophies were very popular in nineteenth-century Britain because the trophies evoked feelings of national pride. Yet not every visitor reacted in this way, as is illustrated by the following. After visiting an exhibition of African war trophies in the Kensington Museum in 1882, the publicist Moncure Conway remarked that '[t]hese African trophies are unpleasantly reminiscent of the worst phase of British policy' (Conway 1882: 71, quoted by Barringer 1998: 22). His opinion clearly differed from that of the exhibition makers.[61]

The chapter also demonstrated that museums, as fields of authority and power, influence people's perceptions of art. Art museums are players in artistic fields, and often reproduce assumptions central to current artistic discourses. The example of the South Meets West and the Les Magiciens de la terre exhibitions showed how the curators, engaged in postmodern debates about aesthetics, selected works that were intended, or could be appropriated, as 'postmodern art'. The exhibitions were influential, but were not received positively by all viewers, as demonstrated by Rikki Wemega-Kwahu's critical comments. The Ghanaian painter objected to the inequality within transnational artistic fields, in which Western-based critics and curators have most economic, social and symbolic power to decide about objects transit and transition and their appropriation as 'art'. His insight leads to the next chapter, which will examine how people have defined art in particular ways in different times and places, often by opposing it to 'non-artistic' categories.

7 'FINE ART': CREATING AND CONTESTING BOUNDARIES

This chapter will further develop one of the main arguments of this book, namely that 'fine art', though defined differently in different times and spaces, is always a category of exclusion. In Chapter 4 we saw that fine art discourses have mostly prioritised the sense of sight, positively evaluating the visual impact of certain types of compositions, colour combinations, textures, and other material qualities. Different forms and features have been promoted by different fine art movements, but in all cases their efficacy has depended on a belief in the 'aesthetic' power of art. In this chapter we shall look closer at different perspectives on aesthetics against the background of particular historical processes. We shall focus on two major approaches, the first based on a belief in the morally uplifting impact of 'timeless beauty', and the second anchored in the conviction that the force of aesthetics can mediate and generate political change.

In Chapters 5 and 6 I argued that the question of whether particular works are considered 'fine art' or not strongly depends on the economic and social dynamics which constitute concrete art worlds. Chapter 5 looked in detail at the influence of market mechanisms on the production and consumption of art. The previous chapter discussed how collecting and display have helped to define 'fine art' through the spatial and discursive recontextualisation of art by intention and art by appropriation. In both chapters, the processual relativist perspective emphasised that transit and transition are central to fine art production. Numerous examples showed that the transformational dynamics which turn objects into 'art' are partially shaped by struggles for power and authority, both within and beyond artistic fields. In this chapter, we shall mainly look at long-term historical processes that have influenced discourses of aesthetics and the social life of 'fine art'.

A central theme weaving through this chapter is that fine art has often been emphatically opposed to other categories of material production, and that the formation of 'art-versus-non-art' discourses has been embedded in changing contexts of power. In previous chapters, we already examined the political implications of discursive practices which made distinctions between 'fine art', 'curiosities', 'primitive art' and 'ethnographic artefacts'. As became clear, these categories reflected and reinforced Western superiority in the context of imperialism and colonial politics. In this chapter, we shall explore classificatory practices creating distinctions between 'art' and 'craft', 'art' and 'kitsch', 'art' and 'propaganda', and 'art' and 'pornography'. As will become clear, these oppositional pairs were central to the development of fine art as a separate domain of professional activity.

The previous chapters have shown that people do not always agree about the artistic status of particular works, and that conflicts about art may reveal wider societal and political tensions. In this chapter, a number of case studies will similarly demonstrate that, in particular socio-historical settings, individuals and groups have strongly criticised dominant practices of artistic exclusivity, and that numerous artists have incorporated 'non-artistic' elements in their work, thereby blurring the boundaries between art and other categories. We shall see that, in various cases, the rejection of dominant notions of art has been a political struggle.

Newly emerging styles and movements have often defined 'aesthetic value' in alternative ways, but have unavoidably created new distinctions between 'art' and 'non-art'. This again underlines the main argument of this chapter, namely that art worlds are by definition exclusivist.

THE BIRTH OF 'FINE ART': ART VERSUS CRAFT

But where did this all begin? When and why did art become a separate discourse and practice? The English word 'art' first appeared in Middle English in the medieval period, and stemmed from the Latin concept of *'ars'*. It was used as a more generic term to identify human skills, opposing them to non-human natural phenomena (see also Chapter 5). Other European languages reflected the same view: as with the English 'art', the term *'kunst'* in German, Dutch and Flemish, *'l'art'* in French and *'l'arte'* in Italian signified a similarly wide range of professional activities. In the medieval setting, the notions of 'art', 'craft' and 'skill' were used interchangeably; one could as easily talk about the art of the butcher as about the art of painting, and both were considered skilful vocations. Like other craftsmen, painters and sculptors were organised in workshops that were regulated by guilds, and commonly consisted of closely related kin who were involved in collaborative production. They were generally led by a more experienced master craftsman who taught his skills to his descendants.

In the late fifteenth century, however, some Italian artists, such as Michelangelo and Leonardo da Vinci, no longer registered with the guilds but set up their own independent studios. These artists presented themselves as producers of something far superior to craft; and their works of 'fine art' were commissioned by powerful patrons, including members of the aristocracy and representatives of the Church. They proudly claimed to possess creative abilities that were far superior to the skills of craftsmen, an image that was reinforced by scholars such as Giorgio Vasari, who described the works and lives of talented fine artists. As a result, 'art' began to be differentiated from 'craft' as a superior form of human dexterity.

Aestheticisation, defined in Chapter 1 as an experiential and discursive process in which socially situated individuals ascribe properties and values to outward phenomena that speak to the senses, is a helpful concept when analysing the birth of fine art. The discourse of fine art produced a specific image of humanity according to which some humans, namely fine artists, possessed God-given, superior creative powers. In this perspective, creativity transformed inactive matter into powerful art, which had the ability to captivate and enchant the viewers. Fine art was thus imagined as an index of supernatural force, which manifested itself through the work of talented artists; a force perceived to be much stronger than the potential impact of craftsmanship.

The many examples of religious imagery in churches all over the world show that 'creativity' has often been perceived as a God-given human ability to represent Christian values and generate feelings of devotion. It should not be forgotten, however, that throughout the centuries numerous theologians have also fervently attacked the concept of human artistic creativity, strongly opposing the production of art. In their view, the very act of representation is morally wrong as it challenges fundamental Christian truths and values (Goody 1997). Other religions, such as Islam, have also imposed restrictions on visual representation for similar reasons. These forms of censorship show the embeddedness of aestheticisation in struggles for religious and political authority.

During the late fifteenth century and the sixteenth century, the new notion of 'fine art' as a category of exclusion spread throughout Europe. It was not only exclusive in terms of its professional self-definition, but also as a politically powerful and emotionally evocative medium of social distinction (Hauser 1968 [1951]: 61; Kempers 1992 [1987]: 15–20; Svašek 1996a: 23, 1997a: 8; White and White 1965; Wolff 1983; see also Chapter 5). Only the rich and powerful (i.e. the Church and the aristocracy) could become art patrons and commission well-known artists to gain prestige. As Nick Prior (2002: 17) noted, 'European courts ... vied for the privilege of patronising renowned artists and competition for prize works was rigorous amongst them.' As art patrons enabled painters and sculptors to create highly valued art works, their artistic status further increased. Prior noted that: 'Court artists such as Bernini and Caravaggio were still treated as artisans, lower middle-class servants, but in the seventeenth and early eighteenth centuries court artists began to enjoy a degree of professional and financial stability' (2002: 17).

It is important to note that, even when perceived as a separate category of 'fine art', the act of painting and sculpture did not yet signify 'individual freedom', as would happen during the late nineteenth century. There was no open market for artworks, and even famous artists were highly dependent on the wishes and expectations of those who commissioned the works.[1] French, Prussian and Habsburg absolute monarchs who ordered royal portraits were depicted as rulers with unlimited political and religious authority (Prior 2002:

19; see also Baxandall 1972). Spatially and discursively contextualised in the royal galleries, they were primarily indexical of their patrons' agency.

During the nineteenth century, with the decline of the power of the Church and aristocracy in Europe, the introduction of industrialisation and the transformation of the art patronage system into a critic-dealer system (see Chapter 5), 'creative' fine art continued to be opposed to 'skilful' craft. The idea that art had special powers was strengthened by Kantian philosophy, which strongly shaped dominant perceptions in fields of fine art. As noted in Chapter 1, during the late eighteenth century, the German idealist philosopher Immanuel Kant had developed a theory of 'aesthetics' to explore the nature of enchanting phenomena. He believed in the necessity of 'indifferent judgement', a process by which people can divest themselves of influences and so make their judgements impartial. He defined 'art' as a category of objects with *inherent* and *timeless* beauty, which had the ability to create experiences of indifferent judgement by connecting individuals to the realm of 'the transcendental'. According to this view, beauty was an objective quality of art and the ability to induce experiences of the transcendental (which he linked in the *Third Critique* to the effects of poetry) was a central defining feature.

While, according to Kantian art historians, all humans had the ability to connect to the transcendental through experiences of natural phenomena (for example by watching a stunning sunset), only those who could recognise artistic quality could experience timeless beauty in art. In other words, only knowledgeable art professionals had the authority to decide what was 'art' and what not, and their classifications were, they claimed, based on well-informed but impartial judgements. The claims to objective knowledge clearly reflected the intellectual climate of the nineteenth century. As with anthropology, art history modelled itself after the natural sciences in its aim to 'objectively' map the production of skilfully made works of art, which had the quality of timeless beauty. As will be discussed in more detail later in this chapter, in the nineteenth century, the urge for timeless beauty was strengthened by a search for the authentic, generated by a disillusion with the social effects of mass-production and a desire to escape the drabness of modern life.

The distinction between aesthetically powerful art and skilful craft was also institutionalised through the educational system. As noted earlier, fine artists were initially trained in the private studios of established master artists. From the sixteenth century onwards, art education became more standardised, with the establishment of art academies, first in Rome (1588) and later in Paris (1664), Vienna (1692), St Petersburg (1764), London, Prague (1799) and Amsterdam (1870) (Kotalík 1979: 15; White and White 1965: 5–6). In these academies, students learned to distinguish themselves from craft producers and see their own products as instances of timeless beauty. Furthermore, when art producers became increasingly dependent on relatively impersonal market forces during the nineteenth century, their self-image was also strongly shaped by the idea that non-commercial artistic authenticity distinguished their work from commercially produced craft (see Chapter 5). As will be discussed in more detail when analysing the art/kitsch dichotomy, the ideal of the non-commercial artist was central to Modernist avant-garde ideology, propagated during the first decades of the twentieth century by art critics such as the American Clement Greenberg.

FROM 'LOW' TO 'HIGH' CRAFT: CLAIMING ARTISTIC STATUS

In the art-versus-craft perspective, art was thus imagined as a domain of pure creativity and artists as free individuals who were supposedly unharmed by the devastating influences of financial and functional constraints. Craft, by contrast, required skill and a commercial mind, but no creativity. A related assumption, namely that authentic craftsmen produced 'tradition' and artists strove for originality, portrayed craft as a non-innovative realm of material production.[2]

The discourse that places 'craft' outside the domain of 'art' has reinforced the high status of art and has strengthened the use of artworks as signifiers of social prestige. In reality, however, the boundaries between art and craft have been blurred. Howard Becker, Vera Zolberg (1990: 154) and others have argued that artworks are often not as non-commercial or unique as their producers may claim. As demonstrated in Chapter 5, many fine artists create series of rather similar looking works for both commercial *and* artistic reasons. This may, of course, not be to the liking of their audiences who wish to believe in the myth of unique creative invention. A Dutch expatriate who had bought a painting by a well-known Ghanaian artist, for example, told me in 1990 how shocked he was when he accidentally saw an exhibition by the same artist in an airport lounge in Europe. 'My painting showed a colourful abstraction of rooftops, and I valued it highly', he said. 'But the paintings in the exhibition were all strikingly similar to mine. Rooftops everywhere! I felt betrayed and could no longer enjoy my painting so when I returned home I took it off the wall.' His reaction clearly shows a longing for something unique, for something different from mass-produced goods.

In line with the art-versus-craft discourse, uniqueness is generally not expected in the craft trade; consumers tend not to feel cheated when they discover a bowl similar to the one they just bought in another shop.[3] Some craftsmen, however, intentionally create 'unique pieces' and claim a superior 'artistic' status. Becker (1982: 277) introduced the term 'artist-craftsmen' to denote artisans with 'higher ambitions than ordinary craftsmen', who 'may share audiences, institutions, and rewards with ordinary craftsmen' but also 'feel some kinship with fine-art institutions'. Some artist-craftsmen intentionally break the constraints of functionality, producing visually attractive artefacts that are otherwise useless. This positions them more in the field of artists, who normally stay away from the production of useful items, such as cups and saucers.

Talking about their work, artist-craftsmen often show a mixture of craft and art approaches. The American Stan Welsh, for example, noted in a potter's handbook (which the significant title *The Craft and Art of Clay*):

[m]y initial interest in ceramics began with a desire to make pots, on the wheel; later I coiled big sculptures. My current sculptures are influenced by my interest in vessel forms. I use low-fire clay and a core 05 matt glaze very thick to create a monochromatic unified form. Most of my work is autobiographical. I believe Jack Kerouac and the Beat Poets' idea of 'first thought, best thought', and I try to stay true to that in my work. (in Peterson and Peterson 2003: 246)

Welsh's words clearly reflected his double identity. On the one hand, he offered technical information, which is typical to the crafts. On the other, he mentioned his source of inspiration (his autobiography) and claimed artistic integrity ('I try to stay true to that'), which is common amongst contemporary artists. His reflections clearly undermine the existence of a strict distinction between art and craft.

Artist-craftsmen have also claimed artistic status through institutional action, actively creating a professional field which incorporated craft into the domain of art. From the 1970s onwards, for example, British organisations have attempted to upgrade craft as a form of artistic innovation (Attfield 2000). The state-funded Crafts Advisory Committee and the Crafts Council, in particular, aimed to 'both preserve ancient craft techniques while at the same time to develop a contemporary aesthetic and a critical language with which to evaluate it on equal terms with fine art' (2000: 66). A new distinction between *'fine* craft' and 'industrial design' meant to underline the artistic aspirations of the more innovative craftsmen.[4] The marketing of fine craft was stimulated by new galleries that presented ceramic artefacts as art, thus encouraging a particular process of transit and transition.

During the 1980s, the Crafts Council continued its attempts to raise the status of craft to art by introducing new terms which emphasised the aesthetic value of the products. Functionality was no longer the major criterion. Exhibition catalogues described ceramic works as 'empty vessels' or as 'new work in clay' instead of as 'pottery', and crafts organisations and courses began to use the terms decorative *arts* and applied *arts* (2000: 67). The changing classificatory practices were related to wider social and economic developments in Britain. The crafts producers' claims to artistic status were made in the context of the urbanisation of the crafts profession. Whereas in the 1960s and 1970s numerous individuals had moved to the countryside to open up craft shops in an attempt to escape the commercial pressures of modern society, by the 1980s a new generation of artisans appeared who were not attracted by the romantic image of rural tradition. By contrast, they worked in city-based studios and cultivated the ideology of creative innovation. Interestingly, they adopted the commercial strategies of successful fine artists by promoting and selling their works through art galleries.

At the same time, numerous regionally based artisans reacted to the growing interest by the heritage industry in local history and 'authentic' products, and began to reproduce local craft traditions. Consequently, a new division was created between creative, innovative fine craft, and regionally produced artefacts which claimed the status of 'local tradition'. Chapter 5 demonstrated that markets of art and souvenirs often diversify, due to commercial limitations and possibilities, and changing interests and abilities of artefact producers. The above has shown that, in the case of ceramics production in Britain, the market roughly diversified into different segments dealing in (1) mass-produced functional items for daily use, (2) locally produced 'traditional' forms of pottery, often bought as souvenirs, and (3) works of 'fine craft', sold and displayed as art. In the latter case, the production and trade undermined the strict art/craft dichotomy.

FEMINIST APPROPRIATIONS OF CRAFT

As noted in the introduction to this chapter, in some cases the rejection of dominant notions of art has been part of a political struggle. As we shall see in this section, in the 1970s, feminist artists and art critics in Western Europe and the United States deconstructed the art/craft opposition as an ideological classification that reinforced female inequality. As part of their resistance, they appropriated elements of craft into their art.

In 1978, in the article 'Art Hysterical Notions of Progress and Culture', the art critics Joyce Kozloff and Valerie Jaudon attacked Modernist aesthetic ideology for its formal rigidness and its rejection of figurative art, ornamentation, decoration and handicraft. As will be explained in more detail below, Modernist artists often aimed for formal clarity, aestheticising it as a sign of purity and authenticity. Kozloff and Jaudon's criticism of this perspective was shared by artists in the United States, who established the Pattern and Decoration Movement. Representatives of the movement, in which women took a leading role, argued that Modernist aestheticians had misrepresented craft as a culturally inferior domain of production. In particular, handicrafts that were popular amongst women, such as knitting, embroidery and patchwork, had been denied the label 'art' (Broude 1994: 208–11).

The categories 'craft' and 'art' had clearly been used as ideological tools to separate and hierarchically classify domains of 'female' and 'male' forms of cultural production. As the artist Judy Chicago stated, 'I think the historical distinction is – if men do it it's art and if women do it it's craft. I think there's a tremendous amount of sexism and racism and classicism in the traditional distinctions between art and craft' (Parker and Pollock 1987).[5] Attacking the gendered art/craft opposition, representatives of the Pattern and Decoration Movement began to incorporate elements of craft in their art. In 1979, Chicago produced the work *The Dinner Party*, an installation which included needlework, pottery and china painting. The work consisted of an open triangular table covered with embroidered cloths and set with 39 place settings, each commemorating an ancient goddess or an important woman in Western history. Four hundred women had worked on the project, doing technical and historical research and making individual pieces. Consequently, the collaborative project also attacked the Modernist image of the artist as a lone genius. The 39 table settings and 999 additional names on the floor were devoted to women of historical importance, but who were commonly written out of male-centred historiography. Chicago's installation represented them as honoured guests. *The Dinner Party* also referred to female sexuality. Each of the 39 plates was decorated with a butterfly/vagina design (Stein 1994)

The installation was a catalyst for feminist debate. Some women, clearly influenced by the perspective of Modernist aesthetics, thought it to be too decorative and, ironically, classified it as craft. Others were offended by its sexual symbolism and rejected the work as 'pornography'. Again others, in particular non-Caucasian women artists, claimed that the work reflected the very specific 'gaze' of a white, heterosexual, middle-class woman, because the list of important women did not include any person of non-Caucasian origin. The controversy shows the political efficacy of *The Dinner Party*, and points out the diversity of opinion within the American feminist movement. The work was clearly able to stimulate discussions about gender and other inequalities.

Another American artist who was central to the establishment of the Pattern and Decoration Movement was Miriam Shapiro (Broude 1994). Like Chicago, she regarded the use of decorative patterns and fabric as a liberating move away from the formal and ideological constraints of Modernism. Her work *Garden of Paradise* (1980), for example, was a canvas shaped in the form of a heart. Along the edge, she had painted a pattern in red, purple and black, and the middle section was covered with flowery fabric. The colourful heart-shaped work not only used craft-like elements, but also questioned the boundaries between art and kitsch. As we shall see in the next section, the art/kitsch dichotomy was central to Modernist aesthetics.

KITSCH: CLASS DIVISIONS AND AESTHETIC PREFERENCE

As with the art-versus-craft perspective, the opposition of art to 'kitsch' produced fine art as a category of pure artistic genius. The birth of the category of kitsch took place in the context of nineteenth-century modernisation, characterised by the Industrial Revolution, large-scale migration from rural areas to urban centres, and the establishment of class-based societies in the Western world. The economic opportunities offered by industrial capitalism created a growing lower and upper middle class, whose members had enough money to acquire mass-produced 'luxury' goods. As already pointed out in the previous section, as a result of increasing industrialisation, mass-produced furniture, textiles, prints and other goods had become more affordable, and manufacturers responded to the aspirations of the new consumer groups.

The new middle classes (the *nouveaux riches*, the bourgeoisie and the petit bourgeoisie) wished to enjoy and show off their acquired status and wealth. Many acquired what they regarded as an 'aristocratic' taste, and bought expensive-looking, decorative furniture and figurative paintings which depicted their ideals. In France, for example, the middle classes rejected Impressionism and preferred a sugary, somewhat idealised form of Realism (Čelebonović 1974). They decorated their bourgeois homes with damask wall hangings, brocade curtains and dark oak, heavily carved, machine-made pieces of furniture, which were often lacquered or enhanced with zinc plating (Boidi and Etal 1988). Factory-produced designs were often over-decorative versions of the more expensive handmade originals. Also popular were porcelain statuettes, prints and paintings, which depicted members of the establishment at parties, families in their middle-class homes, and Romantic scenes of nature.

In the field of craft, numerous critics deplored the supposedly detrimental influence of mass production on design. While some critics, such as the art historian John Ruskin, rejected the modern means of craft production and promoted a return to medieval technology, others, such as Karl Marx, stated that the new technologies should be transformed so that they would serve all people, and not just the middle and upper classes. In Britain (followed by several other countries), the debate led to the establishment of the Arts and Crafts Movement, which aimed to restore the status of the crafts. In the catalogue produced on the occasion of the first exhibition, one of the organisers lamented the 'misapplication of machinery' (Crane 1888a: 6) and, in an essay on decorative painting, he urged decorative painters[6] to 'find again the lost thread, the golden link of connection and intimate association with the sister arts and handicrafts, whereof none is before or after another, none is greater or less than the other' (1988b: 38). In other words, the separation of the crafts and the fine arts, which had happened in Italy in the fifteenth century, had to be undone. As was discussed at the beginning of this chapter, similar feelings led in the 1970s to the production of 'traditional' crafts.

During the second half of the nineteenth century, the increasing middle-class consumption of art and craft was heavily criticised by experts and members of the aristocracy, who saw proper aesthetic appreciation as a defining feature of their own class identity. Commenting on an exhibition of English painting that opened in 1862, the British art critic Tom Taylor lamented the poor taste of the new patrons, who, in his view, lacked the refinement of the aristocracy and the landed classes. He stated in *The Fine Arts Quarterly Review* that '[t]he irresistible influence of "the demand" in art tends daily to stifle more and more all aspiration to whatever does not appeal to immediate and obvious sources of pleasure in minds of no high or special culture' (Taylor 1863, quoted in Nead 1988: 166). Texts such as these opposed images of true and serious art to what they saw as the fake pretensions and low desires of the rapidly growing bourgeoisie.

The term 'kitsch' appeared in the late nineteenth century to dismiss factory-produced artefacts and middle-class artworks because of their appeal to popular taste.[7] Their popularity automatically signified vulgarity, oversentimentality and pretentiousness. This rather elitist moral judgement was rather common amongst art historians during the twentieth century, especially before the 1980s. Aleksa Čelebonović (1968: 281) claimed, for example, that manufacturers and buyers of kitsch were generally 'content with modified substitutes which are accordingly thought of as more beautiful: the vacuum is filled by semblance and false showiness'. Matei Calinescu (1987) has argued that kitsch offers an 'aesthetics of deception and self-deception' because of its power to easily respond to people's dreams and desires. The philosophers Herman Broch (1968 [1950–51]), who introduced the term 'kitsch-man' (*kitschmensch*) and Ludwig Giesz have explored people's positive experience of kitsch. Giesz (1968: 165, 167; see also Giesz 1971 [1960]) argued that there is 'a specific inclination in man to produce kitsch or to take pleasure in it'; the basic preconditions of kitsch are 'man's quest for happiness' and 'his escape into distraction'.

Over time, ownership of kitsch was not just restricted to the middle classes (Dorfles 1968a). Ongoing industrialisation, the slowly improving socio-economic conditions of the working class in the west, and the availability of cheap labour elsewhere broadened the market. New materials and innovative production techniques pushed down the prices of mass-produced household goods, clothes, prints and other products, which meant that members of the working classes could now afford the cheaper consumer products. Not surprisingly, Marxist scholars have argued that the modern desire to own kitsch has partly been generated by alienation, a state of detachment and disempowerment, which was caused by a lack of control over production processes (see also Chapter 3 and Miller 1987: 36). In this perspective, ownership of kitsch was a form of emotional and material compensation, an escape from the routines of modern life. Furthermore, responding to the desire for a more colourful lifestyle, kitsch turned the workers' attention away from the reality of everyday life, thus depoliticising them and strengthening their disempowerment.[8]

KITSCH AS THE OPPOSITE OF AVANT-GARDE ART

The above made clear that 'kitsch' is not a neutral classification. It categorises certain types of artefacts as providers of an easy, morally weakening catharsis, which makes them radically different from art. This rather negative perception of kitsch was also apparent in the reactions of some of my students at Queen's University Belfast. In 2001 and 2003 I asked those who did the module 'Anthropology of Art' to bring a kitsch object to class and to describe why they thought the item to be 'kitschy'. Evidently, the students were not representative of just any student body. Most of them were local, Northern Irish students, and the remaining 30 per cent came from England or the Republic of Ireland. The majority of the students were female. The selected artefacts ranged from a porcelain statuette of a little girl to colourful plastic items and a dragon-shaped cigarette lighter with glowing red eyes. An English female student who presented a fake Louis Vuitton glasses case gave the following explanation:

If you are smart enough to know that it's crap then you can call it kitsch. My younger sister brought me this glasses case when she went to visit my other sister in China. It was a joke; she wanted me to understand just how fake things in China can be. If you open the case you can see the smudging of the Louis Vuitton logo. It is so big and bulky and it is falling apart. It is the most unrealistic fake I know of. It still makes me smile every time I take it out of my bag because people may think that I am trying to convince myself and others that it looks real when it is obviously a fake. It's like a practical joke my sister played on me that repeats itself every time I see it. I don't even like the design. It's a piece of junk, but because I know that, it is funny and kitsch.

A Northern Irish female student held up a small plastic thumb which, before it had broken, could be wound up and then let go to jump. She explained:

This thing is an example of what I call kitsch. It is a bit of a joke but a bit macabre as well. If it was accompanied by music and had a light inside it would be superb kitsch! Kitsch is really good when it is excessively bad.

She also noted that she found it 'difficult to describe something as kitsch when it has an important meaning to someone else – it is as if [the very act of calling something kitsch] mocks tastes and sentiments'.

What seems to be central in these students' reflections is that kitsch should not be taken seriously because it is fake, inauthentic and ultimately something to be ashamed of. It is not only made of low-quality material, but also pretends to be something it is not. As long as kitsch's ugliness is recognised, kitsch can be enjoyed – not for aesthetic reasons, but rather tongue-in-cheek, as a funny joke. In this perspective, people's emotional attachment to kitsch or, even worse, their genuine aesthetic appreciation of it, is a rather painful matter.

The perception of kitsch as the ultimate fake, as an embarrassing lie which is only valuable once it has been uncovered as a lie, is partly rooted in early twentieth-century avant-garde ideology. The students' reaction in Belfast demonstrated that this discourse has been widely influential, even reaching people who have had little or no interest in the avant-garde movement. The main advocator of the kitsch-versus-art perspective was the American art critic Clement Greenberg (1909–94), who attacked conventional art for its shallow academicism and accused it of containing kitschy elements. In 1935, in the essay 'Avant-Garde and Kitsch', he claimed that kitsch was 'deceptive', and that it had 'many different levels and some of them are high enough to be dangerous to the naïve seeker of true light' (Greenberg 1935, quoted in Marquis 1991: 93). In other words, kitsch had entered and polluted the domain of art.

Greenberg opposed kitschy, deceptive conventional art to avant-garde painting and sculpture, which, he claimed, expressed genuine sensations.

Modernist, avant-garde visual artists, he argued, were essentially anti-traditional, non-commercial and innovative, and their creative experiments resulted in unique, authentic pieces. By contrast, kitschy art was simply fake, based on imitation and relying on popular sentimentalism. In this perspective, kitsch producers were the opposite of avant-garde artists, as the former simply offered easily saleable clichés. It aestheticised avant-garde art as a visual medium which offered experiences of the authentic – of morally lifting expressions of honesty and splendour – to both artists and viewers. His theory reinforced Kantian notions of aesthetics as a realm of beauty and truth.

Greenberg's kitsch/art opposition strongly promoted avant-garde artistic styles, in particular American Abstract Expressionism. His plea for free expression not only criticised the corrupting effects of kitsch on American cultural consumption, but also attacked the anti-avant-garde policies in Nazi Germany and the Soviet Union. This shows that his approach had a clear political intention, promoting the American Dream of freedom and individuality. In the 1940s and 1950s, he became immensely influential in the American art world and 'taught a generation not only how to look at art but also how to talk about it knowingly and, above all, judgmentally' (Marquis 1991: 92). Judging what was valuable art and what should be considered useless kitsch, he pushed the careers of particular artists, promoting their works as masterpieces. As Marquis (1991: 92) noted, Greenberg was an influential actor in the competitive artistic field of contemporary art, '[h]is relentless and often solitary drumbeat accompanied the Abstract Expressionists on their triumphal march to prominence'.

One of Greenberg's protégés was Jackson Pollock, who became famous for his gesture paintings, such as *Autumn Rhythm* (1950). The work is made up of rhythmic trails of oil and enamel paint, apparently poured on the surface of the canvas. Photographs of the artist at work, which appeared in *Life* magazine, helped to popularise Pollock as a Bohemian rebel, a tortured man who just lived for his art and dripped colour over large surfaces in an act of frenzy. While various critics rejected his drip paintings as artistically completely incompetent works, a growing group of people valued them as important aesthetic works, created through ritual acts in which the artist liberated his suppressed unconsciousness (Cox 1982 [1977]: 83–94). This reading of his work was of course partially influenced by the increasing popularity in American society of psychoanalysis.

By defining the Abstract Expressionists as purely creative and non-commercial art producers, Greenberg ironically denied his own involvement in the selective marketing of Abstract Expressionism in the American art market.[9] His extremely negative judgement of kitsch as the opposite of avant-garde art not only denied the down-to-earth commodity status of the latter, it also propagated a strongly elitist view of culture, assuming that the masses who enjoyed kitsch were culturally inferior because they failed to recognise the shallowness of their own personal tastes, values and sentiments. This again shows that art functioned as a tool of social distinction, classifying only some, and not other people's, sensorial experiences as valuable and relevant. Transit and transition were central to this process, as only those artefacts that were thought to trigger the right responses were presented and spatially contextualised as authentic pieces.

POSTMODERNITY: INCORPORATING KITSCH INTO ART

The art/kitsch dichotomy was deconstructed as a Modernist ideal during the second half of the twentieth century. As already noted in Chapter 3, in the 1970s, certain artists and intellectuals proclaimed the 'death of the avantgarde' and, identifying themselves as 'postmodernists', they challenged the now conventional Modernist boundaries between art and non-art. They undermined the myth of artistic purity and innovation by arguing that all acts of creation are necessarily citation and pastiche. Following earlier artistic trends, such as 1950s Pop Art, numerous artists who defined themselves as postmodernists in the 1980s turned their attention to expressions of popular culture and began to incorporate popular imagery in their works. Some of them were particularly interested in kitsch.

The American artist Jeff Koons is known for his deliberately kitschy works of art, including his 1988 *Michael Jackson and Bubbles*, a white-and-golden porcelain statue of the famous American pop singer with his pet monkey. Two years earlier, his ephemeral sculpture *Puppy*, exhibited in front of the New York Rockefeller Center, attracted large crowds of people. The image of a Highland Terrier had been made of 70,000 geraniums, begonias and other colourful flowers. According to the art critic Andrew Graham-Dixon (2000: 16), it was 'the triumph of Koons-style kitsch, a deliberately vulgar art with nothing to say'. The critic noted that in Koons's world, 'art exists not so much to redeem us from the mundanity and banality of everyday existence but to reconcile us to it, even immerse us in it' (2000: 16).

The artist's studio in Manhattan showed the type of mundane things that inspired the artist. When Graham-Dixon visited it in 1999, he saw inflatable elephants, piles of magazines, cut-out pictures of doughnuts and Coca-Cola bottles, and 'panels from cereal packets showing cartoon cats and dogs and other cheery characters contently munching away at their milky mush of choice – all pure unadulterated Koonsiania' (2000: 16). The artist's work procedures undermined another Modernist assumption, namely that artists should work alone in quiet contemplation or in a genuine passionate frenzy, and be the sole creators of their products. By contrast, Koons worked with 25 assistants who realised his designs. In an interview with the art journal *Flash Art*, the artist explained: 'I have assistants because if I made the sculptures and paintings myself I really would be able to make only one object, or one painting a year. So the important thing to me is really just to be able to achieve the finished result I'm looking for, and be able to move on' (Kontová and Politi 1997: 108).

Calinescu (1987) has regarded the reappearance of kitschy elements in high art as a form of ironic connoisseurship. In his view, postmodern aesthetics has transformed bad taste into an expression of superior refinement, and therefore belittles both those who abhor kitsch for its supposed insincerity (the Modernist stance), and those who are truly moved by it (the cultural ignorati).[10] Koons, however, has denied that his work intends to be ironic, and has stressed that he is truly enchanted by kitsch (Rosenblum 1992). His positive evaluation of kitsch reflects the view of the sociologist Jacqueline A. Gibbons, who, referring to Bourdieu, has deconstructed the art/kitsch divide as a class-biased regime of taste that is rooted in the aesthetic theories of Plato and Kant, which reject the value of immediate sensation. By contrast, Gibbons (1997: 66) argued that '[a]s an artistic genre, Kitsch clearly embodies the warmth of family and ties of friendship; it also symbolizes personal nurturance needs and broadly held cultural values'.

The Czech artist Milan Kunc has incorporated kitschy imagery in his work for different reasons. Denying that his work has anything to do with easily understandable fake art, he has argued that his realism is multi-dimensional and offers 'real content', exploring the meaning and impact of modern icons (van Adrichem 2005). In 1964, Kunc was thrown out of the Academy of Fine Arts in Prague because of 'lack of talent'. This was, of course, the official reason; more likely, he had to leave because he failed to work in a politically correct style. In 1969, he emigrated to West Germany. In Dusseldorf, the multi-media artist Joseph Beuys selected him as an art student in his studio, but Kunc had felt rather alienated amongst his left-wing peers. In an interview with Petr Volf (2006), he recalled how he had been the only student in the class who had direct knowledge of everyday life under communism, and who had made figurative works, a style rejected by his peers as old-fashioned.

In the Ost-Pop series (1977–79), Kunc mixed images of capitalist consumption goods with communist symbols. *Coca-Cola Hammer* (1979), for example, showed the distant heads of a crowd of people carrying a red flag. The painting was dominated by two red hammers with the word 'Coca-Cola' painted over them, the c's resembling hammers and sickles. He intended to draw the attention to 'consumism' (people's desire to consume for consumption's sake), and argued that this ideology had shaped both capitalist and communist societies. On both sides of the Iron Curtain, he argued, those in power used propagandistic measures to feed people's desires and thus stay in power. *Schöner Wohnen* (1979) depicted a domestic scene with a large piece of 'luxurious' furniture in the shape of a hammer and sickle, including a comfortable sofa, two televisions and various cupboards. A vase and a bookstand in the shape of communist stars were placed on top of the cupboards, and an abstract painting hung on the wall. A woman leaned against the piece of furniture, while smoking a cigarette and sipping a drink, and a man sat on the sofa, reading his newspaper.

The above shows again that art production must be analysed from a processual relativist perspective, which is sensitive to a variety of historical factors. In Kunc's case, his experience of life in both the communist East and the capitalist west was of major importance. He managed to explore contemporary icons, dreams and desires through a figurative style, which incorporates elements of the world he critically explores. As such, he has undermined the art/kitsch opposition. The successful social life of his works, their appearance in prestigious private and museum collections, is directly related to the increasing influence of postmodern art critics on the artistic establishment during the 1980s and 1990s.

The critic Boris Groys noted that Kunc's work foretold the changes which would take place in Central and Eastern Europe ten years later, after the end of state socialism. He argued that the end of the Cold War and the introduction of capitalism in the post-socialist states had brought about the 'diffusion of everyday Western and Eastern signs', a visual clash which had already appeared in Kunc's Ost-Pop series (Groys 2005). After the political change in Czechoslovakia, Kunc explored the impact of the free market on post-socialist desires. In 1992, he painted the work *Penetration of the Dialectic (Young East European Lovers in the Caribbean for the First Time)*, described as follows by Donald Kuspit:

[T]he young lovers still carry the hammer (his) and sickle (hers) in their heads, having traded their Communist paradise for a Caribbean paradise – a real material paradise, where red is not the colour of the failed social revolution but of the successful sexual revolution (of passion rather than social planning). However idyllic their embrace, they are secretly linked by barbed wire, not love. Prisoners of passion indeed! They are also tempted by the American Express Card proffered by a crab, Kunc's version of the snake in paradise. (Both the card and the crab are the green colour of American money.) The card is no doubt on their minds because they made the trip to paradise on credit: Eastern Europe being economically bankrupt as well as a social lie, who will pay the price for the holiday when it comes due in the socialist future? (2005: 277)

In Broch's terminology, the painting explored the dreams and desires of post-socialist 'kitsch-man', cleverly exploited by the tourist industry. Kunc's ironic visual comments on the similar emptiness of communist and capitalist propaganda leads us to the next section.

ART VERSUS PROPAGANDA

As with 'art', 'craft' and 'kitsch', the word 'propaganda' has had different meanings over time. This section will show that, while some discourses have construed 'propaganda' as the antithesis of 'art', others have claimed that all art is necessarily political. Not surprisingly, the different views have attributed different types of agency to art. To gain a better insight into these classifica-tory practices, it is necessary to take a processual relativist perspective which emphasises the impact of historical context.

The original connotation of propaganda, 'the systematic propagation of beliefs, values or practices', was coined when the Vatican established the Congregation for the Propagation of the Faith (*Congregatio de Propaganda Fide*) in 1622, with the aim of undermining Protestant Reformist religious efforts. During the following three centuries, the term was used in various European languages to refer in more general terms to the spreading of political and religious ideas, and (especially after the introduction of print capitalism) to commercial advertising. In these contexts, 'propaganda' was a descriptor of disseminating practices, and was not yet associated with negative notions of purposeful distortion, ideological oppression and anti-aesthetic tendencies (Clark 1997).

This changed when, during the First World War, state institutions began to use the mass media to call for citizen participation in the war effort. Visual images in newspapers, on posters and in the cinema became highly effective tools of political and emotional management which reached large audiences, both within and beyond state boundaries, and propaganda came to be seen as the manipulation of reality. As Toby Clark (1997: 7–8) noted, '[t]his wartime perception of propaganda's links with censorship and misinformation was compounded by its increased application as psychological warfare, waged against the morale of enemies'. In other words, visual imagery became an active agent of state power.

The reconceptualisation of propaganda as an emotionally powerful but dangerous medium of political control was reinforced during the Second Word War, when Nazi Germany was accused of being a ruthless propaganda machine.[11] This understanding of propaganda was further strengthened with the onset of the Cold War, when Stalinist policy in the Eastern bloc was heavily criticised for its purposeful distortion of reality. Ironically, however, capitalist democracies, united as 'the West', denied their own use of the public media for political purposes, which was, in fact, an inherent part in their own Cold War propaganda. Representing their own political systems as completely transparent fields of truth and honesty, they emphatically associated the term 'propaganda' with the oppressive forces of fascist and communist totalitarianism (Clark 1997: 8; see also Cockroft 1974; Goldfarb 1982).

Particularly in the United States, contemporary art became an important medium which disseminated ideas about the anti-propagandistic quality (and thus the moral and political superiority) of Western democracy. Interestingly, the discourse of propaganda as 'intentional lying' partly overlapped with the discourse of kitsch as the production of fake art. As noted earlier, from 1939 onwards, the American art critic Clement Greenberg had warned of the devastating influence of kitsch on avant-garde artistic values, which he saw reflected not only in American mass culture, but also in fascist and communist art.[12] In his view, kitsch was a helpful propagandistic tool as it kept 'a dictator in closer contact with the "soul" of the people' (Greenberg 1968 [1939]: 123). As we saw in the previous section, 40 years later this view would also be expressed by Kunc, albeit in a visual language that would not have been acceptable to the purist aesthetician Greenberg. Obviously, they had different opinions of the aestheticising power of particular artistic styles.

COLD WAR PROPAGANDA AND ART: TWO PERSPECTIVES

In the context of the Cold War, the image of avant-garde aesthetics as a realm of freedom and experimentation was further politicised. Western non-figurative art was discursively construed as the direct opposite of Eastern bloc propaganda (Guilbaut 1983; Lash 1968; Lindey 1990; Svašek 1996a, 1997d). American art policy consisted of consciously promoting Abstract Expressionism as a sign of creative liberty which could only flourish in capitalist democracies. CIA officials clearly realised that 'the promotion of American *free*, advanced art could be used as a cultural weapon' (Lindey 1990: 10). Paradoxically, some commentators regarded Modernist abstract art as an undesirable, un-American cultural expression. The conservative Congressman George Dondero, for example, made a speech in 1949, entitled 'Modern Art – Shackled to Communism', in which he emphasised that Russian formalist artists had been of major importance to the development of West European and American Modernist styles, and that numerous American Abstract Expressionists had left-wing sympathies. The FBI created files about the subversive activities and works of six members of the New York school, ready to accuse them of communist conspiracy (Craven 1999: 96).[13]

Yet, as the Cold War persisted, the ideology of the American avant-garde (whose members intended to break away from reactionary forces and conventional stylistic forms,[14] was further aligned with the US government's ideals of post-war liberalism, which valued notions of individual freedom and responsibility. As such, Abstract Expressionism was actively used to portray America as the land of freedom and opportunity, opposing it to oppression and censorship in Soviet-dominated Central and Eastern Europe. In other words, in the context of Cold War politics, the art/propaganda dichotomy was itself a political tool.

By contrast, in the Eastern bloc, communist officials rejected all avant-garde developments as deplorable *bourgeois* propaganda, but, at the same time, blurred the categories of propaganda and art. In this perspective, 'propaganda' had extremely positive connotations, at least as long as the propagated message agreed with communist ideals. To assure this, art worlds in the Eastern bloc were strongly politicised. The following case study demonstrates how this process took place in Czechoslovakia during the Stalinist period. We focus on three interrelated levels of politicisation, namely the organisational dynamics in the art world, the creation of social groups and hierarchies, and the formation of public artistic discourse. It is argued that, despite the introduction of centralisation and censorship, total politicisation was never realised (Svašek 1996a).

Soon after the Communist coup of 1948, the Czechoslovak art world was restructured according to the Soviet model, which meant that avant-garde art was no longer tolerated, and that artists and critics who wished to remain influential needed to (at least outwardly) accept communist ideals. Chapter 5 argued that art worlds are open-ended social spheres in which artists, dealers, buyers, critics and other specialists form cooperative networks and compete for economic, cultural and social symbolic capital. It highlighted the importance of art historians, who provide normative models for the interpretation of art. Not surprisingly, the politicisation of the Czech art world after the Communist coup meant that critics who had propagated avant-garde art were sidelined by communist colleagues who now dominated the scene. The latter established the official communist art journal *Výtvarné Umění* ('The Visual Arts'), which propagated the politicisation of art. In the first issue, the editor Václav Jícha stated:

For the first time in the history of our visual arts, a magazine is being published which will interpret the organic needs of our time, fight for an art that will be a reflection of life in its historical reality, educate and change people in the socialist spirit, and draw its inspiration from the everyday life of our people, showing their power to build socialism in our country. (Jícha 1950: 1)

The keywords used to mark anti-socialist art were 'cosmopolitanism' and 'formalism' (Jůza 1993: 27). Communist aestheticians applied these political terms to the arts, arguing that, in a class-divided society, artists, just like other workers, had 'entered the fully developed world of capitalist commodity production' (Fischer 1963 [1959]: 52). Instead of seeing this as a positive development, they claimed that this had turned artists into cosmopolitan competitors who simply served the international bourgeoisie by creating formalist works which mystified the social reality of class domination (Svašek 1996a: 39–43; see also Chapter 3).

Jícha (1950: 1) stated that it was the duty of *Výtvarné Umění* to 'fight against the survival of bourgeois cosmopolitanism and formalism, which by its non-national and cultural terrorism suffocates the life sources of national power'. One of the main tasks of the journal, he pointed out, was to propagate the method of Socialist Realism, which, in the words of the Minister of Information and Culture Václav Kopecký, required a 'higher, more beautiful, and thus truer art' (Kopecký, as quoted by Jícha 1950: 1).

The journal provided examples of artworks that were considered ideologically sound and, during the Stalinist 1950s, its pages were particularly dominated by images of 'people at work'. Most artworks of this genre featured male workers between the ages of 20 and 50, wearing flat caps with their shirtsleeves rolled up past their elbows. As often as not, they held hammers, smelting pots or miner's lamps to further symbolise their status as workers. Women were similarly portrayed as workers or as working housewives in simple clothing. To complete the familial image of the new socialist state, children dressed in the uniform of the communist movement were frequently presented as symbols of the future. People were also pictured in folk costumes, which shows that the communists recognised the emotional potential of 'folklore'. Instead of emphasising the historical roots of the nation, as the Czech nationalists had done (see Chapter 6), communist discourse construed the folk culture as the opposite of decadent bourgeois culture.[15] Another recurrent theme was the fight against the Nazis during the Second World War, and the subsequent liberation by the heroic communist Red Army (Svašek 1995).

The people portrayed in the ideologically correct artworks showed either concentration (at work or political meetings), happiness (at demonstrations and celebrations, and at work), admiration (when meeting a political leader) or gratitude (for the liberation by the Red Army and Stalin's leadership). Their faces and body language served as ideal examples of how people should behave and organise their emotions, so as to strive to embody the virtues of socialist citizens (Svašek 1996a: 44; see also Haraszti 1987 [1983]: 61–3).

Transit and transition were central to the politicisation of art. Only ideologically correct paintings and statues appeared in public, emphatically contextualised as 'true art'. Artists were also approached through *Výtvarné Umění*, which strongly discouraged them from continuing to work in avant-garde styles. The artist František Hudeček, for example, was praised for his painting *Near the Cutting Machine* because it 'discard[ed] the speculative constructivist method which he had used in his work for a number of years' (Šolta 1950: 118). Examples of Western art were given to prove the futility of cosmopolitan imagery. A reproduction of a Surrealist painting by the British painter Edward Wadsworth was accompanied by the comment:

An example of where decadent art has already led. It is hard to understand why this play with several abstract stakes is called *Coast*. In truth, this surface 'decoration' is nonsense. Where there is no content, it is not possible to speak of form, nor to speak of art. (1950: 124)

The above has shown that, while in the West, the term 'propaganda' was used as an accusation of cultural and political oppression, in the Eastern bloc, art and propaganda were not necessarily each other's opposites. Ideally, 'art' and 'politics' merged, but this was only acceptable when the political content of the artworks agreed with the principles of socialism. When this was the case, it was argued, the right images would be perceived in a correct way, triggering the right feelings and inspiring people to take politically correct actions.

DOMINATION AND RESISTANCE IN THE CZECH ART WORLD

It is important to note that 'propaganda' is not simply a linguistic label that has been applied to different phenomena in different contexts. Propaganda is a field of concrete practice, in which powerholders have the economic, political and possibly military means to shape society and influence human behaviour. In the Czechoslovak case, the communists were indeed powerful enough to drastically transform the organisation of the art world, restructuring it along the lines of the example set by its Soviet neighbour.[16] After the 1948 coup, the existing art associations and private galleries were closed down, and a new communist Art Union (*Svaz československých výtvarných umělců*) was established, which centrally controlled the production, exhibition and sale of art. All artists were made members of the Art Union, and all forms of public protest were suppressed. While retaining their official membership of the Art Union, however, some stubborn artists escaped its control by forming illegal art groups and organising secret exhibitions outside the official structures. Stifled by official censorship and scared of the Secret Police, they were forced to engage in 'hidden' artistic discourse by showing their politically unacceptable works outside the public sphere.

When asked in 1995 to describe the atmosphere in the Czech art world during the 1950s, the painters (and twin sisters) Květa and Jitka Válová said:

KV: It was very bad.

JV: We couldn't exhibit because they wouldn't let us.

MS: Because you made a different kind of art?

KV: Yes, we made different things, we didn't work in a realistic vein.

MS: Did you try to exhibit?

KV: No, it was clear [that we couldn't]. There were still art associations up until 1950, but even when we took things along they never showed them at any of the exhibitions. There was no point in trying.

MS: Were there a lot of young artists who had similar difficulties?

JV: Yes, a lot.

KV: Those who stood for something. The rest just licked arses and copied nature. They weren't artists.

In 1954, together with some artist friends, the sisters established the unofficial art group Trasa ('Route'), whose members secretly met in their studios and frequently mounted exhibitions. Their illegal activities automatically assumed a political meaning, even though their works were often meant to be non-political. Yet the fact that these artists offered alternative views to official Socialist Realist imagery made their works into counter-propaganda. Their activities created a space of dissent, proving that it was still possible to hold and express views that differed from the official doctrines (Svašek 1996a: 71–8, 1997d).[17]

Paradoxically, after the end of state socialism in 1989, Western curators and art dealers emphasised the political message of unofficial art, and promoted a romantic image of 'dissident artists' as morally superior beings who had greatly suffered and endured communist afflictions. In 1990, the German foundation Niedersachsen Hannover, for example, financed the exhibition Tradition and Avant-gardism in Prague. The catalogue spoke of the moral integrity and the political significance of the participating artists. The sculptor Aleš Veselý, one of the artists chosen for the exhibition, objected to this view. Tired of the label 'dissident', he claimed that the political conditions under which he had lived were less important than his works' artistic value. He preferred a 'normal' catalogue in which the artworks were simply evaluated as aesthetic objects. The sculptor Stanislav Kolíbal similarly argued that the appearance of artworks in unofficial spaces had not automatically given them artistic quality. Referring to his own work, he said with noticeable irritation that '[t]he West should accept it without a need for compassion, and with respect for its value' (Svašek 1996a: 205).

The political efficacy of particular artworks depends on a variety of factors, including the organisational set-up of possibly overlapping artistic and political fields, the intentions of those who exhibit the works and the expectations of the viewing public. As Clark (1997: 13) noted, 'art can become propaganda through its function and site, its framing within public or private spaces and its relationship with a network of other kinds of objects and activities'. In the same vein, propaganda can lose its sharp political angle. While a portrait of Stalin displayed in a Czech factory in 1950 would have evoked genuine feelings of admiration (amongst communist believers) or anger and fear (amongst the persecuted), the same portrait, hanging in a smoky bar in Prague in 1992, would most probably have triggered ridicule and laughter.

ART AND PROPAGANDA: FEMINIST AND OTHER PERSPECTIVES

During the 1960s, the Modernist belief that artists should concentrate on purity of form and refrain from expressing political views was increasingly criticised. In 1967, the British artist John Latham expressed his criticism by destroying a copy of Greenberg's collected essays *Art and Culture* (1961), which he had borrowed from St Martin's School of Art in London. He chewed the book's pages and dissolved them in acid, keeping the remains in a jar (Clark 1997: 125–6).[18] Several artists in the United States, Europe and Argentina turned away from the more conventional artistic media of painting and sculpture, and began making conceptual art, 'work in which the idea is paramount and the material form is secondary, lightweight, ephemeral, cheap, and/or "dematerialised"' (Lippard 1973: vii). In many cases, they were highly critical of the social and political establishment, and called for radical change. Communication and the distribution of ideas were regarded as essential to the artistic process.

In the United States, numerous artists (conceptual artists as well as painters and sculptors) turned against the ideal of 'apolitical art' during the Vietnam War, and used their art as a form of protest against American imperialism. During the same period, Civil Rights activists and minority artists began to use art as a political tool to struggle against racial inequality, and feminist artists redefined art as a weapon against male domination (Lippard 1973: 126–32). In 1980, the American art critic Lucy Lippard attacked the negative definition of propaganda inherent in Modernist aesthetics in the article 'Some Propaganda for Propaganda' in the feminist magazine *Heresies*. She argued that artists should produce 'positive propaganda' by using the political potential of art to criticise oppression and inequality (Clark 1997: 9).[19]

In Britain, after having worked as a professional photographer for seven years, Jo Spence began to question her authority to represent other people's lives through what is commonly regarded as an objective medium. She gave up her career and began to use photography as a critical medium to examine the power of representational practices. She noted in 1979: 'The question of which represents who in our society, how they do it, and for what purpose, is something which has come to dominate my practical and theoretical work' (Spence 1985). From 1982 onwards, she criticised the power of the male-dominated medical establishment through photographs that documented her struggle against breast cancer, refusing orthodox treatment. Spence commented in 1985:

My aim is to try to help for a bridge between work on health struggles, and work on the visual image, which seem to me to be totally related. One refers to our bodily and social self, the other to our psychic self. Just as the body is fragmented through representation, so it is fragmented and parcelled up as a variety of specialities within discourses of health. (Spence 1985)

One of the photographs from the series *From My Family Album* shows her naked breasts, one of them partly covered with a bandage. On the cancerous breast, she has written the question 'Property of Jo Spence?'

The Palestinian artist Mona Hatoum, who decided to stay in Britain when the war broke out in the Lebanon in 1975, discovered the political potential of art when she studied at the Byam Shaw School of Art in London. In an interview with Michael Archer, she explained that she became increasingly politically conscious: 'The Slade politicized me. I got involved with feminist groups, I became aware of class issues, I started examining power structures and trying to understand why I felt so "out of place"' (Archer 1997: 9; see also Archer et al. 1997). During the mid 1980s, when she met the artist Rasheed Araeen, she became politicised in terms of her sense of cultural difference. In 1977, Araeen had addressed issues of racism in the performance *Paki Bastard: Portrait of the Artist as a Black Person*. In *A Thousand Bullets for a Stone* (1988), Hatoum criticised Israeli politics in the West Bank and Gaza. She projected a newspaper image on two walls of a woman who confronted a soldier with a gun, while, in the background, children were throwing stones at him. On the floor in front, she placed stones which were labelled and numbered. She did, however, move away from making direct political statements through her art. She explained: 'When you present someone with a statement in an artwork, once they get it, they either agree with you or dismiss your argument and move on to the next thing – no need to look again' (Archer 1997: 13). As Toby Clark (1997: 153) noted, '[l]ike Jo Spence, she acts out inner dramas of her personal history that express political concerns of alienation and division'.

The above cases have again demonstrated that contextual factors, including international political dynamics and the intricacies of people's own life-histories, influence people's perceptions of art. We have also seen that, in all cases, the people involved were engaged in aestheticisation. Each group connected particular sensorial experiences to particular abstract values. The communists believed that Socialist Realism would move people to participate in the communist revolution; the Abstract Expressionists were convinced that abstraction and formal purity would lead to the authentic; and feminists thought that their work would activate viewers to strive for gender equality. The examples of Spence and Hatoum, however, made clear that the messages of individual works are often complex and multi-layered.

PORNOGRAPHY VERSUS ART? 'PRE-PORNOGRAPHIC' EXPRESSIONS

This section explores the final dichotomous discourse discussed in this chapter, namely the 'art-versus-pornography' construction. We shall see that particular historical developments have shaped the changing notions of 'pornography', and that some artists have incorporated pornographic imagery in their work in an attempt to push the boundaries of art.

In 1968, Ugo Volli claimed that pornography is 'an essentially non-aesthetic phenomenon for mindless consumption' (1968: 225).[20] Classifying pornography as the direct opposite of art, he defined it as a mentally stupefying form of commoditisation – as a powerful but amoral force which merely evoked lust and desire. Volli contrasted the supposedly negative impact of pornography with art's ability to generate morally uplifting aesthetic experiences through the purifying force of quiet contemplation. His view reflected the historically specific Modernist ideals of artistic purity. To understand this, it is necessary to look at the etymology of the word 'pornography'.

Hunt (1993: 13) has convincingly argued that 'pornography' is not a neutral and timeless description but rather a 'cultural battle zone' in which people express changing and conflicting ideas about the production and social life of erotic imagery. The word stems from the Greek '*pornē*' (prostitute) and '*graphein*' (to write), and was coined in 1850 by the German art historian C.D. Müller in his *Handbuch der Archäologie der Kunst*. Looking for a term to classify obscene objects in museum collections, he translated the Greek term '*pornographos*' ('whore painters', from a second-century Greek book on prostitution) into '*Pornographen*', or 'pornographers' in the English translation (Kendrick 1987: 11–12). The word 'pornographers' became a term for producers of erotic artefacts as well as for learned men who wrote about the life and medical conditions of prostitutes, and 'pornography' categorised erotic texts and visual imagery.

It is not surprising that Müller turned to Greek sources to find a term for sexually explicit images. Scholarly interest in ancient Greek history had grown when eighteenth-century archaeological excavations had resulted in spectacular findings. Digging up the city of Pompei, excavators had discovered lascivious frescos and sculptures; a particularly shocking image was a marble statue of a satyr who had sex with a goat. King Charles decided to hide it from public view and entrusted it to the royal sculptor Joseph Canart, who placed it in the secret collection of the Royal Museum of Portici. Other disturbing findings were also stored in places that were closed to the general public, such as, during the nineteenth century, in the Collection de l'Enfer (in the

Bibliothèque Nationale de Paris), and the Private Case (in the British Library) (Hunt 1993: 9).

Interestingly, some commentators compared the explicit representations of sexuality in the works of the ancient Greeks with the absence of such imagery in contemporary European art. In 1780, Maréchal stated, for example, that '[a]ncient relics ... are full of objects so indecent, if we compare them to modern compositions, that the brush or needle of our Artists hardly dares to reproduce them for us' (1780: 24–5, quoted by Kendrick 1987: 8–9). The widespread appearance of obscene images in Greek society was explained away by these scholars as a sign of their childlike innocence and, following Rousseau, of their supposed closeness to nature. Other commentators emphasised the mystical and symbolic function of the images, undermining the idea that the Greeks would have created the images primarily for erotic reasons (Kendrick 1987: 10).

When the collections of ancient erotic artefacts grew, learned scholars began to catalogue the objects for scientific purposes, claiming that the images did not affect them physically. As M.L. Barré noted in 1877 in the catalogue of the 'Pornographic Collection' of the National Museum of Naples, '[i]n the exercise of his holy office, the man of science must neither blush nor smile, we have looked upon our statues as an anatomist contemplates his cadavers' (quoted in Kendrick 1987: 15). In this context, it is important to note that, from the early Renaissance onwards, the 'Greek period' began to be seen as a central phase in the history of European civilisation. This idea was further developed by nineteenth-century evolutionists, who did everything they could to create a clear-cut distinction between refined eroticism in classic European art and society, and primitive sexual urges in non-European material culture. Burland (1973) has pointed out that many African erotic artefacts were damaged or destroyed by European missionaries and government officials during the colonial period, and that, up to the second half of the twentieth century, Western ethnographic museums collected but did not display such artefacts in public. Ethnographers who had access to the hidden collections saw the artefacts as proof that the more primitive races were slaves to their animal instincts and passions. Spatially and discursively recontextualised, these hidden objects were made into signifiers of non-Western inferiority.

Explicit sexual imagery had been taboo in European art for several centuries. Erotic imagery, however, was often produced with the aim of criticising the political and religious establishment. In 1524, engravings by the Italian artist Marcantonio Raimondi, which showed couples in 16 different positions of love-making, were banned.[21] In an act of subversion, Pietro Aretino reproduced them as illustrations in a booklet of sonnets, *Sonnetti Lussuriosi*, and these were taken out of circulation by order of the pope. This happened at the time when 'fine art' emerged as a professional domain of discourse and practice, separate from 'craft'. The art historian Giorgio Vasari (1987 [1550]), a highly influential critic at the time, strongly condemned the insulting engravings, emphatically placing them outside the domain of the fine arts. Art was not supposed to sexually arouse the viewers, but rather to enchant them and stimulate feelings of respect for the religious and political establishment.

Aretino's work was, however, popular amongst a small elite of upper-class males, who, in the following two centuries, managed secretly to get hold of various reproductions of the original engravings. Only a select but growing group of buyers were involved in the transit of erotic pictures and stories. The invention and improvement of printing techniques allowed for their spread throughout Europe, albeit on a small scale and only amongst certain members of the educated elite.[22] The works gained political efficacy when, through their interest in forbidden imagery, sixteenth-century humanists and seventeenth-century libertines expressed their revolt against religious orthodoxy, political authority and conventional morality (Hunt 1993: 25; Kendrick 1987: 58–9). As agents of rebellion, many representations criticised the hypocrisy of the Church, and were not or no longer primarily aimed at sexual arousal.

In 1746, for example, the title page of *Vénus dans le cloître ou la Religieuze an chemise*[23] showed an angel with its hand between the legs of a half-naked, reclining woman. In 1748, the Frankfurt edition of *Histoire de Dom B-, portier des Charteux* included an illustration in which a monk was having sexual intercourse with a prostitute, while he was mounted by a fellow monk (Jacob 1993: 186). The erotic images often portrayed prostitutes. These women interacted with men from all walks of life, so narratives about them could convincingly reveal the double standards of the religious and political establishment. Pornographic pamphlets also targeted political powerholders. They were, for example, given out during the French Revolution, and aimed to trigger anti-royalist feelings (Hunt 1993: 33–5).

Kendrick (1987) has argued that the engagement with sexual imagery between 1500 and 1800 should be called 'pre-pornographic', as it was limited to certain social circles. As noted earlier, erotic images such as Aretino's were relatively rare, the hygienic surveys of brothels and the museum catalogues were only available to expert scholars, and the obscene archaeological collections were not accessible to the general museum public. A radically different understanding of sexually explicit imagery began to appear, however, when pornography was no longer produced for political reasons and became a mass-produced commodity available to all classes. According to Kendrick, the birth of 'the pornographic', pushed governments to take a more active role in the protection of their citizens from the force of immorality. In Hunt's words, 'pornography as a regulatory category was invented in response to the perceived menace of the democratization of culture' (1993: 12–13). The new government policies reflected a rather elitist and gendered view. The underlying assumption was that, unlike educated men, women and lower-class men lacked control over their unruly passions, and were therefore unable to guard themselves against the power of sexually evocative imagery.

Highly relevant to the theme of this chapter, Modernist notions of art as realm of purity fed the new understanding of pornography. As Kendrick (1987: 31) noted, '[i]t was when contemporary art joined in the pornographic battle that the modern concept of "pornography" had its origin'. Today, the *Shorter Oxford English Dictionary* reflects this new understanding, defining it as '[t]he explicit description or exhibition of sexual subjects or activity in literature, painting, films, etc., in a manner intended to stimulate erotic rather than aesthetic feelings'. The notion of pornography as 'the anti-aesthetic' was rooted in Modernism's bias against mass culture, a phenomenon which, as we saw earlier, was also apparent in the kitsch-versus-art dichotomy. Like kitsch, pornography was classified as a form of mindless consumption and instant satisfaction, fed by physical desire. This perspective reinforced the Cartesian idea that bodily functions were distinct from (and inferior to) mental capabilities, and placed 'art' in the realm of the reserved and rational mind.

The dominant high-culture view was that low- and mass-cultural media, like pornography, moved their subjects in their individual particularity, provoking through their appeal to the senses a physical, often sexual response. The high arts were perceived as those which invoked a disinterested stasis, suspending their subjects in moments of (the idea of) universal intellectual apprehension. (Pease 2000: 76).[24]

This perspective on art clearly reflected Kantian notions of aesthetics as a non-judgemental experience of beauty and truth, and fed middle-class concerns about the uncivilised and polluting disposition of the working class. Their anxiety resulted in state censorship on moral grounds, leading in the twentieth century to government policies which weighed the principle of 'freedom of expression' against the 'harm principle', imposing restrictions if it was proved that third parties were negatively affected by pornographic imagery (Copp and Wendell 1983).

Paradoxically, the acceptance of Kantian aesthetics by middle-class art lovers *also* stimulated the incorporation of pornographic imagery into high art. Their emphasis on the significance of form (which could only be properly valued by those who had sufficient mental power) made them susceptible to any form perceived as 'beautiful in itself'. The idea was that mental control could hold off 'a collapse into the pornographic', which meant that male members of the upper classes could safely appreciate erotic works, at least as long as they were also beautiful (Pease 2000: 74). In Britain, Aubrey Beardsley's pen-and-ink drawings of male and female nudes, erect penises, masturbation and homoerotic scenes, became popular amongst certain members of the middle class during the first three decades of the twentieth century. They were acceptable because of their form, their stylised beauty.

There were, however, limits to what could appear in public. While the book *Salome*, written by Oscar Wilde and illustrated by Beardsley (published in 1894), was sold openly, Beardsley's *Lysistrata* series (1896) was only sold under the counter (Wilson 1973 [1972]: 24). Central to this form of targeted censorship was the idea that only those with the knowledge and sensitivity to perceive the images as 'art' would not be morally corrupted by them. Access to the images thus emphasised class and gender distinctions, as women and members of the lower classes were thought to lack this perceptual power. Roughly 100 years later, moral discourses about the accessibility of erotic imagery had radically changed, as will be shown in the next section.

BEYOND MODERNISM: PORNOGRAPHY AS ART

In February 1997, the Dutch Groninger Museum launched an exhibition of works by the American artist Andres Serrano, which included erotic photographs from the series *A History of Sex* (1996). The evocative series had been commissioned by the museum in an attempt to attract a large number of visitors. The public relations marketing manager, José Selbach,[25] explained in 2004 that photo exhibitions rarely tempted large crowds, and that the museum had hoped that the series would interest a large group of people. As it turned out, the exhibition got even more response than the museum had wished for. *A History of Sex* triggered a stormy public debate about the power of sexually explicit images, in which conflicting ideas about artistic freedom and state censorship were fervently defended by different groups of people.

As already pointed out in Chapter 4, by 1997 Serrano was already a controversial artist. In 1989, his work *Piss Christ* had angered members of the Catholic and Anglican churches, who claimed that he had disrespected Christian values. In 1997, the artist provoked a much wider group of people, who could not accept the sexual explicitness of his photographs. *A History of Sex* included images such as 'Red Pebbles' (a naked woman holding a horse's elongated penis), 'The Fisting' (a woman with her fist inserted into a man's anus) and 'Christiaan and Rose' (a heterosexual couple with the woman wearing a strap-on penis). Angry commentators stated that the works were plain pornography and had nothing in common with art. Many reproduced Modernist notions of fine art as a domain of aesthetic purity, and argued that artists and other actors responsible for public images should take responsibility for the negative impact that these morally debatable images might have on innocent viewers.

A wave of protests appeared in the public media when the Groninger Museum decided to use the photograph 'Leo's Fantasy' to advertise the exhibition throughout the country (Heijne 1997; Jansen van Galen and Van Roosmalen 1997; Zandbergen 1997: 18). The photograph was a close-up of a woman peeing into a man's mouth (see Figure 9). Motivated by different ideologies, church groups, feminists and elderly people protested against the image, which they regarded to be tasteless, disgraceful and offensive. Some argued that the museum could exhibit whatever it wanted, because people could choose not to see the exhibition; yet it should not have the authority to confront people with visual imagery outside the exhibition space. Anti-pornography activists emphasised the potential power of sexual imagery. They stated that the advertisement was extremely dangerous because it would provoke sexual harassment and threaten public safety. The museum received several bomb threats, and a Molotov cocktail which was thrown into the building damaged the entrance hall. The issue was addressed in the Dutch Lower Chamber and the matter was eventually taken to court. Before the outcome of the court case (which, ironically, supported the museum's freedom of choice), the Groninger Museum decided to pull back and withdraw the poster, replacing it with a more neutral, text-based advertisement.

Figure 9 'Leo's Fantasy' (from the series *A History of Sex*, 1996), by Andres Serrano. Cibachrome/plexiglass (152 × 126 cm). Photograph by John Stoel. Collection Groninger Museum. Courtesy of the Groninger Museum

The commotion around Serrano's works attracted an unusually large number of visitors to the exhibition: 10,000 on the opening day alone and a total of 90,000. The museum's strategy to increase its visitor numbers had clearly been successful. Serrano himself was also pleased with the unfolding scandal because it further increased his visibility in the art world. When the series was exhibited in 1997 in New York in the Paula Cooper art gallery, a reviewer wrote that, 'Tout le art world is talking about this show', and remarked that, 'Insofar as glorifying sex at the margins of society is concerned, Serrano now reigns supreme' (Paul 1997). The photographs were successful art commodities; editions of three prints (60×49 inches) were sold for $10,000 each.

Serrano was not the first to produce images of sexually explicit scenes as 'art'. As noted earlier, throughout the history of fine art, numerous works had expressed mainly male erotic fantasies, mostly portraying women as passive sexual objects of the male gaze. These works were mostly often within the limits of the dominant artistic canon, however, and were generally not as explicit as Serrano's scenes. Furthermore, as noted earlier, artists who did produce erotic works, such as Beardsley or Gustav Klimt, only showed them to a limited audience. Yet, especially from the 1970s onwards, partly as a result of the sexual revolution, an increasing number of mainly American artists began to exhibit explicit sexual imagery in public places. Robert Mapplethorpe, for example, became famous for his photographs of male nudes and gays in sadomasochist outfits. In *Self-Portrait* (1978), he posed for the camera while penetrating himself anally with a bull-whip. Richard Meyer claimed that:

Mapplethorpe refutes what Susan Sontag has described as the 'supertourist' stance of documentary photography in which the photographer becomes 'an extension of the anthropologist, visiting natives and bringing back news of their exotic doings and strange gear'. Rather than reporting on the 'exotic doings of others', the 1978 *Self-Portrait* presents Mapplethorpe himself as the object of photographic curiosity, as the sadomasochistic 'native' in the midst of using his own 'strange gear'. (Meyer 2002: 197–8, quoting Sontag 1977: 41–2)

Not surprisingly, many members of the public were shocked by the work. In 1989, when US Senator Jesse Helms found out that the photographer had been supported financially by public funds from the National Endowment for the Arts, he began a campaign to prohibit the use of such funds for the creation and display of obscene imagery.

A second example will show that some artists have blurred the boundaries of three domains of objects, namely art, pornography and kitsch. The American artist Jeff Koons, discussed earlier in the chapter in connection with his postmodern appropriation of kitsch, created heterosexual erotic scenes inspired by eighteenth-century French Rococo imagery (by François Boucher and Jean Honoré Fragonard). In the late 1990s, he produced a series of contemporary works entitled *Made in Heaven*. The works showed him and his wife, the Italian porn star and member of parliament Ilona Staller, having sexual intercourse. In the painting 'title', for example, Koons looks ecstatically up while Staller gives him a blow job. Commenting on the series, Andrew Graham-Dixon (2000: 18) noted:

this is apparently another ... attempt to purify something potentially damaging – pornography, this time [instead of kitsch] – And transform it into something as serenely innocent and enjoyable as a children's game ... The heavily made-up artist and his blonde consort, cherubically shorn of all her pubic hair, looked as though they might almost be made of plastic: a Thunderbird puppet making love to a Barbie doll.

Both Graham-Dixon and Helms claimed that the artists, while playing with the emotional efficacy of sexual imagery, broke the boundaries of pornography and art through their particular aesthetic approaches. While, in Mapplethorpe's case, this was done through an 'anthropological', exoticising gaze, Koons kitschified the topic. No doubt, however, this understanding of their work expressed the views of only a select group of people, familiar with and supporting the latest developments in the Western art world. The examples show again that art can be controversial and that not all people share the same aesthetic preferences.

The incorporation of pornographic images into art has signified the postmodern desire to break down distinctions between high and low culture. Many contemporary viewers, however, do not recognize Mapplethorpe's and Koons's objects as 'postmodern art', especially when presented outside the context of artistic settings. This became clear when I asked anthropology students at Queen's University Belfast to look at 35 slides which showed sexually explicit representations.[26] Many of these students were locals from Northern Ireland, which, compared to the rest of Britain, is relatively conservative, with many people identifying themselves as Catholics or Protestants.

The slides included 'ethnographic objects', 'classical', 'modern' and 'postmodern' works of 'fine art', as well as some photographs of paintings and objects, which I had taken in the Amsterdam Red Light district.[27] Amongst the works were two works by Koons from the series *Made in Heaven*. As part of the exercise, the students had to first define the concept of pornography. Subsequently, while looking at the individual slides, they were asked to respond to four questions, namely, (1) 'Does this object/image have aesthetic qualities?', (2) 'Does this object/image send out an erotic message?', (3) 'Do you regard this object/image as pornographic?', and (4) 'Would you like to own and display this object/image?' In their answers, they could choose between 'not at all', 'no', 'yes' or 'certainly', and some scribbled extra comments next to their responses to further explain their reaction.

Many students defined pornography as an offensive phenomenon, which is not surprising considering the fact that most were from Northern Ireland (for comparison see Locher 1997). A male student, aged 21, wrote:

Pornography is often a portrayal of sexuality/sexual behaviour in a disturbing, immoral manner, intended to excite those who come into contact with it in a sexual way. This is maybe a rather simplistic view but this is how the majority interpret it without really knowing much about the subject. But society has given pornography a very negative label, and rightly so I think.

The student clearly reproduced a Modernist understanding of pornography, regarding it as a harmful phenomenon, and it is likely that his views were also shaped by his religious background. Some noted that people might get pleasure out of pornography, but most added that it could also have negative effects, for example, when shown to children. This also reflected a growing concern in Britain about the sexual abuse of children, and the accessibility of pornography on television and the internet.

Interestingly, many respondents maintained a distinction between art and pornography in their answers. A female student, aged 21, commented after the exercise that, looking back at her answers, she noticed that whenever she had decided that an object was 'pornographic' she had thought that it lacked aesthetic qualities. At the same time, she had felt that none of the aesthetic images were pornographic (which she defined as obscene and offensive), although many sent out erotic messages. The distinction between 'pornographic' and 'erotic' is relevant here, as 'the erotic' is generally regarded as a positive and harmless mode of sexuality. Lynda Nead (1993) noted that the discourse of 'erotic art' as a non-corruptive form of sexual imagery was generated in the context of the 1960s and 1970s, when the sexual mores relaxed in many Western urban regions. Erotic art 'became the site where new ground might be won for sexual freedom within legitimate culture, or which confirmed the corruption of traditional public life through permissiveness' (Nead 1993: 150–1). Associated with love and sincerity (as opposed to the profit-oriented status of pornography), and artistic beauty (as opposed to the ugliness of porn), it marked the boundaries of acceptable sexual representation in modern Western culture.[28] Through their supposed ability to recognise the quality of erotic art, consumers could distinguish themselves, on the one hand, from the uncivilised, morally corrupted porn-consumers, and, on the other, from rigid, conservative moralists. Evidently, 'erotic art', 'pornography' and 'art' are positions in a cultural battle, rather than markers of objective categories of objects.

Not surprisingly, all students decided that the two works by Koons were 'pornographic', and only a tiny minority thought that they had aesthetic quality. Interestingly, most students regarded Koons' images as more pornographic and less aesthetically pleasing than the photographs taken in the Red Light district. Amongst the latter was a wall painting taken in a sex club of two female strippers who showed their bodies to imaginary viewers (see Figure 10). A female student, aged 22, decided that this image was pornographic and lacked aesthetic qualities, and her added comment was simply: 'I don't like it.' By contrast, her reaction to Koons's work was phrased in more explicit terms. She found them *very* pornographic, having *no aesthetic qualities whatsoever*. Reacting to the statue, she wrote that she would not like to possess the object because it was 'shameful, [you would] feel like a pervert if you had it displayed in your home'. Her reaction illustrates that emotions often function as moral judgements – prescribing how one should (or should not) behave in specific situations. In the words of Michelle Rosaldo (1983: 136):

Insofar as all emotional states involve a mix of intimate, even physical experience, and a more or less conscious apprehension of, or 'judgement' concerning, self-and-situation, one might argue that emotions are, by definition, not passive 'states' but *moral* 'acts'. (original emphasis)

Commenting on the exercise as a whole, the same student emphasised: 'I would not display images of a sexual nature in my home as it's not right. People would judge you by this.' This clearly points out that objects and images appear in morally framed and gendered social contexts. The fact that most students were from Northern Ireland suggests that religious beliefs also influenced the students' reactions, even though none of them mentioned this. Another female student, aged 22, wrote in a reaction to Koons's statue: 'Just as I wouldn't want a stranger shagging in my house I wouldn't want this. It's intrusive.' Her reaction defined sex as a private affair, that should not take place in front of an audience.

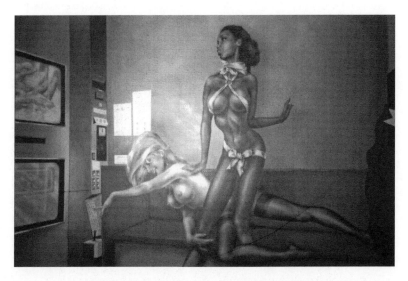

Figure 10 A mural at the entrance of a sex club in the Red Light district in Amsterdam, 2000 (photograph by Maruška Svašek)

Various female students reacted strongly to images which suggested male domination. In a reaction to an image of Bacchus embracing a female nude, a 22-year-old respondent noted: 'Girl seems distressed, it's not very nice.' Another 20-year-old female stated that: 'I would not like to own this object. Bachhus has a perverse facial expression.' In response to the exercise, she explained: 'I tend to condemn art that shows females as victims, and cannot own an object which displays the violence intrinsic to the sexual act itself, because it aggresses me every time I look.' This clearly reflected the idea that both men and women should agree to and enjoy having sex, an opinion that has strongly been pushed by the feminist movement since the 1960s.

What surprised me most was that the students wished to own surprisingly few of the works, and quite a few did not want to possess any of them, even if they thought they had aesthetic quality. This again was characteristic of the type of students participating in the exercise. Although speculating, I am quite sure that anthropology students at, for example the University of Amsterdam (where I studied myself), would be more interested in owning ethnographic artefacts or works of art, even if they were sexually explicit. Although in the Belfast study there were differences in aesthetic preference, most students who said they would like to own and display particular works chose the less explicit images, such as two paintings by the *fin-de-siècle* artist Gustav Klimt. *Danae* shows a woman asleep, with one bare breast, and *Friends* depicts two half-naked women asleep, embracing each other. Both paintings were highly stylised and decorative. In a reaction to the latter work, a 20-year-old female student wrote that she enjoyed it because of the 'colours, shapes, movement – lust of the senses shown AND stimulated/aroused *in a calm, peaceful way*' (italics mine). She explained that she only liked non-intrusive works, which showed warm affection. In her comments, she distinguished deplorable aggressive pornography from acceptable erotic art. Her reaction demonstrates how people may use discourses of the erotic versus pornography to position themselves as sexual but responsible subjects. As Kathy Myers (1987 [1982]) pointed out:

Images themselves cannot be characterised as either pornographic or erotic. The pornographic/erotic distinction can only be applied by looking at how the image is contextualised through its mode of address and the conditions of its production and consumption.

The importance of context to meaning and efficacy leads on to the next section, which discusses how feminist artists have appropriated sexually explicit imagery in acts of emancipation and self-realisation. The section also again demonstrates that artists may push the boundaries of art as part of their political struggles.

FEMINIST CRITIQUE AND EXPRESSIONS OF FEMALE SEXUALITY

As pointed out in Chapter 3, from the 1970s onwards, feminist art historians and artists have argued that, from the fifteenth century, the fine arts have been dominated by 'the male gaze', a perspective which objectifies women as spectacles and projections of sexual fantasy. One of the genres deconstructed by feminist art historians is 'the female nude', a genre which, through its erotic imagery, questions the distinction between art and pornography. J.A.D. Ingres' *The Great Odalisque*, made in 1841, exemplifies the politics of male-dominated representation of the female body. The painting shows a female nude, her reclining body turned away from the viewer. Yet 'the glimpse of her breast and the expanse of her buttocks and thighs emphasise her sexual availability' (Betterson 1996: 252). Her smooth body, visible behind a drawn curtain, and her gaze at the viewer present the woman as a passive object of male desire. As Rosemary Betterson noted:

Under the guise of disinterested aesthetic contemplation, the spectator/owner was given a privileged access to the spectacle of the naked female body, a sight normally tabooed in Western culture. (1996: 253)

Debates on the corrupted male gaze and critical discussions about the harmfulness of pornography during the 1970 and 1980s created an atmosphere in which it was hard for female artists to represent images of women that were regarded acceptable within feminist circles. Artists who intentionally depicted stereotypes of females in an attempt to critically uncover them, such as Cindy Sherman, were frequently accused of undermining the feminist project. The argument was that their works would simply reinforce the male gaze. Yet, as Rosemary Betterson (1996: 18–19) pointed out:

The nervousness about the body in feminist art of the 1980s has been replaced by its full-blooded embrace – sometimes literally – as sexually explicit and transgressive art practices run riot. The shift away from a totalizing view of pornography as sexual exploitation has been paralleled by a move towards the exploration of a range of sexualities.

In the last three decades, various female photographers have offered alternatives to male pornography, producing a wide variety of images which express sexual desire (Gibson 1997). The works range from rather 'innocent' romantic depictions of male nudes, to humorous portrayals (for example, of a man peeing in a hotel sink), to 'hard-core' images, such as a close-up shot of an erect penis held by a leather-gloved female hand. Lesbian artists have also explored their sexuality (Boffin and Fraser 1991). In the series *Dream Girls*, Deborah Bright (1991: 151) made photomontages of stills from old Hollywood movies, inserting images of herself as a butch-girl into the photographs, giving shape to her childhood and adolescent fantasies. In the series *Celestial Bodies*, Jean Fraser (1991) combined texts that discussed the erotic life of nuns with photographs of two nuns and a female nude having a picnic. In the work 'Transgression-devotion', a nun touches another nun's upper thigh, subtly expressing their sexual relationship. Other lesbian photographers have chosen to be more explicit, for example through shots of female sexual organs. The examples again demonstrate that 'art' is a changeable category, and that one should contextualise art production to be able to understand why artists make particular works. Their aims and artistic choices are related to power struggles and social changes which influence the public debate and affect what is regarded 'acceptable' in particular art worlds.

CONCLUSION

The above has shown that 'art' is inherently a category of exclusion, and that, at different times and in different places, 'art' has been opposed to various 'non-artistic' categories, such as 'craft', 'kitsch', 'propaganda' and 'pornography'. The processual relativist analysis emphasised the embeddedness of classificatory practices in specific historical processes, such as the enactment of power by the Church and the aristocracy during the Renaissance, and, during the seventeenth and eighteenth centuries, humanist and libertine resistance to religious orthodoxy, political authority and conventional morality. The constant improvement of printing techniques was also influential, as were processes of urbanisation, industrialisation and the formation of class-based societies during the nineteenth century. In the nineteenth and twentieth centuries, the influence of capitalist and communist ideologies also strongly shaped people's notions of 'art' and 'non-art'. Obviously, the analysis in this chapter limited itself to describing some major connections between societal processes and the classification of 'art', leaving out many other relevant influences.

One of the major arguments in this chapter was that, although different artistic styles have been promoted in different socio-historical and political settings, their efficacy has depended on a widespread belief in the exceptional quality and power of fine art. I situated the birth of this idea in late fifteenth-century Italy, when the art/craft distinction began to project the view that artists, through their creativity, produced works that were far superior to craft. During the eighteenth century, this idea was linked to a belief in the aesthetic force of art, which meant that art could connect viewers to the transcendental, pushing them beyond the limitations of their own judgemental perception, generating experiences of timeless beauty, truth and morality.

The art/kitsch discourse, formed in the context of industrialisation and class formation, linked the idea of beauty and morality to the idea of 'proper' and 'improper' forms of consumption. In this perspective, proper consumers recognised the quality of timeless beauty because, through mental effort, they were able to avoid the dangers of easy bodily satisfaction. Lovers of kitsch were by definition mentally weaker persons whose consumer preferences were influenced by instinct and passion, instead of rational consideration and non-judgemental experience. The art/kitsch dichotomy thus justified socio-economic inequalities, portraying the lower classes as less-developed beings.

The notion of unrefined and polluting consumption was also central to the art-versus-pornography discourse. Whereas kitsch was thought to have a detrimental effect, because it responded too easily to lower-class sentiments, pornography was regarded as dangerous because it evoked their sexual desires. The art-versus-pornography perspective reinforced class division, as the higher classes used it to imagine themselves as morally superior beings who had evolved beyond animal instincts, and who could easily connect to the realm of the transcendental without being distracted by animal instincts.

The chapter demonstrated that postmodernists and feminists strongly objected to the notion of aesthetics as a realm of transcendence and timeless quality. Instead, they convincingly argued that aesthetic value is actively created in art worlds, and that 'art' and 'non-art' are thus socially constructed categories. The latter view opened up the possibility for artists to intentionally play with the idea of art without pretending to create anything with inherent values, and this resulted in the incorporation of elements in their work that were previously regarded as 'non-art'. This implied that, especially during the last three decades, the boundaries between art, craft, kitsch and pornography have become increasingly blurred.

As was shown, other artists criticised art-versus-propaganda notions of the transcendental, which imagined 'politics' as a field of action that was by definition judgemental and therefore amoral. These artists argued, by contrast, that all art is necessarily political, as players in the art world make choices which reflect and reproduce their understanding of the world. While in some contexts, such as Stalinist Czechoslovakia, political art became a strategic propagandistic tool in the hands of powerful politicians who aimed to control society at large, in others, such as the 1970s feminist movement, it was rather a medium of critical reflection which deconstructed dominant ideologies. In both cases, art's potential to make people think and bring them to political action was defined as its major aesthetic value.

The examples in this chapter have shown that the creation of domains of 'art' and 'non-art' has been strengthened by particular commoditisation processes, which clearly links this chapter to the discussion in Chapter 5. We have seen that the development of different markets for art and craft not only linked up particular producers, dealers and consumers, but also created a price difference, in which works of art were generally valued higher than works of craftmanship. This increased when craft began to be mass-produced, but decreased when a new market was established for 'high craft' and when 'traditional styles' increased in value as they became collectors' items. Kitsch was in itself a result of mass production, but certain, especially older and less available objects have gained enormous value as collectibles. The market for pornography is varied and has evolved from a secretive production of images and texts for a small elite into the development of large-scale trade networks across the globe. Appropriated as art, kitsch and pornography now also appear in high-brow museums and galleries, valued as art and therefore much more expensive than kitsch and pornography by intention.

As noted earlier, political aims, such as feminist struggles for gender equality, have played an important role in the creation of more inclusive artistic trends. It must not be overlooked, however, that economic motives have also played their part. In the booming art market in the 1960s and 1980s, 'dealers and collectors began looking beyond established artistic institutions for promising new forms and creators', commoditising new types of products as high art (Zolberg and Cherbo 1997: 2). The desire to own and invest in 'something different' generated a strong interest in, for example, works made by asylum inmates, prison inmates, serial killers and children, and these have been moved to and sold in gallery settings. Yet, unlike some of the other boundary-breaking art forms, what has been called 'outsider art'

(Zolberg and Cherbo 1997) has often reinforced the myth of the artist as a creative genius who operates in the margins of society.[29]

The next chapter will examine another case of object transit and transition, namely of Fante flags and Fante flag-makers who were taken from Ghana to Northern Ireland. The analysis will again show the value of the processual relativist approach.

8 PROCESSUAL RELATIVISM: FANTE FLAGS IN NORTHERN IRELAND

In this last chapter, I present a detailed case study which ties up the main arguments of this book and shows the advantages of what I have loosely termed 'processual relativism'. As pointed out in the previous chapters, this approach stresses the processual nature of artefact production, interpretation and experience, and combines the analysis of historically situated signifying practices with an interest in aestheticisation, commoditisation and efficacy. This chapter focuses on a project which brought Fante flags and their makers from Ghana to Belfast. As we shall see, the flags were recontextualised in an art gallery setting, and the flag-making process was transformed into a series of community events which served specific social, educational and political goals.

As argued throughout this book, the study of transit and transition in local, national, and transnational fields of power can create valuable insights into the social life of artefacts. This chapter further explores the analytical value of the concept of 'interculturality' that was briefly introduced in Chapter 4, and argues that a focus on intercultural transaction and translation offers a useful perspective on the ways in which people interact, communicate or fail to communicate through artefact-related behaviour. As pointed out in Chapter 4, Fred Myers (2002) used the notion of 'intercultural space' in his study of the production, circulation and consumption of Australian Aboriginal painting and ritual performance, which formed a heterogenous field of practice and representation. The case study presented in this chapter similarly shows that, during the Fante flag project, artefacts were produced, used and valued by a variety of individuals with rather different aims and outlooks.

'The intercultural' should not be misunderstood as a point of contact between two or more static, separate cultures. As pointed out in Chapter 3, this essentialist identity–place approach to culture has been heavily criticised during the past four decades, and has been replaced by perspectives which define culture as dynamic processes of signification, identification and objectification. Some of these approaches have emphasised that human understanding of material realities involves sensorial experience and physical sensations which affect interpretation processes, and vice versa.

Obviously, processes of intercultural transaction and translation are partly shaped by interactions between and amongst individuals who physically move in and out of different locations and social settings, engaging or refusing to engage with each other. As we shall see in this chapter, their intersubjectivity implies a two-way process of perception and interpretation, in which people experience and give meaning to each other's actions, words and physicality. In the example of the Fante flag project, flag-making was central to these dynamics.

TALKING IN COLOUR: AFRICAN FLAGS OF THE FANTE

On 21 October 2003, the art curator Shan McAnena officially opened the exhibition Talking in Colour: African Flags of the Fante in the Naughton Gallery, an L-shaped exhibition space, which is part of and sponsored by Queen's University Belfast. The gallery (which was recently given a museum status) has become known for its diverse exhibition policy and its outreach programme, which offers tours and workshops to schools, community and public groups. Some of these events are rather spectacular, such as the Parade of the Dead in 2005, in which local artists, performers, school children and various other groups participated.[1]

The Naughton Gallery's involvement in community events mirrors Queen's University's outreach policy, but also reflects a global trend in the museum world. As Fred Myers (2002: 256) noted:

The more general effort to make museums 'eventful' should be recognised as part of their emerging structure, a movement that is making museums something more like public forms than temples of civilisation as they enter into spaces of the bourgeois public sphere in which controversial interpretative exhibitions might be held and symposia might bring interlocutors face to face.

Chapter 6 gave examples of how, in recent years, various museums have created active dialogues with different communities, thus turning the museum space from a more conventional exhibition area into an arena of public debate and critical reflection. The Naughton Gallery is one of the more active art centres in Belfast that have frequently used dialogical exhibition practices.

The Talking in Colour project was truly eventful, and not only brought Ghanaians to Northern Ireland, but also invited local African migrants to the opening ceremony.[2] It included several public lectures,[3] the making of flags by community groups, flag-making by local artists, as well as some social events (see Figure 11). The project was part of a larger festival, the annual Belfast Festival at Queen's, which offers a series of exhibitions, concerts, films, theatrical performances and other shows.

As emphasised by the title of the exhibition, Talking in Colour aestheticised Fante flags as things that were worth seeing, partly because of their extreme colourfulness. The bright colour combinations unavoidably stimulated the

Figure 11   Talking in Colour photo session in the African Cultural Centre, Belfast, 2003. Photograph by Maruška Svašek

visitors' sense of sight, so it is not surprising that various visitors I talked with during the exhibition mentioned their brightness as something extraordinary. As argued in Chapter 4, however, physiology alone can not explain why particular artefacts are thought to be remarkable and attractive. To be able to understand that, it is necessary to look at the performative context in which they gain secondary agency, in this case in the context of the gallery.

Talking in Colour was made up of three, relatively separate displays. The main exhibition consisted of 20 flags that had been made by the flag-makers Akwesi Asemstim and Baba Issaka prior to their arrival to Belfast (see Figure 12). The flags had been commissioned by the Naughton Gallery and were copies of existing items. Also included was one visibly old, used flag, about 100 years old. This flag demonstrated that Fante flag-making was an old tradition; it also showed that flags wore out through ritual use and natural decay. A brightly coloured, newly made *Asafo* uniform drew attention to the fact that company uniforms are normally worn during *Asafo* celebrations and rituals.

As emphasised in Chapter 6, uses of space and techniques of display must be critically analysed if one wants to understand the politics of exhibition-making. Techniques of display intentionally frame objects, often stimulating viewers to see them as instances of either 'art' or 'culture'. In the main gallery, explanatory texts and a documentary about Fante flag-making provided more background information about the local meanings and practices of Fante flag-making, and its rootedness in *Asafo* company activities.[4] The show had an 'ethnographic' feel to it, an impression that was reinforced in the catalogue, which did not classify the flags as 'art' (nor deny that it was

Figure 12   View of the Talking in Colour exhibition at the Naughton Art Gallery in Belfast, 2003. Photograph by Maruška Svašek

possible to do so), but rather compared Fante flag-making to flag-making traditions in Britain and Ireland. The catalogue also provided information about the *Asafo* companies, describing them as 'militia groups which existed long before the arrival of the white men but which were manipulated and organised by the Europeans to further their own colonial and commercial ambitions' (McAnena 2003: 5).[5] This and other background information made clear that Fante flags did not normally appear in the context of an art gallery, and seemed to suggest that they were 'culture'. Yet the very fact that the exhibition took place in an art environment, and the static display of the flags as objects made by named persons, also stimulated visitors to perceive the objects as works of art.

The presentational ambiguity in the Naughton Gallery exemplified how, since the 1980s, an increasing number of curators (art historians and anthropologists) have challenged rigid classifications of artefacts as *either* art *or* culture (see the discussion of Clifford's art/culture system in Chapter 6). Challenging conventional distinctions was an important aim of the Belfast Festival in 2003. One of the themes chosen by the organisers was to question the boundary between art and craft. As discussed in the previous chapter, the blurring of boundaries was a central aim of postmodern theory. Evidently, Asemstim and Issaka were not conscious of the new subtext of their works, as they were unfamiliar with postmodern aesthetic debates; neither were most of the visitors. This again shows that art worlds create knowledge and values that may be quite specific. As outsiders, the two flag-makers relied on their own expectations, and thought that their main aim was to show their skills and demonstrate the richness of Fante traditions. In the context of the Belfast Festival, however, their work was reinterpreted as boundary-undermining expressions.

Paradoxically, fixed notions of 'art-versus-craft' and 'art-versus-culture' were, perhaps unintentionally, reinforced in the second part of the display, which consisted of 13 artefacts made by local Northern Irish artists who had been asked to draw inspiration from the Fante flag tradition. This second batch of flags hung down from the balustrade of the corridor which led to the main gallery. Their peripheral location, their absence from the catalogue and the title of the project (Talking in Colours: African Flags of the Fante) signalled that the local Irish flags were not the main attraction of the show. Interestingly, in this part of the exhibition, no information had been provided about the intended meaning of the flags. This reflected a key assumption in contemporary fine art, namely that aesthetic objects can 'speak for themselves' and need no explanation beyond their own presence (see Chapters 6 and 7). The absence of explanatory texts also signified that the local works of art were not as exotic as the Fante flags. In other words, it emphasised the idea of cultural difference.

Apart from the spatial and discursive separation of local and Fante objects, the Northern Irish flags also differed in terms of their material characteristics. Unlike the Fante flags, they showed a considerable variety of size, material, technique and style. While all objects were undoubtedly flag-like artefacts, only one artist had made a flag that closely resembled the design of the Fante flag. This diversity increased the impression that the Fante flags, by contrast, formed a relatively homogeneous cultural tradition.

The possibility of intercultural communication and mutual exchange between Northern Irish and Fante forms of visual expression was, however, central in the third part of the exhibition. This display consisted of 19 flags that had been produced by a number of Northern Irish community groups in cooperation with the two flag-makers.[6] As McAnena (2003: 10) explained in the exhibition catalogue:

On arrival in Belfast, the flag-makers worked with seventeen different groups across the social and political divide – from homeless teenagers to senior citizens, from the women of the Patchwork Guild to people with learning difficulties – to make flags that embody the spirit of the particular association.

The reference to 'the social *and* political divide' is highly relevant and refers to the situation in Northern Ireland, which has been scarred by conflicts between Unionists and Nationalists. Interestingly, the tensions have been visually expressed by local flag and banner traditions, as well as by the painting of murals (Jarman 1997, 1999), which means that, in the local context, the activity of 'flag-making' directly refers to the conflict between 'essentially different' Protestant and Catholic communities. The Northern Irish organisers of the Fante flag project, however, transformed 'flag-making' into an activity which celebrated cultural difference and promoted interculturality, not only between Northern Irish locals and the Ghanaians, but *also* between members of different local communities. Again, this was a subtext unknown (and irrelevant) to Asemstim and Issaka.

On the day of the opening, the community flags were displayed on the walls of the stairs leading to the gallery. The display differed in several ways from the other two shows. The names of the individuals who had worked on the flags were not mentioned, just the names of the group they belonged to. The artefacts were thus presented as community flags which expressed the collective identity of the group; as products of collective effort. This clearly signalled that these flags belonged to a different category. While the Fante flags were presented as an ethnic tradition and the local artists' flags emphasised artistic idiosyncrasy, the community flags intended to demonstrate the 'rich cultural diversity' within Northern Ireland, as many, rather different groups had produced a flag. As visual signifiers of 'unity in diversity', these products objectified the political discourse of reconciliation and cross-community activity, and also resonated with recent attempts by Northern Irish institutions to promote anti-racism.[7] The politically charged messages were intended for all people in Northern Ireland; to reach a wider audience, the community flags were moved to a public location in the city centre after the opening night.

HISTORICAL AND ETHNOGRAPHIC BACKGROUND: THE *ASAFO* COMPANIES

To be able to understand how and why the meaning, value and efficacy of the *Asafo* flags changed when they were recontextualised as gallery exhibits and community products, it is essential to take a processual relativist approach and first examine their place in the dynamic context of Fante history. Not pretending to give a complete analysis of Fante flag-making throughout the centuries (partly because not much is known about it), the following details will make clear that Fante flag-making is a centuries-old vibrant tradition which has been influenced by changing policies, economics and other factors.

Fante people migrated in the fourteenth and fifteenth century to what is today the coastal region of the West African state of Ghana. The migrants established a number of states, each headed by a Chief (*Ohen*). The individual states were united by a King (*Oman-hen*), but the Fante did not form, as the neighbouring Asante had done, a strong, centrally governed political union. Matrilineal kin groups or *abusua* were central to Fante social, economic and political life, with the exogamous *abusua* controlling the inheritance of land and property, and deciding about chiefly succession. Matrilineal ancestral spirits were thought to be the 'real owners of the land and the people', and their protection was sought in elaborate rituals (Christensen 1954: 127). With the establishment of the Gold Coast colony and the subsequent independence of Ghana, the political power of the King and his Chiefs decreased.

While matrilineal descent organised the Fante politically, the military *Asafo* system was structured patrilineally. Men in particular identified themselves strongly with their *Asafo* alliances. As Christensen noted, 'the oath, taken by every [*Asafo* company] member, to answer the call of his officers takes precedence over all other affiliations, including the ties of the *abusua*' (1954: 107).The *Asafo* military organisation (*sa* meaning 'war' and *fo* 'people') was, and still is, constituted by distinct companies. In the different states the number of companies has varied from 2 to 14, and in some of the bigger towns as many as seven companies have been established. For centuries, companies have produced colourful flags for ritual and military purposes, similar to the ones that were exhibited in the Naughton Gallery in Belfast. The myth that explains the origin of the Fante flag tradition tells of a flag-bearer who led the Fante people to the coastal area, and describes how, after their arrival, female migrants were so enthusiastic about their new homeland that they took off their clothes and waved them like flags in the wind.

Alternative explanations of the origin of *Asafo* and their flag traditions have been given by various academics. Eva Meyerowitz (1974: 87–93) claimed that the new Fante states had included members of other ethnic groups that influenced Fante politics and social organisation. According to Meyerowitz, one of the elements that was incorporated into Fante life was the *Asafo* military system, which had been one of the central organisational features of the Afutu people. Other authors have argued that organisational forms similar to *Asafo* were quite common among all the Akan (Christensen 1954: 108; see also DeGraft Johnson 1932: 309–10). Numerous authors have suggested that the Fante flag tradition resulted from the creative appropriation by the Fante of European flag traditions. *Frankaa*, the Fante word for 'flag', is thought to have derived from the English 'flag' or the Dutch *vlaggen* ('flags'). The flag tradition itself can thus be regarded as an instance of intercultural translation.

The patrilineal *Asafo* is as hierarchical as the matrilineal *abusua*. The confederation of all companies is commanded by the chief commander or *Tufohen*, a term that can be roughly translated as 'chief of the gunners'. The individual companies are known as *etsikuw*, which can be literally translated as a 'group of heads', and a number of set positions structure them. The senior officer (*Supi*) is the commander, who is responsible for the company flags, the drums and other equipment such as gunpowder. Several junior officers hold the position of *Asafohen* and command smaller groups of company members. The *Frankakitanyi* (*franka* means 'flag', *kitaa* 'hold' and *nyi* stands for 'person') is the official flag-bearer, who is guarded by the *Asikamahen* or chief scout guards. His position is elected, and so is the position of *Akyerema*, or drummer, who beats the company drum when the group needs to be assembled or instructed during battle and ritual activities (Christensen 1954: 106–9; Sarbah 1968: 11–12). In the past, women used to function as a supply corps to the frontlines as well as a kind of unarmed home guard (McCarthy 1983: 20).

As noted earlier, *Asafo* patrilineal alliance has been of major importance
to Fante men and continues to be so today. Around the age of 18, boys are
initiated into their father's company, and relationships between fathers
and sons are understood in terms of shared physicality, spirituality and
company membership. Fathers are believed to be the main provider of blood
to embryos, and the prime source of their spiritual power (*egyabosom*) and
soul (Christensen 1954: 127). This makes the loyalty between fathers and
sons particularly strong. Patrilineal ideology is also reflected in the internal
politics of the companies. The key positions of *Supi* and *Asafohen* are inherited
patrilineally, and sons are believed to directly inherit their fathers' military
competence and bravery (1954: 108–9). Especially in the past, *Asafo* groups
frequently confronted each other in violent clashes, which often led to injuries
and killings. Men were obliged to take part in these struggles, even if it meant
that they would face their own matrilineal kin in battle.

Asafo companies used to be active in the fields of military defence, politics,
religion and society generally, and, before the increase of British influence
that led to the establishment of Gold Coast Colony in 1874, military defence
was their major task (Christensen 1954). Company officers were expected
to defend their patrilenial group when inter-company violence occurred,
but they also formed strong alliances with their rival companies when war
broke out with non-Fante groups. The companies had considerable political
influence as they were consulted when a new *Omanhen* was being installed.
As a result of colonisation, however, they lost most of their military and
political influence, and their pre-colonial power base was not fully restored
after independence.

It is important to note, however, that the political changes did not
undermine the *Asafo* system of patrilineal alliance and territorial rivalry.
Company members have also continued their involvement in society, providing
communal labour and assisting in cases of emergencies. At the same time,
changing religious beliefs resulting from missionary activities have failed to
undermine the Fante belief in ancestral powers. Despite widespread conversion
to Christianity and Islam, *Asafo* flags are still regarded as seats of patrilineal
spirits, and the *posuban* (the sacred shrine in which the Fante flags are kept, see
below), has remained central to *Asafo* symbolism and ritual practice.

FLAG-MAKING: PRODUCTION AND ICONOGRAPHY

Asafo flags have social lives, being ordered and made, and moving in and
out of particular social and spatial contexts. While some flags are ordered
collectively by *Asafo* companies, it is mostly individual men who commission
flags as part of their initiation as company members or leaders. Young men
who are to be installed as company officers normally approach a flag-maker
to order a flag, which will become collective company property after their
initiation. Those who commission a flag need to select a design and discuss
the various possibilities with the flag-maker. There is considerable similarity

between the iconography of flags, both within and amongst the companies. In a recent study of flags in the towns of Abandze and Kormantse, Kwame A. Labi (2002: 31) noted that 'many motives are shared by different companies' as they are based on well-known Fante proverbs.

Asemstim and Issaka told me that, these days, they normally show photographs of flags they made earlier to their customers as examples. Their clients either order copies of existing designs, or – less frequently – propose alternatives. The final product is, by and large, based on an existing iconographic repertoire, which is, however, broadened through occasional innovation. While this approach ensures the continuation of a recognisable visual genre, it also leaves considerable room for variety and change. As radically new designs must be approved by the *Tufohen*, the politics of representation is ultimately controlled by the highest authority within the company. This shows that, as was argued throughout this book, object production must be analysed as an activity which may reinforce existing power relationships. At the same time, however, Fante flag production is strongly shaped by generic rules and by the preferences and expectations of the producers and users of the flags.

In Chapter 6 it was argued that spatial politics is central to object transit and transition. Fante flags are normally kept in company shrines (*posuban*) or in boxes under the beds of flag-dancers or company elders, who control their appearance in public (cf. Labi 2002: 31). Before the introduction of cement during the colonial period, shrines were marked by a particular type of tree, but the presence of new building materials and the increasing influence of European traders and British colonial representatives inspired the Fante to build large cement shrines in the shape of forts and ships. During the colonial period such images alluded to the influence and status of the British rulers; in a process of cultural translation, they were at the same time transformed into signifiers of *Asafo* authority. Shrines have also been decorated with life-size sculptures and reliefs, which depict people and events central to company history and identity. This obviously increases their agency as markers of *Asafo* identity.

Due to the harsh climate and the limited durability of cotton cloth it is hard to find flags that are over 150 years old, and the older ones often have almost turned to dust. Many shrines store hundreds of flags, and new flags are added as long as sons are born who will take up company membership. *Asafo* members regard their flags as the 'soul and embodiment' of their companies. They are included in all company activities, and company members are required to swear to defend them. Considered to be sacred artefacts, the flags have considerable agency (Labi 2002: 29). In Chapter 4, I provided several examples of holy or sacrosanct objects' performative agency. Sacred objects are often used as powerful communicative instruments; they actively evoke specific emotional responses, pushing people to take particular forms of social and political action. Before looking in more detail at the performative power of the Fante flags, I shall briefly discuss the influence of European military traditions on *Asafo* practices.

Even though it is not clear when the practice of flag-making started, scholars seem to agree that the making of heraldic flags and banners was related to the arrival of the Europeans, which started with a visit by Portugese traders in 1471 (Adler and Barnard 1992: 7, 10). It is very likely that the Fante were directly inspired by the European custom of national flags and company banners, which expressed pride, identified collectivities and marked ownership. One of the first reports that mentioned Fante flags was written in 1693 by an English trader, who visited Christiansborg Castle after it had been captured from the Danish by the Fante General Akwamu. The report noted the presence of a 'white [flag] with a black man painted in the middle brandishing a scymitar' (1992: 11). In 1732, Barbot observed that Fante who lived under the protection of Europeans would carry the national flag of their protectors into battle with them (Labi 2002: 29). Both occasions can be regarded as acts of interculturality in which, for strategic or other reasons, 'alien' traditions were actively translated and incorporated.

The *Asafo* companies were also influenced by other European military traditions. They adopted some of their practices, such as marching in procession, and the use of regimental colours, names, numbers, mottos and uniforms to identify different companies. Company numbers and colours began to appear on the flags, as well as depictions of scenes which revealed other changes. A flag made by Issaka, which was on display in the Naughton Art Gallery, was clearly a copy of an old flag that had been made during the colonial period. It showed a British administrator behind a table full of coins, who held up a sign with the words 'Come for pay'. Opposite him three members of 'No. 1' Company (from Agona Nkwanta) waited in line for their payment, holding a gun, an axe and a spade. These artefacts symbolised the work traditionally done by members of *Asafo* companies as part of their duty to their patrilineage – protection, construction and sanitation. The flag imagery demonstrated that, in the colonial period, this was also done as wage labour for British employers.

Fante flag-makers were clearly intrigued by European imagery. Numerous flags show 'European' figures, such as dragons and lions, which appear in heraldic poses, complete with crowns and extended tongues. The influence of European military iconography was also demonstrated by images of the Union Jack in the left-hand corner of many flags. After independence, the Ghanaian national flag was also frequently depicted.

As noted earlier, the visible impact of British culture did not completely transform *Asafo* practices. As Christensen noted, '[w]hile the influence of the European powers along the coast on the culture of the Fante cannot be dismissed, it is felt that the company system is an outgrowth of the military tradition of the Akan, and not a copy of the European military pattern' (1954: 108; see also DeGraft Johnson 1932: 309–10). In other words, the Fante did not passively copy European traditions but selectively incorporated certain 'foreign' elements without radically changing their own beliefs and practices. A clear sign of this is the importance of proverbs to flag imagery. The use of proverbs is an important element in Fante everyday speech, and flag symbolism concentrates on those proverbs that can be used to challenge and insult rival companies. To give a contemporary example, one of the flags exhibited in the Naughton Gallery in Belfast pictured the proverb 'When the cat is dead the rats will take over.' Rats are perceived as highly intelligent animals, and the company that had commissioned the flag associated itself with this animal. The flag also showed the image of a dead cat (the rival company) and the image of the rival company's shrine, overrun by rats. The depiction of the victory of the rats over the cats was a direct challenge to the rival company.

FANTE FLAGS: PERCEPTION, POWER AND EFFICACY

Yet how and why do Fante flags challenge rival company members, and how and why do they generate company pride? How are pieces of textile turned into powerful agents? Chapter 4 pointed out that objects and images are often able to evoke memories and emotions, subsequently generating social action. This means that object perception is not just a matter of encoding and decoding messages, but that it involves complex processes that cannot be explained by semiotics alone. The perspective of object agency helps to explain why objects become effective in certain socio-historical and spatial settings. Central is the ways in which they are used by primary agents (i.e. people) to manipulate other beings. Of equal importance is their embeddedness in 'aestheticisation', a process in which people value their experience of objects and often connect it to abstract ideas.

From Powerless Objects to Seats of Spiritual Force

How can the perspectives of aestheticisation and object agency be used to explain the significance of the Fante flags in concrete contexts? Let us first look at the ways in which the Fante normally transform newly made flags into powerful agents. According to the Fante, *Frankaa* only become efficacious when, after completion, libation is poured over them. At that moment, patrilineal ancestral spirits enter the flag and use their spiritual power (*tumwum*) to strengthen and protect not only the new officer, but also the company as a whole. The Fante also believe that when the commissioning officer dies, his spirit increases the *tumwum* of the flag he once ordered.

The above shows that the discourse of *tumwum* constructs the 'spiritual force of the ancestors' as a protective and guiding power. Indirectly, it justifies the authority of the *Tufohen* and the *Supi*, who are regarded as representatives of the patrilineage. *Tumwum* also refers to bodily experiences of ancestral power. Flag-dancers, believed to be sensitive to the demands made by different ancestral spirits, use their sensitivity to decide which flag they will pick to dance with, and claim that they feel their force when handling it. The flag-maker Asemstim, who is officer in the No. 1, Benti Company in Kromantze, occasionally stands in as flag-dancer, and he assured me that whenever he dances with a flag, he can physically feel its power. When I asked him how this feels, he made movements as if he was subtly pulled into different directions. The fact that flags are thought to come to life through rituals and dancing acts means that active bodily interaction with the flags is thus central to how people perceive and experience them.

Labi (2002: 30) described flag-dancing as an athletic performances 'that involves somersaulting, spinning around, leaping in the air, and twirling the flag'. Bearing in mind that most Fante only see company flags when they are used in dances, it may be clear that their perceptual experience of flags contrasts considerably with the ways in which visitors to the Naughton Gallery experienced the exhibits. In Chapters 4 and 5, several case studies pointed out that experiential transformations are part and parcel of transit and transition, especially when ritual objects are appropriated as objects to be statically displayed. In the case of the Talking in Colour exhibition, the visitors' perceptions were shaped by a familiarity with traditions of gallery display, which emphasise visual experiences. Their understanding of the exhibition was also framed by a belief in the significance of artistic and cultural heritage. Expecting to see authentic works with aesthetic value (after all, the works had been chosen by a respected and knowledgeable art historian), they anticipated being enchanted by beautiful artefacts. For that, they did not need to touch or dance with the flags. Properly socialised as art lovers, they took on a contemplative attitude and quietly experienced the works' aesthetic force.

From 'Ayefie' to 'Beauty' and Back: Intercultural Space

Normative concepts of 'beauty' and 'skill' – central defining features of 'high-art' discourses – are not altogether insignificant in relation to the flag-making process. When I asked Asemstim and Issaka whether they used specific terms to judge and compare individual flags, they stated that flag-makers needed to acquire sewing skills, a sense of colour and composition, and knowledge about the proper kind of imagery used for flag designs. Apprentices normally acquire this knowledge within two years, as they are trained by master flag-makers (sons mostly learn from their fathers or from another patrilineal male relative). The two flag-makers used the term *ayefie* ('beauty', also used for 'beautiful' women or 'beautiful' landscapes) as a normative concept to judge the visual and technical qualities of flag designs. They stressed, however, that it was the flags' *tumwum* (spiritual power) and not their beauty which made them truly effective.

During the community projects, I observed how Asemstim and Issaka used their skills to create visually attractive compositions. They advised the participants on choice of colour (sometimes simply ignoring the participants' own suggestions), showed them the templates they had brought from Ghana, cut out the selected images in colourful cotton and moved them over the flag surface until they had found a satisfactory composition. I got the impression that, in putting the images together, they tried to find a balance in the shapes, sizes and colours of the individual pieces. Especially during the first community projects, Asemstim and Issaka showed what seemed to be genuine enthusiasm for the results, which were of course to them, at least to some extent, rather uncommon.

One of the school classes with whom they did a project chose, for example, to include images of a computer and a football shoe on their flag. Although this was uncommon subject material to the two flag-makers, they reacted with humour, and were visibly enchanted by the end product. They were really engaged in the making of this particular flag, which was the third flag they worked on. The day before they had assisted in the making of two flags with women from the Northern Ireland Patchwork Guild. In this case, the emphasis had been more on the teaching of the flag-making technique, and there had also been a more conscious exchange of knowledge, as the women patchworkers had brought some samples of their own products. The flag-makers studied those with interest and complimented the ladies, and received compliments about their own work in return. After the workshop, the unfinished flags were completed by the women themselves, who used their own application technique.

It was interesting to compare the enthusiasm of Asemstim and Issaka with the body language of an Ashanti relative of the textile merchant who had coordinated the project on the Ghanaian side. He initially posed as one of the flag-makers' 'assistants', but it soon became clear to me that he did not know much about flag-making. He just stood there, politely watching, and hardly interfered. He also began telling me about Ashanti beliefs when I asked about the *tumwum* of the flags. At that point, the two flag-makers protested, saying that he was not referring to Fante traditions at all. It seemed that the 'assistant' had simply taken the opportunity to come to Europe. When I jokingly suggested to the flag-makers that their 'assistant' might be a conman, the flag-makers did not respond but smiled politely.

The enthusiasm of the two flag-makers did wear off, however, after several days, when they tired of being taken from one community to another to produce community flag after community flag. The time pressure made them feel weary as well. During the workshops, they started working on the flags but were asked to finish them during their 'spare time'. They were provided with sewing machines in their Belfast accommodation and, by the end, they said they had to work throughout the night to finish everything before the opening of the exhibition. Even though the organisers said that the community flags did not have to be perfect, and that they did not need to spend so much time on them, Asemstim and Issaka simply could not rush and do a bad job. The only concession they made was to only sew the image on one side of the flag instead of on both. This was not problematic at all, of course, as the flags were not waved or danced with, but stuck on the wall.

I visited Asemstim and Issaka several times in their temporary home in Belfast, and the lounge in which they worked – the floor, the couch and the chairs – were increasingly covered with little colourful threads. Finished and unfinished flags were lying everywhere. They told me they had never worked as hard in their lives, and that they would need at least three weeks off to recover when they returned to Ghana. Despite their complaints about the workload, however, when the flags were finally finished, they said they were satisfied with the results and that they had a sense of accomplishment.

They also enjoyed seeing their own flags displayed together in the main exhibition. I met them one afternoon in the gallery, and they sat side by side, chatting and looking at the display. Interestingly, they had not know each other before the project, and their personal differences (for example, Asemstim was a Christian and Issaka a Muslim) were underplayed during their stay in Belfast. Their shared identity as Fante flag-makers was accentuated throughout the trip. The project provided an occasion to observe each other's approaches to flag-making, to discuss photographs of flags they saw in the book *Asafo! African Flags of the Fante* (Adler and Barnard 1992), and to evaluate how their flags were recontextualised by the Naughton Art Gallery. Fascinated by the fact that these flags are normally kept in company shrines and only appear in public during ritual occasions, I asked them whether they felt that a taboo had been broken. They both declared that their flags were just pieces of textile without any *tumwum*, because they had not been spiritually empowered. They were, however, proud of their products, because they were beautiful and made with skill.

Politics of Objects in Space

As noted earlier, the spatial recontextualisation of the Fante flags in a quiet, well-lit gallery was crucial to visitors' experiences of the exhibits. In the Fante setting, space was equally important, but in a rather different way. Patrilineal residence patterns divide many Fante towns into separate territories. Interestingly, yet unknown to the two flag-makers, the territorial use of space was quite similar in Belfast, where many areas are predominantly Catholic or Protestant. In the Fante case, particular territories are controlled by single *Asafo* companies, and flag-dancing parades frequently cross these territorial boundaries. There are fascinating parallels with the situation in Belfast. Protestant and Catholic groups, such as lodges of the Orange Order and divisions of the Ancient Order of Hibernians parade with banners in the streets to mark certain historical and ritual occasions, and problems occur frequently when participants march or intend to march through each other's territory (Jarman 1997, 1999). The catalogue of the exhibition mentioned these similarities, arguing that:

[t]he parallels and differences in the evolution, design and use of flags in Northern Ireland and Ghana, together with the delight in the Fante's condensation of identity into such a beautifully simple visual solution was the trigger for the project. (McAnena 2003: 10)

In the Fante case, armed company members, who accompany their flag-dancer and protect the company flag he is carrying, sing abusive songs which express their own bravery and ridicule their competitors. On temporary transit through quarters controlled by rival groups, the flags strongly increase their power to challenge and insult. Evidently, an analysis which solely focuses on the insulting iconography of the flags misses out an important aspect of communication through matter: flag-dancing is a multi-sensorial experience, as colourful flags and singing, dancing, sweating and shouting bodies move through time and space. In the past, the spatial politics of flag celebrations frequently led to intercompany violence.

From the eighteenth century onwards, the British slowly secured their involvement in internal Fante affairs and tried to stop the violent outbursts between the *Asafo* companies. In the nineteenth century, the new rulers implemented policies that aimed to regulate company celebrations to reduce the power of the flags. The control of space was vital to their efforts. In 1850, the judicial assessor, James Fitzpatrick, proclaimed that all celebrations organised by *Asafo* companies should take place outside the towns. He forbade celebrations on Sundays, and specified the hours during which they should start and end. One of his aims was to avoid the fights that regularly broke out between the different companies during the annual harvest festivals (McCarthy 1983: 155). The British also tried to control flag design to undermine the flags' potentially explosive effect. In 1859, when a serious fight occurred between No. 1 Company Bentil and No. 3 Company Intin in the town of Cape Coast, the British Mayor of Cape Coast wrote a letter to the Chief Justice suggesting that the custom of *Asafo* flag design should be regulated. He explained that:

Each company has its flag; but besides its regular 'company flag', each company has in addition a variety of fanciful flags with devices on them, intended to represent some event or circumstance connected with the history of the company that carries them, or of some rival company. When making their grand customs, each company, if it has no quarrel with any others, passes through the various quarters of the town with its original 'company flag', but when there is a desire to convey defiance or insult, a company, in passing through the quarter inhabited by the company whom it is desired to annoy, will there display a flag having some device ostentatiously offensive. In the same way, whilst each company has its war songs, which, without being offensive to other companies, are, of course, self-laudatory, each has also a habit of exciting rival companies by singing insulting songs at the same time that the objectionable flags are paraded. From time immemorial these flags and songs have been the cause of ill-feeling, strife, and bloodshed, as has unfortunately been the case in the present instance. (quoted in Sarbah 1968: 12)

In a reaction to the letter, the Chief Justice decided that, to avoid outbreaks of violence, flag designs would have to be sent to the town hall for approval by the Governor 'who, if he disapproved, will substitute some other in its place' (1968: 14). Accepted patterns and colours would have to be registered in the secretary's office in the fort, and the use of other designs would be prohibited and punished (1968: 14).

Even though the new policy was never fully successful, the incident provides evidence of the potential force of the flags, which not only challenged other companies but also resisted colonial control. The British, however, were relatively successful in exploiting the lack of political unity amongst the Fante and gaining control over the coastal areas. They 'organized the Asafo warriors into efficient military units', which helped them to 'bring together an army for a quick reaction to any threat from the interior' (Adler and Barnard 1992: 8). Several factors were crucial, including the declining authority of the chiefs, the continued fear of their arch-enemies the Ashanti, the increasing dependence on overseas capital and the internalisation of new values by a growing class of aspirant bourgeoisie (McCarthy 1983: 143). As we shall see in the next section, the latter two factors helped to stimulate the flags' commodity potential.

MARKETS FOR FANTE FLAGS

Chapter 5 pointed out that the growing demand for primitive art in the West has led to the diversification of artefacts which are commoditised as authentic African art. Not surprisingly, some art traders have set their eyes on the Fante flags, seeing them as skilfully-made colourful works which may appeal to Western buyers. As we shall see, the traders mostly emphasise the beautiful colours of the flags and their simple but effective compositions, claiming that they have culturally specific meanings but also a culture-independent, timeless aesthetic quality. Evidently, they react to the expectations of Western consumers and use particular marketing strategies to catch the eye of their potential customers. This agrees with earlier findings, namely that commoditisation influences aestheticisation, and vice versa.

The flags began to enter the primitive art market on a more regular basis during the late twentieth century, rapidly gaining commodity value and soon becoming increasingly expensive. Interestingly, within the context of contemporary *Asafo* companies, the flags already go through a brief period of commoditisation when they are sold to Fante customers who commission flag-makers and pay them for their work. Asemstim and Issaka told me that they normally produce one or two flags per week for the Fante market. In 2003, these sales provided them with a weekly salary of about £30–40 sterling.[8]

Once the payment has been made, however, flags become company property and are not expected to be exchanged again. In other words, they are de-commoditised as soon as they are handed over to the companies and stored with the other company flags. The development of a market for old and used flags, however, has meant that many flags have been re-commoditised as they have been taken out of their shrines and sold to outsiders. The tradesmen are commonly Ghanaian middlemen or Western traders who respond to, and help to create, a growing demand for 'authentic' African art. The flags are sold through gallery sales and auctions, as well as through the internet.

Charles Jones African Art is based in Wilmington (North Carolina), and offers a wide variety of African objects, including weapons, masks, furniture, beadwork and Fante flags. The gallery clearly markets the flags as 'art', and 'unconditionally guarantees the authenticity of any work sold' (http://www. cjafricanart.com/Gallery.htm, accessed 26/10/04). As noted earlier in this book, claims to authenticity have been a central feature of the trade in and discourse of art during the last two centuries. The notion of the authentic promotes art specialists as knowledgeable critics who are able to judge the quality of good art. In line with this, Charles Jones African Art provides an appraisal service. In the competing market of primitive art, it also tries to reach potential customers in a large area, holding showings throughout the south-eastern United States.

Stephen Messick,[9] an American collector of African and Chinese artefacts, has mainly sold Fante flags through his website, thus cutting the cost of public shows (http://www.treasurenc.com/sys-tmpl/homagetofanteasafo, accessed 26/10/04). In 2005, the prices of his flags varied between US $200 and US $400. Evidently, their value goes up when the flags move through a chain of sellers and buyers.[10] Feeding the expectations of potential customers, Messick emphasised that his flags carried the marks of authenticity:

I'm lucky to own over 20 fascinating Asafo flags. ... some of the older ones are so worn you can see through them. These flags were USED, not just hung for display. Many were paraded outside in all sorts of weather, hung from poles, and some were even slept on by novice flag-makers! Most therefore have holes, stains, and bleeding of the darker colours.

Again, this shows that authenticity (to own 'the real thing'), is a key concern to many buyers of Fante flags. There is, however, also a market for newly produced flags. Being new and unused, these flags are commonly lower priced than the old and used ones.

Asemstim and Issaka also produced new flags for the foreign market, selling them for double or triple the price of the flags they produced for their Fante customers. Like many other producers of African artefacts, they did not sell these flags directly to foreign customers, but sold them to African middlemen who had connections with foreign buyers (see also Chapter 6).

FIELDS OF INTERCULTURAL TRANSACTION: RELATIONS OF POWER

Shan McAnena contacted one of those African middlemen when she travelled to Ghana to organise the Talking in Colours exhibition. She had not yet any connection with Fante flag-makers and, when she arrived in Accra, she was referred to the textile trader Atta Gyamfi. Their contact was crucial in the process of transit and transition that followed. Gyamfi was of Ashanti ethnic background and mainly exported Kente cloth to Europe and America, but also occasionally dealt in Fante flags. He took McAnena to Asemstim's and Issaka's villages and, when the latter two agreed to make flags for the exhibition and to travel to Northern Ireland for the Belfast project, it was decided that Gyamfi (who had 'foreign' experience and who spoke good English) would be in charge of the organisation and financial arrangement on the Ghanaian side.

Transactions concerning the production, transit and transition of artefacts always take place within fields of power (see in particular Bourdieu's theory of practice, Chapter 6). In the Talking in Colours project, the field was mainly defined by economic power, socio-economic position and professional status. On the one hand, the power hierarchy was defined by long-term economic inequalities between the north (Northern Ireland) and the south (Ghana), and by internal socio-economic differences in Ghana. Coming from Northern Ireland, McAnena was able to fly to Ghana and commission flags for an extremely small amount of money (if compared to the cost of flags in Britain) – she agreed on £25 per flag. The flag-makers, local artisans who mainly produced for local audiences, were happy with the deal, but it made them dependent on Gyamfi. They were considerably less well-off than the Accra-based businessmen, who exported cheap goods to wealthy countries, and they had to accept that Gyamfi would earn a salary just for organising the production of the flags, while they would be doing most of the work. Not surprisingly, however, Asemstim and Issaka jumped at the opportunity to earn some cash and travel to Europe without needing to think about organisational matters, even though it was not yet fully clear to them how much money they would eventually make.

Professional status and experience also shaped the field of power. The Belfast art historian represented a powerful institution; she was employed by Queen's University, which financially supported the Naughton Gallery. Her university alliance signified her position as a respected and influential professional, and her status and experience allowed her to travel to Ghana and set things in motion. By contrast, Gyamfi had proved himself to be a successful textile trader. His previous business experience in America/Europe and his knowledge of English made him an important player in this specialised field, so it was not surprising that other Ghanaians recommended him to McAnena. Asemstim and Issaka were known locally as experienced flag-makers who produced quality flags, and who had already demonstrated their willingness to produce flags for foreign markets. Gyamfi had already bought flags from them in the past, and this made him confident enough to introduce McAnena to the two flag-makers. As he had expected, she was delighted with what she saw.

The art historian asked the flag-makers to produce ten flags each (copies of existing flags) as well as a large banner, and to work with community groups during their three-week trip to Belfast. With Gyamfi, she agreed that they would be paid around £2,130 for their work;[11] it remained unclear, however, whether the middleman would take a percentage of this amount for himself. During their stay in Belfast, Asemstim and Issaka expressed their concern about the financial arrangement; they would have preferred to be paid directly by McAnena. Although the curator felt uncomfortable about the situation, she assured me that there was nothing she could do. As was common practice with art projects, she had signed a contract with Gyamfi, assuming that she could trust the co-organiser. This left the two flag-makers in a vulnerable position. On several occasions, they complained to me that while *they* were doing all the work, they were unsure about the amount of money they would eventually be given. The fact that Gyamfi was an Ashanti (historically the arch-enemy of the Fante) did not help to create confidence. When the textile trader learnt of the flag-makers' worries he was offended, saying that the flag-makers spoiled his good name as a trustworthy businessman.

Even though the dependency of the two flag-makers demonstrated how global economics reflect and sustain inequality, it would be too easy to portray them as purely victims of an unfair system. Referring to the 1988 Aboriginal *Dreamings* performance in the Asia Society in New York, Myers (2002: 273) noted that:

[t]he view of these events simply as moments in a longer history or structure of domination or subjugation, however accurate they might ultimately prove to be, ignores the play and possibilities of the event as a form of social action that is not necessarily reducible to a past or future social state. Not only is there much to learn about the experience of such intercultural transactions by this attention; there also seems to be little alternative. A postcolonial ethnography, one that does not articulate itself within the existing relations of knowledge and power, should attend to these actors' considerations over our own critical judgements.

Asemstim and Issaka, though angered by the workload and their insecurity about payment, also visibly enjoyed their stay in Belfast. As 'stars of the show', they received positive media attention, which increased their status in Ghana. They received many compliments for their craftsmanship, skills and artistic qualities, which seemed to make them proud and happy. They were presented as representatives of Ghana and 'Fante culture', a role they had never had before, which boosted their self-image. The project also allowed them to see their own flags in a new light, as products that could be admired just for their beauty. Their stay also offered other, more unexpected moments of happiness. When McAnena showed them the documentary about flag-making, Asemstim suddenly recognised his deceased father in the film and was overjoyed.

COMMUNITY PROJECTS: POSSIBILITIES AND LIMITATIONS OF
INTERCULTURALITY

The Fante flag project involved the transit and transition of both flags *and*
flag-makers, as it redefined the flag-maker's position in a different social
set-up. In Ghana, they were independent craftsmen who were involved in
a relatively straightforward decision-making process. Normally, they were
contacted by Fante commissioners in their own studios, who communicated
directly with them about the flag designs and prices. Their familiarity with
the commissioners' expectations and their specialised knowledge of flag
iconography gave them considerable authority. Producing flags for *Asafo*
members, they also controlled their own time and could work in peace in
their own workshops.

In Northern Ireland, by contrast, the flag-makers were taken to many
different unfamiliar settings in a relatively short period of time to work with
a wide variety of groups who all had different aims and expectations. The
groups were asked to come up with a flag design that would be representative of their group identity. As the flag-makers did not know anything about
the groups, they lost control over the decision-making process. They had
to respond to ideas offered by participants, accept the roles they were given
and adapt to different styles of communication. A more detailed account
of one of the sessions will demonstrate how their position was shaped in a
particular workshop context, how Fante flag symbolism was appropriated
and combined with non-Fante symbolism, and how other factors influenced
the process of intercultural transaction and translation.

I participated in four of the 17 community projects, namely the sessions
with the Northern Irish Patchwork Guild, with a primary school class at
Malone College, with our own School of Anthropological Studies, and with
Challenge for Youth, a charitable organisation that gives support to socially
deprived youngsters. At the meeting with the women from the Northern
Irish Patchwork Guild, the flag-makers were presented as skilful artisans
who could teach the women a new technique. At Malone College, they
were rather presented as people from a far-away place, who should be
respected and who could teach the children about cultural diversity. At the
School of Anthropological Studies, interacting with the flag-makers had
theoretical significance, as it provided an occasion to be 'co-present' with
'others' and 'interact' through 'co-production'. Evidently, in all sessions, the
attraction was also to enjoy the workshop, as it enabled the participants to do
something 'unusual'. As we shall see, compared to the other three sessions,
the Challenge for Youth session was extremely informal and relatively
unstructured, as it was shaped as an event during which the youngsters
could 'be themselves' and 'explore some of their potentialities' in a safe and
non-authoritarian environment.

Asemstim, Issaka and Gyamfi were taken by car to the Challenge for Youth
address by one of the employees of the Naughton Gallery who also assisted

during the session. I met them in the street and we waited for a while, not knowing where to go. After an enquiry by mobile phone, we were told where the entrance to the building was, and a female social worker waited for us at the door. We walked through the building up the stairs to a room where three girls were half-sitting, half-lying on two couches around a small low table. The flag-makers were not formally introduced at this point, so they just looked around and sat down by themselves on some chairs. Two of the girls, about 16 years old, were very talkative. One of them had a punky outfit and the other was dressed in fancy sports clothes. A third, younger girl was dressed in her school uniform and was very quiet. 'She is new,' the social worker said, 'within a few days she'll be as loud as the others.' The Ghanaians were then introduced by their first names as Baba, Akwesi and Atta. The social worker chatted to the girls, explaining a few things about the project. We then walked for about five minutes to another building, and entered a room with a large table with about ten chairs around it. The employee of the Naughton Gallery had brought boxes with colourful textiles and two sewing machines, and the flag makers sat behind the machines and waited. Having gone through several sessions during the previous days, they seemed a bit bored.

The sporty girl half lay down on the table, the others sat on chairs. The first 10 or 15 minutes just went by with the girls chatting and teasing each other. The social worker then asked them whether they knew where Ghana was, which they did not. One girl asked about the time difference between Ghana and Britain, and Gyamfi responded. They then continued joking and telling stories amongst themselves, now and then making eye contact with the Ghanaians. After a while, the social worker urged the girls to start working on the flag, saying that 'We will have to finish it ourselves and the more we do now the more Baba will be able to help us.'

First they chose the background colour, pink, and then began to come up with ideas for the flag, making some drawings. The sporty girl suggested a devil, but when nobody reacted, she said that she wanted only her own name on it, and to use the flag as a coat. The employee from the Naughton Gallery looked somewhat embarrassed, and Gyamfi seemed uneasy, not really knowing how to react. To get the girls to think about imagery that symbolised their group, the social worker suggested to use the letters 'CFY' (for Challenge for Youth), and asked what the girls were interested in. The girls laughed and discussed (or rather, shouted and joked about) a number of topics, including love, food (one of the girls wanted to be a chef) and sport (another girl does gymnastics). Atta suggested a tortoise with eggs, referring to a Fante proverb, but hearing that, the girls exchanged puzzled looks. They did not ask for an explanation, but the sporty girl did draw a tortoise with eggs, after which the punky one said that the eggs looked like turds, and the others laughed. They did not pay much attention to the Ghanaians, something that was emphatically done in some of the other workshops.

At Malone College, for example, the teacher had stressed time and again how interesting and valuable communication with people with different backgrounds could be. At the beginning of the workshop, he had told his pupils that their 'Ghanaian guests' were going to 'show their culture', that the flag-makers would 'learn about our culture', and that the students would also 'learn something about a different culture'. The teacher further explained that their flag would be exhibited in public, and he suggested that they could use the blue and green colours of the school logo. In response, some children said they could depict the school logo itself. The teacher took the opportunity to explain the meaning of the school logo, which included images of shaking hands. Emphasising that the notion of cultural exchange had a particular local dimension, he extended his discussion of 'cultural exchange' with some words about the necessity of communication between local communities. He explained:

We did not just choose any image when we designed that. A lot of thought has gone into it. Do you see the sea and the land, the blue and the green, and the hands, each symbolising one side of the community?

Talking about the importance of cross-community relations, he linked the flag project to the official educational aims of the college. Being an *integrated* school, which accepted pupils from Catholic, Protestant and other religious (as well as non-religious) backgrounds, the teachers were expected to stimulate peaceful interaction between children from different communities. Referring to both Catholic/Protestant tensions and racism, he transformed the flag-making session into a tool for tolerance and reconciliation. In the classroom setting, the teacher was clearly in a position of (gentle) authority and the pupils (familiar with the philosophy of integrated schools), accepted his interpretation.

By contrast, during the Challenge for Youth session, the girls tried to dominate the scene. Although they did not seem to want to annoy the Ghanaian visitors, they were mainly focused on themselves, trying to impress each other by sharp and funny comments. Stimulated by the social worker, they decided on the image of a gymnast on a trapeze and the symbols of the four playing cards. The punky girl then drew a sword with a snake and two wings, and started cutting the shapes out of textile. Other images that were proposed included a vampire, a devil and a heart. 'Is there something else you do as a group?', the woman from the Naughton Gallery asked, trying to push them beyond popular teenage imagery. Having recently been involved in a football tournament, they decided on the image of a football.

As the workshop progressed, the girls and the social worker began to interact with the Ghanaians. When one of the flag-makers showed them the templates (paper cuttings in the shape of images used on the Fante flags), the girls selected the 'running man' as their 'football player'. Gyamfi said he liked the drawing of the trapeze figure, and Issaka enlarged it and cut it out in cloth. The social worker asked whether the flag could hang with the long sides down, but Gyamfi said that this was uncommon and should not be done. The girls were asked by the flag-makers to select colours for the border of their flag. When one of the girls suggested red, white and blue, they all laughed, and the social worker joked: 'Yes and then a bit of orange as well and we'll know where you come from.' She obviously referred to Unionism and the Northern Irish tradition to mark Protestant and Catholic territories using certain colours. Evidently, the political joke was not understood by the Ghanaians, who just politely smiled. Because of the emotional and political power of particular colour combinations, the organisers of the community projects had been briefed to discourage the participants of the projects from using colours which hinted at political alliances. In line with this request, the employee from the Naughton Gallery made sure that the girls made a different choice.

The above clearly shows the contextual possibilities and limitations of intercultural transaction and translation. In the case of the Challenge for Youth project, the flag was mainly designed by the girls who joked amongst themselves and did not interact much with the flag-makers. The lack of communication was partly caused by the open character of the event and the embeddedness of the girls in their own teenage world. Guided by the social worker and the employee of the Naughton Gallery, they were, however, pushed towards 'respectable' themes which signified the official aim of Challenge for Youth: to keep children of the street, offering them a stimulating social environment. Consequentially, in the case of the Challenge for Youth workshop, the main actors of intercultural translation were the girls, the social worker and the gallery employee. As a result of their negotiations, crucial decisions were made about the eventual flag design.

The knowledge and presence of the flag-makers was, of course, not irrelevant. The girls accepted the Fante image of a 'running man' and the flag was made in the style of the *Asafo* flags: the images were applied horizontally, the flag had a colourful border, and the flag-makers used a specific technique to put the flag together. As a result, the object was also a product of flag-maker–teenager interculturality, and showed considerable similarity with the other 16 community flags.

INTERCULTURAL MEANING: APPROPRIATION OF FANTE IMAGERY

Appropriation through material culture is a common tool of intercultural translation. As noted time and again throughout this book, artefacts and images do not have fixed meanings or impact; as dynamic signifiers and secondary agents they can change meaning and exercise different types of power in distinct social, spatial and material settings. The Northern Irish participants of the community projects actively appropriated Fante visual signifiers, as already illustrated by the example of the 'running man' which was chosen by the girls from Challenge for Youth.[12] A number of other Fante symbols, such as the 'pointing man', were also easily appropriated. The Fante flag-makers used this image to visually highlight the importance of a particular scene on their flags. It appeared, for example, on 'When the

cat is dead the rats will take over' – the man's finger pointing at the rats on
the shrine. The women from the Northern Irish Patchwork Guild used the
image on two flags. On one, the man's finger was directed at the Guild's logo;
on the other, at a patchwork image which portrayed the different Northern
Irish counties. The women followed the Fante example, cutting the image out
of one piece of textile. The pupils from the Assumption Grammar School in
Ballynahinch, by contrast, chose pink material for the arms, legs and head of
the figure, and dressed it in a white outfit. The figure thus became a 'teacher',
with its finger pointing at a blackboard.

Various groups used the space in the top left corner of the flag (often used
by Fante flag-makers to depict the Union Jack or the Ghanaian national
flag), for their own logo. The pupils from Malone College created an image
of the Ghanaian flag, combined with a small green map of Northern Ireland.
The symbol intended to express positive connections between Ghana and
Ireland, and to remind the pupils of their friendly interaction with the two
Ghanaian flag-makers. As with the school class, other groups also aimed to
send messages through their flags, using the artefacts as secondary agents.
The flag of the Homeless Support Team of the Ormeau Centre, for example,
included the image of a white dove with the word 'respect' on it. A red and a
green hand caressed the bird. Around the dove, the words 'Ormeau Centre.
No difference' propagated respect for *all* homeless people in Northern Ireland,
regardless of their community background.

The School of Anthropological Studies had also been invited to create a
flag that summed up the key philosophy of the discipline. One of the Fante
flags in the exhibition pictured the proverb 'Size doesn't matter when the
antelope is king', showing a small antelope on a royal stool with a much
bigger elephant standing next to it. The accompanying text explained that
this design has been popular with small companies who wished to claim
strength and superiority. As a staff member of the School of Anthropological
Studies, I suggested that we could take the antelope to symbolise the status of
anthropology as a relatively small but highly significant discipline. The other
message would be that Northern Ireland may be perceived as a peripheral
place in Britain, but that it produces quality teaching and research which
has international impact. The participants in our workshop combined the
antelope with the image of two figures who pointed at each other (referring
to the intersubjectivity of fieldwork), and the image of a large female figure
with a globe in her belly (referring to embodied knowledge). The latter was
inspired by a fascinating image we found in the book by Peter Adler and
Nicholas Barnard, of a female spirit who breastfed two smaller beings. It
symbolised the proverb 'A good spirit always looks after her young' (Adler
and Barnard 1992: 14). The spirit, Sasabansam or Funtum Yempa, was 'a
powerful and dangerous bush spirit that protects her friends and destroys her
opponents' (1992: 28–9), and, as flag imagery, she assured the protection
of the *Asafo* company. One participant suggested that the female figure with

the globe could be reinterpreted as representing anthropological knowledge. She commented:

The world has been swallowed as a symbol of internalising knowledge about people and places through human understanding. When we are born, we also come into the womb of a world that is pre-formed and births us socially. Socialisation naturalises and shapes our understanding of ourselves and others. Ideas of people, words, technologies, places and cultures in the world are often taken for granted and yet these understand- ings of the world form our being. The world resides within the woman representing the procreational capacity to continue the rebirthing of knowledge. Thus, we grasp an understanding of our social selves through revealing and concealing our rules of engagement, our systems of interaction and our processes of communication.

The participants in our group were not told about contemporary Ghanaian views about the use of spirit images, but Issaka and Asemstim had told me earlier that they would personally never portray the image of the female spirit on a flag, even though it had been a Fante tradition. They argued that, being a Muslim and a Christian, they stayed away from pagan beliefs. They did not object to our appropriation of the image, however, because they only felt responsibility for the skilful production of these flags, not for their design (see Figure 13). In addition, they saw the community flags as harmless, powerless objects without spiritual power or significance. As a result, leaders in the groups had been given permission to use the images and to reinterpret them according to particular disciplinary perspectives.

The group that remained closest to Fante imagery and proverbial meaning was the Northern Ireland African Cultural Centre. Identifying themselves with the Ghanaians as 'pan-Africans', they looked for a Fante symbol that would be relevant to their own predicament in the Northern Irish situation. They chose the image of a two-headed crocodile and a human hand, described in the catalogue as 'an important and well-known symbol in the Akan culture of West Africa'; the text further explained that '[t]his rare natural phenomenon had been adopted as a caution against infighting, [and stands for the proverb] "the two-headed crocodile has but one belly". The hand is all that is left of the man who has been a victim of cooperation' (McAnena 2003: 15). The community flag showed two hands instead of one, a white one and a black one, and intended to propagate peaceful cross-community relations in Northern Ireland. Coming from African migrants, this message was also directed against racism and promoted multiculturalism. The latter was emphasised in the speech made by James Uhomoibhi (the Nigerian director of the Centre) at the opening of the Talking in Colour exhibition. He stated that:

[i]f we can achieve the design, development and final production of the many flags that will be flown in our various groups which also will be exhibited all over Northern Ireland within three weeks, we must then accept that for a common cause of understanding one another, we can design, develop and produce that which will result in peace, progress and development of all sections of the Northern Ireland

community. These flags for us should be a symbol of unity, a symbol of sharing and caring and make us ready to support each other.

Figure 13 One of the Fante flag-makers working on the community flag for the School of Anthropological Studies, 2003. The photograph shows the original image of the Sasabansam or Funtum Yempa spirit in Adler's book, the group's interpretation of it in a drawing (without the suckling twins but with an added globe in her belly) and the flag-makers' translation of our design on the flag (the hair was added later as embroidery)

CONCLUSION

This final chapter has again proved the strengths of processual relativism, an approach that stresses the processual nature of artefact production, interpretation and experience in fields of power. Transit, in this case the movement of objects, object-makers and project managers, between Ghana and Northern Ireland, was clearly essential to Talking in Colour, and transition was inherent as the value, meaning and efficacy of the flags changed as they were moved to an art gallery setting. The flag-making process was also transformed into a series of community events which served specific social, educational and political goals, and the position of the flag-makers was temporarily redefined.

The concept of 'interculturality' was a useful tool of analysis as it helped to unravel complex processes of interaction and translation. Manipulating and communicating through the flags, the individuals involved actively interpreted their own and each others' object-focused intentions, and co-produced new forms and shared meanings. In the process, they questioned as well as reinforced boundary-creating discourses. Overcoming their differences, they undermined essentialist understandings of 'African' and 'European' identity and, stressing similarities, they emphasised their shared humanity and produced positive memories of 'shared productivity'. The latter had been the political goal of the project.

Aestheticisation shaped people's transactions and translations. Seeing particular colours, shapes and movements, individuals had particular sensorial experiences of the flags, and their engagement with the flags was also influenced by the spatial and temporal characteristics of their confrontations. Staring in silence at a flag on display in gallery is quite a different experience to singing and marching behind a flag-dancer who frantically waves the flag in a procession that passes through the territory of rival groups.

Knowledge about the Fante flag tradition, as well as familiarity with art gallery settings and community work, affected the ways in which the different actors experienced and interpreted the Talking in Colour project, and influenced the power the flags had over different individuals. People familiar with 'fine art' traditions expected to be enchanted by the works and looked for experiences of 'beauty'. Those who participated in the community events expected to be distracted from everyday problems, enriched through their confrontation with a different 'culture', or even politically empowered as they felt that the project gave them a collective voice.

As the flags were produced as commodities, and the flag-makers were paid for their active presence in Northern Ireland, commoditisation was also inherent in the process of transit and transition. The project clearly reflected and reproduced North–South economic inequalities, but also provided an opportunity for the Ghanaians to earn some money abroad and increase their social status at home. The trip also increased their consciousness of the specificity of Ghanaian and Fante life, and put the spotlight on their skills and their ability to create 'beautiful artefacts'. The perspective of 'intercultural space' thus provided valuable insights into the complex interplay of commoditisation, aestheticisation and object agency.

9   CONCLUSION

In this book I have taken a processual relativist approach to art and artefacts, stressing the processual nature of object production, signification and efficacy. I have emphasised that 'art' is a changing, historically specific discourse, and that it is therefore analytically wrong to construct it as an objective tool of analysis to compare artefact production in different societies. Instead, the book contextualised particular discourses, practices and experiences of art by showing their embeddedness in social, economic and political processes.

Part 1 explored the emergence of particular approaches to art in anthropology, critically discussing how anthropologists produced and reinforced certain ideas of art in their ethnographic studies, and demonstrating how different political and professional contexts influenced this process. It also rejected non-reflective approaches to art, which deny the effect of anthropologists' own biases on the study of artefacts, and criticised the cultural relativist paradigm, which reifies ideas of bounded culture. Instead, I have proposed in this book a processual relativist approach, which stresses the significance of 'transit' and 'transition' in relation to people's engagement with artefacts. 'Transit' referred to the location or movement of objects over time, and across social or geographic boundaries. 'Transition' examined how the meaning, value and status of those objects, as well as how people experience them, is in turn changed by that process.

The book has also sought to explain how, since the late nineteenth century, anthropological theories of art have themselves been shaped by object transit and transition. The discipline as a whole emerged from early scientific attempts to map the world through the collection and classification of natural and man-made objects. Artefacts were selected, housed and recontextualised in ethnographic museums, then 'aestheticised' as signifiers of scientific truth and agents of professional authority. In the book's analysis of this process, the concept of aestheticisation proved a useful tool.

I have used the concept of aestheticisation in a much broader sense than it has traditionally been used by scholars who define aesthetics as the essence of art. In the context of the processual relativist approach adopted by this book, aestheticisation is the process by which objects are perceived, and the ensuing sensory experience used to provide a basis for descriptions of 'aesthetic experience', which in turn are used to reinforce abstract ideas or beliefs. I have emphasised that the relationship between experience and interpretation is dialectical, as the ways in which people experience objects is often already influenced by their knowledge and expectations. In this perspective, anthropologists themselves are engaged in a similar form of aestheticisation when they turn artefacts into objects of study. By perceiving them in a particular way, stressing certain sensorial information at the expense of other such information, the objects come to stand for specific theories and convictions. Unavoidably, the same charge could be levelled at this book, which aims to present its own view of the material world.

The perspective of aestheticacation adopted by this book takes into account the fact that artefacts may be either originally created as artworks or later appropriated as art, and argues that a belief in 'aesthetic value' underlies the discursive construction of objects as art. Part 2 highlights that, in order to achieve any insights into this process, it is necessary to examine the functioning of art worlds, conceptualised as cooperative networks of art producers, critics, dealers and consumers. When entering art worlds, artefacts are not only discursively constructed but also commoditised as art, moving through chains of dealers and buyers. Presented in galleries, museums and private homes as artworks, they are primarily perceived by sight, triggering interest and admiration in viewers. Objects appropriated as art, however, often lose other meanings and forms of efficacy which may have been central to their existence prior to their transformation into art.

Focusing on the changing impact of artefacts, I used the perspective of object agency. Various case studies showed how individuals often multiply their own agency through artefacts, in a way which is intended to actively manipulate other people's feelings and behaviour. The book highlights the fact that performativity of objects is central to aestheticisation, as objects placed in strategic places necessarily interact with the senses and thereby impact on the viewer. The sensorial experience, often already influenced by existing knowledge and expectations, is interpreted in particular ways, and these interpretations sometimes reinforce particular convictions. As such, they often provide the foundation for aesthetic experience. A prestigious artwork for example, on display in a rich art collector's home, might improve the perception of his social status among visiting guests, or an emotive statue of Christ displayed in a church might stimulate church-goers to give donations. Similarly, in other examples used in the book, a Trobriand canoe design affected the actions of *Kula* partners, and political monuments reminded passers-by of the authority of their government.

In all these cases, the enactment of power was part and parcel of object transit and transition. I used the perspective of field theory to analyse the power dimensions of object transit and transition in evolving art worlds. It showed that the creation of art and aesthetic value is strongly shaped by professional dynamics, characterised by struggles for social, economic and cultural capital. These struggles are, however, also shaped by larger structural processes, such as class formation, gender inequality, discrimination and global inequality. The definition of art and its boundaries is thus a process that needs to be understood by examining artistic discourses and practices against the background of long-term historical change. Processual relativism is one way of taking up that challenge.

NOTES

1   INTRODUCTION

1. The model confronts the analyst with another problematic issue, namely the drawing of boundaries around supposedly exclusive domains of 'art' and 'culture'. Yet how do we define art as a universal category and how does 'art' differ from 'non-art'? How do we define 'culture' and where does one culture end and another begin? Furthermore, in what ways are particular definitions of 'art' informed by specific understandings of 'culture' (and vice versa), and how do specific approaches to art and culture influence the production of ethnographic knowledge about other people's engagement with matter?

2. Defining himself in opposition to scholars such as Maquet (see note 7 and Chapter 2), Anderson noted that 'rather than defining the subject of study as the things that the attuned percipient appreciates via an aesthetic attitude, I use the preceding list of recognition criteria to demarcate the domain of art and then ask "What attitudes do people have regarding them?"' (2000: 8).

3. The first characteristic feature referred to human productivity. Art objects, Anderson argued, were generally produced by human beings. Second, they were mostly created with exceptional physical, conceptual or imaginative skill. Third, he noted that art objects were generally created in a public medium, and that, fourth, they were commonly intended to provoke a sensuous effect. Finally, art objects shared stylistic conventions with other artworks produced during the same period in the same locality (see Anderson 2000: 8, 199). Influenced by the philosopher Morris Weitz (1957), he believed these indicators to be essential to most forms of artistic expression.

4. Its elements of water and soil are in constant interaction. At times, the water more or less follows the route marked by the riverbank, only causing slight changes. At other times, the currents are so strong that they break the banks and change the course of the flow.

5. Delvoye told me this by phone in 2000.

6. James Clifford noted that cultures should not be seen as bounded wholes, but that 'a "culture" is, concretely, an open-ended, creative dialogue of subcultures, of insiders and outsiders, of diverse factions' (1988: 46).

7. In 1971, Jacques Maquet (1979 [1971]) applied the concepts of 'art by destination' and 'art by metamorphosis' in his theory of aesthetic consciousness (see also Maquet 1986: 18). A few years later, Nelson Graburn (1976) used the terminology in his classification of ethnic and tourist art, as did Arjun Appadurai (1986) as part of his commoditisation theory. Shelley Errington subsequently renamed the terms by replacing the words 'destination' and 'metamorphosis' with 'intention' and 'appropriation' respectively, in order to emphasise the active and sometimes aggressive involvement of art producers in the selective nature of the transformation process (1998: 78, 277).

8. The supposed universality of emotions has been fiercely debated by cultural relativist scholars. For an overview of this debate, see Leavitt (1996), Svašek (2005a).

9. Nussbaum (2001) and Wierzbicka (2004) discuss this problem in detail.

2   FROM EVOLUTIONISM TO ETHNOAESTHETICS

1. Other influential evolutionist studies of 'primitive' artefacts were, for example, Pitt Rivers' *The Evolution of Culture* (1906 [1875]), Augustus Hamilton's study of 'the art workmanship' of the Maori Race in New Zealand (1896), and Ernst Grosse's *Die Anfänge der Kunst* (1894), which was translated into English four years later as *The Beginnings of Art* (1898; see Chapman 1985; Firth 1992: 20).
2. Directly reproducing biological methods and terminology, each chapter of *The Decorative Art of British New Guinea* (Haddon 1894) first described the geographical features of particular districts, and then analysed styles of design and ornamentation characteristic to the areas by providing general descriptions of particular stylistic 'species', and presenting concrete examples of 'actual specimens' which could be found in particular museum collections.
3. In Haddon's view, artistic development could consists of '(1) an upward or specialising evolution, or (2) degeneration, or (3) selection, which implies partial elimination and a specialisation of the selected details' (Haddon 1895: 312).
4. To decide the level of progression of a population, anthropologists determined their physical characteristics and the features of their society, and gathered information about the material and technical complexity of the artefacts they produced. Higher levels of complexity (as perceived by the evolutionists) automatically signified 'further advanced' and 'more culture'. Generally, evolutionist theory divided mankind into three main modes of being, namely 'savagery', 'barbarism' and 'civilisation'. 'Savages', who belonged to the realm of nature, lived in bands and tribes, were ruled by kinship, believed in magic and animism, survived through hunting and gathering, were nonliterate, and – of main importance to the topic of this chapter – lacked the abilities to produce works of art. 'Classical' examples of savage tribes that were thought to be extremely little evolved were Hottentots, Pygmies and Australian Aborigines. Barbarism was defined as an evolutionary phase that followed 'savagery'. The category of 'barbarians' included, for example, Chinese populations whose 'archaic' civilisations were characterised by divine kingship, agriculture, literate priesthood and an outlook on life that was mainly defined by religious beliefs. Barbarians were thought to be able to produce works of art, but their 'archaic' artistic products were regarded as relatively inferior repetitive forms, which lacked all signs of individual creativity.
5. Boas criticised, for example, the idea that the strongest development of a style in a particular region always meant that the style had originated in this region; he also disagreed with the idea that styles always take on a special form in specific areas, and he disagreed with the view that styles, once developed by particular people, were unchangeable (1955 [1927]: 4–6).
6. 'When we speak of art, we have to bear in mind that all art implies technical skill. It is therefore an improper use of the term to speak of primitive art when we refer to objects in which the producer does not possess that mastery of technique that makes the product of his labors a work of art' (Boas 1961 [1916]: 4).
7. Raymond Firth noted that these perspectives had mainly been concerned with 'detailed description of form, or with broad problems of style, origin, and development of design' (1973a: v).
8. Even in 1983, Rubin noted that:

    It is still sometimes said that traditional tribal art was a collective rather than an individual creation involving constant repetition of established formulae, to which the individual carver brought little beyond artisanal skill. My own experience with this art, on the contrary, has confirmed for me the assumption that good art is made only by gifted individuals. I am, in fact, struck by the differences rather than the similarities between tribal pieces of the same style (at least in types not standardized for European taste), and especially by the uniqueness of those works I would call masterpieces. For example, of the dozen Grebo masks I have seen no two are alike, though all include the basic constituents. The differences between these masks are just as marked as those between works by anonymous Western artists of the Medieval schools in given regions – any particular school Romanesque sculptors, for example. And the best work is distinguished by unique qualities of expressiveness and invention. (1984: 20–1)

9. Another type of political system which intrigued scholars who were interested in authority-reinforcing art was the Big Man system in Papua New Guinea. In 'Kilenge Big Man Art', Philip Dark (1973: 67) pointed out that:

> [t]he motivation for artistic activity in Kilenge lies with the desire of big men to outstrip their fellows in the social regard of their peers, to enhance their prestige by outdoing their rivals. The activation of artistic activities has its economic and social aspects, for the big man has to see to the mustering of certain resources, such as food, as well as to promote production by the artist. The kind of work the artist will produce is determined, in the large, by the big man, but in detail by the limits of the traditional repertoire of forms comprehended by the artist.

10. Various chapters in d'Azevedo's volume investigated the working procedures and aesthetic perception of individual object producers. William Bascom (1973), for example, analysed film and interview material gathered in 1950, when he had commissioned the master carver Duga of Meka to make a copy of a Shango dance wand. His chapter looked at the artist's working procedures and comments.

11. See also the chapters by Robert Farris Thompson, William Bascom and James H. Vaughan in the same volume (Otten 1971).

12. Influenced by this view, in the early 1970s, numerous anthropologists began to analyse speech-acts, contributing to the new field of sociolinguistics ('the ethnography of speaking').

13. As Dell Hymes (1983: 194) noted:

> 'Ethno' indicates the concern with analysis of cultural systems in their own terms; 'science' refers ambiguously both to the goals of the work itself, and to the assumption that native cultural systems are not imperfect versions of Western science, but products of human rationality and experience in their own right.

Ethnoscientists also used the term 'folk classification'. The concept referred to:

> the referential meaning of terms used by some folk, that is, some group of people ... . Folk systems are used by the common people, have multiple authors (usually unknown), are transmitted informally from generation to generation, and change through time. They are classification systems because they divide the world into named segments. (Kempton 1981: 3)

14. Harold K. Schneider argued that this was highly necessary because:

> scholars who discuss the art of nonliterate people sometimes seem to impute standards on them or, what amounts to the same thing, try to deduce the standards of beauty of a people by analysis of objects from their cultures. In both cases standards of beauty learned in Western cultures are used as a basis for judging what is or is not art in a nonliterate group. (1971 [1956]: 55)

15. Schneider also found that where Westerners would probably have classified a whole object as 'beautiful' or 'ugly', the Pakot would only regard parts or aspect, as aesthetically pleasing. In the case of a carved wooden milk pot, for example, his informants only thought the lip to be *pachigh*.

16. Other empiricist ethnoscientists studied how different groups of people within single cultures classified particular artefacts in different ways. Kempton (1981), for example, conducted a study on subcultural variation in terms for Mexican ceramics in 1974. As with Fischer, Kempton was highly influenced by psychology and claimed to be able to provide data which objectively mapped emic cognitive maps. He presented his informants (from three villages in the state of Tlaxcala and in Mexico City, aged from 4 to 76, and from different social and occupational backgrounds) with miniature samples of the pots and vases, as well as sheets of drawings, and asked them to name the objects and elicit gradings within categories. He also measured and weighed the samples, and explained terminological variation as an effect of different forms of expertise and modernisation.

17. He used so-called 'objective statistical tests' to test theories of the relationship of art styles to social conditions. Clearly influenced by the Culture and Personality school of thought, he noted that 'all sane persons inevitably participate to a considerable extent in the modal personality of the group', and 'the successful artist has a greater than average ability to express the modal personality of his public in his particular art medium' (Fischer 1971: 143).

18. Chapter 7 will discuss in more detail how this shift in anthropology coincided with an attack on Modernist aesthetics.

19. He added that these vague definitions 'commit the fallacy of assuming that certain institutions must, in fact, be universal, rather than recognizing that universality is a creation of definition' (Spiro 1968: 87).

20. See also Chapter 1, notes 2 and 3.

21. Criticising what he saw as the postmodern trend of anti-positivist vagueness, he added that 'it makes no more sense to speak of an eternally and universally "true" meaning of the word than it does to assert that if virtually anything has the potential to be transformed into art, then "art" must be everything' (Anderson 2000: 5).

22. Generalising abstractions have also been used by Harvey Whitehouse (2004: 3) who defined 'art' as behaviour which, like 'ritual', incorporates 'elements which are superfluous to any practical aim, and, thus, are irreducible to technical motivations'. Referring to Edmund Leach's notion of 'aesthetic frills' (1954), he argued that, when a line is drawn from A to B to mark the direction in which to walk, the action is purely technically motivated. When clouds and rainbows are added to the map, the drawing is transformed into an object which may, at least potentially, have aesthetic value. Even though it is hard to argue against this general statement, it is questionable whether it helps to gain a better understanding of art and artefacts in specific socio-historical contexts. Most things in life have more than just technical relevance, and technical objects such as tools and machines are not only designed in particular ways for technical reasons, but also to make them visually attractive to potential buyers and users.

23. He concluded that these components are *not* culture-specific, and 'consequently, aesthetic excellence may be intuitively perceived and discursively analysed cross-culturally' (Maquet 1986).

24. In 1993, Coote participated in a debate with Howard Morphy, Joanna Overing and Peter Gow about the question whether 'aesthetics' can be regarded as a cross-cultural category (Weiner 1994). Not surprisingly, their opinions were directly related to their understanding of 'aesthetics'. Overing and Gow argued that 'aesthetics' was a culturally and historically specific term, and both rejected the motion. Overing saw aesthetics as a typically Western discourse of artistic autonomy. Gow argued that aesthetic discourse and practice create social distinction, something that does not occur in all societies. Morphy and Coote defined aesthetics as a universal human capacity to sense and positively evaluate particular stimuli, properties, forms and ideas. While Morphy and Coote stated that people in societies without 'high art' have the ability to perceive and evaluate the world in an aesthetic manner, Overing objected, claiming that their broad notion of aesthetics was still based on Western values and

assumptions. She claimed, for example, that Morphy's cross-cultural definition of aesthetics assumed a rather particular 'interrelationship between the sensual and the semantic' (1994: 8).

3 FROM VISUAL COMMUNICATION TO OBJECT AGENCY

1. Only the functionalists focused on the workings of power through art, but their system approach reified the notion of bounded culture, and did not account for intra-cultural conflicts and historical change. Defining the 'function' of art as a mechanism of social stability, they assumed that art always justified the political status quo, and ignored forces of antagonism and resistance.

2. Munn (1973) noted that the functionalists had shown little interest in the study of symbols and even less in the symbolism of visual representation, as 'kinship systems' had so far been the dominant focus of research. In 1971, Edwin Ardener had similarly criticised the functionalists for their unawareness of important theoretical findings in linguistic theory (Ardener 1971; Tonkin 1989).

3. Elizabeth Tonkin (1982: 116) similarly postulated that, when analysing semantics, a 'focus on "subject and verb" is more powerful than one on "object" alone, and ... permits kinds of understanding hardly possible with systemic paradigms'.

4. In a study of the religious doctrine of the Jamaa religious movement in Zaire, Fabian examined the interplay between classification and articulation.

5. Peirce's (1839–1914) theory was based on a triadic relationship between 'objects', 'signs' (meaning attached to objects) and 'interpretants' (meaning created in the minds of individual perceivers of objects). Interpretants were signs which themselves called up new interpretants. In Peirce's words, 'There is no exception ... to the law that every thought-sign is translated or interpreted in a subsequent one, unless it be that all thought comes to an abrupt end in death' (Peirce 1958: 52, quoted by Jensen 1995: 22).

6. In racist discourse, for example, the conventional sign for 'monkey' (consisting of the sound or signifier 'monkey' and the mental image of the animal) becomes a signified when connected to the mental image of a black man. The image of 'a black man as a monkey' is then a new sign, which projects a meaning which radically differs from the primary significance of 'monkey'. In this case, the process of secondary signification produces the racist image of blacks as animal-like, uncultured beings (see also Lidchi 1997: 164, 182).

7. In 1994, the artist Vlodek, who lived and worked in Hranice, stated indignantly in a local newspaper: 'The statue of the Russian soldier in Hranice was put up after the occupation by the Soviet Army. Not after the liberation in 1945, but after the occupation in 1968!' (*Hranický Týden* 11 March 1994). Vlodek himself had been approached by a building contractor and a member of the City National Committee with the request to make the statue, but he had refused. The sculptor Rudolf Doležal, who had earlier created a five-metre-high statue depicting Stalin and Lenin, had no objections. People like Vlodek did not accept the official connotation of soldier/girl memorials, and interpreted the image rather as a symbol of Soviet domination.

8. See Lidchi (1997: 185) on Foucault's theory and the ways in which his work contrasts with that of Barthes.

9. For a critique of Foucault's denial of conscious subjective involvement in the production of discursive formations, see Lidchi (1997: 198).

10. Ironically enough, Švec did not really believe in communist values, but he was more than willing to receive 1 million Czechoslovak crowns for his design.

11. Feminist studies, such as those by Kessler (1976), Moore (1994), Behar and Gordon (1995), Ward (1996), Lancaster and DiLeonardo (1997) or Lamphere et al. (1997) do not pay any attention to artefact production. In Ward's (1996) volume *A World*

Full of Women, I found only one reference, namely to Maureen MacKenzie's (1997 [1971]) study of female-produced stringbags in Central New Guinea, in which she emphasised the symbolic, ritual and practical importance of the items.

12. Gender was only a factor in the ways the sand painting skills were taught, with more women than men learning the craft in the context of the domestic household, being taught by their parents and siblings. Men were also taught by clan-relatives who lived in other communities, both on- and off-reservation (Parezo 1993 [1982]: 230).

13. Gender studies were central to the development of a more critical examination of self in society:

> Through feminism, women were among the first to arrive at the realization that the self may only exist within social framing, and so the cliché of the individual vs. society, which had been a male myth all along, was brought into question by feminist women, who now saw the categories as not only interdependent but also problematic. (Broude and Garrard 1994a: 22)

14. Norma Broude and Mary D. Garrard (1994b) pointed out that:

> Feminist art and art history helped to initiate postmodernism in America. We owe to the feminist breakthrough some of the most basic tenets of postmodernism: the understanding that gender is socially and not naturally constructed; the widespread validation of non-'high art' forms such as craft, video, and performance art; the questioning of the cult of 'genius' and 'greatness' in Western art history; the awareness that behind the claim of 'universality' lies an aggregate of particular standpoints and biases, leading in turn to an emphasis upon pluralist variety rather than totalizing unity.

15. Impressionism, Expressionism, Surrealism, Cubism, Abstraction.

16. These artists were, in fact, inspired by much earlier, Modernist artists who had been part of Cubist, Dada and Pop Art movements, and who had incorporated 'non-artistic' fragments in their works through the use of collage techniques and the creation of the category 'objets trouvés'.

17. For example, the architects Charles Jenck and Robert Venturi.

18. He argued that anthropological descriptions of other people's cultures 'must be cast in terms of the interpretations to which persons of a particular denomination subject their experience, because that is what they profess to be descriptors of; they are anthropological because it is, in fact anthropologists who profess them' (Geertz 1973: 15).

19. 'If accorded an autonomous textual space, transcribed at sufficient length, indigenous statements make sense in terms different from those of the arranging ethnographer. Ethnography is invaded by heteroglossia. This possibility suggests an alternative textual strategy, a utopia of plural authorship that accords to collaborators not merely the status of independent enunciators but that of writers' (Clifford 1988: 51).

20. He argued that:

> Modern anthropology, that is, the work of anthropology carried out under the conditions of our time, does not search for truth and reality *behind* cultural representations. The aim now is not to cut through surface manifestations in search of a deeper, perhaps unconscious, reality, but to confront other searches for truth and reality and to negotiate knowledge through critical reasoning. (Fabian 1996: 298)

21. In an earlier book, *The Order of Things*, Foucault had noted: 'it is not that the words are imperfect, or that, when confronted by the visible, they prove insuperably inadequate. Neither can be reduced to the other's terms: it is in vain that we say what we see; what we see never resides in what we say' (1970 [1966]: 9).

22. Judy Attfield similarly argued that artefacts should not be reduced to 'a form of visual imagery that can be decoded so that an object becomes a sign system by virtue of its style, thereby dematerialising it and thus denying it the reality of physical thingness' (2000: 16).

23. In 1987 he complained that, despite increasing mass production and consumption, academics had largely avoided the study of artefacts as material culture (Miller 1987: 3). In their commodified form, he argued, artefacts were even regarded with suspicion because Marxists and conservative traditionalists had turned them into signifiers of corrupting commercialism.

24. The differences lay first and foremost in their contrasting evaluations of the importance of technical and intellectual skills, and the significance of innovation. Not surprisingly, these evaluations were not simply one-off opinions about particular artefacts but reflected wider social, professional and generational concerns which affected attitudes in everyday life.

25. The word 'aesthetics' originated from the Greek *'aisthetikos'*, and can be translated as 'perception'. The adverb *'aistheta'* means 'perceptible things'. The Greek meaning of the concept was therefore much broader than the present-day meaning of the English word 'aesthetics'. The narrow, art-oriented definition was introduced in the mid eighteenth century by German philosophers such as Immanuel Kant, who connected the term to a particular concept of 'beauty' and 'art'. The Kantian approach to aesthetics was adopted (in different versions) by English philosophers during the early nineteenth century. During the nineteenth and twentieth centuries, the majority of philosophers working in the sub-discipline of 'aesthetics' searched for universal, objective definitions of 'aesthetic value', and based their views on assumptions about the nature of beauty as reflected in aesthetic form, content, integrity, harmony, purity and fittingness (Blackburn 1994: 9).

26. Coote noted that '[w]hile our common human physiology no doubt results in our having universal, generalized responses to certain stimuli, perception is an active and cognitive process in which cultural factors play a dominant role' (1992: 247).

27. Discussing the visual qualities of individual animals was a favourite pastime. John Ryle noted that '[w]hen discussing the colour patterns of an animal – as they do for hours – the Dinka sound more like art critics than stockbreeders'(Ryle 1982: 92, quoted in Coote 1992: 251). Coote, by contrast, claimed that '[s]uch discussions are a matter of both appreciation and classification, perhaps more akin to the discussions of antique-dealers or wine connoisseurs than to those of art critics' (1992: 251). In my view, a more apt comparison is probably with more common discussions in urban areas of car models. After all, wine-tasting and antique-dealing are relatively elitist practices.

28. Appadurai's theory also made a distinction between 'singular' and 'homogeneous' commodities, defining the first category as 'commodities whose candidacy for the commodity state is precisely a matter of their class characteristics (a perfectly standardised steel bar, indistinguishable in practical terms from any other steel bar)', and the second as 'those whose candidacy for the commodity state is precisely their uniqueness within some class (a Manet rather than a Picasso; one Manet rather than another)' (1986: 16). Further distinctions were 'primary commodities' (necessities) versus 'secondary commodities' (luxuries), and 'mobile commodities' versus 'enclaved commodities' (1986: 16).

29. Gell stressed that '[i]n place of symbolic communication, I place all the emphasis on agency, intention, causation, result, and transformation. I view art as a system of action, intended to change the world rather than encode symbolic propositions about it' (1998: 6). See also Hirsch 1995.

30. In some respects, Gell's perspective further developed Roy Sieber's insights. Sieber had written that the 'impact on its audience' was 'a crucial part of the study of the arts' (1971 [1962]: 204).

31. Munn argued that:

Walbiri describe all designs as *wiri*, a term meaning 'strong', 'powerful', and also 'important'. In fact, there are distinct classes of designs that differ in relative importance and power, but the general sense of 'efficacious' applies to all of them. (Munn 1973: 33)

She noted that '[e]ach design class is connected with a specific sort of efficacy, but can only aid in attaining the ends desired when created in the right contexts and accompanied by the singing of associated songs' (1973: 34).

4   PERFORMANCES: THE POWER OF ART/EFACTS

1. The *Bedye* or pupil mask, for example, consists of a plaited head covering and is easy to make. Other headpieces are carved from wood, and some, such as the 'healer' or the 'tree' are hard to construct, and may be made by an experienced specialist.
2. 'Throughout the mask festival ... expressions of male superiority abound – in speech ('Hit the women') , in the behavior of the masks, and in the symbolism of the mask outfits and paraphernalia ... . And the central taboo of the masks concerns women: women may not come into close contact with any part of the mask, whether headpiece, paraphernalia, or especially the red fibers. Women are not supposed to know that the masks are costumed men; though of course they are perfectly aware, not only that men are inside the masks, but also who they are' (van Beek 1991: 66).
3. Griselda Pollock (1988: 80) stated that 'the goal of feminism is not to be incorporated as a new -ism to add richness to the pluralism popularly labelled post-modernism. Its base is a mass movement of women for radical social change and this makes it a revolutionary force'.
4. Even though the latter works have increasingly appeared in 'high art' settings since the 1980s, 'Aboriginal art' has often been presented as a separate category of objects. The NGV shop of the National Gallery of Victoria, for example, sells three distinct categories of art posters, namely 'international', 'Australian' and 'indigenous'. So while 'indigenous art', which included 'art by intention' and 'art by appropriation' (see Chapter 1), is labelled 'art', it is not always presented as an 'Australian' cultural expression.

5   MARKETS: ART/EFACTS ON THE MOVE

1. Several scholars have spotted disjunctions between indigenous interpretations and art-critical understandings of artefacts which have been taken by art experts and dealers from indigenous contexts to contemporary art settings (Myers 1991: 30; see also Clifford 1988; Hart 1995; Steiner 1994; Svašek 1997c; Thomas 1991).
2. Other sociologists, such as Diana Crane (1987), Vera Zolberg, Alice Goldfarb Marquis (1991) and Liah Greenfeld (1989), who examined the development of artistic careers in France, the United States and Israel, came to the same conclusion: even though artists' activities cannot be understood by economics alone, their market involvement and the impact of dealers', critics' and collectors' financial strategies must be studied if we want to understand why some artists are more successful than others (see also Moulin 1987; White and White 1965).
3. For a comparison of different analytical perspectives on the production of art and aesthetics in local, national and global art worlds, see Danto (1964, 1981, 1988), De Coppet and Jones (1984), Dickie (1975), Frey and Pommerehne (1989), Morphy (1995) and Steiner (1995).
4. See, for example, Gerbrands (1971 [1957], Olbrechts (1939), Gerbrands (1971 [1957]), Bohannan (1971 [1961]).
5. Evidently, admiration for such 'qualities' was not shared by all Europeans. Roy Porter convincingly demonstrated that Tahitian sexual mores evoked quite different reactions.

The explorer Bougainville and the surgeon Philibert Commerson had visited Tahiti in 1767, and on their return they reported that the island was a 'paradise regained' in which the people 'knew no other god than love' (Commerson 1769, quoted by Porter 1990: 119). James Cook, who visited Tahiti on several occasions, agreed that some Tahitian girls danced naked and had sex with many different men (including the rather eager European sailors), but he denied that this was typical for all Tahitian women, and compared the behaviour of the naked girls to the amoral behaviour of European prostitutes who hung around in harbours back home. The Protestant pastor Johann Reinhold Forster who also joined the expedition abhorred what he saw as extremely sinful, marked it as a sign of 'universal depravity', and denounced the Europeans for their sexual splurges (cf. Porter 1990: 138). As with Cook, he refused to construct an image which simply opposed wild heathens to completely civilised Europeans. The botanist Joseph Banks who accompanied Cook reacted rather differently. Unlike Cook and Porter, he was strongly attracted by the Tahitian girls and welcomed their willingness to have sex. Like Bougainville, he depicted the Tahitians as an exotic, erotic people, thus blending discourses of exoticism and eroticism.

6. In the eighteenth century, the portrayal of particular natives, such as the Polynesian King Kamehameha I, as skilled political beings and authoritative rulers was more or less acceptable in certain social circles, especially amongst those who tried to undermine Rousseau's plea for natural equality (Liebersohn 1999). It was, however, generally regarded as outrageous to portray non-Europeans as producers of fine art.

7. Rousseau's philosophy was based on the idea that in a natural condition, all humans were essentially free and equal, and that primitive people, being closer to nature than the civilised Europeans, were naturally good and deserved the term 'noble savages'. An idealised idea of 'nature' and 'natural sentiments' was central to the discourse of the 'noble savage', and was used as a weapon to criticise 'the artificial, corrupt ways of ancien régime Europe' (Rousseau and Porter 1990: 12). Rousseau claimed that European civilisation had generated egotism as well as social and economic inequalities. To combat this process of degeneration, he believed it was necessary to replace the hierarchical monarchal political systems by egalitarian communities which would ensure conformation to the will of all.

8. In various regions where 'tourist art' has flourished, certain objects have crossed the fuzzy boundary between souvenirs and contemporary art. Some artefacts that were originally produced as souvenirs, such as the West African *statues colons* – wooden statues representing colonial officials and European traders and travellers – have been redefined as 'fine art' in institutional settings, and now appear in important art collections and exhibitions (Werewere-Liking 1988).

9. These are 'imitation things' or 'toys' which were used for children's' play and as adult gambling chips.

10. Firth noted that in the nineteenth and twentieth centuries, 'Oceanic art ... lost much of its dynamic quality: it's forms were flattened, its design impoverished, its inspiration faded' (1992: 34). Yet modernisation and globalisation have also offered new opportunities to artists (cf. Firth 1992: 35; Graburn 1976; Layton 1991 [1981]: 202–11).

11. Marshall noted that '[e]xpectations as to what "eastern" art ought to be were formed very early indeed in the minds of European. A kind of Chinoiserie, thought to be appropriate for all the arts of Asia, was established in sixteenth-century England. When imported Indian textiles did not come up to these expectations, patterns were sent out to guide weavers in future. Most of what were thought to be 'eastern' textile designs were in fact pastiches of European ideas of what an eastern design ought to be' (Marshall 1990: 61).

12. The school curriculum often emphasised the importance of naturalist drawing and the mastering of technical skills. In other cases, students were expected to work according

to local traditions, perceived as unchanging cultural styles, but these styles were taught in school class environments.

13. In the context of the exhibition 'Africa Explores: 20th Century African Art' which was organised by the Centre for African Art in New York, Susan Vogel (1991: 11) used the term 'international art' to classify objects 'made by artists who are academically trained or who have worked under the guidance of a European teacher/patron'. She explained that '[t]hese artists live in cities, often represent their governments in international gatherings, are more widely travelled than other artists, and have a higher standard of living. Their works are shown in exhibitions, and may be sold to foreigners and international businesses as well as to governments and the elite of their own countries. Their works can be concerned with issues of form, and the meanings can be obscured to the uninitiated.' Vogel distinguished this type of art from 'traditional art', 'new functional art', 'urban art' and 'extinct art'.

14. Hughes's concern with 'authenticity' (and thus his ability to participate in the global discourse of 'high art') was also reflected in another interview, in which he discussed the difficulties African artists are faced with. He noted that:

> [S]ome collectors jumble all the various art forms in Africa together, because it is a lot easier than to carefully research their quality. For example crafts, folk art, sign writing fall within the same category as long as they are made by an African. It is ridiculous to the point where even fake poorly made contemporary artworks are valued sometimes as authentic. Whereas genuine contemporary works by trained artists are considered inauthentic, because they have been influenced by Western ideas. We do not condemn modern and post-modern Western artists for being influenced by African art. (personal communication 2005)

15. Hughes' subject matter also includes soccer players, soldiers, musicians and human heads, and his work also includes sculptures, performances, assemblages and digital photography.

6   MUSEUMS: SPACE, MATERIALITY AND THE POLITICS OF DISPLAY

1. Throughout the chapter, concrete case studies will demonstrate that exhibitions cannot but express the intentions of those who curate and control them. Curators consciously aim to influence the imagination of the viewing public, place objects in orchestrated material environments and thus enact representational power. They affect the experience and perception of the visiting public, even though individual viewers may form their own, alternative views. In Lidchi's words, '[i]n museums objects are culturally, spatially, and temporally displaced. They are recontextualised, and new layers of meaning are either superimposed over older ones or re-articulated' (Lidchi 1997: 167).

2. In connection with visual embeddedness, compare, for example, the different visual effect of a red dot on (1) a green background, (2) an orange background, (3) a white background and (4) a black background. Thinking about spatial embeddedness, compare, for example, a chair in a small room packed with furniture with the same chair standing alone in a large room.

3. In 1656, the Tradescant collection classified some of the objects as 'rare curiosities of Art & c.' (Lidchi 1997: 158). The term 'art' referred to 'human skill' and 'the artificial' (in opposition to 'the natural'). The label 'Mechanick artficial Works in Carvings, Turnings, Sowings and Paintings' also classified the objects as products of skill. The paintings to which the label referred ('several curious paintings in little forms, very ancient') were not conceptualised as aesthetic objects, but rather as curiosities (1997: 210).

4. In 1845, for example, the British Museum collection of 'Natural and Artificial Curiosities' was reorganised as the 'Ethnological Gallery'. Some established museums donated their collections of curiosa to the newly founded ethnographic museums. The Ashmolean in Oxford, for example, transferred its 'Cook collection' to the Pitt Rivers Museum when the latter was established in the 1880s. The exhibits were not just objects of ethnographic study, but also served as signifiers of the scientific status of the new discipline.

5. One of the largest collections of ethnographic objects was to be found in the Rijksmuseum voor volkenkunde in Leiden, the Netherlands. It included numerous Japanese artefacts, collected by the geographer and diplomat P.F.B von Siebold (Chapman 1985: 22–4).

6. For further discussion, see also Lidchi (1997: 168).

7. When Pitt Rivers established the Pitt Rivers Museum in Oxford in 1883, for example, one of his conditions was to employ E.B. Tylor as a Reader in Anthropology. In the United States, the American anthropologist Franz Boas, who occupied the positions of assistant curator of ethnology and somatology between 1896 and 1905, also taught at Columbia University.

8. Boas (1907: 921) had insisted that the museum should have three functions, namely of entertainment, education and research. The museums, he argued, should have a close connection with the universities, and should include both exhibition collection and study collections (in Jacknis 1985: 88).

9. The groups of life-size plaster figures showed 'a family or several members of a tribe, dressed in their native costume and engaged in some characteristic work or art illustrative of their life and particular art or industry' (Jacknis 1985: 100).

10. Pitt Rivers, for example, was very annoyed when the staff of the South Kensington Museum, which housed his collection before the establishment of the Pitt Rivers Museum in Oxford, did not follow his instructions. Boas left the National Museum in 1905 after a series of conflicts (Chapman 1985).

11. 'The work has been effected in a most satisfactory manner by a trained corps of sappers of the Royal engineers and a body of nine native workmen under the direction of Lieut H.H. Cole. ... The cast was completed on February 21st, and being packed in suitable sections, arrived at Liverpool early in June via Hoshungbad, Bombay and the Suez Canal' (*Art Journal* 1870: 5, quoted by Barringer 1998: 19)

12. Livingstone abhorred the slave trade, and sent home several accounts which described its horror, as well as a slave yoke to illustrate the cruelty of slavery. It is now owned by the museum in Blantyre in Livingstone's place of birth, and is displayed with a text saying that Livingstone himself took the yoke off a slave's neck (Cannizzo 1998: 155).

13. Currie also intended to civilise the Ovimbundu in more general terms – making them give up the practice of polygamy, live in European-type houses, wear European-type clothes and work in European-type enterprises. He sent material proofs of his successful transformation to Canada, including wooden cups and spoons, and a small violin that had been made in the mission carpentry shop (Cannizzo 1998: 163). These objects meant to show to the wider public that the Western presence in Africa had a positive civilising effect.

14. As Johannes Fabian noted, the idea of tribal identity was a pragmatic concept, and people in the emerging colonies 'gave, or were given, names that changed even as exploration was in progress' (1998: 85).

15. Obviously, while those in control of exhibition-making clearly exercise authority, they are also limited by certain constraints. There are always limits to the budget and existing collections can only include a selection of artefacts. Curators are also influenced by current exhibition trends.

16. Displays of war trophies were very popular as they spoke to images of the British military as an army that was far superior to the wild primitive hordes. Yet such displays also evoked critical comments (see Barringer 1998).

17. During the second phase of nationalism, when most of former colonies gained independence, the establishment of museums also functioned as an act of nation-building.

18. Discussing the collection of ethnographic artefacts from New Guinea, the ethnographer Haddon (see also Chapter 2), for example, claimed with pride that '[f]ortunately for us the art in our Protectorate is more varied in scope than appears to be the case in either the Netherlands or German territory' (Haddon 1894: 3).

19. Colonial aims and racial ideology underlay nineteenth-century British representations of the Chinese, who were considered to be a lazy, lawless race of stupid people, who did, however, produce 'interesting, 'splendid' or even 'magnificent' objects (Pasanin 1998: 28). By contrast, before the Opium Wars, the English had 'considered the Chinese to be a happy pig-tailed race dwelling in fanciful pavilions whose institutions were to be admired' (Paganini 1998: 28).

20. The sharing of symbols was even more important because the people who defined themselves as members of a nation would 'never know most of their fellow-members, meet them, or even hear of them' (Anderson 1991 [1983]: 6).

21. Museums also help to define the boundaries of art. Many artefacts that now appear in anthropological museums were once exchanged in the context of empire-building and colonialism. Nicolas Thomas (1991, 1994) explored the historical conditions of exchange between Europeans and the natives in the Pacific, stressing the importance of the co-presence of locals and explorers/traders/colonial officials during exchange encounters. By contrast, Chris Gosden and Chantal Knowles (2001: 6) emphasised that 'the movement of goods, gifts and ideas ... helped to reinforce difference rather than break it down'.

22. The work, written in Czech, enthusiastically described the Hussite victories over the armies of German crusaders and Roman emperors, and analysed the rise and decline of the Bohemian Kingdom. This kingdom had collapsed in 1620 after the Battle of the White Mountain, when the Czech aristocracy was defeated by Habsburg military forces sovereignty (Holy 1996: 38).

23. The Czech 'national revival' had started by the end of the eighteenth century, when linguists tried to revive the Czech language, which, at the time, was only spoken by peasants. During the nineteenth century, other intellectuals, including historians, composers and fine artists, began to look for a Czech national identity, turning to myths, legends, customs and significant historical events. A major event was the establishment of the National Theatre in 1881, which functioned as a space in which nationalists expressed and enacted their identity. Composers such as Smetana and Dvořák based many compositions on folk tunes.

24. In Prague, the Krasoumná jednota (Fine Arts Association) was founded in 1835, Jednota umělců (Association of Artists) in 1849, Umělecká beseda (Artistic Society) in 1863 and Mánes (named after the painter) in 1887. In 1900, the Klub přátel umělců (Club of Art Friends) was founded in Brno, the capital of Moravia. In 1907, the Sdružení výtvarných umělců (Federation of Visual Artists) was established in Hodonín. The Klub přátel výtvarného umění (Club of Friends of the Visual Arts) was founded in Pilsen in 1910. In Prague, the Skupina výtvarných umělců (Group of Visual Artists) was founded in 1911, and Hollar, an association of graphic artists, was founded in 1917. In Brno, artists established the association Aleš (named after the painter) in 1919 and the Skupina výtvarných umělců (Group of Visual Artists) in 1922. In Pilsen, artists founded the Spolek výtvarných umělců plzeňských (Association of Visual Artists from Pilsen) and Koliba (Shepherd's Hut) in 1923. In 1923, 1925 and 1926, regional artists federations (Sdružení) were formed in Brno, Pilsen, České Budějovice and Olomouc.

In 1937, artists from Olomouc formed the Skupina Olomouckých výtvarných umělců (Group of Artists from Olomouc).

25. Their attempts were temporarily hampered by the failed 1848 revolution, but towards the end of the nineteenth century, the nationalist movement regained strength.

26. These were the Department of Prehistory and Protohistory, the Department of Old Czech History, the Department of Modern Czech History, the Numismatic Department, the National Museum Archive, the Ethnographic Department, and the Department of the History of Physical Education and Sports.

27. 'The placing of royal collections into public or semi-public contexts involved a reconceptualisation of the space of representation as well as of the art works inside. The onus shifted gradually away from co-ordinating enclosed spaces for private pleasure or personal glorification towards an organisation based on the narratives of progress, civil refinement, and moral betterment. These were the idioms of the intelligentsia and its public sphere' (Prior 2002: 33).

28. Over the years, numerous folklore museums have been established, including the Moravský zemský muzeum in Brno, Muzeum Vysočiny in Jihlava, Horácké muzeum in Nové Město na Moravě, Valašské muzeum v přírodě in Rožnov pod Radhoštěm.

29. The mountain Říp lies in what is today North Bohemia. After seeing a flow of milk and honey, Čech decided that this country should belong to the Czech migrants, who had come from the East.

30. The Czech folklorist Jaromír Kubíček (2000) argued recently that the aesthetic value of Moravian folklore is often unwanted or unconscious, and that only a minority of folkloristic products can be regarded as *Lídové umění* (folk art).

31. The latter photograph was entitled *Vyšivačký kurs v Zubři u Rožnova* ('Embroiderer's Course in Zubři u Rožnova').

32. In 1954, the production of folklore was reorganised into a centrally directed industry.

33. Reflecting on common Western museum practices, James Clifford noted in 1988 that:

> Since the turn of the century objects collected from non-Western sources have been classified in two major categories: as (scientific) cultural artifacts or as (aesthetic) works of art. Other collectibles – mass-produced commodities, 'tourist art', curios, and so on – have been less systematically valued; at best they find a place in exhibits of 'technology' or 'folklore' (1988: 222)

34. Some collections of decorative art had evolutionary subtexts about the racial hierarchy of human progression (see also Chapters 1 and 5). In nineteenth-century London, the South Kensington Museum stated that its aim was to 'make the historical and geographical series of all decorative art complete, and fully to illustrate human taste and ingenuity'(Earle 1986: 866, quoted by Clunas 1998: 44), and while it included objects from what were regarded as the more evolved non-European areas, such as China and Japan, it excluded artefacts made by the supposedly primitive African and Australian Aboriginal races who had 'neither art nor history' (Clunas 1998: 44).

35. Clifford explained that:

> [t]he system classifies objects and assigns them relative value. It establishes the 'contexts' in which they properly belong and between which they circulate. Regular movements towards positive value proceed from bottom to top [from the inauthentic to the authentic] and from right to left [from culture to art]. These movements select artifacts of enduring worth or rarity, their value normally guaranteed by a 'vanishing' cultural status or by the selection and pricing mechanisms of the art market. (1988: 223)

36. Even though, especially from 2000 onwards, the museum addressed questions of cultural ownership, the issue remained of relative unimportance to the set-up of its exhibitions. In January 2000, it published guidelines about the repatriation of Canadian First Peoples' cultural materials housed in the Museum of Anthropology, expressing its willingness to consider special access to holdings, loans stewardship arrangements, advice on respectful storage and display, as well as the permanent return of artefacts.

37. In other words, while the impact of art is regarded as an aesthetic force that exists independent of culture, and that (at least potentially) affects all humans, the power of culture is thought to be a contextually specific force, which marks essential difference.

38. Clifford noted that artefacts displayed in the Hall of Asian People at the New York Museum of Natural History, for example, were presented in a *l'art pour l'art* fashion, and the Museum of Modern Art in New York included cultural artefacts such as furniture and home appliances in its permanent exhibition (1999).

39. In 1992, the Royal Tropenmuseum in Amsterdam organised the conference 'How to Display It? The Museological Presentation of Contemporary Non-Western Art' to discuss these trends.

40. In a symposium on 'The Global Issue', published by the journal *Art in America* in July 1989, Brian Wallis argued that museums:

   are for the most part not exhibiting the mundane, but are perpetuating a type of selectivity based on quality. That is in part the defining interest of most museums. If you have a museum exhibition that focuses on, for example, contemporary Native American culture, they are generally trying to find 'the best' of that culture – from an essentially ethnocentric point of view.

41. She also looked at the changed meaning of the genre when pieces were hanging on the walls of the house of an American tourist buyer.

42. Hart also noted that, in the context of the museum, 'the object's maker has gone from being a participant in a collective ritual process to a named and isolated bearer of the mystical spark of artistic creativity' (1995: 138).

43. He noted that:

   [t]ypical postmodern genres such as technology art, media art, feminist art and other installation art works that engage issues and ideas such as sexuality, religion, gender, the body, popular culture, political, social and economic history are yet to take firm roots in Ghana, at least. (Wemega-Kwahu 2002:15)

44. The debates have also been stimulated by calls within the fields of art history and anthropology for more reflexivity (see Chapter 3).

45. Peers and Brown (2003: 2) noted that source communities are cultural groups 'from whom museums have collected: local people, diasporas and immigrant communities, religious groups, settlers and indigenous people, whether those are First Nations, Aboriginal, Maori, or Scottish'.

46. Even though the development of anthropology as an independent professional discipline was closely related to the establishment of ethnographic museums in the nineteenth century, anthropologists began to lose interest in museum practices in the early twentieth century. Between the 1930s and the 1980s, most university-based anthropology departments were no longer involved in the collection and exhibition of ethnographic artefacts, and there was a wide social and cultural gap between the worlds of museums and academia. The study of material culture disappeared from the curriculum and museums were generally regarded as dull and theoretically uninspiring places. In the 1980s, however, this situation began to change, and today, museum- and university-based anthropologists are actively involved in joint projects and theoretical

discussions. As Stocking pointed out, this reorientation was brought about by a number of social and political factors (1985: 10–12). First, the people who, until the 1960s, had been the object of ethnographic representations began to critically assess the ways in which the established museums had confiscated and exhibited artefacts which they considered to be their own cultural property. Intellectuals in the newly established postcolonial states, as well as some self-conscious members of minority groups in the United States, Canada, Australia and other countries, became themselves active collectors, and discussed issues of ownership and representation, attacking established museums for their hegemonic policies. This resulted in a world-wide debate on the rights to repossess cultural property and, in 1970, the Unesco Convention officially prohibited the illegal global transfer of ethnographic and artistic artefacts. Second, the theoretical interest within anthropology in 'representation' and disciplinary history generated a growing body of critical studies of museum practices. Both museum-based and university-based anthropologists reflected on the political aspects of collecting and exhibiting. Since the 1980s, they have organised an increasing number of joint conferences, such as 'How to Display It' in 1992 at the Royal Tropical Institute in Amsterdam (Leyten and Damen 1992).

47. The 1970 Unesco Convention prohibited the illegal transfer of cultural property. In the same year, the Ondaga Indians claimed the Iroquois wampum belts from the New York State Museum (Stocking 1985: 11).

48. The website of the U'mista Cultural Society explained that:

> [a]lthough there was no immediate opposition to the potlatch at the time of initial contact with the white man, such opposition began to grow with the coming of missionaries and government agents. Frustration over unsuccessful attempts to 'civilize' the people of the potlatch led officials, teachers, and missionaries to pressure the federal government into enacting legislation prohibiting the ceremonies. (http://www.schoolnet.ca/aboriginal/umista2/potlatch-e.html, entered 06/02/03)

49. In Clifford's view, the notion of the museum collection was transformed or 'transculturated' in a new, hybrid context, which also responded to commercial and cultural tourism.

50. Active appropriation did not only take part on the side of the Native Canadians: '[a]s a condition for relinquishing the objects, the conservation-minded museum world successfully extended itself into the tribal world' (Clifford 1997: 212).

51. In an analysis of the community-oriented policies of the Chinatown History Museum in New York, its director John Kuo Wei Tchen (1992: 291) noted that dialogue has meant 'engaging with our audiences in mutually exploring the memory and meaning of Chinatown's past'. Instead of talking *at* people, this approach claims to be talking *with* people, giving visitors an active role in the planning and shaping of museum-related activities. As Tchen noted, this has not undermined the position of the curators, but has allowed them to take whatever they learn from the dialogues, creating valuable insights into the history of the Chinese community and their embeddedness in local and national historical contexts. Crucial is the museum's ongoing relationship with the Chinese community, a goal attained through outreach programmes.

52. She also noted that there is 'an ambivalence about sharing power. It is good to be the person who tells the story, and there is a reluctance to relinquish that position' (Peirson Jones 1992: 240).

53. About the performance area, she noted that:

> [t]he aim is here to integrate oral, intellectual, and performance aspects of culture into the static artifact exhibition and to promote intercultural understanding through person-to-person contact. I hope that a wide variety of ethnic minority and other social groups will come in to use this space in ways they determine for themselves – in ways facilitated, rather than prescribed, by museum staff. The

performance is a venue in which cultural diversity can be expressed and celebrated. Adventurous programming in this area will be a key element in making Gallery 33 a true meeting ground of cultures. (Peirson Jones 1992: 229)

54. She noted that:

Objects and images from Britain are mixed with those from 'foreign' cultures and cover a long span of time, from the archeologically known past to the present day. Exhibits have been chosen from the museum's art and local-history collections, thus breaching the traditional (and racist) divide that exists in many museums between ethnographic material (often linked with natural-history collections), on the one hand, and Western art and material culture, on the other. For example, the section on 'The Decorated Body' has thirty-five references, which include Italian plastic surgery, ancient Egyptian face paintings, British Sikh turbans, Japanese, Maori, and British tattoos, African hairstyling, and modern cosmetics. (Peirson Jones 1992: 227)

55. These included a community worker, a journalist, a photographer, an anthropologist, a curator, a librarian and two educators.

56. Legêne's (1998) analysis of four textile female slave dolls, which were taken from Surinam to the Netherlands in 1824, looked at the complex history of the dolls' social life. The historical context in which they were collected was one of colonial expansion. The Kingdom of the Netherlands had been founded after the Napoleonic wars in 1815, and its policy was aimed at the re-establishment of marine power and the expansion of colonial possessions. To demonstrate the Dutch nation's status as a colonial power, King William I established the Royal Cabinet of Curiosities, and members of numerous aristocratic and other powerful families collected objects.

57. Stocking noted that in the nineteenth century, while some objects were part of deliberate collections that took place in the context of colonial politics, others were rather haphazardly collected souvenirs. Integrated into single collections, the meaning linked to the collectors' experiences, investigations and activities is often lost (see also Legêne 1998).

58. At the same time, the use of computer technology has increased the spectacular element of the museum, which increases the risk of 'having to depend on shallow, deracinated images' (Lavine 1992: 146).

59. *Khalsa*, 'the fellowship of the pure', was founded in 1699 by Guru Gobind Singh.

60. Evidently, all interpretations require active signification, meaning that signifiers are connected to signifieds, thus creating signs which reinforce certain discursive formations. This means that although, on a theoretical level, different aspects of curatorship can be easily separated into 'the investigation and handling of matter' and 'the manipulation of visual and material signs', these processes cannot be analysed in isolation from each other.

61. The following account illustrates that, similarly, works of 'art' do not necessarily enchant gallery visitors. Unimpressed by a display of Jo Spence's photographs, one of my students wrote in 2004:

I didn't particularly want to go to this exhibition [Jo Spence at Belfast Exposed], but a friend of mine in Film Studies had to go for some reason and I got dragged into agreeing to sign away half an hour of my life I have since regretted losing. Before walking in I had absolutely no idea of what to expect from the exhibition beyond that it wasn't on the top of my 'To Do' list, as the sun had successfully broken through and it was reasonably warm ... . As I didn't want to be there in the first place I didn't read too much in depth, but skim read the passages and largely ignored the photos. From what I picked up from the passages the artist had led a particularly hard life at times, and had picked up a rather strong Feminist bent, which if I'm honest served only to disengage myself further from the exhibition ... . By the time we left it had clouded over, and while walking to a Taxi rank it began to rain, and I distinctly remember promising myself I wouldn't inflict anything like that on myself for no damn reason again.

7 'FINE ART': CREATING AND CONTESTING BOUNDARIES

1. In France, artists were even regarded as royal 'property', and had to ask the king for permission if they wished to work for someone else (Prior 2002: 30).
2. Traditional craft has, of course, inspired artists, especially in the context of nationalist ideology, as was clarified in Chapter 6.
3. Becker (1982: 279) noted that:

   > People who pay $200 for a small, beautifully turned bowl will not feel cheated if they find there is another more or less like it. What they bought exhibits the virtuoso craftsmanship they pay for. Had they bought the same bowl on the assumption that is was a unique work of art, they *would* feel cheated to find that there were two.

4. Not surprisingly, industrial designers did not accept this redefinition because it undermined their own claims to artistic status. In their view, in their own professional field, it was the designers who were creative and innovative, and who needed craftsmen who just had the technical and physical skills to make copies.
5. This is part of a longer statement in which she explains that she uses a different, genderless definition of art and craft.

   > I do think there's a distinction between art and craft, and I think it's a distinction that needs to be maintained. However I do not think it's the historical distinction. I think the historical distinction is – if men do it it's art and if women do it it's craft ... I think there's a tremendous amount of sexism and racism and classicism in the traditional distinctions between art and craft, and what I use myself as a working distinction is that in art, the technique or the material is in the service of meaning, and in craft, the technique or the material or the process is an end in itself. (Parker and Pollock 1987)

6. Producers of wall paintings and painters of domestic furniture.
7. While some scholars argue that the word 'kitsch' derives etymologically from the English 'sketch', others believe that it was taken from the German verb '*verkitschen*', 'to make cheap' (Dorfles 1968b: 10). The philosopher Tomáš Kulka has looked for a universal definition of kitsch, in which all conditions are context- and culture-dependent. He identified the following three conditions: 'Kitsch depicts objects or themes that are highly charged with stock emotions', 'The objects or themes depicted by kitsch are instantly and effortlesly identifiable' and 'Kitsch does not substantially enrich our associations relating to the depicted objects and themes.'
8. The Marxists attacked sentimental depictions of religious and folkloristic themes as conservative propaganda, and offered, instead, images of the international proletariat, consisting of strong and proud workers who believed in progressive unity. Ironically, much Marxist propaganda contained what can be called kitschy elements. Depictions of working-class families, for example, were often sentimental clichés.
9. As Alice Goldfarb Marquis (1991: 97–8) argued:

   > [h]aving chosen [the painter] Jackson Pollock as the star of his day, Greenberg invested many hours and days in critiquing his work, suggesting improvements, and promoting sales. The critic 'seemed a combination of patron, mentor and career mover', said one observer. Elaine de Kooning [wife of the painter Willem de Kooning] told an interviewer that 'Clem acted as an unpaid p.r. man, furthering the artist's career more than any dealer.'

10. In Calinescu's view, kitsch art is less revolutionary than avant-garde art:

> The kitsch artist mimics the avant-garde only to the extent to which the latter's unconventionalities have proved successful and have been widely accepted or even turned into stereotypes. For kitsch, by its very nature, is incapable of taking the risk involved in any true avant-gardism.

11. On Nazi propaganda and art, see, for example, Thomae (1978) and Wistrich (1995).

12. Hermann Broch claimed in the early 1950s that evil was inherent in kitsch, and that there was a strong relationship between neurosis and kitsch, demonstrated by Hitler's love of kitsch (1968 [1950–1]: 68).

13. Ad Reinhardt, Mark Rothko, Adolph Gottlieb, Robert Motherwell and Lee Krasner.

14. Some defined themselves as 'anti-Stalinist' supporters of the left (Craven 1999: 3).

15. A striking example, which combined all elements of Socialist Realist iconography, was the monumental painting *Thanksgiving of the Czech and Slovak People to Generalissimo Stalin* (*Díkuvzdání českého a slovenského lidu Generalissimu Stalinovi*) by Jan Čumplelík, Jaromír Schor and Alena Čermáková, which was completed in 1952. In line with Stalin's personality cult, it depicted the Soviet leader standing high on a podium surrounded by a mass of jubilant industrial workers, miners, farmers, intellectuals, children and old people. The stairs and the podium were covered in flowers and the people held up well-known communist symbols, such as a painted jug (as a symbol of politically sound folklore), and a model of a locomotive (as a symbol of industrialisation and economic progress). The upper half of the painting was dominated by large billowing Czechoslovak and Soviet flags, symbolising the fraternity of the two nations (Svašek 1996: 45).

16. At the time of the founding of the Czechoslovak Republic in 1918, the Czech art world had been relatively independent from political institutions, as the Republic's democratic ideals did not support a close connection between art and politics (even though it was keen on a positive attitude toward Czech nationalism). Czech artists competed amongst themselves for access to the international art market, and numerous art associations and galleries were established. After a five-year period of censorship during Nazi occupation, the art world continued to promote a wide diversity of styles. The new communist government that was established after the 1948 coup made an end to this.

17. The same happened when, after a short period of relative freedom between 1957 and 1969 (a period ended by the invasion of Czechoslovakia by the Soviet-led Warsaw Pact Army in 1968, and the subsequent 'normalisation' of Czechoslovak society), hardliners in the Communist Party regained control and new unofficial groups were founded. To avoid intervention by the Secret Police, only select groups of personal friends were invited to the secret exhibitions, but one could never be sure just how far their network of information extended. According to the art historian Zdenka Gabalová (1990: 4): '[i]t was a joke at that time that if you had not had your exhibition closed down by the police then you were simply not very good'.

18. A year later, he exhibited the jar together with a request from the library to return the book. As a result, he was dismissed from his teaching position.

19. Judy Chicago and Miriam Shapiro set up the Feminist Art Program at the California Institute of the Arts in 1971. Female sexuality was an important theme in the programme.

20. He further argued that 'pornography is by nature crude and rough and raises no aesthetic or philosophical issues; it does not attempt to defend itself, does not try to hide its morbid character, and does not claim to be an art or a science' (Volli 1968: 224).

21. The original drawings had been made by Giulio Romano.

22. As Lynn A. Hunt (1993: 9–10) noted: '[i]n early Modern Europe, that is, between 1500 and 1800, pornography was most often a vehicle for using the shock of sex to criticize religious and political authorities'.

23. This was the Düsseldorf edition. The French original had been published in 1683.

24. This perspective was also central to the work of Walter Benjamin (1968), who argued that only the mental work of serious concentration led to aesthetic experience. Aesthetic perception required the absorbing of the viewer by the artwork. By contrast, the immediacy of eager consumption perhaps resulted in instant satisfaction, but also gave no space to the agency of the object. In the latter case, it was the viewer who absorbed the work, and not vice versa.

25. Personal communication 2004.

26. The students took the module Anthropology of Art.

27. The 'ethnographic artefacts' included, for example, bark paintings by Australian Aboriginals from Arnhem Land; a wooden statue which represented a Polynesian god of cultivation and fertility; a figure with an erect penis, cut in turf on a chalk hill in Dorset; ceremonial bark-cloth costumes representing forest spirits, made by Cuna Indians in Panama; and figures made of raffia and wood on a mask intended partly as sexual instruction. The images were taken from the book *Primitive Erotic Art* (Rawson 1973). The examples of 'Western art' were mainly taken from the book *Erotic Art of the West* (Melville 1973), and included classical Greek images: *Galatea* by Raphael: *Cupid and Psyche* by Gérard, *Friends* and *Danae* by Gustav Klimt, and others.

28. In this perspective:

> [h]ard-core pornography lacks cultural distinction, its function is merely and solely that of sexual arousal and sensual gratification. Erotic art, on the other hand, takes on the didactic role of high art and lifts the depiction of desire to a higher cultural plane. Desire is thus contained and controlled by the aesthetic. Erotic art arouses, but it is a reflective and enriching form of arousal. (Nead 1991: 144)

29. In the United States, many types of 'outsider art' have, however, become 'insider art' as their production has been increasingly institutionalised, for example through their appearance in the annual Outsider Art Fair (first organised in 1992). These objects have clearly made a transformative journey.

8   PROCESSUAL RELATIVISM: FANTE FLAGS IN NORTHERN IRELAND

1. It was organised on 2 November 2004, and was part of El Dia de Los Muertos – The Day of the Dead exhibition. The exhibition was curated by the art historian Chloe Sayer, who has a large collection of Mexican artefacts which are used in Day of the Dead rituals.

2. Akwesi Asemstim, Baba Issaka and their interpreter, an Ashanti textile trader who had coordinated the project in Ghana, were present during the opening. So were most of the artists, some members of the community groups, and other people who had received an invitation. As is usual during exhibition openings, drinks were offered, and the crowd walked around, chatted and looked at the flags. The official opening started with the entrance of a group of African drummers, dancers and singers, and continued with speeches made by the organiser of the project, Shan McAnena and James Uhomoibhi, the Nigerian director of the Northern Ireland African Cultural Centre. The twelve dancers were visitors from South Africa from Umtapo Centre, based in Durban, KwaZulu Natal. Their performance had been organised by the Northern Ireland African Cultural Centre.

3. One public lecture about the Fante flag-making tradition given by McAnena, and two lectures for art history students about the power of the flags by myself.

4. John Picton (1993: 21) noted that the *ethnographic* interest in the meaning and context of Fante flags has turned the flags into markers of particular narratives. In his view, this has taken the viewers' attention away from the flags themselves.

5. On an earlier trip to Ghana, McAnena had visited the two flag-makers in their home towns, and had commissioned them to each make ten flags that best reflected their skills and the range of flags they normally produced (McAnena 2003: 10).

6. The community groups included the Northern Ireland Patchwork Guild, four secondary school classes, one youth group, two day centres for the elderly, the Northern Ireland African Cultural Centre, the Chinese Welfare Association, the Belfast Travellers' Support Group, the Homeless Support Team, the Northern Ireland Social and Political Archive, and the School of Anthropological Studies.

7. A year before the exhibition was held, increasing outbursts of racism in Belfast led the media to call Belfast 'the racist capital of Europe'.

8. As far as I know, it is not known whether, before the introduction of money, the *frankaa* were exchanged for other goods, or whether flag-making was simply a duty, performed by specialised company officers. As flag-making has become paid employment, flag-makers are not necessarily company members. Asemstim was an officer of No. 1 Benti Company in Kromantze, but Issaka was not associated with any particular *Asafo* company.

9. On his website, Messick described himself, amongst other things, as a former professional social worker, bottle washer, poet, hotel manager, violinist, website editor, flower child and total loser. Messick's proclaimed objective for the site was 'education through art', providing photographs of artefacts (many not for sale) as well as short texts about poverty, political unrest, and violence in a special section called 'A Current Events "Museum"'. His critical text about Ghana accused the Ghanaian government of neglecting the drier inland regions of the North.

10. Messick indicated that he had traded one his flags with a former US ambassador to Ghana for a NgBaka statue, and that several others came from the above-mentioned Charles Jones African Art, or from Duncan Clarke, author of *The Art of African Textiles* (2002 [1997]).

11. Gyamfi was paid £25 per flag, and £500 for the banner. Furthermore, the flag-makers would get a weekly salary of £250 while they were in Belfast, plus a daily allowance of £15. Their flights and accommodation were paid for by the project.

12. Not all groups incorporated 'original' Fante images in their flag designs, but if they did, these had either been provided by Asemstim and Issaka, or were taken from the book *Asafo! African Flags of the Fante*. This book included 210 photographs of Fante flags with brief explanations, and a text which described the flags as 'a wonderfully graphic and kinetic tribal art form' (Adler and Barnard 1992: 7). It had accompanied the exhibition Asafo: The Flags of the Fante Regiments, organised in 2003 in the Museum of Modern Art in Oxford. I had been given the book by a colleague, and took it to some of the community events, where participants leafed through it for inspiration.

BIBLIOGRAPHY

Adams, Jacqueline 2001 'The Makings of Political Art', *Qualitative Sociology* 24(3): 311–48.

Adler, Peter and Barnard, Nicholas 1992 *Asafo! African Flags of the Fante*. London: Thames and Hudson.

Adrichem, Jan van 1985 'Gecontroleerde waanzin. De ambivalente schilderijen van Milan Kunc' ('Controlled Madness: The Ambivalent Paintings of Milan Kunc'), *Museumjournaal* 1.

al-Khalil, Samir 1991 *The Monument: Art, Vulgarity and Responsibility in Iraq*. Berkeley and Los Angeles: University of California Press.

Ames, Michael M. 2003 'How to Decorate a House: The Renegotiation of Cultural Representations at the University of British Columbia Museum of Anthropology', pp. 171–80 in Laura Peers and Alison K. Brown (eds) *Museums and Source Communities: A Routledge Reader*. London and New York: Routledge.

Anderson, Benedict 1991 [1983] *Imagined Communities: Reflections on the Origin and Spread of Nationalism*. London: Verso.

Anderson, Richard L. 1979 *Art in Primitive Societies*. Englewood Cliffs, NJ: Prentice Hall.

—— 2000 *American Muse: Anthropological Excursions into Art and Aesthetics*. Upper Saddle River, NJ: Prentice Hall.

Anderson, Richard L. and Field, Karen L. (eds) (1993a) *Art in Small-scale Societies. Contemporary Readings*. Englewood Cliffs, NJ: Prentice Hall.

—— (1993b) 'New Directions: The Beholder's Share', pp. 388–9 in Richard L. Anderson and Karen L. Field (eds) *Art in Small-scale Societies: Contemporary Readings*. Englewood Cliffs, NJ: Prentice Hall.

Appadurai, Arjun 1986 'Introduction: Commodities and the Politics of Value', pp. 3–63 in Arjun Appadurai (ed.) *The Social Life of Things: Commodities in Cultural Perspective*. Cambridge: Cambridge University Press.

Archer, Michael 1997 'Interview: Michael Archer in Conversation with Mona Hartoum', p. 31 in Michael Archer, Guy Brett and Catherine de Zegher (eds) *Mona Hatoum*. London: Phaidon.

Archer, Michael, Brett, Guy and de Zegher, Catherine (eds) 1997 *Mona Hatoum*. London: Phaidon.

Arderner, Edwin 1971 'Introductory Essay: Social Anthropology and Language', pp. ix–cii in E.W. Ardener (ed.) *Social Anthropology and Language*, ASA Monograph 10. London: Tavistock Publications.

Art Crime (n.d.) 'Piss Christ', http://renewal.org.au/artcrime/pages/serrano.html (accessed October 2006).

Art in America (1989) Special Issue 'The Global Issue', July.

Arts Law (n.d.) 'Piss Christ Exhibition 97.4', http://artslaw.com.au/reference/piss974/ (accessed 17/11/2004).

Attfield, Judy 2000 *Wild Things: The Material Cultures of Everyday Life*. Oxford: Berg.

Babcock, Barbara A. 1997 'Mudwomen and Whitemen: A Meditation of Pueblo Potteries and the Politics of Representation', pp. 420–39 in Louise Lamphere, Helena Ragoné and Patricia Zavella (eds) *Situated Lives: Gender and Culture in Everyday Life*. New York and London: Routledge.

Barber, Karin 1986 *The Popular Arts in Africa*. Birmingham: Centre of West African Studies.

Barré, M.L. 1877 *Musée Secret*, vol. 8. Naples: National Museum of Naples.

Barringer, Tim 1998 'The South Kensington Museum and the Colonial Project', pp. 11–27 in Tim Barringer and Tom Flynn (eds) *Colonialism and the Object: Empire, Material Culture and the Museum*. London and New York: Routledge.

Barthes, Roland 1977 *Image Music Text*. London: Fontana Press.

—— 1980 [1956] 'Myth Today', pp. 93–149 in *A Barthes Reader*, edited by Susan Sontag. London: Vintage.

Bascom, William 1969 'Creativity and Style in African Art', pp. 98–119 in D.P. Biebuyck (ed.) *Tradition and Creativity in Tribal Art*. Berkeley: University of California Press.

—— 1973 'A Yoruba Master Carver: Duga of Meko', pp. 62–78 in Warren L. d'Azevedo (ed.) *The Traditional Artist in African Societies*. Bloomington: Indiana University Press.

Bastian, Adolf 1860 *Der Mensch in der Geschichte* (Mankind in History). Leipzig.

—— 1871–73 *Ethnologische Forschungen* (Ethnological Researches). Leipzig.

Baxandall, Michael 1972 *Painting and Experience in Fifteenth-century Italy*. Oxford: Oxford University Press.

Becker, Howard S. 1982 *Art Worlds*. Berkeley: University of California Press.

Behar, Ruth and Deborah A. Gordon 1995 *Women Writing Culture*. Berkeley: University of California Press.

Ben-Amos, Dan 1977 'Introduction: Folklore in African Society', pp. 1–36 in Bernth Lindfors (ed.) *Forms of Folklore in Africa: Narrative, Poetic, Gnomic, Dramatic*. Austin: University of Texas Press.

Benjamin, Walter 1968 'The Work of Art in the Age of Mechanical Reproduction', *Illuminations*, trans. Harry Zohn. New York: Schocken Books.

Bennett, Tony 1995 *The Birth of the Museum: History, Theory, Politics*. London and New York: Routledge.

Berger, John 1972 *Ways of Seeing*. London: BBC.

Betterson, Rosemary 1996 *An Intimate Distance: Women Artists and the Body*. London and New York: Routledge.

Bevers, Ton (ed.) 1993 *De kunstwereld. Produktie, distributie en receptie in de wereld van kunst en cultuur* (The Artworld: Production, Distribution and Reception in the World of Art and Culture). Hilversum: Verloren.

Binkley, David A. and Darish, Patricia J. 1998 ' "Enlightened but in Darkness": Interpretations of Kuba Art and Culture at the Turn of the Twentieth Century', pp. 37–62 in Enid Schildkrout and Curtis A. Keim (eds) *The Scramble for Art in Central Africa*. Cambridge: Cambridge University Press.

Blackburn, Simon 1994 *The Oxford Dictionary of Philosophy*. Oxford: Oxford University Press.

Blackman, Margaret B. 1993 [1980] 'Master Carpenters' Daughters: Women Artists of the Northwest Coast', pp. 233–46 in Richard L. Anderson and Karen L. Field (eds) *Art in Small-scale Societies: Contemporary Readings*. Englewood Cliffs, NJ: Prentice Hall.

Boas, Franz 1961 [1916] 'Representative Art of Primitive People'. In *Holmes Anniversary Volume*. Washington: Bryan Press.

—— 1955 [1927] *Primitive Art*. New York: Dover Publications.

—— n.d. Frederic Ward Putnam Papers: Correspondence. Harvard University Archives, Cambridge, MA.

Boffin, Tessa and Fraser, Jean (eds) 1991 *Stolen Glances: Lesbians Take Photographs*. London: Pandora.

Bohannan, Paul 1971 [1961] 'Artist and Critic in an African Society', pp. 172–81 in *Anthropology and Art: Readings in Cross-cultural Aesthetics*, in Charlotte M. Otten (ed.) New York: Natural History Press.

Boidi, Adriana and Etal, Sassone 1988 *Furniture from Roccoco to Art Deco*. Cologne: Evergreen.

Bolz, Peter 1999 'Erstehung und Geschichte der Berliner Nordamerika-Sammlung', pp. 23–49 in Peter Bolz and Hans-Ulrich Sanner (eds) *Indianer Nordamerikas: Die Sammlungen des Ethnologischen Museums Berlin*. Berlin: Staatliche Museen zu Berlin, Preussischer and G+H Verlag.

Bourdieu, Pierre 1977 *Outline of a Theory of Practice*, trans. Richard Nice. Cambridge: Cambridge University Press.

—— 1979 'Symbolic Power', *Critique of Anthropology* 4(3–4): 77–85.

—— 1984 [1979] *Distinction: A Social Critique of the Judgement of Taste*. London and New York: Routledge and Kegan Paul.

—— 1993 *The Field of Cultural Production: Essays on Art and Literature*. New York: Columbia University Press.

Bourdieu, Pierre and Darbel, Alain 1969 *L'Amour de l'art: le musée et son public*. Paris: Editions de Minuit.

Bright, Deborah 1991 'Dream Girls', pp. 144–54 in Tessa Boffin and Jean Fraser (eds) *Stolen Glances: Lesbians Take Photographs*. London: Pandora.

Broch, Herman 1968 [1950–51] 'Notes on the Problem of Kitsch', pp. 49–67 in Gillo Dorfles (ed.) *Kitsch: An Anthology of Bad Taste*. London: Studio Vista.

Broude, Norma 1994 'The Pattern and Decoration Movement', pp. 208–25 in Norma Broude and Mary D. Garrard (eds) *The Power of Feminist Art: The American Movement of the 1970s*. History and Impact. New York: Harry N. Abrams.

Broude, Norma and Garrard, Mary D. (eds) 1994a *The Power of Feminist Art: The American Movement of the 1970s. History and Impact*. New York: Harry N. Abrams.

—— 1994b 'Introduction: Feminism and Art in the Twentieth Century', pp. 10–29 in Norma Broude and Mary D. Garrard (eds) *The Power of Feminist Art: The American Movement of the 1970s. History and Impact*. New York: Harry N. Abrams.

—— 1994c 'Conversation with Judy Chicago and Miriam Shapiro', pp. 66–85 in Norma Broude and Mary D. Garrard (eds) *The Power of Feminist Art: The American Movement of the 1970s. History and Impact*. New York: Harry N. Abrams.

Brydon, Anne 2001 'High Art Down Home: An Economic Ethnography of a Local Art Market by Stuart Plattner', *Ethnology* 23(1): 326–9.

Burland, Cottie 1973 'Africa, South of the Sahara', pp.197–251 in Philip Rawson (ed.) *Primitive Erotic Art*. London: Weidenfeld and Nicolson.

Calinescu, Matei 1987 *Kitsch: Five Faces of Modernity – Modernism, Avant-garde, Decadence, Kitsch, Postmodernism*. Durham, NC: Duke University Press.

Campbell, Shirley 2001 'The Captivating Agency of Art: Many Ways of Seeing', pp. 117–35 in Christopher Pinney and Nicholas Thomas (eds) *Beyond Aesthetics: Art and Technologies of Enchantment*. Oxford: Berg.

—— 2002 *The Art of Kula*. Oxford: Berg.

Cannizzo, Jeanne 1998 'Gathering Souls and Objects: Missionary Collections', pp. 153–66 in Tim Barringer and Tom Flynn (eds) *Colonialism and the Object: Empire, Material Culture and the Museum*. London and New York: Routledge.

Čelebonović, Aleksa 1968 'Notes on Traditional Kitsch', pp. 280–9 in Gillo Dorfles (ed.) *Kitsch: An Anthology of Bad Taste*. London: Studio Vista.

—— 1974 *The Heyday of Salon Painting: Masterpieces of Bourgeois Realism*. London: Thames and Hudson.

Chadwick, Whitney 1990 *Women, Art and Society*. London: Thames and Hudson.

Chapman, William Ryan 1985 'Arranging Ethnology: A.H.L.F. Pitt Rivers and the Typological Tradition', pp. 15–48 in George W. Stocking (ed.) *Objects and Others: Essays on Museums and Material Culture*. Madison: University of Wisconsin Press.

Christensen, James Boyd 1954 *Double Descent Among the Fanti*. New Haven, CT: Human Relations Area Files.

Clark, Toby 1997 *Art and Propaganda in the Twentieth Century: The Political Image in the Age of Mass Culture*. London: Everyman Art Library.

Clarke, Duncan 2002 [1997] *The Art of African Textiles*. London: Grange.

Clifford, James 1988 *The Predicament of Culture: Twentieth-century Ethnography, Literature, and Art*. Cambridge, MA: Harvard University Press.

—— 1989 'Interview with Brian Wallis', *Art in America* (Special Issue 'The Global Issue') July: 86, 151, 152.

—— 1991 'Four Northwest Coast Museums: Travel Reflections', pp. 212–54 in Ivan Karp and Steven D. Lavin (eds) *Exhibiting Cultures: The Poetics and Politics of Museum Display*. Washington and London: Smithsonian Institution.

Clifford, James and Marcus, George E. (eds) 1986 *Writing Culture: The Poetics and Politics of Ethnography*. Berkeley: University of California Press.

Clunas, Craig 1998 'China in Britain: The Imperial Collections', pp. 41–51 in Tim Barringer and Tom Flynn (eds) *Colonialism and the Object: Empire, Material Culture and the Museum*. London and New York: Routledge.

Cockroft, Eva 1974 'Abstract Expressionism, Weapon of the Cold War', *Artforum* June: 39–41.

Cohen, Abner 1974 *Two-dimensional Man: An Essay on the Anthropology of Power and Symbolism in Complex Society*. Berkeley: University of California Press.

Cole, Herbert M. and Ross, Doran H. 1977 *The Arts of Ghana*. Los Angeles: Museum of Cultural History, University of California.

Commerson, Philibert 1769 'Lettre de M. Commerson, docteur en medicine', *Mercure de France*.

Congressional Record, 18 May 1989, http://www.csulb.edu/~jvancamp/361_r7.html (accessed 16/11/2004).

Conway, M. 1882 *Travels in South Kensington*. London: Trubner.

Cooks, Bridget R. 1997 'Complicated Shadows: Challenging Histories of Cultural Representation in Contemporary Art', *Focaal* 29: 25–36.

Coote, Jeremy 1992 ' "Marvels of Everyday Vision": The Anthropology of Aesthetics and the Cattle-keeping Nilotes', pp. 209–44 in Jeremy Coote and Anthony Shelton (eds) *Anthropology, Art and Aesthetics*. Oxford: Oxford University Press.

Coote, Jeremy and Shelton, Anthony (eds) 1992 *Anthropology, Art and Aesthetics*. Oxford: Oxford University Press.

Copp, David and Wendell, Susan 1983 *Pornography and Censorship*. Buffalo, NY: Prometheus Books.

Cox, Annette 1982 [1977] *Art-as-Politics: The Abstract Expressionist Avant-garde and Society*. Epping: Bowker Publishing Co.

Crane, Diana 1987 *The Transformation of the Avant-garde*. Chicago: University of Chicago Press.

Crane, Walter 1888a 'Preface', pp. 5–10 in *Catalogue of the First Exhibition* (The New Gallery). London: Arts and Crafts Exhibition Society.

—— 1888b 'Of Decorative Painting and Design', pp. 29–38 in *Catalogue of the First Exhibition* (The New Gallery). London: Arts and Crafts Exhibition Society.

Craven, David 1999 *Abstract Expressionism as Cultural Critique: Dissent during the McCarthy Period*. Cambridge: Cambridge University Press.

Crew, Spencer R. and Sims, James E. 1991 'Locating Authenticity: Fragments of a Dialogue', pp. 159–75 in Ivan Karp and Steven D. Lavine (eds) *Exhibiting Cultures: The Poetics and Politics of Museum Display*. Washington and London: Smithsonian Institution Press.

Danto, Arthur C. 1964 'The Artworld', *Journal of Philosophy* 61: 571–84.

—— 1981 *Transfigurations of the Commonplace: A Theory of Art*. Cambridge, MA: Harvard University Press.

—— 1988 'Artifact and Art', pp. 18–32 in Suzanne Vogel (ed.) *Art/Artifact: African Art in Anthropology Collections*. New York: Center for African Art and Preston Verlag.

d'Azevedo, Warren L. (ed.) 1973 *The Traditional Artist in African Societies*. Bloomington: Indiana University Press.

Dark, Philip 1973 'Kilenge Big Man Art', pp. 49–69 in Anthony Forge (ed.) *Primitive Art and Society*. London: Oxford University Press.

De Coppet, Laura and Jones, Alan 1984 *The Art Dealers: The Powers behind the Scenes Tell How the Art World Really Works*. New York: Potter.

DeGraft Johnson, J.C. 1932 'The Fanti Asafu', *Africa* 5: 307–22.

Delcourt, Jean Paul and Scanzi, Giovanni Franco 1987 *Potomo Waka*. Milan: Editions Lediberg.

Dickie, George 1975 *Art and the Aesthetic: An Institutional Analysis*. Ithaca, NY: Cornell University Press.

DiMaggio, Paul J. (ed.) 1986 *Nonprofit Enterprise in the Arts: Studies in Mission and Constraint*. New York: Oxford University Press.

Dockstader, Frederick J. 1973 'The Role of the Individual Artist', pp. 113–25 in Anthony Forge (ed.) *Primitive Art and Society*. London: Oxford University Press.

Dorfles, Gillo (ed.) 1968a *Kitsch: An Anthology of Bad Taste*. London: Studio Vista.

—— 1968b 'Introduction', pp. 9–12 in Gillo Dorfles (ed,) *Kitsch: An Anthology of Bad Taste*. London: Studio Vista.

Duncan, Carol 1991 'Art Museums and the Ritual of Citizenship', pp. 88–103 in Ivan Karp and Steven D. Lavine (eds) *Exhibiting Cultures: The Poetics and Politics of Museum Display*. Washington, DC and London: Smithsonian Institution.

Errington, Shelley 1998 *The Death of Authentic Art and Other Tales of Progress*. Berkeley: University of California Press.

Fabian, Johannes 1975 *Taxonomy and Ideology: On the Boundaries of Concept Classification*. Lisse: Peter de Ridder Press.

—— 1978 'Popular Culture in Africa: Findings and Conjectures', *Africa* 48(4): 315–34.

—— 1984 'Cultuur versus praxis – over ideologie in de antropologie' ('Culture versus Praxis – About Ideology in Anthropology'), in Ton Lemaire (ed.) *Antropologie en ideologie* (Anthropology and Ideology). Groningen: Konstapel. Reprinted in *Critical Essays 1971–1985*, University of Amsterdam: ASC, pp. 19–40.

—— 1996 *Remembering the Present: Painting and Popular History in Zaire*. Berkeley: University of California Press.

—— 1997 [1978] 'Popular Culture in Africa: Findings and Conjectures', pp. 18–28 in Karin Barber (ed.) *Readings in African Popular Culture*. Bloomington and Indianapolis: Indiana University Press and Oxford: James Currey.

—— 1998a *Moments of Freedom: Anthropology and Popular Culture*. Charlottesville and London: University Press of Virginia.

—— 1998b 'Curios and Curiosity: Notes on Reading Torday and Frobenius', pp. 79–108 in Enid Schildkrout and Curtis A. Keim (eds) *The Scramble for Art in Central Africa*. Cambridge: Cambridge University Press.

Fabian, Johannes and Szombati-Fabian, Ilona 1980 'Folk Art from an Anthropological Perspective', pp. 247–93 in I.M.G. Quimby and S.T. Swank (eds) *Perspectives on American Folk Art*. New York and London: W.W. Norton and Company.

Fagg, William 1963 *Nigerian Images*. London: Lund Humphries.

Feest, Christian F. 1984 'The Arrival of Tribal Objects in the West from North America', pp. 85–98 in William Rubin (ed.) *'Primitivism' in 20th-century Art*. New York: Museum of Modern Art.

Fernandez, James 1971 [1966] 'Principles of Opposition and Vitality in Fang Aesthetics', in Carol F. Jopling (ed.) *Art and Aesthetics in Primitive Societies: A Critical Anthology*. New York: E.P. Dutton and Co.

—— 1973 'The Exposition and Imposition of Order: Artistic Expression in Fang Culture', pp. 194–220 in Warren L. d'Azevedo (ed.) *The Traditional Artist in African Societies*. Bloomington: Indiana University Press.

Fienup-Riordan, Ann 1996 *The Living Tradition of Yup'ik Masks: Agayuliyararput* (Our Way of Making Prayer). Seattle: University of Washington Press.

—— 2003 'Yup'ik Elders in Museums: Fieldwork Turned on Its Head', pp. 28–41 in Laura Peers and Alison K. Brown (eds) *Museums and Source Communities: A Routledge Reader.* London and New York: Routledge.

Firth, Raymond 1973 'Preface', pp. v–vii in Anthony Forge (ed.) *Primitive Art and Society.* London: Oxford University Press.

—— 1992 'Art and Anthropology', pp. 15–39 in Jeremy Coote and Anthony Shelton (eds) *Anthropology, Art and Aesthetics.* Oxford: Oxford University Press.

Fischer, Ernst 1962 'Künstler der Dan, die Bildhauer Tame, Si, Tompieme und Son, ihr Wesen und ihr Werk' ('Dan Artists: The Sculptors Tame, Si, Tompieme and Son, Their Life and Work'), *Baessler Archiv*, Neue Folge, 10.

—— 1963 [1959] *The Necessity of Art.* New York: Penguin Books.

Fischer, John L. 1971 'Art Styles as Cultural Cognitive Maps', pp. 140–60 in Charlotte M. Otten (ed.) *Anthropology and Art: Readings in Cross-cultural Aesthetics.* New York: Natural History Press.

Flores, Toni 1985 'The Anthropology of Aesthetics', *Dialectical Anthropology*, 27–41.

Forge, Anthony 1973a (ed.) *Primitive Art and Society.* London: Oxford University Press.

—— 1973b 'Style and Meaning in Sepik Art', pp. 169–91 in Anthony Forge (ed.) *Primitive Art and Society.* London: Oxford University Press.

Foucault, Michel 1970 [1966] *The Order of Things.* London: Tavistock.

—— 1972 *The Archeology of Knowledge and the Discourse on Language.* New York: Pantheon.

—— 1980 *Power/Knowledge*, edited by C. Gordon. New York: Pantheon.

—— 1982 'Afterword: The Subject and the Power', in H.L. Dreyfus and P. Rabinow (eds) *Beyond Structuralism and Hermeneutics.* Chicago: University of Chicago Press.

—— 1983 [1973] *This Is Not a Pipe.* Berkeley: University of California Press.

Fraser, Douglas 1966 [1941] 'The Heraldic Woman: A Study in Diffusion', pp. 36–99 in Douglas Fraser (ed.) *The Many Faces of Primitive Art.* Englewood Cliffs, NJ: Prentice Hall.

—— 1971 'The Discovery of Primitive Art', pp. 20–36 in Charlotte M. Otten (ed.) *Anthropology and Art. Readings in Cross-cultural Aesthetics.* New York: Natural History Press.

—— (ed.) 1974 *African Arts as Philosophy.* New York: Interbrook.

Fraser, Jean 1991 'Celestial Bodies', pp. 76–85 in Tessa Boffin and Jean Fraser (eds) *Stolen Glances: Lesbians Take Photographs.* London: Pandora.

Freedberg, David 1989 *The Power of Images.* Chicago: University of Chicago Press.

Freeman, C.R. Boyd 1923 *The Uncivilised Irish Samples of Catholic 'Culture'.* London: Protestant Truth Society.

Frey, Bruno S. and Pommerehne, Werner W. 1989 *Muses and Markets: Explorations in the Economics of the Arts.* Cambridge, MA: Basil Blackwell.

Fusco Coco 2002 [1991] 'Shooting the Klan: An Interview with Andres Serrano', http://www.communityarts.net/readingroom/archive/files/2002/09/shooting_the_kl.php (accessed 16/11/2004).

Gabalová, Zdenka 1990 'Peripeties of Czechoslovakia's Art', pp. 1–10 in Barbara Benish and Zdenka Gabalová (eds) *Dialogue Prague–Los Angeles.* Los Angeles: Benish.

Gans, Herbert 1974 *Popular Culture and High Culture: An Analysis and an Evaluation of Taste.* New York: Basic Books.

Gauguin, Paul 1985 *Noa Noa: Gauguin's Tahiti*, ed. and introduced by Nicholas Wadley. Oxford: Phaidon. (Orig. 1920, New York: N.L. Brown.)

Geertz, Clifford 1973 'Thick Description: Towards an Interpretative Theory of Culture', in *The Interpretation of Cultures: Selected Essays.* New York: Basic Books.

—— 1983 [1977] 'Art as a Cultural System', in *Local Knowledge. Further Essays in Interpretative Anthropology.* New York: Basic Books.

—— 1985 *Local Knowledge. Further Essays in Interpretative Anthropology*. New York: Basic Books.

Gell, Alfred 1992 'The Technology of Enchantment and the Enchantment of Technology', pp. 40–63 in J. Coote and A. Shelton (eds) *Anthropology, Art and Aesthetics*. Oxford: Clarendon Press.

—— 1998 *Art and Agency: An Anthropological Theory*. Oxford: Clarendon Press.

Gerbrands, Adrian A. 1966 *Wow-Ipits: Eight Asmat Woodcarvers of New Guinea*. The Hague: Mouton.

—— 1971 [1957] 'Art as an Element of Culture in Africa', pp. 366–82 in Charlotte M. Otten (ed.) *Anthropology and Art: Readings in Cross-cultural Aesthetics*. New York: Natural History Press.

Gibbons, Jacqueline A. 1997 'Kitsch: Artistic Text or Cultural Anathema?', *Focaal* 29: 57–66.

Gibson, Ann Eden 1997 *Abstract Expressionism: Other Politics*. New Haven, CT and London: Yale University Press.

Giesz, Ludwig 1968 'Kitsch-man as Tourist', pp. 156–74 in Gillo Dorfles (ed.) *Kitsch: An Anthology of Bad Taste*. London: Studio Vista.

—— 1971 [1960] *Phänomenologie des Kitsches* (Phenomenology of Kitsch). Munich: Wilhelm Fink Verlag.

Goldfarb, Jeffrey 1982 *On Cultural Freedom: An Exploration of Public Life in Poland and America*. Chicago: University of Chicago Press.

Goody, Jack 1997 *Representations and Contradictions: Ambivalence Towards Images, Theatre, Fiction, Relics and Sexuality*. Oxford: Basil Blackwell.

Gosden, Chris and Knowles, Chantal 2001 *Collecting Colonialism: Material Culture and Colonial Change*. Oxford: Berg.

Graburn, Nelson (ed.) 1976 *Ethnic and Tourist Arts: Cultural Expressions from the Fourth World*. Los Angeles: University of California Press.

Graham-Dixon, Andrew 2000 'Kitsch and Tell', *Sunday Telegraph Magazine*, 17 September, pp. 15–18.

Greenberg, Clement 1968 [1939] 'The Avant-Garde and Kitsch', pp. 116–26 in Gillo Dorfles (ed.) *Kitsch: An Anthology of Bad Taste*. London: Studio Vista.

—— 1961 *Art and Culture*. Boston, MA: Beacon Press.

Greenfeld, Liah 1989 *Different Worlds: A Sociological Study of Taste, Choice, and Success in Art*. Cambridge: Cambridge University Press.

Grosse, Ernst 1894 *Die Anfänge der Kunst* (The Beginnings of Art). Freiburg i. B., Leipzig: J.C.B. Mohr.

Groys, Boris 2005 'Cheerful Post-modernism', http:/www.milan-kunc.com (accessed 02/11/05).

Guilbaut, Serge 1983 *How New York Stole the Idea of Modern Art: Abstract Expressionism, Freedom, and the Cold War*. Chicago: University of Chicago Press.

Haddon, Alfred Cort 1894 *The Decorative Art of British New Guinea: A Study in Papuan Ethnography*. Dublin: The Academy House.

—— 1895 *Evolution in Art, As Illustrated By the Life-histories of Designs*. London: Walter Scott.

Halle, David 1993 *Inside Culture: Art and Class in the American Home*. Chicago: University of Chicago Press.

Hamilton, Augustus 1896 *The Art Workmanship of the Maori Race in New Zealand*. Dunedin, NZ: Fergusson and Mitchell.

Haraszti, Miklos 1987 [1983] *The Velvet Prison: Artists Under State Socialism*. New York: Basic Books.

Hart, Lynn M. 1995 'Three Walls: Regional Aesthetics and the International Art World', pp. 127–50 in George E. Marcus and Fred R. Myers (eds) *The Traffic in Culture: Refiguring Art and Anthropology*. Berkeley: University of California Press.

Haskell, Francis 1993 *History and Its Images: Art and the Interpretation of the Past.* New Haven, CT and London: Yale University Press.

Hatcher, Evelyn Payne 1985 *Art as Culture: An Introduction to the Anthropology of Art.* Lanham, MD: University Press of America.

Hauser, Arnold 1968 [1951] *The Social History of Art.* London: Routledge and Kegan Paul.

Heijne, Bas 1997 'Lipstick op het doek. Kunstvernieling, een lange traditie' ('Lipstick on the Canvas: Art Destruction, A Long Tradition'), *NRC Handelsblad, Cultureel supplement,* 28 February: p. 1.

Herskovits, Melville J. 1948 *Man and His Works: The Science of Cultural Anthropology.* New York: Alfred A. Knopf.

Hilton-Simpson, Melville 1911 *Land and Peoples of the Kasai.* London: Constable and Co.

Himmelheber, H. 1935 *Negerkünstler.* Stuttgart: Strecker and Schröder.

—— 1960 *Negerkunst und Negerkünstler.* Braunschweig: Klinckhardt and Biermann.

Hirsch, Eric 1995 'The Coercive Strategies of Aesthetics. Reflections on Wealth, Ritual and Landscape in Melanesia', *Social Analysis* 38: 61–71.

Holy, Ladislav 1996 *The Little Czech and the Great Czech Nation: National Identity and the Post-Communist Transformation of Society.* Cambridge: Cambridge University Press.

H.O., Paul 1997 'Andres Serrano at Paula Cooper', http://www.artnet.com/ Magazine/ features/ho/ho3-11-97.asp (accessed 16/11/2004).

Honour, Hugh 1979 *Romanticism.* London and New York: Penguin Books.

Hunt, Lynn Avery 1993 'Introduction: Obscenity and the Origins of Modernity, 1500–1800', pp. 9–45 in L.A. Hunt (ed.), *The Invention of Pornography: Obscenity and the Origins of Modernity, 1500–1800.* New York: Zone Books.

Hymes, Dell H. 1983 *Essays in the History of Linguistic Anthropology.* Amsterdam and Philadelphia: John Benjamins Publishing Co.

Impey, Oliver and MacGregor, Arthur (eds) 1985 *The Origins of Museums: The Cabinet of Curiosities in Sixteenth- and Seventeenth-century Europe.* Oxford: Clarendon Press.

Ives, J. 1773 *A Voyage from England to India, in the Year 1754.* London.

Jacknis, Ira 1985 'On the Limitations of the Museum Method of Anthropology', pp. 75–111 in George W. Stocking (ed.) *Objects and Others. Essays on Museums and Material Culture.* Madison: University of Wisconsin Press.

Jackson, Michael 1989 *Paths Toward a Clearing: Radical Empiricism and Ethnographic Inquiry.* Bloomington: Indiana University Press.

Jacob, Margaret C. 1993 'The Materialist World of Pornography', pp. 157–202 in L.A. Hunt, *The Invention of Pornography: Obscenity and the Origins of Modernity, 1500–1800.* New York: Zone Books.

Jansen van Galen, John and Van Roosmalen, Marcel 1997 'Het fatsoens-debat' ('The Decency Debate'), *Haagse Post/de Tijd* 7 March: 24–31.

Janson, H.W. 1962 *History of Art: A Survey of the Major Visual Arts from the Dawn of History to the Present Day.* London: Thames and Hudson.

Jarman, Neil 1997 *Material Conflicts: Parades and Visual Displays in Northern Ireland.* Oxford: Berg.

—— 1999 *Displaying Faith: Orange, Green and Trade Union Banners in Northern Ireland.* Belfast: Institute of Irish Studies, Queen's University Belfast.

Jensen, Klaus Bruhn 1995 *The Social Semiotics of Mass Communication.* London: Sage.

Jícha, Václav 1950 'Na novou cestu', *Výtvarné Umění* 1(1): 1–2.

Johnston, Harry H. 1908 *Georg Grenfell and the Congo,* 2 vols. London: Hutchinson and Co.

Jordan, Glenn and Weedon, Chris 1995 *Cultural Politics: Class, Gender, Race and the Postmodern World.* Oxford: Basil Blackwell.

Jules-Rosette, Bennetta 1984 *The Messages of Tourist Art: An African Semiotic System in Comparative Perspective.* New York: Plenum Press.

Jůza, Vilém 1993 'Smutná léta padesátá. Druha avantgarda' ('The Sad 1950s: The Second Avant-Garde'), pp. 27–34 in Jiří Vykoukal (ed.), *Záznam nejrozmanitějších factorů České malířství 2. poloviny 20. století ze sbírek galerií* (Record of the Most Varied Examples of Czech Painting of the Second Half of the Twentieth Century from the Gallery Collection). Prague: Národní galerie.

Karp, Ivan and Lavine, Stephen B. (eds) 1991 *Exhibiting Cultures: The Poetics and Politics of Museum Display*. Washington, DC and London: Smithsonian Institution.

Karp, Ivan, Kraemer, Christine Mullen and Lavine, Stephen D. 1992 *Museums and Communities: The Politics of Public Culture*. Washington, DC and London: Smithsonian Institution Press.

Kempers, Bram 1992 [1987] *Painting, Power and Patronage: The Rise of the Professional Artist in the Italian Renaissance*, trans. Beverley Jackson. London: Allen Lane.

Kempton, Willett 1981 *The Folk Classification of Ceramics: A Study of Cognitive Prototypes*. New York: Academic Press.

Kendrick, Walter 1987 *The Secret Museum: Pornography in Modern Culture*. Berkeley: University of California Press.

Kessler, Evelyn S. 1976 *Women: An Anthropological View*. New York: Holt, Rinehart and Winston.

Kiernan, V.G. 1990 *Noble and Ignoble Savages*, pp. 86–116 in G.S. Rousseau and Roy Porter (eds) *Exoticism in the Enlightenment*. Manchester: Manchester University Press.

Kirschenblatt-Gimblett, Barbara 1990 'Objects of Ethnography', pp. 386–443 in Ivan Karp and Steven D. Lavine (eds) *Exhibiting Cultures: The Poetics and Politics of Museum Display*. Washington, DC and London: Smithsonian Institution Press.

Kontová, Helena and Politi, Giancarlo 1997 'Jeff Koons: Ten Years Later', *Flash Art* 195: 102–8.

Kopytoff, Igor 1986 'The Cultural Biography of Things: Commoditization as Process', pp. 64–91 in Arjun Appadurai (ed.) *The Social Life of Things. Commodities in Cultural Perspective*. Cambridge: Cambridge University Press.

Kotalík, Jiří 1979 *Almanach Akademie výtvarných Umění v Praze* (Almanac of the Academy of Fine Arts in Prague). Prague: Akademie výtvarných umění v Praze and Národní Galerie.

Kozloff, Joyce and Jaudon, Valerie 1978 'Art Hysterical Notions of Progress and Culture', *Heresis: A Feminist Publication on Art and Politics* 4 (Winter): 28–42.

Kubíček, Jaromír 2000 *Vlastivěda Moravská Země a Lid*, Svazek 10 (Local History and Geography of Moravia and its People, Vol. 10). Brno: Ústav Lidové Kultury ve Strážnici Muzejní a Vlastivědná Společnost v Brně.

Kulka, Tomáš 1996 *Kitsch and Art*. University Park: Pennsylvania State University Press.

Kunz, Ludvík 1954 *Česká Etnographie a folkloristika v letech 1945-1952* (Czech Ethnography and Folklore Studies, 1945–1952). Prague: Nakladatelství Československé Akademie Věd.

Kuo Wei Tchen, John 1992 'Creating a Dialogic Museum: The Chinatown History Museum Experiment', pp. 285–326 in Ivan Karp, Christine Mullen Kraemer and Stephen D. Lavine (eds) *Museums and Communities: The Politics of Public Culture*. Washington, DC and London: Smithsonian Institution Press.

Kuspit, Donald 2005 'Fool's Paradise', http://www.milan-kunc.com (accessed 02/11/05).

Labi, Kwame A. 2002 'Fante Asafo Flags of Abandze and Kormantse', *African Arts* 35(4): 28–37.

Lamphere, Louise, Ragoné, Helena and Zavella, Patricia (eds) 1997 *Situated Lives: Gender and Culture in Everyday Life*. London: Routledge.

Lancaster, Roger N. and DiLeonardo, Michaela (eds) 1997 *The Gender/Sexuality Reader: Culture, History, Political Economy*. New York: Routledge.

Lang, Gladys and Lang, Kurt 1988 'Recognition and Reknown: The Survival of Artistic Reputations', *American Journal of Sociology* 94: 79–109.

Lasch, Christopher 1968 'The Cultural Cold War: A Short History of the Congress of Cultural Freedom', in Barton J. Bernstein (ed.) *Towards a New Past: Dissenting Essays in American History*. New York: Pantheon.

Lavine, Steven D. 1992 'Audience, Ownership, and Authority: Designing Relations between Museums and Communities', pp. 137–57 in Ivan Karp, Christine Mullen Kraemer and Stephen D. Lavine (eds) *Museums and Communities: The Politics of Public Culture*. Washington, DC and London: Smithsonian Institution Press.

Layton, Robert 1991 [1981] *The Anthropology of Art*. Cambridge: Cambridge University Press.

Leach 1954 *Political Systems of Highland Burma: A Study of Kachin Social Structure*. London: London School of Economics and Political Science.

Leavitt, J. (1996) 'Meaning and Feeling in the Anthropology of Emotions', *American Ethnologist* 23(3): 514–39.

Legêne, Susan 1998 'Nobody's Objects: Early 19th-century Ethnographical Collections and the Formation of Imperialist Attitudes and Feelings', *Etnofoor* 11(1): 21–39.

Lemon, Alena 2000 *Between Two Fires: Gypsy Performance and Romani Memory from Pushkin to Post-Socialism*. Durham, NC: Duke University Press.

Lévi-Strauss, Claude 1953 'Reply to Comments', in S. Tax et al. (eds) *An Appraisal of Anthropology Today*. Chicago: University of Chicago Press.

—— 1960 *Entretiens avec Claude Lévi-Strauss*. Paris: Plon.

—— 1963 *Structural Anthropology*. New York: Basic Books.

Leyten, Harrie and Damen, Bibi (eds) 1992 *Art, Anthropology and the Modes of Re-Presentation. Museums and Contemporary Non-Western Art*. Amsterdam: Royal Tropical Institute.

Lidchi, Henrietta 1997 'The Poetics and the Politics of Exhibiting Other Cultures', pp. 151–222 in Stuart Hall (ed.) *Representation: Cultural Representations and Signifying Practices*. London: Sage.

Liebersohn, Harry 1999 'Images of Monarchy: Kamehameha I and the Art of Louis Choris', pp. 44–64 in Nicholas Thomas and Diane Losche (eds) *Double Vision: Art Histories and Colonial Histories in the Pacific*. Cambridge: Cambridge University Press.

Lindey, Christine 1990 *Art in the Cold War: From Vladiwostock to Kalamazoo, 1945–1962*. New York: Amsterdam Books.

Lippard, Lucy R. 1973 *Six Years: The Dematerialization of the Art Object from 1966 to 1972*. Berkeley: University of California Press.

Locher, David A. 1997 'Art, Obscenity, and Interpretation: Sexual Beliefs in the United States', *Focaal* 29: 67–80.

Lyotard, Jean-François 1984 [1979] *The Postmodern Condition: A Report on Knowledge*, trans. Geoff Bennington and Brian Massumi. Minneapolis: University of Minnesota Press.

Lucie-Smith, Edward 1995 [1969] *Movements in Art Since 1945: Issues and Concepts*. London and New York: Thames and Hudson.

McAnena, Shan 2003 'Introduction', pp. 5–8 in Naughton Gallery (ed.) *Talking in Colour: African Flags of the Fante*. Belfast: Queen's University Belfast.

McCarthy, Mary 1983 *Social Change and the Growth of British Power in the Gold Coast: The Fante States 1807–1874*. Lanham, MD: University Press of America.

MacClancy, Jeremy (ed.) 1997 *Contesting Art. Art, Politics and Identity in the Modern World*. Oxford: Berg.

MacKenzie, Maureen 1997 [1971] 'Androgynous Objects: String Bags and Gender in Central New Guinea', pp. 144–8 in Martha Croonfield Ward (ed.) *A World Full of Women*. Boston and London: Allyn and Bacon.

Malinowski, Bronislaw 1984 [1922] *The Argonauts of the Western Pacific*. Prospect Heights, IL: Waveland Press.

Malraux, André 1967 [1965] *Museum without Walls: The Voices of Silence*, trans. Stuart Gilbert and Francis Price. London: Secker and Warburg.

Maquet, Jacques 1979 [1971] *Introduction to Aesthetic Anthropology*. Malibu, CA: Undena Publications.

—— 1986 *The Aesthetic Experience: An Anthropologist Looks at the Visual Arts*. New Haven, CT and London: Yale University Press.

Marcus, George E. and Myers, Fred R. (eds) 1995 *The Traffic in Culture: Refiguring Art and Anthropology*. Berkeley: University of California Press.

Marquis, Alice Goldfarb 1991 *Art Biz: The Covert World of Collectors, Dealers, Auction Houses, Museums, and Critics*. Chicago: Contemporary Books.

Marshall, P.J. 1990 'Taming the Exotic: The British and India in the Seventeenth and Eighteenth Centuries', pp. 46–65 in G.S. Rousseau and Roy Porter (eds) *Exoticism in the Enlightenment*. Manchester: Manchester University Press.

Melville, Robert 1973 *Erotic Art of the West*. London: Weidenfeld and Nicolson.

Meyer, Richard 2002 *Outlaw Representation: Censorship and Homosexuality in Twentieth-century American Art*. Boston, MA: Beacon Press.

Meyerowitz, Eva 1974 *The Early History of the Akan States of Ghana*. London: Red Candle Press.

Miller, Daniel 1987 *Material Culture and Mass Consumption*. Oxford: Basil Blackwell.

Milton, Kay and Svašek, Maruška 2005 *Mixed Emotions: Anthropological Studies of Feeling*. Oxford: Berg.

Mitchell, Jon 2006 'Performance', pp. 384–401 in Christopher Tilley, Webb Kane, Susanne Kuechler, Michael Rowlands and Patricia Spyer (eds) *Handbook of Material Culture*. London: Sage.

Moore, Henrietta L. 1994 *A Passion for Difference: Essays in Anthropology and Gender*. Cambridge: Polity.

Morphy, Howard 1991 *Ancestral Connections: Art and an Aboriginal System of Knowledge*. Chicago: University of Chicago Press.

—— 1992. 'From Dull to Brilliant: The Aesthetics of Spiritual Power among the Yolngu', pp.181–208 in J. Coote and A. Shelton (eds) *Anthropology, Art and Aesthetics*. Oxford: Clarendon Press.

—— 1994 'For the Motion', pp. 3–9 in James Weiner (ed.) *Aesthetics is a Cross-cultural Category: A Debate Held in the Muriel Stott Centre, John Rylands University of Manchester, on 30th October 1993*. Manchester: Group for Debates in Anthropological Theory, University of Manchester.

—— 1995 'Aboriginal Art in a Global Context', pp. 211–39 in Daniel Miller (ed.) *Worlds Apart: Modernity through the Prism of the Local*. London: Routledge.

Moulin, Raymonde 1987 *The French Art Market: A Sociological View*. New Brunswick, NJ: Rutgers University Press.

Mount, Marshall Ward 1973 *African Art: The Years since 1920*. Newton Abbot: David and Charles.

Munn, Nancy D. 1962 'Walbiri Graphic Signs: An Analysis', *American Anthropologist* 64: 972–84.

—— 1973a 'The Spatial Presentation of Cosmic Order in Walbiri Iconography', pp. 193–220 in Anthony Forge (ed.) *Primitive Art and Society*. London: Oxford University Press.

—— 1973b *Walbiri Iconography: Graphic Representation and Cultural Symbolism in a Central Australian Society*. Chicago: University of Chicago Press.

Myers, Fred R. 1991 'Representing Culture: The Production of Discourse(s) for Aboriginal Acrylic Paintings', *Cultural Anthropology* 6(1): 26–62.

—— 2002 *Painting Culture: The Making of an Aboriginal High Art*. Durham, NC: Duke University Press.

Myers, Kathy 1987 [1982] 'Towards a Feminist Erotica', pp. 283–96 in Hilary Robinson (ed.) *Visibly Female: Feminism and Art Theory Today – An Anthology*. London: Camden Press.

Nead, Lynda 1988 *Myths of Sexuality: Representations of Women in Victorian Britain*. Oxford: Basil Blackwell.

—— 1993 '"Above the Pulp-line": The Cultural Significance of Erotic Art', pp. 144–55 in Pamela Church Gibson and Roma Gibson (eds) *Dirty Looks: Women, Pornography, Power*. London: British Film Industry.

Nightingale, Eithne and Swallow, Deborah 2003 'The Arts of the Sikh Kingdoms: Collaborating with a Community', pp. 55–71 in Laura Peers and Alison K. Brown (eds) *Museums and Source Communities: A Routledge Reader*. London and New York: Routledge.

Nochlin, Linda 1989 *Women, Art and Power and Other Essays*. Boulder, CO: Westview Press.

—— 1999 [1975] *Representing Women*. London: Thames and Hudson.

Nussbaum, Martha 2001 *Upheavals of Thought: The Intelligence of Emotions*. Cambridge: Cambridge University Press.

O'Hanlon, Michael 1989 *Reading the Skin: Adornment, Display and Society Among the Wahgi*. London: British Museum Publications.

—— 1993 *Paradise: Portraying the New Guinea Highlands*. London: British Museum Press.

Olbrechts, F.M. 1939 'Ivoorkunst-expeditie van de Rijksuniversiteit te Gent en van het Vleehuis-museum te Antwerpen. Voorlopig verslag over de werkzaamheden: November 1938-Januari 1939' ('The Ivory Coast Expedition of Ghent University and the Antwerp Vlesshuis Museum: Preliminary Report of Activities'), *Kongo-Overzee* 5: 177–87.

Oliva, Achille Bonito 1980 *The Italian Trans-Avantgarde*. Milano: Giancarlo Politi.

Otten, Charlotte 1971 'Introduction', pp. xi–xvi in Charlotte Otten (ed.) *Anthropology and Art: Readings in Cross-cultural Aesthetics*. New York: Natural History Press.

Overing, Joanna 1994 'Against the Motion', pp. 9–16 in James Weiner (ed.) *Aesthetics is a Cross-cultural Category: A Debate Held in the Muriel Stott Centre, John Rylands University of Manchester, on 30th October 1993*. Manchester: Group for Debates in Anthropological Theory, University of Manchester.

Paganini, Catherine 1998 'Chinese Material Culture and British Perceptions of China in the Mid-nineteenth Century', pp. 28–40 in Tim Barringer and Tom Flynn (eds) *Colonialism and the Object: Empire, Material Culture and the Museum*. London and New York: Routledge.

Parezo, Nancy J. 1993 [1982] 'Navajo Sandpaintings: The Importance of Sex Roles in Craft Production', pp. 220–32 in Richard L. Anderson and Karen L. Field (eds) *Art in Small-scale Societies: Contemporary Readings*. Englewood Cliffs, NJ: Prentice Hall.

Parker, Rozsika 1984 *The Subversive Stitch: Embroidery and the Making of the Feminine*. London: Women's Press.

Parker, Rozsika and Pollock, Griselda (eds) 1987 *Framing Feminism: Art and the Women's Movement, 1970–85*. London and New York: Pandora.

—— 1995 *Old Mistresses: Women, Art and Ideology*. London: Pandora.

Paudrat, Jean-Louis 1984 'The Arrival of Tribal Objects in the West: From Africa', pp. 125–78 in William Rubin (ed.) *'Primitivism' in 20th-century Art*. New York: Museum of Modern Art.

Pearce, Susan 1987 'Ivory, Antler, Feather and Wood: Material Culture and the Cosmology of the Cumberland Sound Inuit, Baffin Island, Canada', *Canadian Journal of Native Studies* 7(2): 307–21.

Pease, Allison 2000 *Modernism, Mass Culture, and the Aesthetics of Obscenity*. Cambridge: Cambridge University Press.

Peers, Laura and Brown, Alison K. (eds) 2003a *Museums and Source Communities: A Routledge Reader*. London and New York: Routledge.

—— 2003b 'Introduction', pp. 1–16 in Laura Peers and Alison K. Brown (eds) *Museums and Source Communities: A Routledge Reader*. London and New York: Routledge.

Peirson Jones, Jane 1992 'The Colonial Legacy and the Community: The Gallery 33 Project', pp. 221–41 in Ivan Karp, Christine Mullen Kraemer and Stephen D. Lavine (eds) *Museums and Communities: The Politics of Public Culture*. Washington and London: Smithsonian Institution Press.

Peltier, Phillipe 1984 'The Arrival of Tribal Objects in the West: From Oceania', pp. 99–124 in William Rubin (ed.) *'Primitivism' in 20th-century Art*. New York: Museum of Modern Art.

Perry, Gillian (ed.) 1999 *Gender and Art*. New Haven, CT: Yale University Press.

Perry, Gillian and Rossington, Michael (ed.) 1994 *Femininity and Masculinity in 18th-century Art and Culture*. Manchester: Manchester University Press.

Peterson, Susan and Peterson, Jan 2003 *The Craft and Art of Clay: A Complete Handbook*. London: Laurence King Publishing.

Phillips, Ruth B. 2003 'Community Collaboration in Exhibitions: Toward a Dialogic Paradigm – Introduction', pp. 155–70 in Laura Peers and Alison K. Brown (eds) *Museums and Source Communities: A Routledge Reader*. London and New York: Routledge.

Picton, John 1993 'Eine Fante-Fahne ist ein Gegenstand in der Welt' ('A Fante Flag is an Object in the World'), pp. 21–36 in Kay Heyner (ed.) *Tanzende Bilder. Fahnen der Fante Asafo in Ghana* (Dancing Images – Flags of the Fante Asafo in Ghana). Bonn: Kunst und Ausstellungshall der Bundesrepublik Deutschland.

Piteri, Rita 'The Andres Serrano Controversy' http://home.vicnet.net.au/~twt/serrano. html (accessed 16/11/2004).

Pitt Rivers, A.H.L.F. 1875 [1906] *The Evolution of Culture and Other Essays*, edited by J.L. Myres. Oxford: Clarendon Press.

Plattner, Stuart 1996 *High Art Down Home: An Economic Ethnography of a Local Art Market*. Chicago and London: University of Chicago Press.

Pollock, Griselda 1988 *Vision and Difference: Femininity, Feminism and the Histories of Art*. London: Routledge.

—— 1992 *Avant-garde Gambits 1888–1893: Gender and the Colour of Art History*. London: Thames and Hudson.

Pomian, Krzysztof 1990 *Collectors and Curiosities: Paris and Venice, 1500–1800*, trans. Elizabeth Wiles-Portier. Cambridge: Polity.

Porter, Roy 1990 'The Exotic as Erotic: Captain Cook at Tahiti', pp. 117–44 in G.S. Rousseau and Roy Porter (eds.) *Exoticism in the Enlightenment*. Manchester: Manchester University Press.

Presiosi, Donald 1989 *Rethinking Art History: Meditations on a Coy Science*. New Haven, CT and London: Yale University Press.

Price, Sally 1989 *Primitive Art in Modern Places*. Chicago: University of Chicago Press.

Prior, Nick 2002 *Museums and Modernity: Art Galleries and the Making of Modern Culture*. Oxford: Berg.

Rattray, R.S. 1927 *Religion and Art in Ashanti*. London: Clarendon Press.

Rawson, Philip (ed.) 1973 *Primitive Erotic Art*. London: Weidenfeld and Nicolson.

Robinson, Hilary (ed.) 1987 *Visibly Female: Feminist Art Today – An Anthology*. Camden Press: London.

Rosaldo, Michelle Z. 1984 'Towards an Anthropology of Self and Feeling', pp. 137–57 in R.A. Schweder and R.A. LeVine (eds), *Culture Theory: Essays on Mind, Self and Emotion*. Cambridge: Cambridge University Press.

Rosenblum, Robert 1992 *The Jeff Koons Handbook*. London: Thames and Hudson.

Ross, Doran 2001 'George Hughes: Portfolio', *African Arts* 34(1).

Rousseau, G.S. and Porter, Roy 1990 *Exoticism in the Enlightenment*. Manchester: Manchester University Press.

Rowe, William and Schelling, Vivian 1991 *Memory and Modernity: Popular Culture in Latin America*. London: Verso.

Rubin, William (ed.) 1984a *'Primitivism' in 20th-century Art*. London: Thames and Hudson.

—— 1984b 'Modernist Primitivism: An Introduction', pp. 1–81 in William Rubin (ed.) *'Primitivism' in 20th-century Art*. London: Thames and Hudson.

Ryle, John 1982 *Warriors of the White Nile: The Dinka*. Amsterdam: Time-Life.

Said, Edward W. 1978 *Orientalism*. New York: Pantheon.

Sarbah, John Mensah 1968 *Fanti Customary Laws*. London: Frank Cass and Co.

Saussure, F. de 1959 *Course in General Linguistics*, trans. C. Bally and A. Sechehaye. London: Owen.

Schneider, H.K. 1971 [1956] 'The Interpretation of Pakot Visual Art', pp. 55–63 in C.F. Jopling (ed.) *Art and Aesthetics in Primitive Societies*. New York: Dutton.

Scott, James 1990 *Domination and the Arts of Resistance: Hidden Transcripts*. New Haven, CT and London: Yale University Press.

Searle, J.R. 1969 *Speech Acts: An Essay in the Philosophy of Language*. Cambridge: Cambridge University Press.

Sieber, Roy 1971 [1962] 'The Arts and Their Changing Social Function', pp. 203–11 in Charlotte M. Otten (ed.) *Anthropology and Art: Readings in Cross-cultural Aesthetics*. New York: Natural History Press.

—— 1973a 'Art and History in Ghana', pp. 70–96 in Anthony Forge (ed.) *Primitive Art and Society*. London: Oxford University Press.

—— 1973b 'Approaches to Non-Western Art', pp. 425–34 in Warren L. d'Azevedo (ed.) *The Traditional Artist in African Societies*. Bloomington: Indiana University Press.

Silver, H.R. 1983 'Calculating Risks: The Socio-Economic Foundations of Aesthetic Innovations in an Ashanti Carving Community', *Ethnology* 20: 101–14.

Šolta, Vladimír 1950 'K některým otázkám socialistického realismu ve výtvarném umění' ('About Some Quesitons Concerning Socialist Realism in the Fine Arts'), *Výtvarné Umění* 1(3): 108–32.

Sontag, Susan 1977 *On Photography*. New York: Dell Publishing.

Spanjaard, Helena 1988 'Free Art: Academic Painters in Indonesia', pp. 103–32 in P. Faber (ed.) *Art from Another World*. Rotterdam: Museum of Ethnology.

—— 1998 'Het Ideaal van een moderne Indonesische Schilderkunst. De creatie van een nationale identiteit 1900–1995' (The Ideal of Modern Indonesian Painting. The Creation of a National Identity), unpublished dissertation, Leiden University.

—— 2003 *Modern Indonesian Painting*. Singapore: Sotheby's.

—— 2004 *Exploring Indonesian Modern Art. The Collection of Dr. Oei Hong Djien*. Singapore: SNP Editions.

Spence, Jo 1985 *Jo Spence: Review of Work 1950–85*. Cambridge: Cambridge Darkroom.

Spiro, Melford E. 1968 'Religion. Problems of Definition and Explanation', pp. 85–126 in M. Banton (ed.) *Anthropological Approaches to the Study of Religion*. London: Tavistock Publications.

Stein, Judith E. 1994 'Collaboration', pp. 226–45 in Norma Broude and Mary D. Garrard (eds) *The Power of Feminist Art: The American Movement of the 1970s. History and Impact*. New York: Harry N. Abrams.

Steiner, Christopher B. 1994 *African Art in Transit*. Cambridge: Cambridge University Press.

—— 1995 'The Art of the Trade: On the Creation of Value and Authenticity in the African Art Market World', pp. 151–65 in George E. Marcus and Fred R. Myers (eds) *The Traffic in Culture: Refiguring Art and Anthropology*. Berkeley: University of California Press.

Stloukal, Karel 1994 *Národní museum. The National Museum. Nationalmuseum. Musé Nationa*. Praha/Prague: Nakladetelství Granit.

Stocking, George W. (ed.) 1985 *Objects and Others: Essays on Museums and Material Culture*. Madison: University of Wisconsin Press.

—— 1987 *Victorian Anthropology*. New York: Free Press.

—— 1992 *The Ethnographer's Magic and Other Essays in the History of Anthropology*. Madison: University of Wisconsin Press.

—— 1995 *After Tylor: British Social Anthropology 1888–1951*. Madison: University of Wisconsin Press.

Strathern, Andrew and Strathern, Marilyn 1971 *Self-decoration in Mount Hagen*. London: Duckworth.

Sturtevant, William 1969 'Does Antrhopology Need Museums?', *Proceedings of the Biological Society of Washington* 82: 619–50.

Svašek, Maruška 1990 'Creativiteit, Commercie en Ideologie. Moderne Kunst in Ghana, 1900–1990' ('Creativity, Commerce and Ideology. Modern Art in Ghana'), unpublished MA thesis, University of Amsterdam.

—— 1995 'The Soviets Remembered: Liberators or Aggressors?', *Focaal: Journal of Anthropology* 25: 103–24.

—— 1996a 'Styles, Struggles and Careers: An Ethnography of the Czech Art World, 1948–1992', unpublished PhD thesis, University of Amsterdam.

—— 1996b 'What's (the) Matter? Objects, Materiality and Interpretability', *Etnofoor* 9(1): 49–70.

—— 1997a 'Visual Art, Myth and Power. Introduction', *Focaal: Journal of Anthropology* 29: 7–24.

—— 1997b 'Gossip and Power Struggle in the Post-Communist Art World', *Focaal: Journal of Anthropology* 29: 101–22.

—— 1997c 'Identity and Style in Ghanaian Artistic Discourse', pp. 27–61 in Jeremy MacClancy (ed.) *Contesting Art: Art, Politics and Identity in the Modern World*. Oxford: Berg.

—— 1997d 'The Politics of Artistic Identity: The Czech Art World in the 1950s and 1960s', *Contemporary European History* 6(3): 383–403.

—— 2002 'Contacts: Social Dynamics in the Czechoslovak State-Socialist Art World', *Contemporary European History* 11(1): 67–86.

—— 2005a 'Introduction: Emotions in Anthropology', in Kay Milton and Maruška Svašek (eds) *Mixed Emotions: Anthropological Studies of Feeling*. Oxford: Berg.

—— 2005b 'The Politics of Chosen Trauma: Expellee Memories, Emotions and Identities', pp. 195–214 in Kay Milton and Maruška Svašek (eds) *Mixed Emotions: Anthropological Studies of Feelings*. Oxford: Berg.

—— forthcoming 'Moving Corpses: Emotions and Subject–Object Ambiguity', in Helena Wulff (ed.) *Emotions: A Cultural Reader*. Oxford: Berg.

Szombati-Fabian, Ilona and Fabian, Johannes 1976 'Art, History and Society: Popular Painting in Shaba, Zaire', *Studies in the Anthropology of Visual Communication* 3(1): 1–21.

Taylor, Tom 1863 'English Painting in 1862', *Fine Arts Quarterly Review* 1(May): 14–15.

Thomae, Otto 1978 *Die Propaganda-Maschinerie: Bildende Kunst und Öffentlichkeitsarbeit in Dritten Reich*. Berlin: Gebr. Mann Verlag.

Thomas, Nicholas 1991 *Entangled Objects: Exchange, Material Culture and Colonialism in the Pacific*. Cambridge, MA: Harvard University Press.

—— 1994 *Colonialism's Culture: Anthropology, Travel and Government*. Oxford: Polity Press.

—— 2001 'Introduction', pp. 1–12 in Christopher Pinney and Nicholas Thomas (eds) *Beyond Aesthetics: Art and Technologies of Enchantment*. Oxford: Berg.

Thompson, Robert Farris 1973 'Yoruba Artistic Criticism', pp. 19–61 in Warren L. d'Azevedo (ed.) *The Traditional Artist in African Societies*. Bloomington: Indiana University Press.

Tilley, Christopher (ed.) 1990 *Reading Material Culture: Structuralism, Hermeneutics and Post-Structuralism*. Oxford: Basil Blackwell.

Tonkin, Elizabeth 1982 'Language Versus the World: Notes on Meaning for Anthropologists', pp. 108–22 in David Parkin (ed.) *Semantic Anthropology* (ASA Monograph 22). London: Academic Press.

—— 1989 'The Semiotics of Edwin Ardener', in Thomas A. Sebeok and Jean Umiker-Sebeok (eds) *The Semiotic Web*. Berlin: Mouton de Gruyter.

Torday, Emil 1925 *On the Trail of the Bushongo: An Account of a Remarkable and Hitherto Unknown African People, Their Origin, Art, High Social and Political Organisation and Culture, Derived from the Author's Personal Experience Amongst Them*. London: Seely, Service and Co.

Toynbee, Arnold J. 1954 *A Study of History*, vol. 9. London: Oxford University Press.

van Beek, Walter 1991 'Enter the Bush: A Dogon Mask Festival', pp. 56–73 in Susan Vogel (ed.) *Africa Explores: 20th-century African Art*. New York: Center for African Art and Munich: Prestel.

Vasari, Giorgio 1987 [1550] *The Lives of the Artists*, trans. George Bull. Harmondsworth: Penguin. (First published Firenze: Lorenzo Torrentino, 1550.)

Vaughan, James H. 1973 'əŋkyagu as Artists in Marghi Society', pp. 162–93 in Warren L. d'Azevedo (ed.) *The Traditional Artist in African Societies*. Bloomington: Indiana University Press.

Vequaud, Yves 1977 *The Art of Mithila: Ceremonial Paintings from an Ancient Kingdom*. London: Thanes and Hudson.

Vogel, Suzanne (ed.) 1988 *Art/Artifact: African Art in Anthropology Collections*. New York: Center for African Art and Preston Verlag.

——— (ed.) 1991 *Africa Explored: 20th-century African Art*. New York: Center for African Art and Munich: Prestel.

Volf, Petr 2006 'Jsem Angažovaný Blázen' ('I Am a Committed Fool'), http://www.jedinak.cz/stranky/txtjunc last (accessed September 2006).

Volli, Ugo 1968 'Pornography and Pornokitsch', pp. 224–50 in Gillo Dorfles (ed.) *Kitsch: An Anthology of Bad Taste*. London: Studio Vista.

Ward, Martha Coonfield 1996 *A World Full of Women*. Boston and London: Allyn and Bacon.

Watson, Peter 1992 *From Manet to Manhattan: The Rise of the Modern Art Market*. New York: Random House.

Weiner, A.B. 1977 *Women of Value, Men of Renown: New Perspectives in Trobriand Exchange*. St Lucia: University of Queensland Press.

Weiner, James (ed.) *Aesthetics is a Cross-cultural Category: A Debate Held in the Muriel Stott Centre, John Rylands University of Manchester, on 30th October 1993*. Manchester: Group for Debates in Anthropological Theory, University of Manchester.

Weitz, Morris 1957 'The Role of Theory in Aesthetics', *Journal of Aesthetics and Art Criticism* 15(1): 27–35.

Wemega-Kwahu, Rikki 2002 'The Contemporary African Artist: Between Past and Present, Local and Global', unpublished paper, presented at the Conference 'The State of the Art(s): African Studies and American Studies in Comparative Perspective', University of Cape Coast.

Werewere-Liking 1988 *Statues Colons: Statuettes Paintes d'Afrique de l'Ouest*. Paris: Nea-Arhis.

White, Harrison and White, Cynthia 1965 *Canvases and Careers*. New York: John Wiley.

Whitehouse, Harvey 2004 *Modes of Religiosity. A Cognitive Theory of Religious Transmission*. Walnut Creek, CA: AltaMira Press.

Wierzbicka, A. 2004 'Emotion and Culture: Arguing with Martha Nussbaum', *Ethos* 31(4): 577–600.

Wilterdink, Nico 2000 *In deze verwarrende tijd. Een terugblik en vooruitblik op de postmoderniteit* (In This Confusing Time: A Look Back and a Look Ahead at Postmodernity). Amsterdam: Vossiuspers AUP.

Williams, Nancy 1976 'Australian Aboriginal Art at Yirrkala: The Introduction and Development of Marketing', in Nelson H.H. Graburn (ed.) *Ethnic and Tourist Arts: Cultural Expressions from the Fourth World*. Berkeley: University of California Press.

Wistrich, Robert S. 1995 *Weekend in Munich: Art, Propaganda and Terror in the Third Reich*. London: Pavilion.

Withers, Josephine 1994 'Feminist Performance Art: Performing, Discovering, Transforming Ourselves', pp. 158–73 in Norma Broude and Mary D. Garrard (eds) *The Power of Feminist Art: The American Movement of the 1970s – History and Impact*. New York: Harry N. Abrams.

Wolff, Janet 1981 *The Social Production of Art*. London: Macmillan.

—— 1983 *Aesthetics and the Sociology of Art*. London: Allen and Unwin.

Yegenoglu, Meyda 1998 *Colonial Fantasies: Towards a Feminist Reading of Orientalism*. Cambridge: Cambridge University Press.

Zandbergen, Gijs 1997 'Andres Serrano haalt gewoon de schouders op', *De Volkskrant* 26 February: p. 18.

Zolberg, Vera 1990 *Constructing a Sociology of Art*. Cambridge: Cambridge University Press.

Zolberg, Vera L. and Cherbo, Joni Maya 1997 *Outsider Art: Contesting Boundaries in Contemporary Culture*. Cambridge: Cambridge University Press.

INDEX

Compiled by Mary Warren